Neo-Confederacy

Neo-Confederacy

A Critical Introduction

EDITED BY EUAN HAGUE, HEIDI BEIRICH,
AND EDWARD H. SEBESTA

FOREWORD BY JAMES W. LOEWEN

University of Texas Press ⟡ *Austin*

Chapter 2, "The U.S. Civil War as a Theological War: Neo-Confederacy, Christian Nationalism, and Theology," was first published by the University of Toronto Press as Edward H. Sebesta and Euan Hague, "The U.S. Civil War as a Theological War: Confederate Christian Nationalism and the League of the South," in *Canadian Review of American Studies* 32.3 (2002): 253–283, and is reproduced with permission.

Chapter 7 was originally presented at the Association of American Geographers Annual Meetings in 2002.

Parts of Chapters 3, 4, 6, and 10 were presented by their authors at the Association of American Geographers Annual Meetings in 2005.

Permission to reproduce the lyrics to "Lest We Forget" in Chapter 9 was granted by Robert Lloyd.

Lyrics for songs by the Free South Band are reproduced by permission of Cornelius "Popcorn" Robertson, www.freesouth.net.

Requests for permission to reproduce material from this work should be sent to:
Permissions
University of Texas Press
P.O. Box 7819
Austin, TX 78713-7819
www.utexas.edu/utpress/about/bpermission.html
♾ The paper used in this book meets the minimum requirements of ANSI/NISO Z39.48-1992 (R1997) (Permanence of Paper).

Library of Congress Cataloging-in-Publication Data

Neo-confederacy : a critical introduction / edited by Euan Hague, Heidi Beirich, and Edward H. Sebesta. — 1st ed.
    p.   cm.
    Includes index.
    ISBN 0-292-72162-5 ISBN 978-0-292-72162-3
    1. Whites—Southern States—Ethnic identity.   2. Confederate States of America—In popular culture.   3. Social movements—United States.   4. Conservatism—United States. I. Hague, Euan.   II. Sebesta, Edward H.   III. Beirich, Heidi.
F220.A1N46 2008
305.809'07509045—dc22
                                                        2008030194

To Cliff and Irene, who taught me the value of education

To Steven, whose love and support have helped make this book possible

Contents

PART II. **Practicing Neo-Confederacy**

Foreword: A Connected Fringe

JAMES W. LOEWEN

Although the Confederate States of America lasted only four years, its impact has continued for almost a century and a half. Today its romance, ideology, and symbolism still sway millions of men and women—and boys and girls—across the nation and around the world.

If its appeal were just a harmless atavism, then no one would mind that the ratio of Confederate to Union Civil War reenactors is two to one. No one would care when high schools, even in Northern states, name their athletic teams "Rebels" and "Colonels" and wave Confederate flags at football games.

But there's a darker side to the neo-Confederate revival. In 1995 I chatted with a flag vendor at a flea market near Brattleboro, Vermont. He displayed more Confederate flags than any other single item, but not the usual battle flag of the Army of Northern Virginia. Embroidered across them were the words "If the South had won, we'd have no trouble now." Consider that phrase for a moment. Who is "we"? Exactly what "trouble" would we not have? The implications are chilling. "What does this mean?" I asked him. "If the South had won, we'd have no trouble now," he answered. "I can read it," I replied, "but what does it *mean?*" "I don't know," he parried. "It's my best seller." In 1999, at North High School in Appleton, Wisconsin, conflicts between Mexican Americans and whites were a frequent occurrence. On the day after whites had defaced a Mexican flag at North, white students came to school "wearing Confederate Battle Flag symbols hanging from pockets on shirts and on car antennas," according to reporter Kathy Nufer. For decades Appleton had been a sundown town, requiring African Americans to be outside its city limits after dark, and residents of such towns frequently own and display Confederate flags. Although it no longer enforced this rule in the 1990s, the fact that students already owned these symbols and saw this conflict as their chance to use them probably derived from Appleton's sundown past.[1]

In various ways, Southern white culture, more broadly defined, wields huge influence, even dominance, over our nation. From music to NASCAR to barbecue, the "Southernization of America" has come a long way since John Egerton used that phrase back in 1974.[2] Around that time, I met a neighbor of mine in Vermont walking out of our woods with a small tape recorder in hand, repeating words when prompted. "What language are you learning?" I asked. "Southern," he replied with some embarrassment. Anxious to improve his standing in a country and western band he played in, Paul was learning to say "lack" for "like," "dai-oun" for "down," and "love" with at least two syllables.

Again, this seems benign—tasty, even—but it has a darker side. From 1964 to 2008, only two candidates for president from outside Dixie were successful. One of them, Richard Nixon, won partly owing to his "Southern strategy," appealing to white voters by using coded language that implied he would go slowly on civil rights. The other, Ronald Reagan, kicked off his 1980 general election campaign at that most Southern of all locations, the Neshoba County Fair. This is a traditionally white venue in the Mississippi county whose law enforcement officers had notoriously helped to kill three civil rights workers in 1964. Reagan never mentioned that tragic event, although some of the perpetrators and their relatives and friends were in his audience. Instead, he focused his remarks on the need for "states' rights," a code phrase for getting the federal government to leave race relations alone.

Unfortunately, Confederate symbolism and ideology inevitably come with white supremacy baggage. Hague, Sebesta, and Beirich show that neo-Confederates also are anti-immigrant, homophobic, and profoundly anti-democratic, and that's with a small "d." (They are profoundly anti-Democratic as well.)

This book performs three crucial functions. First, it shows the nuts and bolts of neo-Confederate ideology, often in its adherents' own words. Their own words make many neo-Confederates look nuts indeed. These are Americans who heroize John Wilkes Booth, not despite but because he assassinated Abraham Lincoln. They glorify Confederate cavalry leader Nathan Bedford Forrest, not despite but because he later led the Ku Klux Klan. And they seriously propose to secede again from the evil anti-white empire that they believe the United States of America has become.

Many Americans believe some of the claims made by neo-Confederates about our past. Probably half of all Americans think the Confederacy seceded for states' rights, for example. Certainly neo-Confederates say so. In reality, South Carolina proclaimed why it was leaving the United States in 1860, and it was for slavery—and *against* states' rights—as their "Declaration of the

Immediate Causes Which Induce and Justify the Secession of South Carolina from the Federal Union" made clear.

The present volume also performs a second crucial function: it points to historical realities like these—facts that undercut the many neo-Confederate claims that do *not* look nuts to too many miseducated Americans today. Most important of all, by providing evidence of neo-Confederate linkages to important foundations, Republican politicians, and professors at major universities, the essays published herein show that even when neo-Confederates *are* nuts, we must not dismiss them as on the fringes of society. Republican leaders like former attorney general John Ashcroft, Senator Trent Lott, and Richard Quinn, former spokesperson and campaign organizer for John McCain, have ties to some of the nuttiest and most racist neo-Confederate organizations and publications. John Shelton Reed, former president of the Southern Sociological Society, repeatedly wrote (under a pseudonym) for *Southern Partisan*, the pro-Confederate magazine that sells T-shirts with Abraham Lincoln's visage over the words "Sic semper tyrannis," the quotation that John Wilkes Booth shouted right after murdering him. Donald Livingston, a professor of philosophy at Emory University, is "currently engaged in a book-length study on the moral, legal, and philosophical meaning of secession," according to his department's web site, but judging from his description in these pages, Livingston is more likely to advocate secession than study it. The Ludwig von Mises Institute at Auburn University and the Rockford Institute in Illinois are among institutions with connections to the neo-Confederate movement. One of *Neo-Confederacy*'s most interesting chapters details how, in the late 1990s, the neo-Confederates took over an important organization, the Sons of Confederate Veterans.

What will they take over next? Nothing, if Hague, Sebesta, and Beirich have their way. For knowledge is power, and this book provides the necessary information for anyone to stop neo-Confederates dead in their tracks, using their own words against them. Hague, Sebesta, and Beirich have done the heavy lifting. In the process, they have created an essential tool for those who work to bring justice and healing across racial and sectional divides in America.

Notes

1. Nufer, Kathy W. "Racial Tensions Mount at North," *Appleton Post-Crescent*, 24 September 1999.

2. Egerton, John. *The Americanization of Dixie: The Southernization of America.* (New York: Harper's Magazine Press, 1974).

Acknowledgments

I would like to thank Steve Davis, Andy Matranga, Jamey Essex, and Tracy Edwards, who completed papers on neo-Confederacy in courses at Syracuse University. They offered new ideas and insights for which I am grateful. Don Mitchell, John Agnew, Jim Glassman, John Western, and John Mercer were sources of ideas, suggestions, and encouragement. At DePaul University many thanks are due to the Geography Department's supportive environment and my colleagues Pat McHaffie, Alex Papadopoulos, Win Curran, Alec Brownlow, Maureen Sioh, and Kim Diver. Laura Carter, Andrea Craft, Kristin Wood, Denise Rogers, Mary Devona, D. J. Forbes, Jennifer Rodríguez, Joe Menard, and Jenny Hampton were called upon to proofread, make photocopies, scan documents, and track down references, often on short notice. Their work is greatly appreciated. I am also grateful to have received DePaul University Research Grants and Competitive Research Leave to complete this book. Michael McMullan at the *Memphis Commercial Appeal* and Jenny Warburg helped to track down photographs. Bill Bishel at University of Texas Press patiently supported this project from proposal to publication, and the anonymous reviewers he enrolled to evaluate the book provided positive feedback and numerous valuable suggestions. My co-contributors were always responsive and gracious when I requested revisions on countless occasions. Thanks are also due to Mark Potok and Nancy McLean for providing copies of their essays, to Teun van Dijk for answering my emailed questions about the League of the South's discourse, and to Eric Schramm for copyediting the manuscript. My family has always been there to answer my questions and hear my frustrations. Last, writing and compiling this book would not have been possible without the intellectual and emotional support of Carrie.

Euan Hague

***

I would like to thank the volunteers who have helped me investigate neo-Confederacy. These seemingly ordinary, everyday persons proved to be quite extraordinary but must remain nameless. Knowing that they would never receive recognition, they took risks and received no rewards other than the knowledge that they were aiding the fight against prejudice. I could not have done this without them. As long as our republic has citizens like these, there is hope.

Edward H. Sebesta

***

I would very much like to thank the Southern Poverty Law Center for allowing me to concentrate a large part of my research and writing efforts on the neo-Confederate movement over the past seven years, in particular Chief Trial Counsel Morris Dees and CEO J. Richard Cohen. I would also like to thank all of my colleagues in the Intelligence Project, particularly my editor and frequent co-author Mark Potok, all of whom have helped our department to create a body of knowledge on this movement. I would not have been able to contribute to this volume without their patience and assistance.

Heidi Beirich

Neo-Confederacy

Introduction: Neo-Confederacy and the New Dixie Manifesto

EUAN HAGUE, EDWARD H. SEBESTA, AND HEIDI BEIRICH

Neo-Confederacy

Contemporary neo-Confederacy made its first mainstream appearance on 29 October 1995 when the *Washington Post* published the "New Dixie Manifesto."[1] The authors were Thomas Fleming and Michael Hill, two of twenty-seven people who had founded a new nationalist organization, the Southern League (later renamed League of the South), on 25 June 1994 in Tuscaloosa, Alabama.[2] Identified by the Southern Poverty Law Center's (SPLC) Mark Potok as the "ideological core" of neo-Confederacy,[3] the League of the South (LS) advocates secession from the United States and the establishment of an independent Confederation of Southern States (CSS).[4] The CSS would contain fifteen states—four states more than seceded to form the Confederate States of America (CSA), which led to the Civil War (1861–65), the additional states being Oklahoma, Missouri, Kentucky, and Maryland.[5]

The New Dixie Manifesto was a clarion call to arms in which Hill and Fleming described themselves as representing "a new group of Southerners . . . calling for nothing more revolutionary than home rule for the states established by the U.S. Constitution." Comparing "American Southerners" to, amongst others, Scots and Ukrainians, the manifesto charged that the United States had treated "American Southerners" with "exploitation and contempt," and that a "renewed South" was both necessary and achievable. Among its specific points, the manifesto espoused the following:

• home rule for "Southerners"
• states' rights and devolved political power
• local control over schooling, in opposition to federal desegregation decrees
• removal of federal funding and initiatives from Southern states

- a Christian tradition in opposition to modernity
- support for Confederate symbols

In addition, the manifesto expressed the following views:

- that "Southerners" are maligned as "racist" and "anti-immigrant" by hypocritical, prejudicial Northerners
- that the South should be left alone on the issues of race
- that race relations are better in Southern states than in Northern ones
- that the United States is a "multicultural, continental empire" run by elites in Washington, Wall Street, Hollywood, and the Ivy League.

The New Dixie Manifesto proclaimed that education policies, historical interpretations, federal programs, and opposition to Confederate iconography together constitute efforts to "rob" "Southerners" of their very existence, an active project of discrimination resulting in "cultural genocide."[6]

Letters critical of the manifesto soon appeared in the newspaper, one stating that Fleming and Hill had presented "questionable arguments."[7] Another claimed that the vision of the U.S. South that the manifesto proposed would require a process of "ethnic cleansing" to change the demography of the region, which, like much of the United States, is "polyglot, eclectic, syncretic and generally mixed and messy."[8] Whether or not by coincidence, the topic was revisited in the newspaper six weeks later on the occasion of the death of Andrew Lytle, one of the Southern (or Nashville) Agrarians. The conservative syndicated columnist George Will introduced readers to the heirs of the Agrarians' intellectual tradition, namely the Southern League and one of its founding directors, Clyde Wilson, a conservative academic at the University of South Carolina and a leading proponent of neo-Confederacy. Will praised the Southern League's "admirable seriousness about the intellectual pedigree of a particular cultural critique of American modernity," and told readers how to contact the organization for those who "believe America is becoming too homogenized, that regional differences are being blurred and ancient passions are growing cold." In addition, Will recommended the League's publication, *Southern Patriot*, which "bristles with quirky agitation against 'Yankee hegemony.'"[9]

Four months later, on 5 May 1996, National Public Radio's *Weekend Edition* broadcast an interview with Southern League president and manifesto co-author Michael Hill.[10] In response to Diane Roberts's questions about democracy, Hill said:

You know, the South has never bought into the Jacobin notion of equality. The South has always preferred a natural hierarchy. You're always going to have some violations of people's rights, for whatever reason, but we just believe that a natural social order left to evolve organically on its own would be better for everyone.

Hill's position, as we review in Chapter 4, is consistent with not only neo-Confederacy, but a nineteenth-century notion of social Darwinism. Explaining the neo-Confederate movement in London's *Guardian* newspaper, Roberts later wrote:

The Southern League [is] a burgeoning organisation of mostly middle-class, often academic, certainly angry, white men. . . . Their mission is to alert like-minded "neo-Confederates" to "heritage violations." . . . The Southern League's agenda is, as their board members describe it, "paleo-conservative." They want the South to return to the "order" it once had before the "disruption" of the Civil Rights Movement.[11]

Critical of this emergent neo-Confederate ideology, and exposing some of its more unpalatable tenets, Pulitzer Prize–winning author and journalist Tony Horwitz described neo-Confederacy in his book *Confederates in the Attic* as a "loosely defined ideology" that pulls together "strains of Thomas Jefferson, John Calhoun, the Nashville Agrarians . . . and other thinkers who idealized Southern planters and yeoman farmers while demonizing the bankers and industrialists of the North."[12] After a conversation with neo-Confederate Manning Williams in Charleston, South Carolina, Horwitz concluded that much of neo-Confederacy's discourse and ideology was "little more than a clever glide around race and slavery, rather like the slick-tongued defense of the Southern 'way of life' made by antebellum orators."[13]

Another journalist who has written on neo-Confederacy is Peter Applebome, who, in his book *Dixie Rising*, identified its proponents:

In hoary, century-old Confederate organizations and freshly minted, modern-day variations on the same theme, at conferences and Civil War reenactments, in cyber-space and the real world, the South is full of Lost Cause nostalgia, angry manifestos, secessionist verbiage, and assorted movements harking back to various elements of the Dixie of old. . . . The neo-Confederate groups are not a monolith. They range from hard-right and overtly racist politics to a relatively benign mix of monument polishing, history, nostalgia, and agrarian conservatism suspicious of both big government and big business.[14]

We concur with Applebome's evaluation, except for his assertion that some of these groups are benign. James W. Loewen and others have demonstrated the perniciousness of monuments to white supremacy throughout the United States: such commemorative efforts, however nostalgic, aid in the construction and maintenance of what geographer Richard Schein identifies as "racialized landscapes—American cultural landscapes that are particularly implicated in racist practice and the perpetuation of (or challenge to) racist social relations."[15] Our sense that Applebome's identification of the influence of neo-Confederacy is somewhat downplayed in these comments is confirmed just a few pages later. Exploring the close working relationships between advocates of neo-Confederacy, such as *Southern Partisan* owner Richard Quinn, and high-ranking members of the Republican Party, such as Ronald Reagan and Strom Thurmond, Applebome explains that "it's hard to know these days where the Confederacy ends and the Republican party begins."[16]

Thus neo-Confederacy may be more closely entangled in the corridors of power in the United States than it first appears. In the late 1990s, the *Washington Post*'s Thomas B. Edsall revealed a series of connections between elected Republican Party officials and the Council of Conservative Citizens (cc c), including Georgia congressman Robert L. Barr Jr.'s keynote speech to the ccc meeting in Charleston on 6 June 1998.[17] After initial denials, Barr admitted he had spoken to the ccc and distanced himself from the group, whose members, Edsall explained, "view intermarriage as a threat to the white race" and propose deporting nonwhites from the United States.[18] Edsall described how other leading Republican politicians, including Mississippi senator Trent Lott, North Carolina senator Jesse Helms, and Mississippi governor Kirk Fordice, had ties to the ccc. When the story broke, Lott initially stated that he had "no firsthand knowledge" of the ccc, but evidence emerged that in 1992 Lott had attended the group's meeting, telling those present in his keynote speech that they "stand for the right principles and the right philosophy."[19] Lott subsequently tried to distance himself from the ccc, members of which confirmed that Edsall's stories were accurate before articulating their opposition to immigration, racially integrated schools, affirmative action, and their fight to protect "such symbols of southern heritage as Confederate monuments and public displays of the Confederate flag."[20]

Despite such mainstream media attention, the debate over neo-Confederacy was perhaps more in evidence in alternative media sources and on the Internet.[21] The focus in such forums often extended beyond neo-Confederate views on race and states' rights issues. Richard Shumate, writing in *Southern Voice* in 1994, warned that "some of the people who are leading the charge to preserve Confederate heritage, known collectively as the neo-Confederate movement, are often openly, and passionately, homophobic."[22] Citing the overlapping interests of the Sons of Confederate Veterans (scv), Georgia's state representatives, and outspoken conservative leaders such as Pat Robertson and Pat Buchanan, Shumate explained that "while neo-Confederates leaders labor long and hard to veil any racist sentiments among their members (though in many cases, the veil wears pretty thin), disdain for gays and lesbians is, in contrast, often expressed openly and boldly."[23]

Writing in the Jewish newspaper *Forward* in 1995, Ira Stoll reviewed the major magazine of neo-Confederacy, *Southern Partisan*, a publication of the Foundation for American Education (discussed in Chapter 1). Highlighting its interviews with well-known Republican Party figures such as Trent Lott, Dick Armey, and Phil Gramm, Stoll explained:

> Some experts say the ties between politicians and the neo-Confederate movement offer insight into the Republican attempt to shift power to the states—an effort consistent with Confederate ideas. The *Southern Partisan* connection, they say, raises the prospect that the new GOP leadership and the presidential candidates may lend credibility to a group tinged with racism and historical carelessness.

One of Stoll's experts was Princeton University historian James McPherson, who said: "If this neo-Confederate point of view begins to forge back into the mainstream, it could undercut support for civil rights."[24] Brian Britt, in the on-line forum *Z Magazine*, concurred, explaining that neo-Confederacy was a worldview that

> encompasses history, literature, museums, reenactments, monuments, battle-fields, and organizations dedicated to the principles and founders of the Confederate States of America. Neo-Confederacy intersects with white supremacy, the Christian Right, the Populist Party, and the states' rights movement. To an increasingly diverse set of Americans, neo-Confederate culture supplies a regionally- and historically-grounded message of right-wing righteousness and urgency. Neo-Confederate culture presents two faces to the world: one of heritage and another of hate. Heritage bespeaks the mythical past of the antebellum South and its valiant defenders, but this gentility often adjoins angry right-wing extremism.[25]

At the time neo-Confederacy was evidently becoming a factor in U.S. politics. In a hotly contested Senate race in Illinois in 1998, the Republican challenger Peter Fitzgerald defeated incumbent Democrat Carol Moseley-Braun, an African American, but not before a Moseley-Braun campaign advertisement showed Fitzgerald standing beside a Confederate battle flag.[26] Fitzgerald "angrily denied Moseley-Braun's allegation that he [was] associated with neo-Confederate groups such as the Rockford Institute."[27] In Georgia, congresswoman Cynthia A. McKinney, also an African American, identified her 1996 electoral opponents as "a rag-tag group of neo-Confederates,"[28] and in Alabama, state senator Charles Davidson joined the neo-Confederate League of the South. "Make no mistake," David Goldfield subsequently warned in his book *Still Fighting the Civil War*, referring to elected officials such as Davidson, "these are not the much-maligned 'redneck' elements; these are southern leaders proving that the shelf-life of southern history extends considerably beyond its expiration date."[29] Examining neo-Confederate magazines like *Southern Partisan*, Goldfield explained that these publications romanticized the Old South and distorted the events of both the Civil War and Reconstruction, producing a neo-Confederacy that valorized white men, "as well as the racial and gender implications derived from those views."[30] Neo-Confederacy thus was seen to comprise a belief in, and the need for, social hierarchy, be this racial or gendered, with white men being dominant. To this, we contend, should be added hierarchies based on class, religion, and sexuality. Believers in neo-Confederacy, Goldfield explained, "are not fringe people." Their worldview and activities have "a broader white support in the South, within the Republican Party and among some evangelical Protestants."[31]

One of the most sustained encounters with this iteration of neo-Confederacy did not come in the South. The city of Rockford, Illinois, just ninety miles northwest of Chicago, became embroiled in a lawsuit about racial segregation and unequal school funding in the late 1980s. Federal Judge P. Michael Mahoney stated that through sophisticated tracking of student performances, school administrators in Rockford had "raise[d] discrimination to an art form," and ruled that Rockford must desegregate its schools, hire more minority teachers, build new facilities, and implement a host of other requirements.[32] Rockford had to levy additional taxes to pay for the costs. These measures attracted the attention of the Rockford Institute and its leader, Thomas Fleming, co-author of the New Dixie Manifesto.

On 16 February 1998, Fleming and his colleagues hosted a rally denouncing taxation, school integration, and the federal court's rulings. Alongside school board members at this event was one of the city's most prominent politicians, Republican congressman Don Manzullo. Exposing Fleming's neo-Confederate beliefs and founding membership in the League of the South, the *Rockford Register Star* explained that Fleming "compared the school desegregation case with historical injustices that caused acts of banditry and insurrection."[33] The newspaper subsequently revealed that "three members of the Rockford School Board say they will use whatever stage is offered to denounce court-ordered school taxes and judicial interference in local school systems. To them, it doesn't matter if the offer is from the founder of a neo-Confederate organization that has been accused of implicit racism."[34] Manzullo stated that he had no knowledge of Fleming's neo-Confederate connections,[35] although a year earlier, in February 1997, he had criticized the Rockford desegregation ruling in Fleming's *Chronicles* magazine.[36] Chastising "activist federal judges," Manzullo advocated limiting the power of the judiciary to make decisions "that would have the effect of raising taxes."[37] Manzullo again appeared in *Chronicles* three months prior to attending Fleming's February 1998 anti-taxation rally, this time attacking the United Nations as an organization that hindered U.S. sovereignty and had "outlived much of its usefulness and overreached its bounds."[38] Manzullo's claim of ignorance about Fleming thus seems disingenuous, particularly given Fleming's repeated assertions of his advocacy of neo-Confederacy in the mid-1990s. Writing in the *National Review* in July 1997, for example, Fleming outlined his reasons for membership in the Southern League (League of the South) and argued that "secession is as American as bootleg whisky and draft riots."[39] After listing numerous secessionist movements in U.S. history, Fleming maintained that "the United States remained, basically, a federal union down to the 1960s, when activist judges and ambitious politicians of both parties decided that the Constitution had outlived its usefulness."[40]

It was evident that something was happening in U.S. political culture that was fusing separatism, nationalism, Confederate heritage, and a politics that looked through a lens of race and ethnic identity. This neo-Confederacy, Christopher Centner explained to readers of *Skeptic* magazine, not only united a range of political positions, but was also pulling together numerous factions whose members often overlapped. These included the "heritage defenders" in groups like the Sons of Confederate Veterans and United Daughters of the Confederacy, "agrarian romantics" who positioned themselves as the intellectual heirs of the 1930s Southern Agrarians, libertarians connected with organizations such as the Ludwig von Mises Institute, "Christian soldiers" who voiced a fundamentalist religion and a belief in biblical literalism, and "racists."[41]

Researching Neo-Confederacy

It was this emerging example of nationalism and racially coded politics that led us (Hague, Sebesta, and the Southern Poverty Law Center) to pursue a sustained collaboration examining neo-Confederacy.[42] Our research was first published in 2000, when Sebesta's essay in *Scottish Affairs* argued:

> Neo-Confederacy is a reactionary movement with an ideology against modernity conceiving its ideas and politics within a historical framework of the U.S. Civil War (1861–1865) and the history of the American South. This includes more than a states' rights ideology in opposition to civil rights for African-Americans, other ethnic minorities, women and gays, though it certainly includes all these things. Opposition to civil rights is just a part of a world view desiring a hierarchical society, opposed to egalitarianism and modern democracy.[43]

Later that year the Southern Poverty Law Center (SPLC), an organization well known for its monitoring of, and legal contests with, militia, patriot, and other racial supremacy groups, identified the League of the South as a "hate group." This designation by the SPLC was made on the basis of a group's ideology as expressed in official publications or by the group's leaders. Hate groups, the SPLC maintains, have beliefs or practices that attack or malign an entire class of people for their immutable characteristics.

The SPLC argued that the neo-Confederate League of the South, founded by Michael Hill, Thomas Fleming, Clyde Wilson, and others in 1994, is racist in its belief that African Americans are inferior to whites and is therefore a hate group. Further, the SPLC report identified the League of the South at the forefront of a neo-Confederate movement that also included the CCC and sections of the SCV and UDC. It noted that the 1990s neo-Confederacy had precedents in, and connections to, the White Citizens' Councils of the 1950s and in this most recent version, neo-Confederacy was "unabashedly political and beginning to show its naked racism."[44]

This revitalized neo-Confederacy, anthropologist Paul Shackel explains, began to inform numerous debates, most prominently about the placement of Confederate flags in states like South Carolina.[45] It also influenced efforts by the SCV to reinterpret the Civil War as a struggle for national independence and sovereignty, a reinterpretation in which SCV authors "never mention slavery."[46] When politicians in the South did mention slavery, and condemned it, furious neo-Confederate sympathizers bombarded local media outlets. In April 1998, Governor James S. Gilmore III of Virginia criticized slavery in a statement that also proclaimed Confederate Heritage Month. Patrick S. McSweeney, a former chairman of Virginia's Republican Party, joined the neo-Confederate Heritage Preservation Association (HPA) in disparaging the governor's remarks.[47] Led in Virginia by R. Wayne Byrd Sr., who stated that Gilmore's comments were "an insult," the HPA was formed in 1993 and was, Shackel explains, "one of the first nationwide neo-Confederate organizations to develop in the post–civil rights era." With members in forty-nine states, the HPA actively lobbies state officials, often successfully, to declare Confederate Heritage months.[48] Through these and other similar groups, best-selling political commentator Kevin Phillips noted, "southerners have bred a new cultural and political phenomenon: neo-Confederates," whose "upsurge goes beyond mere nostalgia."[49] Although it is this recent neo-Confederacy that forms the major part of our analyses, neo-Confederate activism has a lengthy history in the United States.

Neo-Confederacy: A Recurrent Practice

It may be a truism to say that neo-Confederacy is practiced differently by different people in different places at different times. Although the latest version of neo-Confederacy emerged in the mid-1990s, the term "neo-Confederate" has an extensive history. James McPherson, for example, has described the efforts of "Neo-Confederate historical committees" operating between the 1890s and 1930s to make sure that history textbooks presented a version of the Civil War in which

> secession was not rebellion but rather a legal exercise of state sovereignty; the South fought not for slavery but for self-government; the Confederate soldiers fought courageously and won most of the battles against long odds but were finally worn down by overwhelming numbers and resources.[50]

These committees were drawn from members of the United Daughters of the Confederacy, the United Confederate Veterans, and the Sons of Confederate Veterans. Another historian, Nancy MacLean, has utilized "neo-Confederacy" to identify the reactionary right-wing politics that coalesced in the 1950s in opposition to Supreme Court rulings mandating racial desegregation.[51] Both usages are consistent with our own: McPherson's as it refers to major proponents of neo-Confederate beliefs and the central components of neo-Confederate understandings of the Civil War, and MacLean's referring to similar actors in conservative politics, whom we examine in Chapter 1.

Despite these varied attributions of "neo-Confederacy" from the period immediately after the Civil War to the present, there are a number of consistencies in neo-Confederate thought—its racist, patriarchal, heterosexist, classist, and religious undertones—that form the basis of a conservative ideology that centers upon social inequality and the maintenance of a hierarchical society. At the core of neo-Confederacy is an active promotion of the political legacy of the short-lived nineteenth-century Confederate States of America, comprising states whose secession resulted in the Civil War. Proponents of neo-Confederacy regularly look to these events, the Confederacy's leadership, and the pre–Civil War "Old South" for theological, philosophical, and cultural precedents and, in many cases, behavioral role models.

The major ideologues of the recent revival of neo-Confederacy are, as we outline in Chapter 1, almost all activists who identified themselves as paleoconservatives, decided to split from mainstream U.S. conservatism, and solidified their views around a vision of the South as "a priceless and irreplaceable treasure that must be conserved."[52] Hostile toward today's multicultural society and focused around organizations such as the League of the South and Council of Conservative Citizens, neo-Confederacy can also be said to inform more mainstream heritage organizations such as the Sons of Confederate Veterans and United Daughters of the Confederacy and, arguably, prominent politicians such as Trent Lott and Strom Thurmond. Proponents of neo-Confederacy also overlap with those advocating a racial, white nationalism, such as Jared Taylor and his *American Renaissance* magazine.[53]

Outline of the Book

Neo-Confederacy intertwines a range of political thought, theology, and historical interpretation into a call for the recognition of a specific Southern U.S. culture and various assemblages of what that culture means for the control of people and resources. In this volume, contributors draw on documents published by neo-Confederate activists to explore how neo-Confederate ideology constructs a worldview that we contend is patriarchal, ethnocentric, intolerant, and racist, but a worldview that operates utilizing a complex discourse, a language that at face value appears to laud cultural rights and freedoms, heritage preservation and celebration, local control over institutions, and Christianity.

Due to the diversity of actors and positions within neo-Confederate organizations, this collection is not intended to be comprehensive. Rather, we hope to illustrate the kinds of activities and politics that permeate this sector of the political right. Our intention is to give readers an understanding of neo-Confederacy, its development and ideologies. Further, we demonstrate the convergence of conservative thought with heritage preservation activism, popular commemorative processes, and theological beliefs, which together articulate neo-Confederacy at the start of the twenty-first century.

Neo-Confederate ideology influences Hollywood movies such as *Gods and Generals* (2003), college football games and mascots, museum displays, musical and theatrical performances, literature, religious beliefs, statuary and monuments, school textbooks, and multiple other aspects of everyday life in the United States. Many recent books about the role of memory and commemoration in the South note the growing presence of neo-Confederate interpretations of the past. When a statue of Abraham and Tad Lincoln was unveiled in Richmond, Virginia, in 2003, for example, the event was attended by "neo-Confederates wav[ing] signs bearing the slogan: 'Lincoln: Wanted for War Crimes.'"[54] The Southern Poverty Law Center's "Intelligence Reports" regularly provide details of the latest actions by neo-Confederate sympathizers.[55]

Two theoretical understandings underpin our collection as a whole. The first, as prominent geographer David Harvey has asserted, is "that no social order can change without the lineaments of the new already being present in the existing state of things."[56] Neo-Confederacy is an attempt to change the social order. Proponents of neo-Confederacy argue that American cultural, educational, political, and religious practices must be changed, and the ultimate aim of the League of the South, as noted, is the secession of fifteen states to create a new Confederacy. Such neo-Confederate contentions, however, did not appear out of the blue with the New Dixie Manifesto in 1995. We have to look to the past to understand the beliefs that coalesced into what became neo-Confederacy in the 1990s.

As examined in Chapter 1, many neo-Confederates identify themselves as "paleoconservatives" who, believing in what they consider to be authentic conservatism, became disillusioned with the direction that conservative politics took in the 1960s. In terms of religious perspectives, proponents of neo-Confederacy maintain that the Civil War was a theological struggle between orthodox Christian Confederate troops and heretical Union soldiers. This is examined in Chapter 2. Chapter 3 traces neo-Confederate understandings of gender and sexuality to the antebellum plantation household in which the white male planter represented the head, and his family and slaves the rest of the body, in an organic conceptualization of gender and race relations. Race is the crux around which neo-Confederacy turns, which is the subject of Chapters 4 and 5. Chapter 4 explores the self-image of many neo-Confederates, that of Anglo-Celtic ethnicity. The authors argue that this is a synonym for whiteness and show how in the 1970s and 1980s academics like Grady Mc-Whiney were integral in developing the Celtic South thesis that understands the (white) residents of the Southern states, both past and present, to be Celtic. Chapter 5 quotes neo-Confederate authors and publications at length, demonstrating that neo-Confederacy entails hostility toward social equality, multiculturalism, civil rights, school desegregation, affirmative action, and immigration. Utilizing ideas about ethnicity and race, proponents of neo-Confederacy maintain that ethnic and cultural groups are distinct and two or more groups cannot co-exist in the same space on equal terms.

The second part of the book examines processes of the production of neo-Confederate culture. This pertains to our second theoretical tenet, that culture is not an object that can be simply identified and then described. Rather, culture comprises on-going processes that must be explained. Saying that "culture" is the reason for something does not offer an understanding of how and why an event occurred or a belief developed. Indeed, saying something is "cultural" typically curtails rather than enhances debate. Consequently, cultural geographer Don Mitchell argues that when examining cultures, the critical questions to ask are "*who* produces culture—and to what end? . . . [and] *why* is it produced" (original emphasis). The result of such questioning is an assessment of how the practices of politics and culture are entwined in a relationship. Thus, our examinations in Part 2 address "the production of [neo-Confederate] 'culture' and its use" in promoting and disseminating a neo-Confederate ideology.[57]

Chapter 6 examines efforts to ensure that the Confederate flag remains flying high over the South, promoted by groups and activists such as the Council of Conservative Citizens, the League of the South, and controversial restaurant owner Maurice Bessinger. Bessinger's signature barbecue sauce was removed from the shelves of national chain stores like Wal-Mart after revelations about his neo-Confederacy appeared in local newspapers following a dispute that centered on flying the Confederate battle flag without a permit. Chapter 7 utilizes theories of nationalism that argue education is central to the reproduction of the idea of a nation. A nation does not just exist; rather, it is continuously reproduced through everyday processes, from the circulation of national heroes on currency and rallying behind national sports stars, to the mundane reproduction of the nation in banal imagery, such as television weather maps that suggest the weather stops at the U.S. borders with Canada and Mexico. Inculcating the next generation is always critical to nationalist projects, and the need to perpetuate neo-Confederacy leads proponents to homeschool their children and to teach peers about what they consider to be the truth about U.S. history.

Chapter 8 identifies the lineaments of current neo-Confederate literature in the nineteenth-century South, examining the fiction and poetry that has become the neo-Confederate curriculum for the educational practices discussed in Chapter 7. Another area of the ongoing practice of producing neo-Confederate culture is the subject of Chapter 9: music. Here the authors review examples such as *Stonewall Country,* a musical about Confederate general "Stonewall" Jackson, and performers like the Free South Band, whose CDs are widely available on neo-Confederate web sites.

The last chapters argue that neo-Confederacy is neither as benign nor as marginalized as some commentators have implied. Chapter 10 is a work of investigative journalism that demonstrates just how far neo-Confederacy has penetrated into mainstream Confederate heritage groups like the Sons of Confederate Veterans. Many active Civil War heritage enthusiasts now identify with neo-Confederate ideology. The result is that the SCV, which has almost 30,000 members, including some prominent public figures, now espouses an increasingly activist neo-Confederate political agenda. Finally, the afterword looks briefly at the reaction of neo-Confederates to the re-election of President George W. Bush in 2004 and notes the extent to which neo-Confederacy and neo-Confederate publications have moved beyond the South to gain a place within national U.S. conservatism. As proponents of neo-Confederacy establish think tanks like the Abbeville and Stephen D. Lee Institutes, the belief system is attracting members of the Republican Party and mainstream heritage groups like the SCV and UDC.[58] Given that these organizations have greater resources, in terms of outreach, membership, and finances, neo-Confederacy is a worldview that is continuing to develop and attract proponents throughout the United States. As a result, we believe it is time for a sustained analysis of neo-Confederacy.

Notes

1. Hill, Michael, and Fleming, Thomas. "New Dixie Manifesto: States' Rights Will Rise Again," *Washington Post,* (29 October 1995): C03. Copyright permission was sought to reproduce the manifesto. It was not received.

2. The Southern League changed its name to the League of the South in 1997 following the threat of legal action for trademark and copyright infringement by The Southern League of Professional Baseball Clubs, Inc. See Hill, Michael. "Name Changes: Principles Remain the Same," *Southern Patriot,* 4.4 (1997): 25–26. The foundation date of the Southern League is from "Partisan Conversation—Michael Hill:

The Southern League," *Southern Partisan*, 14 (4th quarter 1994): 34–37. The size of the initial foundational meeting is noted in League of the South, *The Grey Book: Blueprint for Southern Independence*. (College Station, TX: Traveller Press, 2004): vii. The president of the League of the South since its foundation has been Michael Hill. Hill also publishes under his full name, James Michael Hill, and J. Michael Hill.

3. Potok, Mark. "Of Hate and Heritage," *Intelligence Report*, 99 (2000): n.p.

4. League of the South. *The Grey Book: Blueprint for Southern Independence*. (College Station, TX: Traveller Press, 2004): vii.

5. For discussion of the origins and development of the League of the South, its positions and claims to territory, see Hill, Michael. "President's Note," *Southern Patriot*, 4.3 (1997): 26; Sebesta, Edward H. "The Confederate Memorial Tartan: Officially Approved by the Scottish Tartan Authority," *Scottish Affairs*, 31 (2000): 55–84; Hodges, Sam. "Southern Heritage: Cultural Genocide? Secession Seen as Remedy," *Atlanta Journal and Constitution*, (21 April 1996): 1R; Southern Poverty Law Center. "A League of Their Own," *Intelligence Report*, 99 (2000): 13–17; Webster, Gerald R. "If First You Don't Secede, Try, Try Again: Secession, Hate and the League of the South," *Spaces of Hate: Geographies of Discrimination and Intolerance in the U.S.A.*, ed. Colin Flint. (New York: Routledge, 2004): 137–164. See also Chapter 6.

6. Hill and Fleming, "New Dixie Manifesto," (1995): C03.

7. Brown, Victor Ivy. "Letter to the Editor: No Claim to Twain," *Washington Post*, (4 November 1995): A15.

8. Padgett, Lawrence. "Letter to the Editor: Dream Dixie," *Washington Post*, (14 November 1995): A18.

9. Will, George F. "Save Your Confederate Money, Boys," *Washington Post*, (28 December 1995): 23. Variants of Will's essay also appeared in the *Chicago Sun-Times*, *Tampa Tribune*, *New Orleans Times-Picayune*, *Atlanta Journal-Constitution*, and numerous other publications.

10. Roberts published other essays critical of the League. See "A League of Their Own," *Southern Exposure*, 25.1&2 (1997): 18–23; "Real Lives: Ghosts of the Gallant South," *The Guardian (G2 section)*, (22 July 1996): 14; "The New Dixie Manifesto," *Utne Reader*, January–February (1998): 67–69, 101–103; "Your Clan or Ours?" *Oxford American*, 29 (1999): 24–30.

11. Roberts, "Real Lives," (1996): 14. Michael Hill subsequently attacked Roberts in 1998 as pursuing a "hysterical crusade" against the nineteenth-century Confederacy and the League of the South: "Roberts and her liberal allies set themselves in the place of God and judge our organization according to their own definitions of 'sin.'" Hill, Michael. "Modern-day Jacobinism Lives on the University of Alabama Campus . . ." (Monroe, LA: League of the South News Service, 7 July 1998). On-line: http://www .dixienet.org/ls-press-releases/rebut-rbts.html [accessed 18 October 2002].

12. Horwitz, Tony. *Confederates in the Attic: Dispatches from the Unfinished Civil War*. (New York: Vintage, 1998); "Rebel Voices," *Wall Street Journal*, 95.83 (28 April 1995): A1, A7; "Death in Dixie," *New Yorker*, 72.4 (18 March 1996): 64–70, 72–77; "Rebel Voices: The Faces of Extremism Wear Many Guises—Most of them Ordinary," *Wall Street Journal*, 95.83 (28 April 1995): A1, A7.

13. Horwitz, *Confederates in the Attic*, (1998): 69–70.

14. Applebome, Peter. *Dixie Rising: How the South Is Shaping American Values, Politics, and Culture*. (New York: Times Books, 1996): 117–118.

15. Schein, Richard H. "Normative Dimensions of Landscape," *Everyday America: Cultural Landscape Studies after J. B. Jackson*, ed. Chris Wilson and Paul Groth. (Berkeley: University of California Press, 2003): 203; Loewen, James W. *Lies Across America: What Our Historic Sites Get Wrong* (New York: Touchstone, 2000). For analyses of the location of monuments to the Confederacy throughout the U.S. South, see, amongst others, Mills, Cynthia, and Simpson, Pamela H., eds. *Monuments to the Lost Cause: Women, Art, and the Landscapes of Southern Memory.* (Knoxville: University of Tennessee Press, 2003); Savage, Kurt. *Standing Soldiers, Kneeling Slaves: Race, War, and Monument in Nineteenth-Century America.* (Princeton, NJ: Princeton University Press, 1999); Gulley, H. E. "Women and the Lost Cause: Preserving a Confederate Identity in the American Deep South," *Journal of Historical Geography*, 19.2 (1993): 125–141; Radford, J. P. "Identity and Tradition in the Post–Civil War South," *Journal of Historical Geography*, 18.1 (1992): 91–103; Foster, Gaines M. *Ghosts of the Confederacy: Defeat, the Lost Cause, and the Emergence of the New South, 1865–1913.* (New York: Oxford University Press, 1987); Winberry, John J. "'Lest We Forget': The Confederate Monument and the Southern Town-scape," *Southeastern Geographer*, 23.2 (1983): 107–121. For assessment of the vitriolic dispute about the location of a statue to African American tennis star Arthur Ashe alongside those of Confederate leaders on Richmond's Monument Avenue, see Leib, Jonathan I. "Separate Times, Share Spaces: Arthur Ashe, Monument Avenue and the Politics of Richmond, Virginia's Symbolic Landscape," *Cultural Geographies*, 9.3 (2002): 286–312. The bas-relief sculpture of Confederate leaders at Stone Mountain is examined by Essex, Jamey S. "'The Real South Starts Here'—Whiteness, the Confederacy, and Commodification at Stone Mountain," *Southeastern Geographer*, 42.2 (2002): 211–227.

16. Applebome, *Dixie Rising*, (1996): 120. Richard Quinn, campaign manager for Senator John McCain's presidential campaign in 2000, was a former editor of *Southern Partisan*. In the USPS Statement of Management Ownership and Circulation for 2004–2005, Quinn is listed as a co-owner of the magazine, alongside Charles Hamel. See Chapter 1 for further discussion of *Southern Partisan*.

17. Edsall, Thomas B. "Barr Spoke To White Supremacy Group," *Washington Post*, (11 December 1998): A23.

18. Edsall, Thomas B. "Barr Rejects Racial Views of Group He Visited; He Says He Had No Idea of Stands," *Washington Post*, (12 December 1998): A04.

19. Quoted in Edsall, Thomas B. "Lott Renounces White 'Racialist' Group He Praised in 1992," *Washington Post*, (16 December 1998): A02.

20. Edsall, Thomas B. "Controversial Group Has Strong Ties to Both Parties in South," *Washington Post*, (13 January 1999): A02. Other Republican Party officehold-ers, such as Congressman Charles Sharpe of South Carolina, were also CCC members. The Republican National Committee chairman Jim Nicholson subsequently called on GOP members to cut their ties with the CCC. See also Edsall, Thomas B. "Conservative Group Accused Of Ties to White Supremacists," *Washington Post*, (19 December 1998): A08; Edsall, Thomas B. "GOP Chairman Denounces 'Racist' Group; Nicholson Urges Party Members to Resign From Council of Conservative Citizens," *Washington Post*, (20 January 1999): A04; Edsall, Thomas B. "Conservative Group Ends E-Mail Postings; Recent Messages Backed Anti-Jewish Views," *Washington Post*, (29 January 1999): A06; Edsall, Thomas B. "Resolution Targets Council Of Conservative Citi-

zens," *Washington Post*, (30 January 1999): A06; Edsall, Thomas B. "Another Republican Retreats From Council of Conservative Citizens," *Washington Post*, (7 March 1999): A12; Edsall, Thomas B. "With 'Resegregation,' Old Divisions Take New Form; Conservative Group Evokes South's Segregationist Past," *Washington Post*, (9 April 1999): A03.

21. Many of the journalists researching these stories were contacted by Edward Sebesta, who provided information and documentation about neo-Confederacy. For an examination of neo-Confederacy on the Internet see McPherson, Tara. "I'll Take My Stand in Dixienet—White Guys, the South and Cyberspace," *Race in Cyberspace*, ed. Beth E. Kolko, Lisa Nakamura, and Gilbert B. Rodman. (New York and London: Routledge, 2000): 117–131.

22. Shumate, Richard. "Stars, Bars, and Homophobia," *Southern Voice*, (31 March–6 April 1994): 1, 15.

23. Ibid.

24. Stoll, Ira. "Meanwhile in Dixie, Southern Partisan Whistles Old Tune," *Forward*, 98.31049 (13 October 1995): 1–2.

25. Britt, Brian. "Neo-Confederate Culture," *Z Magazine*, (December 1996). Online: http://www.zmag.org/Zmag/articles/dec96britt.htm [accessed 27 January 1999 and 2 December 2004].

26. Howlett, Debbie. "Moseley-Braun Trails Fitzgerald," *USA Today*, (4 November 1998): 6A.

27. Rotzoll, Brenda Warner. "First Lady Makes Third Blitz for Local Dems," *Chicago Sun-Times*, (1 November 1998): 9. The Rockford Institute is based in Rockford, Illinois, and is closely associated with Thomas Fleming and the magazine *Chronicles*. We discuss this below and in Chapter 1.

28. Kirkpatrick, David D. "Police Seek Warrant to Arrest Congresswoman," *New York Times* (4 April 2006): A20.

29. Goldfield, David. *Still Fighting the Civil War* (Baton Rouge: Louisiana State University Press, 2002): 302.

30. Ibid., 303.

31. Ibid.

32. For a full review of this case, and some background to Rockford, see Austin, Elizabeth. "A River Knifes Through It: Nature Split Rockford First, but It Has Taken a Desegregation Lawsuit to Truly Divide the City," *Chicago Tribune*, (27 September 1998): 10.

33. Sweeny, Chuck, and Emerson, Judy. "New Confederates Spark Outrage in Rockford," *Rockford Register Star*, (15 March 1998): 1A, 4A-5A. The local newspaper, the *Rockford Register Star*, covered this debate extensively—see Sweeny, Chuck. "Dixienet: Cyberspace Southern Style," *Rockford Register Star*, (15 March 1998): 4A; Emerson, Judy. "Southern-born Prof Calls League Racist," *Rockford Register Star*, (15 March 1998): 5A; Sweeny, Chuck. "'An Unconscionable Act' or 'Courage to Do the Right Thing'?" *Rockford Register Star*, (16 March 1998): 1A, 4A; Manzullo, Don. "Manzullo says League of the South articles Were Unfair to Him, Misleading Readers," *Rockford Register Star*, (22 March 1998).

34. Sweeny, "'An Unconscionable Act,'" (1998): 1A, 4A.

35. Manzullo, "Manzullo Says League."

36. Manzullo, Don. "Judicial Taxation without Representation," *Chronicles: A*

Magazine of American Culture, 21.2 (1997) 36–37. This issue of *Chronicles* magazine contained articles by a "who's who" of 1990s neo-Confederacy and paleoconservatism, including Thomas Fleming, Samuel Francis, Franklin Sanders, Mark Malvasi, and Paul Gottfried.

37. Manzullo, "Judicial Taxation," (1997): 36–37.

38. Manzullo, Don. "Cultural Revolutions," *Chronicles,* 21.12 (1997): 6–7. After a seven-year hiatus, Manzullo returned to publishing in *Chronicles* in 2004. Again writing in the "Cultural Revolutions" section (*Chronicles* 28.5 [2004]: 7), Manzullo outlined a proposal to reduce the amount of taxation paid by U.S. manufacturers who produced goods within the United States.

39. Fleming, Thomas. "America's Crackup," *National Review,* 49.14 (1997): 48.

40. Ibid., 64.

41. Centner, Christopher M. "Neo-Confederates at the Gate: The Rehabilitation of the Confederate Cause and the Distortion of History," *Skeptic,* 9.3 (2002): 60–66.

42. The earliest result of these discussions initiated by Sebesta was Mark Potok's "League's Course Threatening," *Montgomery Advertiser,* 23 October 1997. This was written in response to Michael Hill's "League Sets Honorable Course," *Montgomery Advertiser,* 7 October 1997. The League of the South web site described Potok's essay as "slanderous, inflammatory and highly inaccurate" and assured neo-Confederate activists that Potok's commentary "borders on actionable libel and a legal review by the League's attorney's is pending." See "Letter to the Editor by Anti-Southern Bigot Marc Potok, as Printed in the 'Montgomery Advertiser'—October 23, 1997" On-line: http://www.dixienet.org/ls-press-releases/potok-slander.html [accessed 2 November 1997]. As of October 2007, no legal action had occurred.

43. Sebesta, Edward H. "The Confederate Memorial Tartan," (2000): 55–56. Sebesta's argument was subsequently attacked by Ray, Celeste. "Comment on 'The Confederate Memorial Tartan,'" *Scottish Affairs,* 35 (2001): 133–138, but it had already made inroads in Scotland—see Ascherson, Neal. *Stone Voices: The Search for Scotland.* (New York: Hill and Wang, 2002).

44. Southern Poverty Law Center. "Rebels with a Cause," *Intelligence Report,* 99 (2000): 9. Neo-Confederates reacted angrily to this SPLC report—see "In Defence of the League of the South," *Southern Patriot,* 7.5 (2000): 12–14; League of the South, "A Message to the Southern Poverty Law Center and Its Leftist Allies." On-line: http://www.dixienet.org/ls-press-releases/LS-special-reports/splc.htm [accessed 15 September 2000 and 3 February 2002]; "A League of the South Special Report on the Southern Poverty Law Center (Part One)." On-line: http://www.dixienet.org/ls-press-releases/LS-special-reports/splc-special.htm [accessed 15 September 2000]; "A League of the South Special Report on the Southern Poverty Law Center (Part Two)." On-line: http://www.dixienet.org/ls-press-releases/LS-special-reports/splc-special2.htm [accessed 18 February 2001]. These virulent reactions by neo-Confederates to negative coverage echo similar denunciations by white supremacist Citizens' Councils of the 1950s to journalists critical of their campaigns—see McMillen, Neil R. *The Citizens' Council: Organized Resistance to the Second Reconstruction (1954–1964).* (Urbana: University of Illinois Press, 1971).

45. See Webster, Gerald R., and Leib, Jonathan I. "Whose South Is It Anyway? Race and the Confederate Battle Flag in South Carolina," *Political Geography,* 20.3 (2001): 271–299.

46. Shackel, Paul A. *Memory in Black and White: Race, Commemoration, and the Post-Bellum Landscape*. (Walnut Creek, CA: AltaMira Press, 2003): 183.

47. Cain, Andrew. "Confederate History Month Has a New Angle; Gilmore Repudiates Virginia Slavery," *Washington Times*, (10 April 1998): A1. See also Hsu, Spencer S. "Slavery 'Abhorred,' Gilmore Says; Words Anger Confederate Defenders; Event Upsets Rights Groups," *Washington Post*, (10 April 1998): C01; Boyd, Thomas M. "The Curse of Slavery," *Washington Post*, (2 May 1998): A19.

48. Shackel, *Memory in Black and White*, (2003): 184.

49. Phillips, Kevin. *American Theocracy: The Peril and Politics of Radical Religion, Oil, and Borrowed Money in the 21st Century*. (New York: Viking, 2006): 140.

50. McPherson, James M. "Long-Legged Yankee Lies: The Southern Textbook Crusade," *The Memory of the Civil War in American Culture*, ed. Alice Fahs and Joan Waugh. (Chapel Hill: University of North Carolina Press, 2004): 64–78. The reference to "neo-Confederate" is on p. 76, the extended quote on p. 68.

51. MacLean, Nancy. "Neo-Confederacy against the New Deal: The Regional Romance of the Modern American Right." Paper presented at conference entitled "The End of Southern History? Reintegrating the Modern South and the Nation" (Atlanta: Emory University, 2006).

52. Wilson, Clyde. "Introduction: Should the South Survive?" *Why the South Will Survive*, Fifteen Southerners. (Athens: University of Georgia Press, 1981): 1.

53. For example, Jared Taylor has contributed to the League of the South's *Southern Patriot*, as have authors like Michael W. Masters who have ties to both neo-Confederate and white nationalist organizations. For an overview of Taylor's beliefs, see the interview conducted in 1999 by Nieli, Russ. "Jared Taylor," *Contemporary Voices of White Nationalism in America*, ed. Carol M. Swain and Russ Nieli. (Cambridge: Cambridge University Press, 2003): 87–113.

54. Fahs, Alice, and Waugh, Joan. "Introduction," *The Memory of the Civil War in American Culture*, ed. Alice Fahs and Joan Waugh. (Chapel Hill: University of North Carolina Press, 2004): 1. In addition to those texts mentioned in this chapter and elsewhere in this book, contests over the memory of the Civil War and Confederate States of America are also addressed by Ayers, Edward L. *What Caused the Civil War? Reflections on the South and Southern History*. (New York: W. W. Norton, 2005); Mills, Cynthia, and Simpson, Pamela H., ed. *Monuments to the Lost Cause: Women, Art, and the Landscapes of Southern Memory*. (Knoxville: University of Tennessee Press, 2003); Blair, William. *Cities of the Dead: Contesting the Memory of the Civil War 1865–1914*. (Chapel Hill: University of North Carolina Press, 2004); Blight, David W. *Race and Reunion: The Civil War in American Memory*. (Cambridge: Harvard University Press, 2001); Blight, David W. *Beyond the Battlefield: Race, Memory, and the American Civil War*. (Amherst: University of Massachusetts Press, 2002); Brundage, W. Fitzhugh. *The Southern Past: A Clash of Race and Memory*. (Cambridge, MA: Belknap Press of Harvard University Press, 2005); Chadwick, Bruce. *The Reel Civil War*. (New York: Alfred Knopf, 2001); Cobb, James C. *Away Down South: A History of Southern Identity*. (Oxford and New York: Oxford University Press, 2005); Cobb, James C. *Redefining Southern Culture: Mind and Identity in the Modern South*. (Athens: University of Georgia Press, 1999); Cox, Karen L. *Dixie's Daughters: The United Daughters of the Confederacy and the Preservation of Confederate Culture*. (Gainesville: University Press of Florida, 2003); Cullen, Jim. *The Civil War In Popular Culture*. (Washington and

London: Smithsonian Institution Press, 1995); Loewen, James W. *Lies My Teacher Told Me: Everything Your American History Textbook Got Wrong.* (New York: Touchstone, 1996); Neff, John R. *Honoring the Civil War Dead: Commemoration and the Problem of Reconciliation.* (Lawrence: University of Kansas Press, 2005); Savage, Kurt. *Standing Soldiers, Kneeling Slaves: Race, War, and Monument in Nineteenth-Century America.* (Princeton, NJ: Princeton University Press, 1999).

55. The Southern Poverty Law Center's *Intelligence Report* is available from Southern Poverty Law Center, 400 Washington Avenue, Montgomery, AL 36104. At the time of writing, subscription is free.

56. Harvey, David. *Paris, Capital of Modernity.* (New York and London: Routledge, 2006 [2003]): 16. Harvey is drawing upon and paraphrasing nineteenth-century political theorists Claude-Henri de Saint-Simon and Karl Marx in this evaluation.

57. Mitchell, Don. *Cultural Geography: A Critical Introduction,* (Oxford: Blackwell, 2000): xviii.

58. The Abbeville Institute was established by Donald Livingston, a scholar of Hume and member of the League of the South in the 1990s; see Hague, Euan. "Texts as Flags: The League of the South and the Development of a Nationalist Intelligentsia in the United States, 1975-2001," *Hagar: International Social Science Review,* 3.2 (2002): 299-339. Its "objective is to promote a critical study of what is true and valuable in the southern tradition"—Erath, Clara. "The Value of Southern Tradition," *UDC Magazine,* 68.7 (2005): 17. See also "A Report on the Abbeville Institute," *Southern Partisan,* 24.6 (2004) 24-27. The Stephen D. Lee Institute, which lists League of the South founder Clyde Wilson as its dean, is connected to the Sons of Confederate Veterans and offers "a national program to promote better understanding of the core issues which surround our cause." Sullivan, Christopher M. "The Stephen D. Lee Institute," *Confederate Veteran,* 64.1 (2006): 8-9. Similar "institutes" promoting neo-Confederacy have been founded since the mid-1990s. Many are listed in "Confederate Education," *Southern Partisan,* 24.6 (2004): 24-26, and include the Watson-Brown Foundation, the Young-Sanders Center, and the Dixie Writers Guild.

PART I

THE ORIGINS AND DEVELOPMENT OF NEO-CONFEDERACY AND ITS TENETS

CHAPTER 1

Neo-Confederacy and Its Conservative Ancestry

EUAN HAGUE AND EDWARD H. SEBESTA

In this chapter we explore the emergence of neo-Confederacy amongst a group who identify themselves as paleoconservatives.[1] Much of this intellectual effort, developed in a series of writings in the 1980s and 1990s, was located within the Agrarian tradition of Southern thought, a tradition that paleoconservatives envisioned themselves as inheriting and continuing. We focus on a few key figures who articulated a neo-Confederacy that we propose has since spread beyond these self-appointed articulators of paleoconservatism. These individuals became influential precisely because they wrote books, founded think tanks and institutes, published magazines, spoke at conferences, and disseminated their ideological positions and interpretations of the United States. It does not mean that these writers were the only proponents of this conservative ideology—indeed, Nancy MacLean, amongst others, suggests that such opinions were widely held in the 1950s and 1960s by those opposing civil rights.[2]

The Changing Political Landscape and the Reaction to Civil Rights

The changes initiated by the Supreme Court's 1954 school desegregation ruling *Brown v. Board of Education*, the 1955–56 Montgomery Bus Boycott, the activism of Martin Luther King Jr., and legislation such as the 1964 Civil Rights Act and 1965 Voting Rights Act continue to transform U.S. social and political landscapes. In the 1950s and 1960s they were fiercely resisted, not just by police with snarling dogs on the streets of Selma, but also in elite political and intellectual circles. MacLean, for example, argues that defense of the segregationist "racial status quo" was central to the establishment of the *National Review* by William F. Buckley Jr. in 1955. In addition, she notes that books like *The Conservative Mind* (1953) by Russell Kirk and Richard M. Weaver's *Ideas Have Consequences* (1948) contributed philosophical fuel to what was becoming a conservative "common defense of the old hierarchical order."[3] This conservatism, although national, looked to the South for inspiration and precedents and drew on states' rights arguments articulated in the Old South, such as those forwarded in the first half of the nineteenth century by John C. Calhoun. Having embedded itself within this intellectual tradition, conservative proponents opposed desegregation and often participated in (White) Citizens' Councils.[4] These Citizens' Councils initially appeared in Mississippi and grew rapidly after the *Brown* decision. Their newspaper, *The Citizens' Council*, which first appeared in October 1955, repeatedly depicted crude stereotypes; African American civil rights leaders, for example, were commonly portrayed in editorial cartoons as nearly naked, wielding spears, wearing grass skirts, and adorned with bones through their noses or necklaces of teeth.[5] Other illustrations indicated that "Black Supremacy" would result in "riots," "orgies," "arson," "looting," "mutiny," "witchcraft," "murder," and "rape," with explanations that "the Negro is utterly incapable of governing himself, much less anyone else."[6] Flying Confederate battle flags at their rallies, Citizens' Councils routinely invoked the Confederacy in their opposition to civil rights and called on their readers to resist "the evil forces of integration."[7]

One of the most prominent opponents of civil rights was Arizona senator Barry Goldwater, who was the Republican presidential nominee in 1964. Largely a libertarian, he voted against the Civil Rights Act, opposed school integration, and stated that racial desegregation meant that "we are being asked to destroy the rights of some under the false banner of promoting the civil rights of others."[8] Although Lyndon Johnson defeated Goldwater in a landslide, Goldwater's candidacy did have an impact—it made people question not only their own political affiliations, but the meaning of conservatism in the United States. One person who was profoundly affected was the future Republican congressman and senator from Mississippi, Trent Lott. In the traditionally Democratic South, Lott and other white voters experienced what MacLean describes as an "epiphany" and began to think of themselves as Republicans.[9] The result was that, for the first time, five Southern states voted for the Republican candidate, although Goldwater lost forty-four states overall. Subsequently, the South has been reliably Republican in every presidential election save 1976, when Georgia's Jimmy Carter was victorious.

Goldwater's candidacy also led to a division within conservative ranks, roughly between neoconservatives and other conservatives. Neoconservatism emphasized a strong anti-Communist foreign policy, tax cuts, supply-side economics, and global free trade, positions that advocates saw as central to the Republican Party.[10] A theological conservatism (theoconservatism) also emerged, its proponents challenging that neoconservatism failed to advance Christian morality in cultural or social issues.[11] For some, however, there was a third branch: paleoconservatism.

The Paleoconservatives

The 1990s version of neo-Confederacy has origins in an attempt by a group of conservative intellectuals to influence right-wing politics in the United States. Self-identified paleoconservatives, much like theoconservatives, believed that neoconservatives were too driven by economic policy, global trade, a free market ideology, and belief in the international expansion of democratic capitalism. The paleoconservatives, by contrast, were anti-modern reactionaries, nativists hostile toward immigration who proposed a hierarchical social order in which loyalty to family, tradition, and Christianity were paramount. Communities, paleoconservatives believed, should be small, agrarian, and self-regulating, with highly localized economies, as one notable paleoconservative, Joseph Scotchie, argued: "Right-thinking Americans need to take control of their schools, town halls, and other institutions—and, if necessary, to create new institutions, such as charter schools. They also need to rediscover their region's—and the nation's—history, culture, heritage, literature, its heroes, and mythologies."[12] The United States, paleoconservatives contended, has strayed from the path laid by the founding fathers and become morally, culturally, and spiritually bankrupt, a process believed to have accelerated since the 1960s era of civil rights and the beginning of subsequent social changes such as women's liberation, gay and lesbian rights, and other efforts to ensure that the nation practiced the promises of equality and democracy that it preached.

One of the main paleoconservative voices in the late twentieth century was Clyde Wilson. In 1982, alongside his University of North Carolina contemporaries and fellow paleoconservatives Thomas Fleming and Samuel T. Francis, Wilson argued there had been a "quarter century" in which government action had "greatly accelerated the deterioration of community by magnifying the unhealthiest elements of society and besieging the best."[13] The removal of Christianity from public schools and racial desegregation were to blame because "in the name of equality they [the U.S. government] destroy the safety and homogeneity of other people's neighborhoods, not their own."[14] Continuing, Wilson explained that political elites were out of touch with grassroots Americans, perversely "reward[ing]" with welfare and rehabilitation programs those who acted without "virtue and responsibility," such as drug users and single mothers, and lamenting that rather than creating "sound communities" founded upon "strong families," government officials sanctioned "alternative lifestyles" and "gay rights," evidence of societal "sickness," "malignancy," and "retrogression."[15]

Central to the paleoconservative argument was the demand that federal authorities allow local communities, and families in particular, to develop their own social and cultural agendas without intervention. Given the antagonism toward racial integration, equality, and gay rights, opposition to government support for the poor and disadvantaged, and demands for local control over neighborhoods, it is evident that leading paleoconservatives implicitly preferred a racially segregated society inhabited by heterosexual families who live without governmental assistance. Typically, paleoconservatives argued this was the "natural" state of affairs that was being artificially eroded by federal programs and governmental belief in equality—what Thomas Fleming called "being poisoned by the raw chemicals of individual rights."[16]

In the 1980s, with Ronald Reagan as president, the New Right, or neoconservatives, had access to the Republican White House, heralding what Alan Wolfe identifies as a shift in U.S. politics: elements once consigned to the radical right now occupied the political center.[17] To paleoconservatives like Thomas Fleming, Joseph Scotchie, Paul Gottfried, and others, however, the Reagan administration did not deliver suitably conservative social policies, failing to reinstate school prayer or overturn abortion rights that the 1973 *Roe v. Wade* Supreme Court decision assured.[18] Similarly, although Reagan's anti-Communism was welcomed throughout the right, paleoconservatives were less convinced by the model of advocating and imposing U.S.-style democracy across the world. In contrast, self-identified paleoconservatives argued that the United States should not look to build an American Empire, but be a self-sufficient republic, detaching itself from global trade and political agreements, institutions like the United Nations, the North Atlantic Treaty Organization, and the International Monetary Fund.[19] Such an arrangement, they claimed, was the intention of the founding fathers. Having departed from the original rationale for the United States, Clyde Wilson questioned whether "the descendents of the present generation of Americans will be free citizens of a proud republic or merely ciphers in a faceless mass of imperial subjects."[20]

Advocating that a U.S. republic should be built from the grassroots up, rather than imposed by a government in top-down manner—the hallmark of an imperial power—Wilson argued that politicians had lost their sense of responsibility to those who elected them and, as a result, community-level beliefs were determined not by local choice but by federal legislation and imposition. As a result:

> Ordinary Americans, particularly in the largest and most liberal cities, are no longer proud members of self-governing communities. They are cowering nobodies, faceless interchangeable beings without a notion of being masters of their own fate. All this under an imperialist regime which seeks "quality" and "equality" with immense expenditures and police powers.[21]

Wilson, like other self-identified paleoconservatives, consistently argued that hierarchy in terms of class, race, and gender divisions was the basis of social life. Equality and egalitarianism were understood by paleoconservatives as artificial constructs imposed on Americans by policy think tanks in Washington, as was multiculturalism, defined by Scotchie as an "anti-Western, anti-Christian ideolog[y]."[22]

In 1981, many self-identified paleoconservatives contributed to a collection that one of the authors, John Shelton Reed, described as a "'neo-Agrarian' manifesto."[23] *Why the South Will Survive: Fifteen Southerners Look at Their Region a Half Century after "I'll Take My Stand"* contained essays by, among others, M. E. Bradford, Samuel T. Francis, Thomas Fleming, and Clyde Wilson. It positioned these paleoconservatives as the intellectual descendents of Southern Agrarians, a connection further symbolized by the participation of an elderly Andrew Nelson Lytle who, fifty years earlier, had contributed to *I'll Take My Stand*, the seminal text of Southern Agrarian political thought.[24]

The Southern or Nashville Agrarians

The ideological basis for much of the writing by self-proclaimed paleoconservatives and subsequent neo-Confederates was the Southern Agrarians (also termed the Nashville or Vanderbilt Agrarians, having originally met at Vanderbilt University). The Southern Agrarians—Robert Penn Warren, Donald Davidson, John Crowe Ransom, Allen Tate, and Lytle, amongst others—wrote in a context of the rapid industrialization and urbanization in the New South, followed by, in the 1930s, the Great Depression, the Works Progress Administration and programs such as the Tennessee Valley Authority, and a revival of the Ku Klux Klan. In a period identified as the "nadir of race relations" in the United States, the Southern Agrarians articulated dissatisfaction with what they felt was an erosion of distinctive Southern traditions and lifestyles.[25] The group "denounced the corrosive effects of technology and modernism on the South,"[26] and, believing that culture and governance should develop from the grassroots centered on local beliefs and local scale legislation, "championed a traditional society that was religious, more rural than urban, and politically conservative—a society in which human needs were met by family, clanship, folkways, custom, and community."[27] They were also concerned that increasing mass production and consumption within a capitalist system and Fordist industrial society was dehumanizing and that the federal secular state was destabilizing Christianity, undermining the faith upon which U.S. communities had been built. Coming together as "Twelve Southerners" to compile the most famous Southern Agrarian text, *I'll Take My Stand,* these writers offered a vision of an agrarian South that was in danger of losing its cultural identity to industrial development:

> Nobody now proposes for the South, or for any other community in this country, an independent political destiny. That idea is thought to have been finished in 1865. But how far shall the South surrender its moral, social, and economic autonomy to the victorious principle of Union? That question remains open.[28]

The Twelve Southerners mapped their struggle for agrarianism onto the battle for the Confederacy, and it is this source, as much as any other, that became the basis for late-twentieth-century neo-Confederate reinterpretations of the Civil War, its legacy and a vision of the future. *I'll Take My Stand* reiterated many white supremacist beliefs about slavery and people of African descent. Novelist Robert Penn Warren contributed the essay "The Briar Patch," which questioned the utility of educating African Americans and their ability to succeed in mainstream U.S. society.[29] In another essay, Frank Owsley wrote:

> When the [American] Revolution came and the Southern colonies gained their independence, they did not free the negroes. The eternal race question had reared itself. Negroes had come into the Southern Colonies in such numbers that people feared for the integrity of the white race. For the negroes were cannibals and barbarians, and therefore dangerous. No white man who had any contact with slavery was willing to free the slaves and allow them to dwell among the whites. Slaves were a peril, at least a risk, but free blacks were considered a menace too great to be hazarded. Even if no race wars occurred, there was a dread of being submerged and absorbed by the black race.[30]

After the publication of *I'll Take My Stand,* some of the contributors drifted away from Southern Agrarianism, but the core of the group including, amongst others, Davidson, Lytle, Owsley, and Warren, wrote for the *American Review* between 1933 and 1937. Openly sympathetic toward European fascism, the *American Review* provided a venue for the Southern Agrarians to advance their ideology, attack those whom they envisioned as critical of the South, and vigorously defend white supremacy.[31]

The writings of the Southern Agrarians did not elicit popular interest, but many academics interpreted them to represent an essential Southern identity and philosophical tradition.[32] Perhaps the most prominent post–World War II advocate of such ideas was Richard M. Weaver (1910–63). While at Vanderbilt, Weaver espoused an anti-modern conservative philosophy and was connected to leaders of Southern Agrarianism, most notably Ransom and Davidson. Continuing the Agrarian idea, Weaver posited that the antebellum South was a feudal society and, defending Southern racial, class, and gender hierarchies, articulated a vision of a Christian Confederate South. What is important about Weaver's work, much of it published posthumously, is his conceptualization of a Southern nationalist culture with a distinct worldview and, therefore, the need for self-determination to shape a society. Where other advocates of the South defended the Confederacy or segregation, or suggested that the South exhibited certain distinctive characteristics, Weaver created a South that was an integrated whole. Hostile to civil rights, which he interpreted as a Communist attempt to undermine society, Weaver's work gained favor with historians George Core and M. E. Bradford, who, alongside other future advocates of neo-Confederacy, began to promote Weaver as an authentic voice of Southern values and beliefs.[33]

Developing Neo-Confederacy: The 1980s and 1990s

In the 1980s, the self-identified paleoconservatives felt themselves to be increasingly detached from the mainstream conservatism and, embittered by the failure of the Republican Party to adopt their agenda, began to develop their own venues for publishing and promoting their ideology. Arguably the most important group of writers came together around the journal *Southern Partisan,* which, over time, pulled together disparate elements to propagate a neo-Confederate worldview.[34] Clyde Wilson and Thomas Fleming had established *Southern Partisan* in 1979.[35] On the masthead of the magazine were a range of conservative figures from old segregationists and Southern Agrarians to New Right leaders. An editorial in the magazine's first issue established that the publication's *raison d'être* was to ensure the survival of "our identity" and the "Southern tradition." Arguing that these had little "to do with slavery or Jim Crow," it continued:

> We do believe that the greatest struggle lies in the next thirty years and it is up to this generation of Southerners to decide whether or not the South will endure. . . . There are almost no public voices raised in defense of the South and its traditions. *The Southern Partisan* intends to be that voice, a reminder of all that was and is distinctively good about the South.[36]

Contributors to early issues included those who would become some of the leading proponents and developers of neo-Confederate ideology: M. E. Bradford, Thomas Fleming, Samuel T. Francis, Robert W. Whitaker, Clyde Wilson, and John Shelton Reed (writing both under his own name and under the pseudonym J. R. Vanover).[37]

Guided by Fleming and executive editor Richard M. Quinn, *Southern Partisan* brought together numerous individuals advocating Southern nationalism.[38] Article topics ranged widely but typically instructed readers as to the appropriate Southern viewpoint on an issue. Central to this undertaking were efforts to build an encompassing historical narrative that would interpret all American history from a Southern position. Bradford, for example, reinterpreted the American Revolution and subsequent constitutional debates,[39] Whitaker dismissed the Declaration of Independence as mere propaganda written to enlist support from Parisian liberals, and Thomas H. Landess advocated demolishing the Statue of Liberty.[40] In a 1988 issue, Quinn described *Southern Partisan* contributor and former Reagan administration staffer Richard Hines as being "among the first neo-Confederates to resist efforts by the infidels to take down the Confederate Flag,"[41] possibly the earliest use of "neo-Confederate" to describe a conservative activist in the pages of *Southern Partisan.*

Southern Partisan promoted an emergent concept of neo-Confederacy that was simultaneously separatist and appealing to all "copperheads," namely those living outside Southern states who support supposedly Southern principles. Thus, neo-Confederate ideology was targeted not just at those in the South, but aimed at stimulating reactionary politics and bolstering paleoconservative perspectives throughout the United States. As such, some prominent politicians, including many Republicans, agreed to be interviewed in the publication: Phil Gramm, Trent Lott, Jesse Helms, Dick Armey, Jerry Falwell, Pat Robertson, and Phyllis Schlafly. *Southern Partisan* contributors, in particular Quinn, hoped that a Republican Party based in the South would adopt the Southern conservative agenda that *Southern Partisan* advocated, but when most Republican officials supported measures such as the Martin Luther King holiday and 1991 Civil Rights Act, Quinn wrote bitterly of these votes as betrayals.[42]

Another *Southern Partisan* strategy was to demonstrate the deep intellectual roots of its agenda, in particular forwarding the principles of Southern nationality and self-determination. Reed, who argued that the Southern Agrarians were nationalists and compared Ransom, Davidson, and Lytle to Gandhi, Kenyatta, and Ho Chi Minh,[43] developed the theme of a modern Southern nationalism in his contributions to *Southern Partisan* under a pseudonym.[44] In turn, Bradford, who published and promoted Weaver, wrote regularly for *Southern Partisan*, advancing ideas that would become fundamental tenets of neo-Confederacy, including the Christianity of the Confederacy and the agrarian basis of Southern society.[45]

This emerging neo-Confederate thought also gained an academic foothold. One particularly important venue was the Intercollegiate Studies Institute (ISI) of Bryn Mawr, Pennsylvania, and its journal, *Continuity*.[46] Edited by Paul Gottfried for much of the 1980s, the journal published articles by, amongst others, editorial board member Grady McWhiney[47] and Clyde Wilson.[48] In a 1984 issue entitled "Recovering Southern History," Bradford analyzed Abraham Lincoln's speeches and concluded:

> Once he was finished in his career, he had left behind him a trail of blood, an emancipation under the worst possible circumstances, and a political example which continues to injure the Republic which he did so much to undermine. It is at our peril that we continue to reverence his name.[49]

Bradford wrote this after his earlier opinions had brought him unwelcome attention, according to Damon Linker:

> In the early days of the Reagan presidency, . . . the administration considered appointing paleoconservative M. E. Bradford to head the National Endowment for the Humanities—a choice that alarmed the neocons, who quickly set out to publicize Bradford's opposition to the 1964 Civil Rights Act, his two-time endorsement of George Wallace for president, and his tendency to refer to Abraham Lincoln as a criminal for his actions during the Civil War. Fearing public scandal and an embarrassing confirmation fight in the Senate, the new administration quickly withdrew Bradford's name. . . . It was a humiliating experience for Bradford and his paleoconservative allies, who from that point forward considered the neocons their mortal enemies.[50]

This rejection of Bradford, say paleoconservatives Gottfried and Fleming, echoing Linker's assessment, led to their own final split from mainstream conservatism and created an "embittered and marginalized minority" of paleoconservatives who positioned themselves as the legitimate inheritors of the Southern Agrarian tradition and sustainers of the tenets of authentic conservative thought.[51] Looking for venues beyond *Southern Partisan* in which to advance their ideas, they soon centered on *Chronicles,* a journal published by the Rockford Institute, a conservative think tank based not in a Southern state but in Rockford, Illinois.

Chronicles became a key vehicle for the views of Fleming and his cohort. Although he was a co-founder of *Southern Partisan,* by 1983 internal disputes had forced Fleming out of the publication, and he became editor of *Chronicles* in 1985. Dismissing many of the existing *Chronicles* contributors, Fleming brought in like-minded colleagues who had contributed to *Southern Partisan,* such as Wilson, Reed, and Francis.[52] Paul Murphy explains:

> The contributors to *Chronicles* betrayed a similar sense of being beleaguered defenders of the Christian order who continue to fight despite being under heavy siege by cultural liberals, black and Hispanic minorities, and the federal government. Most members of the circle identify southernness with a Christian and organic social order built on traditional and patriarchal authority . . . and the aim of some members of the group seems to be a return to the perceived security, peace, and order of the segregated, pre–civil rights American South, one in which the prerogatives of white southerners were unquestioned.[53]

A pivotal moment for this now nascent neo-Confederate movement was the breakup of Communist governments in Eastern Europe and the fall of the Soviet Union in the late 1980s and early 1990s. Nationalist movements throughout the world were boosted by these events, including those in the United States. In a series of *Chronicles* articles on secession, authors implicitly equated the Soviet Union with the United States, arguing that even an imperial superpower with massive resources of governmental power could disintegrate nearly bloodlessly if its population no longer wanted it.[54] As Eastern Europe fractured along ethnic lines, contributors to *Chronicles* argued that ethnicity was the only solid foundation for a nation and that nations based on non-ethnic criteria were fundamentally artificial and unsound:

> Unless it returns to constitutional government, the United States cannot maintain its present territorial integrity except by quelling independent-

minded citizens through terrorist violence. . . . This empire, like Yugoslavia, was never really legitimate and is certain to fall apart, either by a peaceful devolution toward constitutional liberty *or by a process of ethnic rebellions and refined revolts.*[55]

Fleming thus claimed that the United States was not a "real nation" and that ethnic and racial war would soon overtake what he claimed was its "continental empire":

There are only two alternatives for this continental empire that has never been a real nation: either we find the means to decentralize decision-making and restore authority to the old institutions of family and town and country (and even state), or else we lapse into a multifaceted civil war of blacks against Hispanics against whites against blacks against Jews. . . .[56]

According to the League of the South's Joseph Scotchie, paleoconservatives oppose the exclusionary and violent aspects of nationalism and merely advocate a "love of one's own culture, history and heritage."[57] The reality, as the above quotations attest, is very different.

To learn about establishing a successful secessionist political party, *Chronicles* editor Thomas Fleming visited the Northern League (Lega Nord) in Italy to learn about its tactics, operations, and electoral strategies.[58] Calling for an American nationalist movement that paralleled the Lega Nord, Fleming proclaimed that "if there is no movement or party willing to embrace a Lega-like program, then one needs to be formed," adding aggressively, "if that is impossible, my advice is to stockpile ammunition and invest in bullet-proof doors and shutters."[59] Elsewhere, Fleming has argued that social relations within the United States are actually an "ever-spreading race war," predicting that "if middle-class whites prove to be as weak as they sometimes seem, then they will be carved up like so much meat in the abattoir."[60] In turn, League of the South director Jack Kershaw, interviewed in *Southern Patriot,* was asked the following: "Much of what made the South good is agrarian roots. Our population growth is out of control with Yankees and other foreign cultures moving in. What one thing can Southerners do to maintain our society?" Kershaw responded with just two words: "Arm yourselves."[61]

Extreme though these opinions may seem, they were not isolated. The Ludwig von Mises Institute, established in 1982 and based in Auburn, Alabama, draws its membership from university faculties throughout the world. Advocating for Austrian school economics and non-interventionist laissez-faire government, in the mid-1990s the Institute started to pick up neo-

Confederate themes, hosting a 1995 conference entitled "Secession, State and Economy," symbolically held in Charleston, South Carolina, where the first shots of the Civil War were fired. In advertising material for the event, secession was described as the "ultimate challenge to centralized tyranny."[62] Wilson, then director of the League of the South, was among the participants. At another Ludwig von Mises Institute conference, "The Costs of War: America's Pyrrhic Victories," held in 1994, Wilson, Fleming, and Francis all spoke. Despite the Institute's largely libertarian positions, it soon shared both personnel and ideological positions with *Southern Partisan, Chronicles*, and the League of the South.[63]

One member of neo-Confederacy's intellectual wing was Donald Livingston.[64] A philosophy professor at Emory University and expert on the eighteenth-century Scottish philosopher David Hume, Livingston was also connected to the Ludwig von Mises Institute and, in the mid-1990s, began publishing on the right of peoples to secede.[65] He maintained that the Civil War was fought over taxation and the separation of authority between state and federal governments. "When the moral issue of slavery as part of the war effort is subtracted from the equation," he wrote, "we are left with the question of whether Lincoln's war of coercion to suppress secession was morally justified."[66] His answer was that it was not. In 2002 Livingston took his neo-Confederacy national in a major essay in *Harper's Magazine* in which he argued that "freedom and human flourishing might require not more unity and centralization but more division, separation, and diversification." Though probably new to *Harper's* readers, Livingson's arguments merely reiterated familiar paleoconservative and neo-Confederate positions. He maintained that the United States had grown to become a "union of . . . monstrous size" and that immigration meant that "entire ways of life and traditions are melting away." U.S. urban areas were "monster cities" having grown to "dysfunctional size," but all this could yet be averted by a recognition of American states not as constituent components of a United States, but as independent countries, a dream deferred because, between 1861 and 1865, "Lincoln made war on the seceding states on the grounds that they were not and never had been sovereign states. He said they should be thought of as counties in a unitary state . . . [but] he was historically and legally wrong."[67]

In the 1980s and 1990s, these intellectual advocates of neo-Confederacy reached out to grassroots supporters of Confederate heritage and its symbols. Groups like the Sons of Confederate Veterans (scv) began advertising books that defended the Confederacy. Fleming's *Chronicles* carried regular advertisements for Albert Taylor Bledsoe's 1866 Lost Cause polemic *Is Davis a Traitor?* Noting the growing market for pro-Confederate literature, booksellers reprinted nineteenth- and early-twentieth-century texts propounding the Confederacy and upholding slavery, promoting these works in Civil War reenactment circles and among genealogical organizations.[68] As African American demands to remove Confederate symbols and names from public institutions (e.g., schools) grew, the final decades of the twentieth century saw "culture wars" ensue over the meaning of the South and Southern identity.[69] Supporters of neo-Confederacy articulated their position to a wider audience through books and magazines. One of the most important titles was Michael Andrew Grissom's *Southern by the Grace of God*, which asserts, amongst other things, that African Americans "in the mild form of slavery practiced in the South would more fittingly have been called servants."[70] In its eleventh printing at the time of writing, Grissom recommends *Southern Partisan* and the writings of the Southern Agrarians to his readers, and portrays the Ku Klux Klan and other similar Reconstruction-era groups as saviors of the South, a region that he argues was a victim of oppression and cultural erasure.[71] Defenses of slavery are common in neo-Confederate texts as indeed they were in Citizens' Council writings in the 1950s, which themselves often reiterated the "scriptural justifications" for slavery first produced in the nineteenth century.[72] A recent notorious assessment written by neo-Confederates Douglas Wilson and Steve Wilkins, *Southern Slavery: As It Was* (1996), argues for the "biblical principles" underpinning slavery and that abolitionists were "driven by a zealous hatred of the Word of God," in contrast to the Confederate army who likely comprised "the largest body of evangelicals under arms in the history of the world." Slavery in the U.S. South, for Wilson and Wilkins,

> was not an adversarial relationship with pervasive racial animosity. Because of its dominantly patriarchal character, it was a relationship based on mutual affection and confidence. There has never been a multi-racial society which has existed in such mutual intimacy and harmony in the history of the world.[73]

Explaining that slaves held good relationships with their masters in a paternalistic, harmonious, patriarchal society is also the aim of Walter Donald Kennedy in *Myths of American Slavery* (2002).[74] Kennedy is one of the most prolific current authors advocating neo-Confederacy and, alongside his brother James Ronald, wrote what is arguably the best-known book in this neo-Confederate canon, *The South Was Right!* (1991). Claiming on the cover of its revised edition to have sold over 93,000 copies, the Kennedy brothers describe themselves as "die-hard Confederates."[75] Rearticulating a Lost Cause defense of the Confederacy and angrily denouncing the 1965 Voting Rights Act, the authors argue that if secession was good enough for Lithuania, then the former Confederate states should secede once more: "We want every Southerner to awaken to the fact that no force on earth can prevent us from reclaiming our lost estate if and when we decide to free ourselves."[76] The Kennedys followed the success of this book with similar neo-Confederate polemics, including *Why Not Freedom!—America's Revolt Against Big Government* (1995), *Was Jefferson Davis Right?* (1998), and *Reclaiming Liberty* (2005).[77] Others, writing in the same breathless style that typifies much neo-Confederate authorship, include *The Southern Nation: The New Rise of the Old South* (2000) by R. Gordon Thornton and Frank Conner's *The South under Siege, 1830–2000: A History of the Relations between the North and the South* (2002).[78] In the latter, Conner forwards racist arguments about a Jewish conspiracy against U.S. Christians, and contends that this led to the imposition of civil rights in the South. Conner was also a regular contributor to the glossy *Southern Mercury* magazine in 2004, published by the Preservation of American Culture, a group closely connected with the scv. In one issue, Conner maintained that the "conservative white South" is under attack and argued that the weaponry used by "liberals" in this assault is "black civil rights." The scv, as the most powerful and populous Confederate heritage organization, Conner maintained, must save the South and its "white Southerners."[79]

Another neo-Confederate text to gain wide attention was Thomas E. Woods Jr.'s *Politically Incorrect Guide to American History.*[80] Woods, a founding member of the League of the South and contributor to its newsletter *Southern Patriot,* was teaching at Suffolk County Community College on Long Island when he published the book. Like those noted above, Woods contends that slavery was benign.[81] Though denounced in the *Boston Globe* as the work of "ultra-reactionary extremism," the book, assisted by plugs on Fox News, became the eighth-best-selling nonfiction book in the United States in January 2005.[82] Adam Cohen in the *New York Times* stated: "It is tempting to dismiss the book as fringe scholarship, not worth worrying about, but the numbers say otherwise." The *Politically Incorrect Guide to American History,* explained Cohen, was one of many recently published "far-right attacks on mainstream history" that

> are disturbing both because they are so extreme . . . and because they seem intent on distorting the past to promote dangerous policies today. . . . If the 14th Amendment, which guarantees minorities "equal protection of the law," was never properly ratified—as Mr. Woods argues—racial discrimination may be constitutional after all.[83]

Magazines and periodicals have also played a central role in this vibrant and growing advocacy of neo-Confederacy. In 2005, Fleming's *Chronicles* had a print run of 7,000–8,000 copies per issue.[84] Other magazines regularly containing articles promoting neo-Confederacy include the 7,000–8,000 monthly copies of the United Daughters of the Confederacy (UDC) magazine, the foremost venue for the women's heritage group's 20,000 members, and the SCV's *Southern Mercury* and *Confederate Veteran* magazine, serving around 27,000 members.[85] The major venue for neo-Confederacy remains *Southern Partisan*, which published 6,000 copies of each issue in 2005.[86] Funding from the Earhart Foundation has also helped promoters of neo-Confederacy. Between 1995 and 2005 the foundation awarded $10,000 to Clyde Wilson, $8,000 to Thomas Woods, $14,000 to Mark Royden Winchell, director of the League of the South Institute, and $20,000 and $98,000, respectively, to League of the South–affiliated scholars Thomas DiLorenzo and James McClellan.[87]

It is evident, therefore, that neo-Confederacy is making inroads into mainstream U.S. political and cultural venues, and it was within this context that comments made by Senator Trent Lott in 2002 put neo-Confederate views in the spotlight.

Who Has the Authentic Voice of Conservatism?
Trent Lott, Thomas Fleming, and Neo-Confederacy

I want to say this about my state: When Strom Thurmond ran for president, we voted for him. We're proud of it. And if the rest of the country had followed our lead, we wouldn't have had all these problems over all these years, either.

SENATOR TRENT LOTT, ON THE OCCASION OF THE RETIREMENT OF
SENATOR STROM THURMOND, 5 DECEMBER 2002

The storm of controversy over these remarks led to Lott's resignation as his party's leader in the Senate some two weeks afterward. Lott's statement put neo-Confederacy onto front pages and television screens across the United States. While his views on the issue of race were new to many people, independent researchers soon revealed that Lott had a history of using implicit references to racial segregation and the Confederacy to assert a politics that understood race as the defining aspect of U.S. society. In this latest instance, praising the 1948 anti–civil rights presidential campaign of Strom Thurmond, Lott articulated his support for the country's segregationist past. He thus implied that racial integration was the source of the nation's current "problems" and that a return to segregation and legalized racial inequalities would solve America's ills.

In previous years Lott had regularly appeared at Confederate heritage events and spoken with writers from neo-Confederate publications such as *Southern Partisan* and *Citizens Informer.* Activist Edward H. Sebesta operated a web site (*www.templeofdemocracy.com*) that demonstrated Lott's many statements of affection for the Old South and his association with organizations advocating racist perspectives. Major newspapers such as *USA Today* noted Lott's "longtime ties to the Council of Conservative Citizens, a neo-Confederate group that has been accused of racist views," a connection that journalist Ana Radelat showed had existed "since the beginning of his political career."[88] Upon his election to the House of Representatives in 1972 and the Senate in 1988, Lott requested that the desk once used by Confederate president Jefferson Davis (1808–89) be placed in his office. In using the desk, Lott was nodding to conservative supporters with a sense of history and positioning himself as the inheritor of Davis's legacy, given that he had also represented Mississippi in the Senate. In addition, Lott worked to restore U.S. citizenship to Davis, a measure that gained the necessary two-thirds majority in the U.S. Senate and House of Representatives in 1978.[89] At the Confederate Monument in Arlington National Cemetery on 3 June 1979, Lott addressed the United Daughters of the Confederacy, telling them that the injustice of 1868's revocation of Davis's U.S. citizenship had been corrected.[90]

Lott's activities in the first decade of his Washington career piqued the interest of neo-Confederate sympathizers. Interviewed in *Southern Partisan,* he responded to the following question: "At the convention of the Sons of Confederate Veterans in Biloxi, Mississippi you made the statement that 'the spirit of Jefferson Davis lives in the 1984 Republican Platform.' What did you mean by that?"

> I think that a lot of the fundamental principles that Jefferson Davis believed in are very important to people across the country, and they apply to the Republican Party. . . . We have seen the Republican Party become more conservative and more oriented toward the traditional family values, the religious values that we hold dear in the South. And the Democratic Party is going in the other direction. As a result, more and more of The South's sons, Jefferson Davis' descendants, direct or indirect, are becoming involved with the Republican Party. The platform we had in Dallas, the 1984 Republican platform, all the ideas we supported there—from tax policy, to foreign policy; from individual rights, to neighborhood security—are things that Jefferson Davis and his people believed in.[91]

Jefferson Davis and his people, of course, also believed in slavery and white supremacy.

Writing about the Lott affair in *Chronicles* in 2002, Thomas Fleming, self-identified paleoconservative and leading advocate of neo-Confederacy, castigated the senator, stating that Lott was not a true conservative:

> If anyone had any doubts about Trent Lott's lack of political understanding, this recent episode would convince him. A revolution has been going on in the United States, and the Senator from Mississippi still thinks he is living in the 1920's. The first phase of the revolution was largely economic and political—FDR's creation of a centralized high-tax state. The second phase was the social revolution designed to destroy the family (we call this feminism) and local control over community life (the civil rights movement). Overlapping and now outdistancing the social revolution has been the cultural revolution that teaches all Americans to despise the founders of the nation, its constitution and traditions, and the culture and civilization it inherited from several thousand years of European experience.
>
> The vehicles for these revolutions have always been "oppressed minorities"—the poor, the female, the black and brown, the foreign, the morally exotic—whereas in fact the *only* beneficiaries have been a ruling class that owns more and more of the national wealth and controls more and more of the social, political, and cultural power. That ruling class still consists of post-Christian WASPs (like the Bushes and Clintons), but they are joined by ex-Catholic Sicilians and Latinos, African Americans who reject their heritage, and Jews who do not practice their religion.[92]

Fleming's assessment of the Lott affair also indicates a wider disillusionment about the state of the USA. He criticizes the establishment of the welfare state in the 1930s, implicitly opposing government provision of social security, and bemoans the advancements toward equality attained by women and nonwhites in the second half of the twentieth century. Indeed, Fleming suggests that the "European" basis of the United States has been neglected and is now "despise[d]" rather than celebrated.[93] Furthermore, Fleming implies that the gains made by women and ethnic minorities in the United States constitute a "revolution," namely an overthrow of the white, male order that has dominated U.S. economic, cultural, and political life since the formation of the nation in the late eighteenth century. In this manner, despite their differences, one could argue that Fleming and Lott are coming to the same conclusion—things were better in the past under a white, hierarchical, patriarchal society.

Conclusion: Resurgent Neo-Confederacy

The lineaments of the neo-Confederacy, as we have outlined in this chapter, can be found in post–World War II conservatism, in particular following the disastrous presidential candidacy of Barry Goldwater in 1964. Following Goldwater's defeat, many of the individuals most heavily engaged in advancing neo-Confederacy identified themselves as paleoconservatives and articulated their position in books like *Why the South Will Survive*, positioning themselves as the inheritors of Southern Agrarian thought. Essays by Thomas Fleming, Samuel T. Francis, Clyde Wilson, Robert Whitaker, M. E. Bradford, and others constructed a worldview centered upon a historical reinterpretation of the Confederate States, the U.S. Civil War, Reconstruction, and their legacies. More than merely Lost Cause enthusiasm, neo-Confederacy underpins a historical narrative on which an anti-modernist, anti-egalitarian belief system is built. Recruiting and politicizing supporters from a range of Confederate heritage organizations and conservative positions, proponents of neo-Confederacy have situated themselves as the legitimate voice of the South and the sustainers of supposedly authentic American conservatism.

Notes

1. A sampling of paleoconservative views can be found in Scotchie, Joseph, ed. *The Paleoconservatives: New Voices of the Old Right.* (New Brunswick, NJ: Transaction Publishers, 1999). Scotchie is a neo-Confederate sympathizer, has been a League of the South member, and is closely associated with paleoconservatism. He has published essays in *Southern Partisan* that are hostile toward immigrants; see, for example, "The Truth about Immigration," *Southern Partisan*, 15 (2nd Quarter 1995): 38–39, 54, and "Apocalypse How," *Southern Partisan*, 19 (4th Quarter 1999): 35–36. In a positive *Southern Partisan* review of Scotchie's *The Paleoconservatives* 19 (4th Quarter 1999): 37–39), William J. Watkins Jr. explains that the book "is part history and part manifesto" in which essays by M. E. Bradford, Russell Kirk, Samuel Francis, Thomas Fleming, Paul Gottfried, and others "delight and instruct."

2. MacLean, Nancy. *Freedom Is Not Enough: The Opening of the American Workplace.* (Cambridge, MA: Harvard University Press, 2006).

3. Ibid., 45. See Kirk, Russell. *The Conservative Mind, from Burke to Santayana.* (Chicago: H. Regnery, 1953); Weaver, Richard. *Ideas Have Consequences.* (Chicago: University of Chicago Press, 1948).

4. The moniker "White" was generally applied to Citizens' Councils by the press and historians. With the exception of at least one local division, most branches and the national organization identified themselves as "Citizens' Councils." See McMillen, Neil R. *The Citizens' Council: Organized Resistance to the Second Reconstruction, 1954–64.* (Urbana: University of Illinois Press, 1971); Bartley, Numan V. *The Rise of the Massive Resistance: Race and Politics in the South during the 1950s.* (Baton Rouge:

Louisiana State University Press, 1969); Wilhoit, Francis M. *The Politics of Massive Resistance*. (New York: George Braziller, 1973); Lewis, George. *Massive Resistance: The White Response to the Civil Rights Movement*. (London: Hodder Arnold, 2006).

    5. See, for example, *The Citizens' Council* 4.2 (1958): 1. *The Citizens' Council*, later shortened to *The Citizen*, was the newspaper published by Citizens' Councils

    6. The cartoon listing these features of "Black Supremacy" appears in *The Citizens' Council*, 5.10 (1960): 2.

    7. "The Carpetbaggers Are Coming—Again!" *The Citizens' Council*, 5.2 (1959): 1–2.

    8. Murphy, Paul V. *The Rebuke of History: The Southern Agrarians and American Conservative Thought*. (Chapel Hill: University of North Carolina Press, 2001): 175.

    9. Quoted in MacLean, Nancy. *Freedom Is Not Enough*, (2006): 73. For further discussion of the Goldwater campaign and its legacy, see Hixon, William B. Jr. *Search for the American Right Wing: An Analysis of the Social Science Record, 1955–1987*. (Princeton, NJ: Princeton University Press, 1992); Phillips, Kevin. *American Theocracy: The Peril and Politics of Radical Religion, Oil, and Borrowed Money in the 21st Century*. (New York: Viking, 2006).

    10. See *inter alia* Steinfels, Peter. *The Neoconservatives: The Men Who Are Changing America's Politics*. (New York: Simon and Schuster, 1979); Peele, Gillian. *Revival and Reactions: The Right in Contemporary America*. (Oxford: Clarendon Press, 1984); Kristol, Irving. *Neoconservatism: The Autobiography of an Idea*. (New York: Free Press, 1995); Frum, David. *Dead Right*. (New York: Basic Books, 1994); Nash, George H. *The Conservative Intellectual Movement in America since 1945*. (Wilmington, DE: Intercollegiate Studies Institute, 1998); Dunn, Charles W., and Woodward, David. *The Conservative Tradition in America*, rev. ed. (Lanham, MD: Rowman and Littlefield, 2003).

    11. Heilbrunn, Jacob. "Neocon v. Theocon: The New Fault Line on the Right," *The New Republic*, 215.27 (1996): 20–24. Heilbrunn maintains that Trent Lott became the focal point for theoconservative activists in Washington. See also Linker, Damon. *The Theocons: Secular America Under Siege*. (New York: Doubleday, 2006).

    12. Scotchie, Joseph. "Introduction: Paleoconservatism as the Opposition Party," *The Paleoconservatives: New Voices of the Old Right*, (1999): 7–8 (see also the rest of this volume and note 1, above); Scotchie, Joseph. *Revolt from the Heartland: The Struggle for Authentic Conservatism*. (New Brunswick, NJ: Transaction Publishers, 2002); Gottfried, Paul, and Fleming, Thomas. *The Conservative Movement*. (Boston: Twayne Publishers, 1988); Whitaker, Robert W., ed. *The New Right Papers*. (New York: St. Martin's Press, 1982).

    13. Wilson, Clyde. "Citizens or Subjects?" *The New Right Papers*, (1982): 124. The connections between Clyde Wilson, Samuel Francis, and Thomas Fleming are examined in Murphy, *The Rebuke of History*, (2001), and Scotchie, *Revolt from the Heartland*, (2002).

    14. Wilson, "Citizens or Subjects?" (1982): 119.

    15. Ibid., 120–121.

    16. Fleming, Thomas. "Old Rights and the New Right," *The New Right Papers*, (1982): 192. Alan Wolfe notes that this ascription of naturalness to human and societal relations is a common conservative "political philosophy" in the United States: "institutions like the family and the arrangement of capitalist political economy are justified

by nature. . . . Patriarchy and profit, in this view, are the condition of the race; to alter either is to disturb the universe and consign oneself to perpetual disappointment." Wolfe, Alan. "Sociology, Liberalism, and the Radical Right," *New Left Review,* 128 (1981): 23. We discuss this ascription in Chapter 4.

17. Wolfe, Alan. "Sociology, Liberalism, and the Radical Right," *New Left Review,* 128 (1981): 3-27.

18. Gottfried, Paul, and Fleming, Thomas. *The Conservative Movement,* (1988); Gottfried, Paul. *The Conservative Movement* (rev. ed., 1993). "The spirit behind the landslide white southern vote for Ronald Reagan in 1984," argues Lewis M. Killian, "was alarmingly reminiscent in several respects of the Ku Klux Klan of the 1920s" — see *White Southerners,* rev. ed. (Amherst: University of Massachusetts Press, 1985): 164.

19. Scotchie, *Revolt from the Heartland,* (2002).

20. Wilson, "Citizens or Subjects?" (1982): 107.

21. Ibid., 116-117. See also Livingston, Donald W. *Philosophical Melancholy and Delirium: Hume's Pathology of Philosophy.* (Chicago: University of Chicago Press, 1998).

22. Scotchie, *Revolt from the Heartland,* (2002): 88.

23. Reed, John Shelton. *One South: An Ethnic Approach to Regional Culture.* (Baton Rouge: Louisiana State University Press, 1982): 113. Lewis Killian, in *White Southerners* (1985), argues that *Why the South Will Survive* proposes a special and distinct status of the South and white Southerners.

24. *Why the South Will Survive: Fifteen Southerners Look at Their Region Half a Century after "I'll Take My Stand."* (Athens: University of Georgia Press, 1981). See also Havard, William C., and Sullivan, Walter, ed. *A Band of Prophets: The Vanderbilt Agrarians after Fifty Years.* (Baton Rouge: Louisiana State University Press, 1982). Neo-Confederate author Thomas Landess argues in "*Pietas* and the Southern Agrarians," *Chronicles,* 24.12 (2000): 43-45, that M. E. Bradford and Clyde Wilson are "intellectual heirs" of the Agrarians.

25. See, for example, Loewen, James W. *Lies Across America: What Our Historic Sites Get Wrong.* (New York: Touchstone, 1999).

26. Dunn and Woodward, *The Conservative Tradition,* (2003): 99. See also Murphy, *The Rebuke of History,* (2001).

27. Tindall, George Brown. *Natives and Newcomers: Ethnic Southerners and Southern Ethnics.* (Athens: University of Georgia Press, 1995): 27.

28. Twelve Southerners, "Introduction: A Statement of Principles," *I'll Take My Stand: The South and the Agrarian Tradition.* (New York: Harper Torchbooks, 1962 [1930]): xx.

29. Warren, Robert Penn. "The Briar Patch," in ibid., 246-264.

30. Owsley, Frank Lawrence. "The Irrepressible Conflict," in ibid., 77.

31. See, for example, the unattributed editorial from 1933 (although the editor of the issue was Seward Collins), "Editorial Notes: The Revival of Monarchy," *American Review,* 1.2 (1933): 247-248, which argued that Hitler's rise to power ended "the Communist threat *forever*" and that the persecution of Jews "if . . . true" was a "negligible" aspect of the Nazi regime.

32. For example, Genovese, Eugene D. *The Southern Tradition: The Achievements and Limitations of an American Conservatism.* (Cambridge, MA: Harvard University Press, 1994).

33. Weaver, Richard M. *The Southern Tradition at Bay*, ed. George Core and M. E. Bradford. (New Rochelle, NY: Arlington House, 1968); Weaver, Richard M. *The Southern Essays of Richard M. Weaver*, ed. George M. Curtis III and James J. Thompson. (Indianapolis: Liberty Press, 1987); Malvasi, Mark G. *The Unregenerate South: The Agrarian Thought of John Crowe Ransom, Allen Tate, and Donald Davidson.* (Baton Rouge: Louisiana State University Press, 1997); Kreyling, Michael. *Inventing Southern Literature.* (Jackson: University of Mississippi Press, 1998).

34. *Southern Partisan,* published by the South Carolina-based Foundation for American Education, has regularly defended itself against accusations of racism. One internal debate ensued in 1986 surrounding an essay entitled "Whistlin' Dixie: Is the White Southerner Ready for Equality?" by J. R. Vanover (*Southern Partisan,* 6.2 [1986]: 61). Vanover (pseudonym of John Shelton Reed) outlined literature he had received from the Southern National Party that called for a "Southern Republic" to "preserve 'white civilization.'" Warren Leamon ("The Long Guilt Trip," *Southern Partisan,* 6:3 [Summer 1986]: 15–18) responded, arguing that "*Southern Partisan* is opposed to bigotry, opposed to white or black supremacist groups." This provoked senior editor Robert Whitaker (*Southern Partisan,* 6.4 & 7.1 [1986–87]: 8) to author "Why I Will Not Denounce Southern Racism or American Imperialism." Whitaker described Vanover's essay as "a standard attack" and Leamon's writing as "containing cutesy-poo wrappings that justify South-bashing with a club that pretends to love us." Whitaker continued: "While it may be blasphemy in our time to say so, I am proud to be white; I like my race (thank you very much) and I pray that my children and their children will retain their whiteness." Whitaker proceeded to argue that the "white race is . . . threatened" as a result of "a flood of third-world immigration." In *Southern Partisan,* 7.2 (Spring 1987): 64, another essay entitled "Racist Drivel" saw its author, Reid Buckley, distance himself from Whitaker, whose opinions he describes as "a gumbo soup of imprecise and absurd racist agglutinations." These contentions resurfaced in 2000–2001 as a result of former *Southern Partisan* columnist and editor-in-chief Richard Quinn's attachment to the presidential campaign of Senator John McCain and the appointment of John Ashcroft as U.S. attorney general. *Southern Partisan* (20–21, 4th Quarter 2000/1st Quarter 2001) reviewed these debates.

35. The first two issues were identified as *The Southern Partisan* on their covers. Future issues referred to these first printings as *The Southern Partisan Quarterly Review.* The magazine did establish a consistent identity and name, *The Southern Partisan,* although not a consistent numbering system. For discussion of the development of *Southern Partisan,* see *inter alia,* Scotchie, "Introduction: Paleoconservatism as the Opposition Party," *The Paleoconservatives,* (1999): 1–15; Scotchie, *Revolt from the Heartland,* (2002); and Murphy, *The Rebuke of History,* (2001). A collection of essays from *Southern Partisan* was collected as Smith, Oran P. *So Good a Cause: A Decade of Southern Partisan.* (Columbia, SC: Foundation for American Education, 1993).

36. Anonymous editorial entitled "Foreword," *Southern Partisan,* 1.1 (1979): n.p. This is described in the issue as the first publication of *Southern Partisan,* but there is no volume or edition number listed.

37. Many of John Shelton Reed's essays for *Southern Partisan* and *Chronicles,* including those originally published under his pseudonym J. R. Vanover, are collected in *Whistling Dixie: Dispatches from the South.* (Columbia: University of Missouri Press,

1990). His decision to use the pseudonym is explained in Bullard, Chrys. "101 Things Everyone Should Know about the John Shelton Reed Professorship and the Man Who Inspired It," *Carolina Connections*, (Winter 2004). On-line: http://carolinafirst .unc.edu/connections/winter2004/reed.html [accessed 15 November 2004]. Bullard quotes Reed: "I was writing opinion pieces that weren't scholarly in nature, so I decided to use a pseudonym and picked J. R. Vanover—my first and last initials along with my grandmother's maiden name."

38. The relationship between *Southern Partisan* and the Republican Party was evidenced after John Ashcroft, the former Missouri senator who had been nominated to become U.S. attorney general, was shown to have made comments in *Southern Partisan*—see "Senator John Ashcroft: Missouri's Champion of States' Rights and Traditional Southern Values," *Southern Partisan*, 18 (2nd Quarter 1998): 26–29. As a result of these public controversies, the hope that *Southern Partisan* would become a vehicle to introduce Southern nationalist politics in the Republican Party was over, as was Quinn's editorship. At the time of writing, Quinn remains a co-owner of *Southern Partisan* (see usps *Statement of Management Ownership and Circulation*, *Southern Partisan*, 24.5 [2004/2005]: 34).

39. Bradford, M. E. "Not So Democratic," *Southern Partisan*, 1.2 (1980): 9–13. Bradford published similar views: "A Dike to Fend Out the Flood: The Ratification of the Constitution in Massachusetts," *Chronicles*, 11.12 (1987): 16–23.

40. Whitaker, Robert W. "Declaration vs. Constitution," *Southern Partisan*, 3.3 (1983): 16–19; Landess, Thomas. "The Statue of Liberty Is Falling to Pieces, and I'm Glad," *Southern Partisan*, 4.3 (1984): 8.

41. Quinn, Richard. "Partisan View," *Southern Partisan*, 8.1 (1988): 5. Quinn was discussing the efforts by Hines to support Jesse Helms and prevent George H. W. Bush from "disenfranchis[ing] entirely the conservative wing of the North Carolina G.O.P." Hines had formerly been a state representative in South Carolina.

42. Quinn, Richard. "The Quota President," *Southern Partisan*, 11 (3rd Quarter 1991): 5; Quinn, Richard. "Martin Luther King Day," *Southern Partisan*, 3.4 (1983): 4.

43. Reed, John Shelton. "For Dixieland: The Sectionalism of *I'll Take My Stand*," *A Band of Prophets: The Vanderbilt Agrarians after Fifty Years*, ed. William C. Havard and Walter Sullivan. (Baton Rouge: Louisiana State University Press, 1982): 52.

44. Vanover, J. R. [John Shelton Reed]. "Why No Southern Nationalism?" *Southern Partisan* 2.1 (1981): 32, and "Why No Southern Nationalism, Part II?" *Southern Partisan* 2.2 (1982): 44.

45. See for example, M. E. Bradford, "The Theology of Secession," *Southern Partisan*, 11 (4th Quarter 1991): 20–24.

46. The isi was founded in 1953 by Frank Chodorov; an early president was William F. Buckley Jr. At the time of writing, the isi president was T. Kenneth Cribb Jr., who has held the position since 1989. Deputy chief counsel to Ronald Reagan's 1980 presidential campaign, Cribb has been an advisor and contributor to *Southern Partisan* since the mid-1990s. See "T. Kenneth Cribb, Jr." http://www.isi .org/about/our_history/t_kenneth_cribb.html [accessed 24 October 2007].

47. McWhiney, Grady. "Continuity in Celtic warfare," *Continuity*, 2 (1981): 1–18; "Conservatism and the Military," *Continuity*, 4–5 (1982): 93–126; "Historians as Southerners," *Continuity*, 9 (1984): 1–31. In addition to his contributions to *Continuity*,

McWhiney was central to the development of the Celtic South thesis (see Chapter 4) and was a director of the League of the South from its founding in 1994 until ill health forced him to step down in 2001. He died in 2006.

48. Wilson, Clyde. "American Historians and Their History," *Continuity*, 6 (1983): 1–16.

49. Bradford, M. E. "Lincoln and the Language of Hate and Fear: A View from the South," *Continuity*, 9 (1984): 108.

50. Linker, Damon. *The Theocons: Secular America under Siege.* (New York: Doubleday, 2006): 59–60. A similar story is recounted by George H. Nash in *The Conservative Intellectual Movement in America since 1945.* (Wilmington, DE: Intercollegiate Studies Institute, 1998): 338.

51. Gottfried and Fleming, *The Conservative Movement*, (1988): 58.

52. Fleming is first listed on the masthead as editor in the June 1985 edition. For the development of *Chronicles*, see Scotchie's "Introduction: Paleoconservatism," (1999), *Revolt from the Heartland*, (2002), and Murphy's *The Rebuke of History*, (2001).

53. Murphy, *The Rebuke of History*, (2001): 218.

54. See, for example, *Chronicles* theme issues on "Secessions," 15.1 (1991); "The Days of Empire—Come and Gone?" 17.2 (1993), "Nationalism in Western Europe," 17.11 (1993), and "*E Pluribus Unum:* Regionalism—Alive and Kicking," 19.8 (1995). Articles included Fleming, Thomas. "New World Disorder," *Chronicles*, 16.7 (1992): 14–16, and Hoppe, Hans-Hermann. "Nationalism and Secession," *Chronicles*, 17.11 (1993): 23–25. In one Fleming column, the status of Estonia within the Soviet Union was paralleled with that of South Dakota and Alabama in the United States, and in another readers were offered a choice for the American future: "devolution or revolution"—see, respectively, "Cultural Revolutions," *Chronicles*, 15.11 (1991): 6, and "April 19, 1995," *Chronicles*, 19.8 (1995): 10–13.

55. Washburn, Michael. "Southern League," *Chronicles*, 19.6 (1995): 7 (emphasis added).

56. Fleming, Thomas. "A League of Our Own," *Chronicles* 17.2 (1993): 15.

57. Scotchie, *Revolt from the Heartland*, (2002): 98. Scotchie is identified as a League of the South member in the section "Books" in the organization's publication *Southern Patriot*, 4.2 (1997): 48, and in the column "More Books by ls members," *Southern Patriot*, 5.3 (1998): 8–9.

58. Fleming, Thomas. "Divorce Italian style," *Chronicles*, 15.1 (1991): 12–16; "Letter from Italy," *Chronicles*, 15.11 (1991): 41–44; "New world disorder," *Chronicles*, 16.7 (1992): 14–16; "Italian lessons," *Chronicles*, 17.11 (1993): 12–15; "Cabbages and worms," *Chronicles*, 21.1 (1997): 8–11; "Hanging with our friends," *Chronicles*, 21.4 (1997): 10–13; "The Lega Nord," *Chronicles*, 21.8 (1997): 7; "In the time of the breaking of nations," *Chronicles*, 24.1 (2000): 10–13. For analysis of connections between the Lega Nord and proponents of neo-Confederacy, see Hague, Euan, Giordano, Benito, and Sebesta, Edward H. "Whiteness, multiculturalism and nationalist appropriation of Celtic culture: The case of the League of the South and the Lega Nord," *Cultural Geographies*, 12.2 (2005): 151–173; Giordano, Benito, Hague, Euan, and Sebesta, Edward H. "Asserting Celtic roots—The use of Celtic culture in the nationalist campaigns of the Lega Nord and the League of the South," *Canadian Review of Studies in Nationalism*, 31.1–31.2 (2004): 23–36.

59. Fleming, "A League of Our Own," (1993): 15.

60. Fleming, Thomas. "Equality or Privilege: Gored on the Horns of the American Dilemma," *Chronicles* 18.8 (1994): 14. Despite such pronouncements, Fleming is incongruously described by his sympathetic colleague Joseph Scotchie as a man who "counsels against a nationalism that scapegoats ethnic or racial minorities, one that is built on the hatred of 'the other'"—see *Revolt from the Heartland*, (2002): 98.

61. Massey, Ross. "Interview with Jack Kershaw," *Southern Patriot*, 9.5 (2002): 7. Here, Kershaw also describes his connections to Agrarians Donald Davidson, Robert Penn Warren, and John C. Ransom. For Kershaw's role in anti-integration activism see Murphy, *The Rebuke of History*, (2001).

62. This information comes from a pamphlet distributed to Mises Institute supporters dated 27 February 1995. Another pamphlet dated 7 March 1995 and titled "Ludwig von Mises Institute's Accomplishments 1995" contained a review of the "seminal and auspicious" secession conference (p. 9). The conference's papers were collected into a book: Gordon, David, ed. *Secession, State and Liberty*. (New Brunswick, NJ: Transaction Publishers, 1998), which contained essays by prominent neo-Confederates Clyde Wilson and Donald Livingston. See also DiLorenzo, Thomas. "Mises, Ludwig von, Institute," *American Conservatism: An Encyclopedia*, ed. Bruce Frohnen, Jeremy Beer, and Jeffrey O. Nelson. (Wilmington, DE: ISI Books, 2006): 575–577. The Institute's official web site is at http://www.mises.org/.

63. Ludwig von Mises Institute members began publishing in magazines like *Chronicles* and *Southern Partisan*. For example, Hoppe, "Nationalism and Secession," (1993): 23–25. Hoppe is identified as "a senior fellow of the Ludwig von Mises Institute" (p. 23).

64. For discussion of Livingston and other intellectuals associated with neo-Confederacy, see Hague, Euan. "Texts as Flags: The League of the South and the Development of a Nationalist Intelligentsia in the United States, 1975–2001," *Hagar: International Social Science Review*, 3.2 (2002): 299–339.

65. Livingston, Donald W. "The Secession Tradition in America," *Secession, State and Liberty*, (1998): 1–33; Livingston, Donald W. "One Nation Divisible," *Chronicles*, 22.2 (1998): 13–17.

66. Livingston, Donald W. *Philosophical Melancholy and Delirium*, (1998): 420.

67. Livingston, Donald W. "Dismantling Leviathan," *Harper's Magazine*, 304.1824 (2002): 16, 17.

68. Sebesta, Edward H., and Hague, Euan. "The U.S. Civil War as a Theological War: Confederate Christian Nationalism and the League of the South," *Canadian Review of American Studies*, 32.3 (2002): 253–283.

69. See, as just one example, Szkotak, Steve. "Latest Civil War Skirmish Stems from Efforts to Rename Public Schools Named after Confederates," *Tuscaloosa News* (Associated Press), (21 December 2003): 7B.

70. Grissom, Michael Andrew. *Southern by the Grace of God*. (Gretna, LA: Pelican Publishing Company, 1989 [1988]): 128. Grissom is one of the most active neo-Confederate authors. His other books include *The Last Rebel Yell*. (Nashville: Rebel Press, 1991), *When the South was Southern*. (Gretna, LA: Pelican Books, 1994), *Farewell to the Accent, or, There Goes the Drawl, Y'all!* (Nashville, TN: Dixie Press, 1996), *Can The South Survive?* (Nashville: Rebel Press, 2001), and *The Southern Book of Quotes: A Compendium of Familiar Quotations and Memorable Utterances Useful to the Pulpit, the*

Lecture Hall, the Stage, the Classroom, the Hustings, and the Parlor. (Wynnewood, OK: Little Dixie Publishing, 2003), co-edited with Christopher Eric McBroom.

71. Grissom, *Southern by the Grace of God,* (1989 [1988]).

72. McMillen, Neil R. *The Citizens' Council: Organized Resistance to the Second Reconstruction, 1954–64.* (Urbana: University of Illinois Press, 1971): 176.

73. Wilkins, Steve, and Wilson, Douglas. *Southern Slavery: As It Was.* (Moscow, ID: Canon Press, 1996): 8, 13, 24. In his *Southern Partisan* review of this book, Byron Snapp recommended keeping a copy "close at hand for reference" and "buy[ing] additional copies to share with your friends" because it presents "facts" that are "historical, thought-provoking, and honest" (*Southern Partisan,* 16 [3rd Quarter 1996]: 54). In contrast, Sean M. Quinlan and William L. Ramsey explain that *Southern Slavery: As It Was* "simply repeats many of the racist arguments advanced by proslavery activists in the 1840s and 1850s. Yet they have retooled those arguments and deployed them in the service of modern neo-Confederate and Christian Reconstructionist arguments" (*Oklahoma City University Law Review,* 30.1 [2005]: 2). Wilkins writes under the names Rev. J. Steven Wilkins, J. Steven Wilkins, and Steve Wilkins. For clarity we refer to him as Steve Wilkins in this book.

74. Kennedy, Walter Donald. *Myths of American Slavery.* (Gretna, LA: Pelican Publishing, 2002).

75. Kennedy, James Ronald, and Kennedy, Walter Donald. *The South Was Right!,* 2nd ed. (Gretna, LA: Pelican Publishing, 1994 [1991]): 8.

76. Ibid., 9.

77. Kennedy, James Ronald. *Reclaiming Liberty.* (Gretna, LA: Pelican Publishing, 2005); Kennedy, James Ronald, and Kennedy, Walter Donald. *Was Jefferson Davis Right?* (Gretna, LA: Pelican Publishing, 1998); Kennedy, James Ronald, and Kennedy, Walter Donald. *Why Not Freedom!—America's Revolt Against Big Government.* (Gretna, LA: Pelican Publishing, 1995).

78. Thornton, R. Gordon. *The Southern Nation: The New Rise of the Old South.* (Gretna, LA: Pelican Publishing, 2000); Conner, Frank. *The South under Siege, 1830–2000: A History of the Relations between the North and the South.* (Newnan, GA: Collards Publishing Company, 2002).

79. Conner, Frank. "Reorganizing the Sons of Confederate Veterans," *Southern Mercury,* 2.3 (2004): 8–11, 27.

80. Woods, Thomas E. Jr. *Politically Incorrect Guide to American History.* (Washington, D.C.: Regnery Publishing, 2004). Its first appearance on the paperback bestseller list came in the *New York Times Book Review* (26 December 2004): 20. It last appeared on that same list on 30 January 2005.

81. Woods's status as one of the founding members of the League of the South (formerly the Southern League) is noted in Woods, Thomas E. Jr. "The Abolitionists," *Southern Patriot,* 2.5 (1995) 36–37. Woods subsequently told Heidi Beirich that he left the League of the South in 1996. In *Politically Incorrect Guide to American History,* Woods acknowledges Clyde Wilson and Donald Livingston as having helped to develop his book.

82. Young, Cathy. "Last of the Confederates," *Boston Globe,* (21 February 2005): A15.

83. Cohen, Adam. "The Difference between Politically Incorrect and Historically Wrong," *New York Times,* (26 January 2005): 16.

84. "Statement of Ownership, Management, and Circulation," *Chronicles*, 29.12 (2005): 9.

85. "Statement of Ownership, Management, and Circulation," *UDC Magazine*, 68.9 (2005): 36. The UDC's membership numbers come from Bluestein, Greg. "Confederate Groups Getting Less Gray," *AP Wire*, (23 May 2006). On-line: http://www.macon.com/mld/macon/14648989.htm [accessed 19 August 2006]. Bluestein notes that UDC membership is getting younger and quotes UDC president Esther Cope: "People across America are learning of their heritage and treasuring it. . . . It's like a cycle. In the '60s it wasn't as popular to learn about your genealogy. And now it's growing. And they're honoring their ancestors by joining these organizations. And we're seeing an upswing as a result." Heidi Beirich contacted Ben Sewell, executive director of the Sons of Confederate Veterans, to ask about the circulation of *Southern Mercury* and *Confederate Veteran*. Sewell would not release circulation figures. The SCV membership figure is taken from a 2006 conversation between Beirich and an SCV official. Earlier published figures had put the SCV's membership somewhat higher, at around 31,000. See McWhirter, Cameron. "Texan Elected as Confederate Group's Leader," *Atlanta Constitution-Journal*, (2 August 2004): 2B; Zengerle, Jason. "Lost Cause," *New Republic*, (2 August 2004) 14, 16, 18–19.

86. "USPS Statement of Management, Ownership, and Circulation," *Southern Partisan*, 24.5 (2004/2005): 34. This is a reduction in circulation—Applebome's *Dixie Rising* (p. 117) identifies the magazine's circulation as "about fifteen thousand" in 1996. In 1982 *Southern Partisan* had been selling around 2,000 copies of each issue—see Richard Quinn. "The New Right Papers," *Southern Partisan*, 2.2 (1982): 4.

87. For full documentation, search the web site of "Media Transparency—The Money behind Conservative Media." On-line: http://www.mediatransparency.org/default.php [accessed 8 February 2007].

88. Radelat, Ana. "Lott Remarks Bring Scrutiny of His Ties to Segregationists," *USA Today*, (12 December 2002): 18A. In the *San Diego Union-Tribune*, Ralph E. Luker noted that Lott had "praised members of the Greenwood, Miss., neo-Confederate Council of Conservative Citizens for their 'right principles' and 'right philosophy'" (12 December 2002). The Council of Conservative Citizens (CCC) is discussed in Chapter 6. At the time of writing, according to its leader Gordon Baum in a conversation with Heidi Beirich, the CCC had 20,000 members. It publishes the newsletter *Citizens Informer*.

89. Lott first introduced the bill to the House of Representatives in the 95th Congress on 16 February 1977 (H.J. Res. 258). He reintroduced the proposal on 3 May (H.J. Res. 433) and again on 24 May 1977 (H.J. Res. 485). On 15 June 1977 Lott reproposed the measure (H.J. Res. 521), doing so again on 25 July 1977 (H.J. Res. 556). An identical measure in the Senate was proposed by Senator Mark Hatfield and co-sponsored by Senators Orrin Hatch and Strom Thurmond (S.J. Res. 16), introduced on 25 January 1977. These measures were signed by President Jimmy Carter and became law on 17 October 1978 (see "Panel in House Votes Citizenship for Davis," *New York Times*, [25 June 1978]: 34; "Carter: The Civil War is Over," *Washington Post*, [18 October 1978]: A12). Jefferson Davis was denied citizenship by the Fourteenth Amendment, ratified on 9 July 1868, which, in addition to granting equal protection for all U.S. citizens, removed such rights from those engaged in "insurrection or rebellion" against the

United States. Confederate general Robert E. Lee had his citizenship posthumously restored by Congress in 1976.

90. Lott, Trent. "Jefferson Davis: In Commemoration of the Restoration of His Citizenship," address delivered on 3 June 1979. Reprinted in *United Daughters of the Confederacy magazine (UDC magazine)*, 43.2 (1980): 15–16.

91. Quoted in Hines, Richard T. "A Partisan Conversation with Trent Lott," *Southern Partisan*, 4.4 (Fall 1984): 44–45.

92. Fleming, Thomas. "Trent Lott and a Few Good Republicans," (2002) (original emphasis). On-line: http://www.chroniclesmagazine.org/HardRight/HardRight 122002.html [accessed 13 November 2003].

93. Mitch Berbrier argues that in the United States "new racists" are revising white supremacist discourse. Instead of direct claims to racial superiority, many articulate a supposed need to recognize and protect European heritage—see "White supremacists and the (Pan-) Ethnic Imperative: On 'European-Americans' and 'White Student Unions,'" *Sociological Inquiry*, 68.4 (1998): 498–516. Along similar lines, Jeffrey Goldfarb notes that "When David Duke, the former Nazi and Ku Klux Klan leader, ran as the Republican candidate for Governor of the State of Louisiana, he campaigned in codes. He did not propagate explicit anti-black or anti-Semitic ideas, but instead celebrated our Christian heritage and our right to sustain it, and defended the equal civil right of whites"—see *Civility and Subversion: The Intellectual in Democratic Society*. (Cambridge: Cambridge University Press, 1998): 146.

CHAPTER 2

The U.S. Civil War as a Theological War: Neo-Confederacy, Christian Nationalism, and Theology

EDWARD H. SEBESTA AND EUAN HAGUE

Religion is central to current invocations of neo-Confederacy. The New Dixie Manifesto, outlined in the introduction, represents the public articulation of neo-Confederacy's central tenets as put forward by two of its major proponents, James Michael Hill and Thomas Fleming:

> On a spiritual level, we take our stand squarely within the tradition of Christianity. This historic faith, though everywhere attacked by the hollow men of modernity, has always been central to the pursuit of personal honor, political liberty and human charity. Asking for only the religious freedoms guaranteed in the Bill of Rights, we oppose the government's campaign against our Christian traditions.[1]

It is not, however, a simple faith in Christianity that neo-Confederacy incorporates. As we have outlined, neo-Confederacy typically looks to the Civil War for lessons and explanations. According to neo-Confederates and their understanding of Christianity, the Civil War was a theological war over the future of the religion, pitting the heretical Union states against the pious, devout Christians of the Confederacy. When intertwined with the separatist positions articulated by groups such as the League of the South (LS), much of neo-Confederacy articulates a commitment to constructing a new Confederation of Southern States based on a reading of Christianity and the Bible that can be identified as Christian nationalist. This is centered upon a theological assessment that interprets the nineteenth-century Confederate States of America (CSA) as having been an orthodox Christian nation. Such reasoning leads to current neo-Confederate claims that the battle flag and other Confederate icons are fundamentally Christian symbols and the assertion that opposition to Confederate symbols and heritage equates with a rejection of Christianity.

The theological war thesis explaining the Civil War originated in the Southern Presbyterian Church of the mid-nineteenth century. Its advocates included Robert Lewis Dabney (1820–1898), professor at Union Theological Seminary in Virginia and the army chaplain of Confederate general Stonewall Jackson; James Henley Thornwell (1812–1862), president of South Carolina College, later professor at Columbia Theological Seminary; and Benjamin Morgan Palmer (1818–1902), founding editor of the *Southern Presbyterian Review,* professor at Columbia Theological Seminary, and later pastor of the First Presbyterian Church in New Orleans. Following the Civil War, the Southern Presbyterian Church published biographies of and writings by Dabney, Thornwell, and Palmer. These works remained outside the more mainstream Lost Cause apologetics for the Confederacy until Southern Agrarian Richard M. Weaver (1910–1963), Christian Reconstructionist Rousas John Rushdoony (1916–2001), and Presbyterian leader C. Gregg Singer (1910–1999) revived interest in these writings after World War II.[2] Subsequently, Sprinkle Publications of Harrisonburg, Virginia, reprinted texts by Southern Presbyterian clergymen dating from the Civil War and postbellum period, and academic historians such as Eugene Genovese reappraised these works in the 1980s and 1990s.

The theological war interpretation was often combined with, amongst other things, defenses of slavery, denunciations of public education and mass schooling, and proposals to maintain a hierarchical and unequal society. Tracing the theological war thesis from its origins to the current iteration of neo-Confederacy at the turn of the twenty-first century demonstrates how belief that the Confederacy was an orthodox Christian nation has gained increasing circulation and acceptance. Though it was once a marginal revisionist reading of the Civil War, we contend that groups as diverse as the Sons of Confederate Veterans (scv), the Christian Reconstructionist Chalcedon Foundation, and the ls now generally accept the theological war thesis. Reaching a broad audience at conferences, through publications and on web sites, neo-Confederate Steve (J. Steven) Wilkins, a founding director of the ls, continues to develop theological interpretations of the Civil War. Operating within this historical trajectory, therefore, neo-Confederate activists have utilized the theological war thesis to promote a Christian nationalist commitment to constructing a new Confederacy.

An examination of every publication in this chronology and tradition is outside the scope of this chapter, and interpretations of Christianity by the far right in the United States are similarly numerous.[3] Others have examined the interrelationships between theological interpretations of Christianity, the Civil War, and biblical justifications for slavery, but the Christian nationalism within current invocations of neo-Confederacy has been little studied.[4] Therefore, this chapter explores how the message currently promoted by neo-Confederates revives mid-nineteenth-century Confederate writings that understood the Civil War to be a theological conflict between Northern heresy and Southern orthodox Christianity.

Current Neo-Confederate Positions

Pledges to "defend the historic Christianity of the South" and advocacy for the creation of an orthodox Christian nation-state are common in neo-Confederate writings.[5] In his essay "Christian Southerners," for example, Michael Hill declares that since the inauguration of the ls, its activists have pushed for "the establishment of a republic based on the Christian principles of our Confederate ancestors," and argues that Christianity was as central to the Confederacy during the Civil War as "Lee, Jackson, Stuart, and Davis."[6] Claiming to continue this Confederate tradition, Hill states that his organization represents "true Southerners" who constitute an "Orthodox Christian" people.[7] Michael Hill thus characterizes present neo-Confederacy and its struggle for Southern independence as a confrontation between Southern Christian principles, which the neo-Confederates themselves represent, and anti-Christian positions attributed to the mainstream United States. Neo-Confederate leaders tell their supporters that the Civil War resulted from a wider, ongoing national conflict between orthodox Christianity and heresy that continues to this day.[8] Hill, for example, identifies Confederate heroes as "uncompromising defenders of the orthodox Christian faith," and interprets the Confederate battle flag as a symbol of Christianity and Western civilization.[9] Opposition to the Confederate States of America is thus seen as a rejection of Christianity, a stance reiterated by Hill: "We intend, God willing, to advance the traditions of the Christian South against the secularising and globalising trends of the modern age."[10] The cause of the Confederacy is both reconfirmed and maintained by neo-Confederates as a strategy to secure Christianity in the United States.

Frank Conner, prominent contributor to the glossy neo-Confederate scv magazine *Southern Mercury* and vituperative author of *The South Under Siege, 1830–2000*, contends that the "war of liberal North against conservative Christian South began in the 1830s; and it continues unabated to this day."

He argues that erasing Christianity is the hidden goal of almost two hundred years of efforts to engender civil rights for African Americans:

> The stated goal of that ideological war has always been to improve the civil rights of blacks—first to free the slaves (in the 19th century) and give them the vote; and then to integrate the blacks into the white Southern culture (in the mid-20th century); and finally to give them preferential treatment, and political control over the Southern whites. But that stated goal was (and still is) intended to mislead the general public. . . . The ideological war has actually been a religious war waged by Northern liberalism to discredit and destroy Christianity first in the South and then in the rest of the nation, and to replace it with secular humanism as the official religion of the U.S. Only when American history is viewed in that light do the relations between the North and the South from the 1830s until now make any sense at all.[11]

The position that the South is a Christian nation under attack from the North is not new. Many of these sentiments originated in the mid-nineteenth century and, in the following section, we review some of these historical precedents.

The Origins of the Theological Interpretation of the Civil War

During and after the Civil War, several prominent Southern clergymen defined the conflict and political debate with abolitionists as theological struggles between Christian orthodoxy and anti-Christian forces. Many clergymen in the South supported secession, delivering sermons and producing pamphlets championing the Confederacy.[12] Within the clergy, historians Francis Butler Simkins and Charles Pierce Roland argue, it was members of the Presbyterian denomination who were widely considered to be "the intellectual elite among Southern churchmen."[13] Presbyterian chaplains, including Thornwell, Palmer, and Dabney, engaged in reviews of the Civil War from a theological perspective. Often published by the presses of the Presbyterian Church, a body of literature developed that asserted the Civil War had been an attack on a Christian South by heretical and atheistic forces of the North. Some contemporaries in the Presbyterian Church condemned this position, however. Robert Livingston Stanton (1810–1885), professor at the Theological Seminary of the Presbyterian Church in Danville, Kentucky, during the Civil War era, wrote that Thornwell gave "eloquent voice to the cause of treason" and that Palmer also was articulate in his support for slavery, secession, and thus "treason."[14] Still, there were others who supported the stances taken by Thornwell and Palmer, such as Frederick A. Ross (1796–1883), a Presbyterian minister in Tennessee and Alabama for over fifty years.[15]

. Texts by Thornwell and Palmer in particular are amongst those that became key to the thesis of a Christian Confederate nation and the theological basis of the war. Between 1871 and 1873 the Presbyterian Committee published Thornwell's complete works, and in 1875 a secular press distributed Palmer's biography of Thornwell.[16] In turn, Thomas Carey Johnson's 1906 biography of Palmer reproduced the New Orleans chaplain's 29 November 1860 Thanksgiving sermon, given in Louisiana three weeks before South Carolina became the first state to secede. Here Palmer argued that slavery "has fashioned our modes of life, and determined all our habits of thought and feeling, and moulded the very type of our civilization," further explaining that it was a religious duty to "defend the cause of God and religion" and, in particular, "to conserve and to perpetuate the institution of domestic slavery."[17] Though condemned by Stanton as "steeped in sin, guilt, and crime" for its exhortation of secession to maintain slavery, Palmer's sermon subsequently became a central text of the theological war thesis.[18]

• Many contemporaries of Thornwell and Palmer sought to assert that Confederate soldiers were more pious than their Union counterparts. For example, Confederate chaplain William W. Bennett (1821–87) explained in his *Narrative of the Great Revival* (1877) that the Confederate soldiers he observed were Christians, contrasting Bible-reading Confederate troops with card-playing Union soldiers. Further, Bennett noted that the "religious sentiments" of Confederate supporters were "deep and strong" and that amongst the troops, "there have been fewer departures from the great cardinal doctrines of the Scriptures than among any other people in Christendom."[19] Both Bennett and another Confederate chaplain, J. William Jones, who served under Robert E. Lee, composed catalogs detailing a revival of Christianity throughout the Confederate army. Although these texts do not advocate that theology was the main issue of the war, they became important sources of evidence for subsequent authors to maintain that, in contrast to the Union, the Confederate States comprised a nation of Christians.[20]

. Arguably the most significant early advocate of a theological perspective of the Civil War was Robert Lewis Dabney, who, according to Simkins and Roland, "for three decades after the fall of the Confederacy in lectures and in books . . . energetically expounded the dogma . . . that the Civil War was a Christian struggle of a justified South against a wicked North."[21] In 1865 Dabney published *The Life and Campaigns of Lieut. Gen. Thomas J. Jackson (Stonewall Jackson)*, in which he argued for secession and states' rights and also described selected Civil War campaigns. The primary purpose of the text was to extol Jackson as a Confederate hero and a pious Presbyterian Christian soldier.[22] Soon after, Dabney wrote on the theological meaning of the Civil War in *A Defense of Virginia and through Her of the South*. Utilizing biblical passages to defend slavery and refute abolitionist arguments, he claimed that slavery was a necessary good for those he identified as depraved lower classes. Dabney asserted, in support for Confederate secession, that "it is only the relation of domestic slavery as authorized by God, that we defend."[23] Further denouncing abolitionism as "infidel" and "anti-scriptural," Dabney maintained that the Bible legitimated slavery, and thus opposition to slavery was tantamount to rejecting Christianity.[24]

Shortly before his death in 1898, Dabney's works were collected into four volumes and published by the Presbyterian Committee of Richmond, Virginia.[25] Throughout his writings, the minister condemned human equality and women's rights as leading to the destruction of the family and, thereafter, of society. Dabney also attacked the immorality of Union soldiers in the Civil War, opposed public schooling (especially of African Americans), and honored Confederate leaders, justifying all his positions using biblical interpretations. In the essays "Geology and the Bible" and "A Caution Against Anti-Christian Science," for example, Dabney wrote that modern science and the theory of evolution were "anti-theological" and that amongst future generations this would result in "a nascent contempt for their father's Bibles" and irreparably damage the South's "Christian households."[26] He further contended that governments were legitimate only if they derived from the will of God.[27] Dabney wrote prolifically, regularly commenting on philosophical and theological topics and was consistently and virulently hostile toward African Americans. Social equality in the South, he argued, would "mix the blood of the heroes of Manassas with this vile stream from the fens of Africa," diluting and weakening the genealogical purity of Confederate blood and thus reducing the once heroic Virginians to a position of servility.[28] By the end of his life, Simkins and Roland assert, Dabney was largely ignored by his contemporaries, considered an advocate of archaic conceptualizations of "chivalry and religious conservatism,"[29] though a few years later he was the subject of a biography by Thomas Cary Johnson.[30]

Restricted largely to Southern Presbyterian venues, this theological war literature was less significant in popular politics than more general Lost Cause apologetics.[31] Yet since the mid-1960s conservative scholars and activists, at times operating within religious circles, have reevaluated and republished these marginal writings. Indeed, in a 1984 preface to Dabney's *Practical Philosophy*, Douglas F. Kelley, professor of theology at the Reformed Theological

Seminary in Charlotte, North Carolina, identifies the nineteenth-century theologian as a "prophet [who] foresaw the life and death struggle that would take place between secular totalitarianism and Christian liberty in America in the latter part of the twentieth century."[32] It is to the trajectory from authors such as Dabney to the neo-confederates of the late twentieth century that we now turn.

The Revival of the Theological Civil War in the 1940s–1960s

Dabney and the other Southern Presbyterians were largely forgotten as the twentieth century progressed and an industrial New South developed. Following the 1929 Wall Street crash, however, scholars began to question the viability of the South's cultural and economic position, and many looked to alternative models of Southern society. Richard King argues that an "anti-New South spirit" pervaded intellectuals such as John Crowe Ransom, Allen Tate, Donald Davidson, and Robert Penn Warren, who became known as the Southern Agrarians.[33] This reactionary group looked back to and defended conservative traditions of the South. Arguing in *I'll Take My Stand* that because religious faith involves submission to God's creation of nature, and that industrialization simplifies nature by turning it into commodities and rendering it artificial, "religion can hardly expect to flourish in an industrial society."[34] To the Southern Agrarians, the regeneration of a religious South mandated a rolling back of industrialization. Following the Agrarians, Richard M. Weaver's (1910–1963) focus on the South constructed it as a pious agrarian region standing in opposition and contradiction to a modern industrial North.[35]

In 1943 Weaver outlined his contention that the Civil War was a clash between an orthodox Christian South and a heretical North: "Southern people reached the eve of the Civil War one of the few religious people left in the Western World. Into the strange personnel of the Confederate Army . . . poured fighting bishops and prayer-holding generals, and through it swept waves of intense religious enthusiasm long lost to history."[36] Weaver further explained that the Confederate military was a Christian army: "Confederate captains not only were conscious of being the standard bearers of chivalry; they also regarded themselves as distinctly a Christian soldiery."[37] Thus establishing that there was a theological dimension to the Civil War, and focusing on the Confederate army and "Southern people" as "distinctly . . . Christian,"

Weaver's work facilitated a revival of theological examinations of the Civil War and serves as a connection between today's neo-Confederates and the Southern Agrarians of the 1930s.[38] Indeed, Kreyling identifies just such a trajectory, extending from the Agrarians and Weaver to Michael Hill and the League of the South.[39]

Following Weaver, other writers revisited the interpretation that the Civil War was a theological war. One of these was C. Gregg Singer (1910–1999), a professor at the Atlanta School of Biblical Studies in 1977 and, after 1987, at the Greenville Presbyterian Theological Seminary.[40] Writing during the civil rights era, Singer explicitly contended that the Civil War was a theological war: "[The] Southern Presbyterian Church saw [the Civil War] as a humanistic revolt against Christianity and the world and life view of the Scriptures. . . . Thornwell, Dabney, and their contemporaries . . . properly read abolitionism as a revolt against the biblical conception of society and a revolt against the doctrine of divine sovereignty in human affairs."[41] As the leader of Concerned Presbyterians, Inc., a dissident faction that condemned heresy in the Southern Presbyterian Church, Singer played a prominent role in establishing the Presbyterian Church in America (PCA) as a distinct denomination in the 1970s. Distancing the PCA from other Presbyterians in the United States, this organization envisaged itself as a successor to the Presbyterian Church in the Confederate States of America (PCCSA), a denomination that had also formed in response to perceived heresy. The PCA drew a direct connection between itself and the PCCSA, stating its intent to "follow the pattern of the Assembly of 1861."[42] Singer further claimed that the PCA continued a legacy dating beyond the PCCSA to Old School Presbyterian orthodoxy, and was following in the footsteps of Thornwell and other leading PCCSA theologians.[43]

As Singer was working to establish the PCA and its historical connections, another religious leader was arguing for the Christian orthodoxy of the antebellum South. Rousas John Rushdoony (1916–2001), founder of the Chalcedon Foundation in 1965 and its newsletter *Chalcedon Report*, initiated the Christian Reconstructionist movement in the United States, advocating the establishment of biblical republics under the rule of God's law, or "theonomy." The people administering these republics would be those Christian Reconstructionists consider to hold orthodox interpretations of Christianity and would, amongst other things, introduce capital punishment for myriad offenses, including stoning for adultery and juvenile delinquency.[44] Rushdoony has attacked the current electoral system for giving too much influence to minority groups and argued that U.S. society should have a civic order based on inequality and social division.[45]

In his interpretation, Rushdoony argued that the Civil War destroyed the early American Republic, which he envisioned as a decentralized Protestant feudal system and an orthodox Christian nation.[46] Union victory, Rushdoony maintained, was a defeat for Christian orthodoxy. Condemning public education and contending that the Civil War was not about slavery but the consolidation and centralization of federal government power, Rushdoony applauded Dabney's defense of slavery.[47] Dabney's views were outlined by Joseph Morecraft III to readers of *The Counsel of Chalcedon*, a publication of the Georgia-based Chalcedon Presbyterian Church, and an anonymous *Chalcedon Report* reviewer of Bennett's 1877 *Narrative of the Great Revival* stated, "What is now needed is a historical study of the Christian efforts at reconstruction which men like Robert E. Lee, and countless other veterans, then began."[48]

, By the mid-1960s, therefore, Weaver, Singer, and Rushdoony had to varying degrees reasserted that the Confederate States fought to preserve orthodox Christianity in the face of heretical abolitionism and that the Civil War was a theological war over the future direction of the United States. Publishing at the height of the struggle for civil rights in the United States, these authors argued that civil rights are anti-Christian and that inequality is God's intended order, drawing on Thornwell, Dabney, and their contemporaries to provide the historical and religious justification for this position. The role of these men in wider conservative and Christian Reconstructionist groups resulted in their views finding a broader audience amongst the religious right and other conservative factions in the United States. Through these overlapping networks, advocates of a self-styled orthodox Christianity began to converge with supporters of Confederate nationalism, as leaders of pro-Confederate and orthodox Christian organizations began to realize that their mutual interests could unify their supporters into larger and more active groups. In the 1970s, Sprinkle Publications began reprinting nineteenth-century Southern Presbyterian texts by Dabney and others, leading to their review and discussion in magazines, books, lectures, videotapes, and other pro-Confederate theological and political venues.[49] By the end of the decade, therefore, reinterpretations of the historical record, founded upon the evidence of a few atypical nineteenth-century texts, claimed that the Confederate Army was populated by theologically driven Christian Reconstructionists fighting to preserve their orthodox Christian nation. Subsequently, some of these nineteenth-century authors, particularly James Henley Thornwell, began to attract academic attention.

Toward a Theological Metaphysics of the Confederacy:
Academic Writings in the 1980s and 1990s

In a *Southern Partisan* interview in 1985, the prominent historian Eugene Genovese announced that his research was increasingly focused on religion in the Old South. Proposing some of the ideas that would occur in subsequent publications, Genovese drew upon conservative scholars such as Richard M. Weaver to argue that "the Old South should be understood fundamentally as a religious society" in which "the defense of slavery was religiously grounded."[50] Reappraising Thornwell, Genovese contended that "Thornwell's defense of slavery may be seen as an extended footnote to his defense of Christian orthodoxy" and thus must be seen as part of a wider theological perspective and understanding of the South and the Civil War.[51] Presenting Thornwell to readers in a review of "the God-fearing, Bible reading, hymn-singing Confederate army," Genovese assessed Southern conservative thought in which "a straight line runs from him [Thornwell] to the Agrarians."[52]

Previous academic analyses of Confederate Presbyterian theologians had been sporadic,[53] but Genovese's comments and the work of historians such as James Oscar Farmer Jr. stimulated further reexamination of Thornwell and other "formidable southern theologians."[54] Pertinent to these studies were three major themes: the theological Civil War and contrast between the orthodox Christian South and the heretical North; reevaluations of modernity from the perspectives of Thornwell and his contemporaries; and complaints about the neglect of Southern intellectual history. Genovese emphasized the centrality of Christian orthodoxy in the antebellum South, suggesting that the consequence was the inevitable political division between Union and Confederacy:

> The political ramifications of southern Christian theology were enormous.
> For at the very moment that the northern churches were embracing theological liberalism and abandoning the Word for a Spirit increasingly reduced to personal subjectivity, the southern churches were holding the line for Christian orthodoxy.[55]

In turn, Farmer suggested that today's Americans, with their "collective anxieties about the kind of civilization we have created," can admire the Old South.[56] Further, for Genovese, Farmer's assessment of Thornwell "clears away a great deal of the rubbish that has long distorted the writing of southern history."[57] In addition to advocating a theological basis for the Civil War, Genovese's analyses imply that this conflict continues to have relevance to late-twentieth-century society. Preempting criticism of his positions as being due to continuing anti-Southern bias in U.S. historical scholarship, Genovese asserts that Presbyterian thinkers such as Thornwell and Palmer, who tried to balance demands for progress with orthodox Christianity and a hierarchical social order, dominate the Southern intellectual tradition.[58] Extending his "straight line" of Southern thought into the late twentieth century, Genovese identifies conservative neo-Confederate historians, including M. E. Bradford and Clyde Wilson, and sociologist John Shelton Reed, as intellectual inheritors of and successors to "the Southern tradition," as are the neo-Confederate publications *Southern Partisan* and *Chronicles: A Magazine of American Culture.*[59]

‣ In arguing that Marxism fails to adequately address religious interpretations of history and that Marx misrepresented the Civil War and the South, Genovese became more explicit in his advocacy of the theological war thesis. Although "it remains commonplace to assume that no honest Christian could be a slaveholder, much less regard slavery as a divinely sanctioned institution," he maintained, nineteenth-century Southern slave owners were Christians who believed slavery was biblically acceptable, and thus the abolitionist declaration that slavery was a sin "was a call to holy war."[60] As a result of such differing theological interpretations of the sinfulness of slavery, argues Genovese, "southerners and northerners were emerging as separate peoples," a division that induced the Civil War.[61] Genovese then proceeds to appraise the theological Civil War thesis, repeating that the North was succumbing to heresy while the South retained orthodox Christianity. Quoting Thornwell's assertion that the major division of the Civil War was not abolitionists opposing slaveholders but radicals against Christians, Genovese concludes with a theological interpretation of the Civil War as a "holy war," because "northerners and southerners . . . disagreed on the essentials of Christian doctrine and morality" and, as a result, "held incompatible visions of . . . social relations."[62] Indeed, Genovese suggests Thornwell and his contemporaries may have been correct in their interpretation of U.S. society:

> We may wonder if [James Henley] Thornwell, [Benjamin Morgan] Palmer, [George Foster] Pierce, and other southerners who pushed for an official Christian Confederacy did not have the last grim laugh. For they had warned that if the Union, based on free labor, the marketplace, and radical democracy, prevailed the ground would be cut from under the churches— that, inexorably, political and social democracy would generate overwhelming pressures for ecclesiastical democracy and, through it, for theological liberalism and eventual unbelief. Southerners insisted that the dissolution of

the family, the collapse of social order, and the repudiation of any concept of legitimate authority must inexorably proceed in step with the eclipse of Christian orthodoxy, which could be sustained only by organic social relations. We may breathe a sigh of relief at the defeat of their proslavery cause. But from our vantage point of our own day, can we, in all honesty, pretend that they had not in fact read the sign of the times?[63]

In this and his other work on the topic, Genovese infers the existence of an antebellum orthodox Christian South and seeks to explore how white elites theologically interpreted slavery and defeat of the Confederacy. Indeed, Genovese notes that he must "bypass the black religious experience" despite its "considerable impact" on such questions.[64] Since the mid-1980s, therefore, Genovese and Farmer, amongst others, have appraised theological interpretations of Southern history and have helped to rehabilitate the pro-slavery Christian theologians of the mid-nineteenth century. Their central focus on Thornwell is also advantageous, given that he died before the war's end. Thus, Thornwell did not leave a legacy of vividly racist postbellum writings: Dabney and Palmer did.[65]

The Theological War in the 1990s: Steve Wilkins and the League of the South

In the last quarter of the twentieth century the theological war thesis and its associated advocacy of a Confederate Christian Southern nationalism found growing appeal not only within academic discourse, but also in neo-Confederate venues such as *Southern Partisan* and conservative religious publications such as *Chalcedon Report*. Since its interview with Genovese in the mid-1980s, *Southern Partisan* regularly outlined the theological Civil War case and orthodox Christian South theses. For example, in a 1991 essay by M. E. Bradford, the prominent conservative historian and pioneer of current neo-Confederacy, the Confederate military is portrayed as a Christian army and their enemies as heretics: "In defeat and in the bondage of enemy occupation, Southerners could think of themselves as people called out to a special witness, a righteous nation surviving in the midst of modernity, sealed forever in its covenant by defeat and freedom from the besetting ambitions of the victorious, progressive North."[66] Indeed, such became the prominence of theological interpretations of the Civil War within neo-Confederate circles that one-time League of the South member Mark Malvasi, a professor of history at Randolph-Macon College in Ashland, Virginia, argued in *Southern Parti-*

san that the contention that the antebellum South was an orthodox Christian nation is "axiomatic," and proceeded to maintain that current U.S. society is failing due to a lack of Christian faith.[67]

Replicating these arguments, Christian Reconstructionist authors drew upon the writings of Dabney, Weaver, and various nineteenth-century Southern Presbyterians to promote the theological war thesis and maintain that during the Civil War a heretical North attacked a Christian South.[68] Such an opinion marks a significant shift in the editorial position of the *Chalcedon Report*. In a 1996 issue devoted to the Civil War, the Chalcedon Foundation balanced articles that promoted neo-Confederate viewpoints, including a comment by League of the South director Steve Wilkins, with those opposing them. Five years later, following a series of articles solely supportive of neo-Confederate perspectives, Wilkins castigated Barry Anderson, a dissenter who criticized the presence of neo-Confederate essays in *Chalcedon Report*. Wilkins joked that Anderson was unable to think clearly, perhaps after "being trapped in a mob of half-crazed females at the shopping mall."[69] Support by the Chalcedon Foundation for neo-Confederate Christian nationalism is also evident in the fact that it posted the March 2000 "Declaration of Southern Cultural Independence" on its web site. In it, Wilkins and his neo-Confederate colleagues state:

> The national culture of the United States is violent and profane, coarse and rude, cynical and deviant, and repugnant to the Southern people and to every people with authentic Christian sensibilities. . . . They have called good evil and evil good; they have everywhere substituted the opinions of men for the decrees of God.[70]

With publications like the *Chalcedon Report* examining the Civil War and people like Steve Wilkins active in both Christian Reconstructionism and neo-Confederacy, the theological war thesis is evident in the historical, political, and theological perspectives of participants in both Christian Reconstructionism and neo-Confederacy. For example, Otto Scott, a regular contributor to both *Chalcedon Report* and *Southern Partisan*, has argued that civil rights and anti-apartheid activists detrimentally reenact abolitionist policies and that nineteenth-century Transcendentalism was a heretical philosophy followed by the Union during the Civil War.[71] Such opinions enabled Scott to speak at the League of the South's second annual National Conference, held on 2–3 June 1995, and to co-produce videotapes outlining neo-Confederate political, theological, and historical interpretations of the Civil War with LS directors Wilkins and Clyde Wilson.

In addition to his role as an LS director, Wilkins is arguably the most prominent member of the current neo-Confederate clergy.[72] A member of the PCA, and resident instructor at the R. L. Dabney Center for Theological Studies based in Monroe, Louisiana, Wilkins writes for almost all the religious publications and groups that advance neo-Confederate and Christian nationalist ideas, interpreting the historical development of the United States as following a heretical trajectory that culminated in the defeat of the Christian Confederate states in the Civil War. Wilkins asserts, in a manner reminiscent of Genovese's assessment, that the cause of the Civil War was theological incompatibility between the North and South, the former having "rejected Biblical Calvinism."[73] In *Southern Patriot,* Wilkins claimed that

> theological disagreement lay at the bottom of the political conflict. To many Southerners, the defense of the Southern Cause became equivalent to a defense of Christendom itself. . . . The War of 1861 . . . was a war of two different world views — one based upon the Bible, the other upon the minds of men. It was a war between two antagonistic faiths between which there was no possibility for compromise. It was a war that continues to this day.[74]

Writing in the Christian Reconstructionist publication *The Counsel of Chalcedon,* Wilkin reiterates that "the War Between the States" was "a true revolution. The foundations of western culture were being broken up and overthrown. . . . Their purpose was not merely to destroy slavery . . . but to destroy Southern culture." Wilkins continues: "There was radical hatred of Scripture and the old theology [and] Northern radicals were trying to throw off this Biblical culture and turn the country in a different direction."[75] The ultimate result of the Civil War, concludes Wilkins, was the Fourteenth Amendment to the Constitution (ratified 1868), which trampled states' rights and created an overly powerful and unconstitutional federal government, because it extended citizenship to African Americans, guaranteeing that the federal government rather than state governments granted the rights of all citizens.[76] Elsewhere, in a book co-written with Douglas Wilson, Wilkins has defended slavery and the discriminatory "Black Codes" of Southern states,[77] claiming that "the Word of God" and biblical Christian orthodoxy are currently threatened by feminism, gay and lesbian rights, and legalized abortion. The way to understand how this has happened, it seems, is "careful study of the War Between the States and the controversies surrounding it. Slavery was one of those controversies."[78] To shield Christianity from these perceived threats, Wilkins and Wilson utilize a theological analysis and draw on Confederate theologians like Dabney to build an argument that defends slavery as biblically justified. "You have been told many times that the [Civil] war was over slavery," Wilkins and Wilson tell their readers,

> but in reality it was over the biblical meaning of constitutional government. The *inflammatory* issue is slavery, however, and so the real issue is obscured in the minds of many. . . . But this "inflammatory" position is the very point upon which the Bible *speaks most directly*, again and again. . . . Our humanistic and democratic culture regards slavery *in itself* as a monstrous evil, and it acts as though this were self-evidently true. The Bible permits Christians to own slaves, provided they are treated well. You are a Christian. Whom do you believe?[79]

Wilkins has also maintained that the Civil War was a struggle between the Confederacy's "old way of Biblical Constitutionalism" and the Union's "'new' way of Humanistic Centralism," slavery being a mere "pretext" used by the Union to force the South into "political subjugation and economic destruction."[80]

Reassessing Dabney's works, Wilkins has argued that Confederate leaders are ideal role models of Christian masculinity.[81] In a lament that the modern Southerner is failing both the South and Christianity because "things which once marked the South are no longer present," Wilkins writes:

> The erosion of Biblical Christianity that has occurred over the last century has left the South a bare shadow of its former self. Many Southerners are now realizing what has been lost in cultural terms but fail to realize the true cause for this loss. It has not been caused by the opposition of the liberals. . . . It has been caused by the rejection of the historic Christian Faith of the Reformation.[82]

The solution to this lack of orthodox Christian faith, for Wilkins, is that residents of the South recover their religious tradition and reinstate this in a revived Confederacy. Indeed, Wilkins is optimistic about this proposal, perhaps signaling the growing popularity and power of neo-Confederate and Christian orthodox movements at the end of the twentieth century:

> Until only a few years ago, it looked as if the vision of the fathers of this nation had died out completely and the legacy of reconstruction would be our nation's epitaph. Today, there are hopeful signs that God's people are waking up to the call of restoring true liberty in Christ to this nation and all its institutions.[83]

By the 1990s, therefore, as collaboration between Confederate heritage and Christian Reconstructionist groups continued, the theological war thesis had become a standard position of neo-Confederacy. On 11 December 1996 at a South Carolina meeting of Christian ministers, Baptist Bobby Eubank spoke in support of the Confederate flag's position above the state capitol.[84] Subsequently published as "The Moral Defense of the Confederate Flag: A Special Message for South Carolina Christians," the oration was distributed at religious meetings.[85] It was also reprinted in *Southern Partisan,* where the authors were described as "Fifteen Ministers"—a deliberate evocation of the 1863 address by ninety-six ministers of the Confederate States giving their reasons for supporting the Confederacy and titled, "An Address to Christians throughout the World."[86] *Southern Partisan* heralded the opinions of the Fifteen Ministers as a call "for a return to orthodoxy and an understanding of the cause for which Confederate Christians fought," urging readers to "find out how you can help in this crusade."[87]

In their essay, the Fifteen Ministers summarize the major points of the theological war thesis, arguing for a Confederate Christian nation. They consider nineteenth-century Confederate leaders and troops as Christian leaders and a Christian army, and assert that the culture of the Bible Belt and religious conservatism in the South stem directly from the Christianity of the Confederate army. The Fifteen Ministers also demand that the Confederate battle flag be recognized as a Christian symbol, namely the Cross of St. Andrew.[88] Before assessing the late twentieth century, the Fifteen Ministers quote Thornwell's declaration that the Civil War was fought between "atheists, socialists, communists, red republicans, [and] Jacobins, on the one side," and Christians, "the friends of order and regulated freedom on the other." For Thornwell, what was at stake was "the progress of humanity."[89] Echoing Thornwell's apocalyptic vision, the ministers assert that "the history of mankind is a struggle or conflict between a moral path and many other paths that lead to darkness, sin, and to the betrayal of truth," and they attack political correctness as the route to immorality and sinfulness:

> We have seen from countless lawsuits, federal regulations and newspaper editorials that the enemies of the P.C. movement are Christians, Western Culture, Dead White Males, supporters of limited government, and (their all-time favorite enemy) *the South.* We are all in the cross-hairs of the P.C. movement—not as "another view" but as "wrong" and even as "evil." . . . If Christians of all races should decide to accept falsehoods defined by a hostile media, Southern Heritage will be defined forever as racist and nothing more than representing slavery. That redefinition of Southern history is dishonest

and it destroys true Southern Heritage. Southern Christians and Christians everywhere cannot support an effort to perpetuate such a lie.[90]

Subsequent *Southern Partisan* issues continued to promote the theological Civil War thesis. LS member Thomas E. Woods Jr., for example, who would later write the best-selling *Politically Incorrect Guide to American History*, asserted in 1997 that this theological conflict is continuing today and that struggles against liberalism, big government, and the New World Order constitute "Christendom's Last Stand."[91]

‘ These essays in *Southern Partisan* mark a general acceptance of the theological war thesis amongst the Confederate heritage community. Indeed, such is the current prominence of the argument that the nineteenth-century Confederacy was an orthodox Christian nation struggling to save Christendom from Union heresy that the Sons of Confederate Veterans (SCV) reprised the theological war thesis in their publication *Confederate Veteran*. Alister C. Anderson, SCV Chaplain-in-Chief, wrote a series of essays forwarding these ideas, arguing that defending Confederate symbols is akin to fighting the Devil and that "the Sons of Confederate Veterans . . . will not succeed in defending our Southern heritage until we as individuals submit to God's authority and offer Him ourselves, our souls and bodies as living sacrifices for His providential plans."[92] Continuing in a subsequent issue, Anderson further stated: "My brother compatriots I ask you to remember that we are soldiers in the Army of God and are organized along the military lines of our soldier ancestors."[93] Succeeding Anderson as SCV Chaplain-in-Chief, John Weaver made national headlines when recounting his view that slavery is biblically justified. His column in *Confederate Veteran*, quoting both Thornwell and Singer, upheld the theological Civil War thesis and argued that "the Confederate flag represents biblical government."[94]

Conclusion: Neo-Confederate Christian Nationalist Theology

In this chapter we have argued that neo-Confederacy and its proponents advocate a theological interpretation of the Civil War, understanding the conflict to have been a struggle between the orthodox Christians of the Confederacy and the heretics of the Union. Such a belief originated within sections of the Presbyterian Church during the Civil War and in the immediate postbellum period amongst some of its prominent clergymen, including James Henley Thornwell, Benjamin Morgan Palmer, and Robert Lewis Dabney. Largely marginalized, these ideas advocated that slavery was God-ordained and that opposition to slavery constituted, therefore, opposition to God.

Although some support for the theological war thesis was evident amongst successors to the Southern Agrarians such as Richard M. Weaver, it was during the civil rights era of the 1960s that C. Gregg Singer and Rousas John Rushdoony drew upon nineteenth-century Presbyterian precedents to again argue that the Civil War was a religious struggle. Academic reappraisal of the Presbyterian theologians, in particular Thornwell, followed in the 1980s and 1990s with the work of Eugene Genovese and James Oscar Farmer Jr. With the theological war thesis gaining attention in both academic and Christian Reconstructionist venues, some proponents began to engage with those interested in Confederate heritage. One such individual was Steve Wilkins, who restated the theological interpretation of the Civil War in numerous publications in the late 1980s and 1990s and became a founding director of the League of the South when this neo-Confederate organization was inaugurated in 1994. By the turn of the twenty-first century, therefore, this once peripheral interpretation of the Civil War as a theological struggle between orthodox Christian Confederate states and heretical Union states has gained credibility and adherents, becoming intertwined with wider Confederate heritage and conservative Christian opinion to become a central tenet of current neo-Confederacy.

Notes

1. Hill, Michael, and Fleming, Thomas. "New Dixie Manifesto: States' Rights Will Rise Again," *Washington Post*, (29 October 1995): C03.

2. For the original proposal of the Lost Cause myth see Pollard, Edward Alfred. *The Lost Cause: A New Southern History of the War of the Confederates.* (New York: E. B. Treat & Co., 1866) and *The Lost Cause Regained.* (New York: G. W. Carleton, 1868). See also the work of Rollin Osterweis: *Romanticism and Nationalism in the Old South.* (New Haven: Yale University Press, 1949) and *The Myth of the Lost Cause, 1865–1900.* (Hamden: Archon Books, 1973).

3. For example: Trelease, Allen. *White Terror: The Ku Klux Klan Conspiracy and Southern Reconstruction.* (New York: Harper and Row, 1971); Wade, Wynn C. *The Fiery Cross: The Ku Klux Klan in America.* (New York and Oxford: Oxford University Press, 1987); Chalmers, David. *Hooded Americanism: The History of the Ku Klux Klan.* (Durham, NC: Duke University Press, 1987); Barkun, Michael. *Religion and the Racist Right: The Origins of the Christian Identity Movement*, rev. ed. (Chapel Hill: University of North Carolina Press, 1997); Bennett, David H. *The Party of Fear: From Nativist Movements to the New Right in American History.* (New York: Vintage Books, 1995); Bushart, Howard L., Craig, John R., and Barnes, Myra. *Soldiers of God: White Supremacists and Their Holy War for America.* (New York: Pinnacle, 1998).

4. See, *inter alia*, Stanton, R. L. *The Church and the Rebellion: A Consideration of the Rebellion against the Government of the United States; and the Agency of the Church, North and South, in Relation Thereto.* (New York, Derby and Miller, 1864); Smith, H. Shelton. *In His Image But . . . Racism in Southern Religion, 1780–1910.* (Durham, NC: Duke University Press, 1972); Wilson, Charles Reagan. *Baptized in Blood: The Religion of the Lost Cause 1865–1920.* (Athens: University of Georgia Press, 1980); Webster, Gerald R. "Religion and Politics in the American South." *Pennsylvania Geographer,* 35.2 (1997): 151–172; Webster, Gerald R., and Leib, Jonathan I. "Whose South Is It Anyway? Race and the Confederate Battle Flag in South Carolina." *Political Geography,* 20.3 (2001): 271–299; Webster, Gerald R., and Leib, Jonathan I. "Political Culture, Religion and the Confederate Battle Flag Debate in Alabama." *Journal of Cultural Geography,* 20.1 (2002): 1–26; Harrill, J. Albert. "The Use of the New Testament in the American Slave Controversy: A Case History in the Hermeneutical Tension between Biblical Criticism and Christian Moral Debate." *Religion and American Culture: A Journal of Interpretation,* 10 (2000): 149–186; Genovese, Eugene D. *"Slavery Ordained of God": The Southern Slaveholders' View of Biblical History and Modern Politics.* 24th Fortenbaugh Lecture. (Gettysburg: Gettysburg College, 1985); Genovese, Eugene D. "Religion in the Collapse of the Union," *Religion and the American Civil War,* ed. Randall M. Miller, Harry S. Stout, and Charles Reagan Wilson. (New York: Oxford University Press, 1998): 74–88; Genovese, Eugene D. "James Thornwell and Southern Religion." *Southern Partisan,* 7.3 (1987): 16–21; Genovese, Eugene D. *The Slaveholders' Dilemma: Freedom and Progress in Southern Conservative Thought, 1820–1860.* (Columbia: University of South Carolina Press, 1992); Genovese, Eugene D. *The Southern Tradition: The Achievement and Limitations of an American Conservatism.* (Cambridge: Harvard University Press, 1994); Genovese, Eugene D. "Marxism, Christianity, and Bias in the Study of Southern Slave Society," *Religious Advocacy and American History,* ed. Bruce Kuklick and D. G. Hart. (Grand Rapids, MI: William B. Eerdmans Publishing, 1997): 83–95; Genovese, Eugene D. *A Consuming Fire: The Fall of the Confederacy in the Mind of the White Christian South.* (Athens: University of Georgia Press, 1998); Fox-Genovese, Elizabeth, and Genovese, Eugene. "The Religious Ideals of Southern Slave Society," *Georgia Historical Quarterly,* 70.1 (1986): 1–16; Fox-Genovese, Elizabeth, and Genovese, Eugene. "The Divine Sanction of Social Order: Religious Foundations of Southern Slaveholders' World View," *Journal of the American Academy of Religion,* 55.2 (1987): 211–233; Fox-Genovese, Elizabeth, and Genovese, Eugene. "The Social Thought of the Antebellum Southern Theologians," *Looking South: Chapters in the Story of an American Region,* ed. Winifred B. Moore Jr. and Joseph F. Tripp. (New York: Greenwood Press, 1989): 31–40; Farmer, James Oscar Jr. *The Metaphysical Confederacy: James Henley Thornwell and the Synthesis of Southern Values.* (Macon, GA: Mercer University Press, 1999 [1986]); Miller, Randall M., Stout, Harry S., and Wilson, Charles Reagan, ed. *Religion and the American Civil War.* (New York: Oxford University Press, 1998).

5. Hill, Michael. "Christian Southerners," *Southern Patriot,* 5.5 (1998): 1–2; Murphy, Martin. "The Principle of Confederation," *Southern Patriot,* 5.1 (1998): 8–9.

6. Hill, "Christian Southerners," (1998): 1.

7. Hill, Michael. "Montgomery 1996: Report from the League President," *Southern Patriot,* 3.3 (1996): 20.

8. See Wilkins, J. Steven. "Theology of the South," *Southern Patriot,* 1.2 (1994): 12; Woods, Thomas E. Jr. "Copperheads," *Southern Patriot,* 2.1 (1995): 3–5.

9. Hill, "Christian Southerners," (1998): 1; Hill, Michael. "The Real Symbolism of the St. Andrews Cross: Christian Liberty vs. the New World Order." On-line: http://www.dixienet.org/dn-gazette/st-andrews-cross.htm [accessed 1 July 2001 and 16 June 2004].

10. Hill, Michael. "What a Way to Begin a Millennium!" *Southern Patriot,* 7.1 (2000): 2.

11. Conner, Frank. *The South under Siege, 1830–2000: A History of the Relations between the North and the South.* (Newnan, GA: Collards Publishing Company, 2002): 76. The accusation of efforts to impose "secular humanism" on the United States refers to the separation of Church and State and the removal of prayer and Christian teaching from public schools. Opposition to "secular humanism" is common on the U.S. right (see Bennett, *The Party of Fear,* [rev. ed., 1995]).

12. Such publications and sermons are collected together and discussed by, amongst others, Snay, Mitchell. *Gospel of Disunion: Religion and Separatism in the Antebellum South.* (Chapel Hill: University of North Carolina Press, 1993); Wakelyn, Jon L., ed. *Southern Pamphlets on Secession, November 1860–April 1861.* (Chapel Hill: University of North Carolina Press, 1996); Fox-Genovese and Genovese, "The Social Thought of the Antebellum Southern Theologians," (1989): 31–40.

13. Simkins, Francis Butler, and Roland, Charles Pierce. *A History of the South.* (New York: Alfred A. Knopf, 4th ed., 1972 [1947]): 158.

14. Stanton, *The Church and the Rebellion,* (1864): 161, 171.

15. Ross, Frederick Augustus. *Slavery Ordained of God.* (Philadelphia: J. B. Lippincott & Co., 1857). On-line: http://www.hti.umich.edu/cgi/t/text/text-idx?c=moa;idno=ABJ1203 [accessed 4 April 2002]; Rogers, Tommy W. "Dr. F. A. Ross and the Presbyterian Defense of Slavery," *Journal of Presbyterian History,* 45.2 (1967): 112–124.

16. Thornwell, James Henley. *The Collected Writings of James Henley Thornwell,* 4 vols., ed. John B. Adger and John Girardeau. (Richmond: Presbyterian Committee of Publication, 1871); Palmer, Benjamin Morgan. *The Life and Letters of James Henley Thornwell.* (Edinburgh: Banner of Truth Trust edition, 1974 [1875]).

17. Quoted in Johnson, Thomas Cary. *The Life and Letters of Benjamin Morgan Palmer.* (Edinburgh: Banner of Truth Trust edition, 1987 [1906]): 209–210.

18. Stanton, *The Church and the Rebellion,* (1864): 169.

19. Bennett, William W. *A Narrative of the Great Revival Which Prevailed in the Southern Armies During the Late Civil War Between the States of the Federal Union.* (Harrisonburg, VA: Sprinkle Publications, 1989 [1877]): 23.

20. See also Jones, William J. *Christ in the Camp or Religion in the Confederate Army.* (Harrisonburg, VA: Sprinkle Publications, 1986 [1887]).

21. Simkins and Roland, *A History of the South,* (1972 [1947]): 405.

22. Dabney, Robert Louis. *Life and Campaigns of Lieut. Gen. Thomas J. Jackson (Stonewall Jackson).* (Harrisonburg, VA: Sprinkle Publications, 1983 [1866]).

23. Dabney, Robert Louis. *A Defence of Virginia, (And Through Her, of the South), in Recent and Pending Contests Against the Sectional Party.* (Harrisonburg, VA: Sprinkle Publications, 1991 [1867]): 99.

24. Ibid., 22.

25. Dabney, Robert Louis. *Discussions, Vol. 1 Theological and Evangelical.* (Harrisonburg, VA: Sprinkle Publications, 1982 [1890]); Dabney, Robert Louis. *Discussions, Vol. 2 Evangelical.* (Harrisonburg, VA: Sprinkle Publications, 1982 [1891]); Dabney, Robert Louis. *Discussions, Vol. 3 Philosophical.* (Harrisonburg, VA: Sprinkle Publications, 1996 [1892]); Dabney, Robert Louis. *Discussions, Vol. 4 Secular.* (Harrisonburg, VA: Sprinkle Publications, 1994 [1897]). A fifth volume was added in 1999—Dabney, Robert Louis. *Discussions, Vol. 5 Miscellaneous Writings.* (Harrisonburg, VA: Sprinkle Publications, 1999).

26. Dabney, Robert Louis. "A Caution against Anti-Christian Science," *Discussions, Vol. 3,* (1996 [1892]): 118, 122. See also Dabney, Robert Louis. "Geology and the Bible," *Discussions, Vol. 3,* (1996 [1892]): 91–115.

27. Dabney, Robert Louis. "Civic Ethics," *Discussions, Vol. 3,* (1996 [1892]): 302–328.

28. Dabney, *A Defence of Virginia,* (1991 [1867]): 353.

29. Simkins and Roland, *A History of the South,* (1972 [1947]): 7.

30. Johnson, Thomas Cary. *The Life and Letters of Robert Lewis Dabney.* (Edinburgh, Banner of Truth Trust edition, 1977 [1903]).

31. For example: Pollard, *The Lost Cause,* (1866).

32. Kelley, Douglas F. "Preface to the New Edition," *The Practical Philosophy.* Robert Lewis Dabney. (Harrisonburg, VA: Sprinkle Publications, 1984): n.p.

33. King, Richard H. *A Southern Renaissance: The Cultural Awakening of the American South, 1930-1955.* (New York and Oxford: Oxford University Press, 1980): 53.

34. Twelve Southerners. "Introduction: A Statement of Principles," *I'll Take My Stand: The South and the Agrarian Tradition.* (New York: Harper Torchbooks, 1962 [1930]): xxiv.

35. Weaver, Richard M. *The Southern Essays of Richard M. Weaver,* ed. George M. Curtis III and James J. Thompson Jr. (Indianapolis: Liberty Fund, 1987); Weaver, Richard M. *The Southern Tradition at Bay,* ed. George Core and M. E. Bradford. (New Rochelle, NY: Arlington House, 1968).

36. Weaver, Richard M. "The Older Religiousness in the South," *Sewanee Review,* 51.2 (1943): 248.

37. Weaver, *The Southern Tradition at Bay,* (1968): 208.

38. These recent studies of Southern theology include those by noted historian Eugene D. Genovese in *The Southern Tradition,* (1994); conservative historian and contributor to *Southern Partisan,* Bradford, M. E. *Remembering Who We Are: Observations of a Southern Conservative.* (Athens: University of Georgia Press, 1985); current associated scholar of the Abbeville Institute and one-time League of the South member Mark G. Malvasi. *The Unregenerate South: The Agrarian Thought of John Crowe Ransom, Allen Tate, and Donald Davidson.* (Baton Rouge: Louisiana State University Press, 1997). Some of these reinterpretations occurred in non-academic, neo-Confederate venues such as that by Thomas Landess, "Is the Battle Over . . . Or Has It Just Begun? The Southern Tradition Twenty Years after Richard Weaver," *Southern Partisan,* 3.2 (1983): 11–19.

39. Kreyling, Michael. *Inventing Southern Literature.* (Jackson: University Press of Mississippi, 1998): 178.

40. Smith, Frank J. *The History of the Presbyterian Church in America.* (Lawrenceville, GA: Presbyterian Scholars Press, silver anniversary ed., 1999): 65; Singer, Gregg C. *A Theological Interpretation of American History.* (Greenville, SC: A Press, 3rd ed., 1994 [1964]). In his assessment *The South under Siege, 1830–2000,* Frank Conner highlights Singer's books as among the "most-important" that he used, saying they are "essential reading for an understanding of the true relations between the North and the South between 1830 and 2000" (p. 714).

41. Singer, *A Theological Interpretation,* (1994 [1964]): 86–87.

42. Richards, John Edwards. *The Historical Birth of the Presbyterian Church in America.* (Liberty Hill, SC: Liberty Press, 1987): 227; Winter, R. Milton. "Division and Reunion in the Presbyterian Church, U.S.: A Mississippi Retrospective." *Journal of Presbyterian History,* 78.1 (2000): 67–86; Smith, *The History of the Presbyterian Church in America,* (1999).

43. Singer, Gregg C. "The Story of Presbyterianism," *Presbyterian Church in America: A Manual for New Members.* (Atlanta: Christian Education and Publications, n.d.): 3–6; The Presbyterian Church split in 1837 into "Old School" and "New School," the more conservative and doctrinal "Old School" becoming most prominent in the South—see, *inter alia,* Genovese, "Religion in the collapse," (1998); Smith, *The History of the Presbyterian Church,* (1999); Richards, *The Historical Birth,* (1987).

44. For more on Rushdoony and Christian Reconstruction see Schultz, Robert. "Rousas John Rushdoony," *American Conservatism: An Encyclopedia,* eds. Bruce Frohnen, Jeremy Beer, and Jeffrey O. Nelson. (Wilmington, DE: ISI Books, 2006): 753–754; Clarkson, Frederick. *Eternal Hostility: The Struggle Between Theocracy and Democracy.* (Monroe, ME: Common Courage Press, 1997); North, Gary, and DeMar, Gary. *Christian Reconstruction: What It Is, What It Isn't.* (Tyler, TX: Institute for Christian Economics, 1991); Rushdoony, Mark Rousas. "Rousas John Rushdoony: April 25, 1916–February 8, 2001, Funeral Eulogy by His Son," *Chalcedon Report,* (16 February 2001): 3–6.

45. Rushdoony, Rousas John. *The Nature of the American System.* (Fairfax, VA: Thoburn Press, 1978 [1965]): 13.

46. Ibid., 4–6.

47. Rushdoony, Rousas John. *This Independent Republic.* (Fairfax, VA: Thoburn Press, 1978 [1964]).

48. Morecraft, Joseph III. "How Dabney Looked at the World," *The Counsel of Chalcedon,* 22.5+6 (2000): 29–38, and "How Dabney Looked at the World, Continued." *The Counsel of Chalcedon,* 22.7+8 (2000): 17–30. For the review of Bennett, see "Book Notices," *Chalcedon Report,* 138 (February 1977): n.p.

49. For a list of these republished titles and discussion of Sprinkle Publications in this endeavor, see the original version of this chapter: Sebesta, Edward H., and Hague, Euan. "The U.S. Civil War as a Theological War: Confederate Christian Nationalism and the League of the South," *Canadian Review of American Studies,* 32.3 (2002): 253–283. In addition, see Byron Snapp's "Interview With Lloyd Sprinkle of Sprinkle Publications," *Southern Partisan,* 14.2 (1994): 28–31.

50. Cathey, Boyd. "Partisan Conversation—Eugene Genovese," *Southern Partisan,* 5.4 (1985): 37–38. Genovese's reevaluation of slavery from the white slaveholders' perspective and his 1990s shift from being "a Marxist," "an atheist, a materialist . . . [and] an ex-Catholic" to being a "committed Christian" is also recounted in an inter-

view in "Appendix A—Eugene D. Genovese and History: An Interview," *Slavery, Secession and Southern History*, ed. Robert Louis Paquette and Louis A. Ferleger (Charlottesville: University Press of Virginia, 2003): 207, 209.

51. Genovese, Eugene D. "Foreword," *The Metaphysical Confederacy* by James Oscar Farmer Jr. (1999): ix.

52. Genovese, Eugene D. "James Thornwell and Southern Religion." *Southern Partisan*, 7.3 (1987): 17.

53. Bishop, Charles C. "The Pro-slavery Argument Reconsidered: James Henley Thornwell, Millennial Abolitionist," *South Carolina Historical Magazine*, 73 (1972): 18–36; Rogers, Tommy W. "Dr. F. A. Ross and the Presbyterian Defense of Slavery," *Journal of Presbyterian History*, 45.2 (1967): 112–124; Smith, *In His Image But*, (1972).

54. Genovese, "Marxism, Christianity, and Bias," (1997): 91. Genovese became central to these efforts at reinvigorating and reinterpreting the theology of the Civil War—see *The Slaveholders' Dilemma*, (1992), *The Southern Tradition*, (1994), and *A Consuming Fire*, (1998). David Brion Davis's 1995 review of Genovese's reassessments of the South in the *New York Review of Books* elicited a strong response from Genovese (see Davis, David Brion. "Southern Comfort," *New York Review of Books*, 42.15 [1995]: 43–46). Kreyling, Michael. *Inventing Southern Literature*. (Jackson: University Press of Mississippi, 1998). Also Farmer's *The Metaphysical Confederacy*, (1999 [1986]) won the Brewer Prize of the American Society of Church History. Lastly, see the discussion by Freehling, William W. "James Henley Thornwell's Mysterious Antislavery Moment," *Journal of Southern History*, 57.3 (1991): 383–406.

55. Genovese, "Marxism, Christianity, and Bias," (1997): 92.

56. Farmer, *The Metaphysical Confederacy*, (1999 [1986]): 3.

57. Genovese, "Foreword," *The Metaphysical Confederacy* by James Oscar Farmer Jr. (1999 [1986]): vii.

58. Genovese, *The Slaveholders' Dilemma*, (1992), and *The Southern Tradition*, (1994).

59. Genovese, Eugene D. *The Southern Front: History and Politics in the Cultural War*. (Columbia: University of Missouri Press, 1995) and *The Southern Tradition*, (1994).

60. Genovese, "Religion in the Collapse," (1998): 74–75.

61. Ibid., 75.

62. Ibid., 84. The quote from Thornwell utilized by Genovese is also used by the Fifteen Ministers in *Southern Partisan*—see below.

63. Ibid., 82.

64. Ibid., 84.

65. Haynes, Stephen. "Race, National Destiny, and the Sons of Noah in the Thought of Benjamin M. Palmer," *Journal of Presbyterian History*, 78.2 (2000): 125–143.

66. Bradford, M. E. "The Theology of Secession," *Southern Partisan*, 11.4 (1991): 25.

67. Malvasi, Mark G. "Christianity and Southern Civilization," *Southern Partisan*, 16.1 (1996): 30. A professor of history at Randolph-Macon College, Malvasi is an important figure in the development of current neo-Confederate thought. His Ph.D. dissertation, "Risen from the Bloody Sod: Recovering the Southern Tradition," was supervised by Eugene Genovese at the University of Rochester and completed in

1991. It was revised, with the aid of a $5,000 grant from the Earhart Foundation, into *The Unregenerate South*, a text one reviewer noted exculpates the racism of Southern Agrarian Donald Davidson, offering instead "high praise" to the poet who led efforts to keep Tennessee racially segregated in the 1950s—see Persky, Joseph, review of *The Unregenerate South: The Agrarian thought of John Crowe Ransom, Allen Tate, and Donald Davidson*, by Mark G. Malvasi. *American Historical Review*, 105.1 (2000): 241-242. Malvasi's neo-Confederate credentials were strengthened in the 1990s by an internship under Clyde Wilson and affiliation with the League of the South Institute, where his video lecture "The Agrarian Tradition and the Crisis of Modernity" remains available for sale via the group's web site. He was a regular contributor to neo-Confederate venues in the 1990s—e.g., "The Agrarians in Retrospect: Southern Tradition and the Modern Age," *Southern Partisan*, 17 (4th Quarter 1997): 16-20; "Letter From Virginia: Arthur Ashe Lives," *Chronicles*, 20.3 (1996): 41-42; "Parenting and the States," *Chronicles*, 21.2 (1997): 40-41.

In 1999 Malvasi received a further $5,000 from the Earhart Foundation and in 2000 was amongst the neo-Confederates who signed a statement supporting flying the Confederate battle flag over the South Carolina state capitol (see "Group 2—Confederate Battleflag: A Symbol of Heritage and Independence," *Southern Partisan*, 20 [2nd Quarter 2000]: 19-21). He has worked on topics central to neo-Confederate discussions, such as slavery, Southern Agrarianism, and paleoconservatives like M. E. Bradford—e.g., "*Quem Patrem?* M. E. Bradford's Southern Patrimony," *Modern Age*, 38.2 (1996): 143-147; Malvasi, Mark G., ed. *History in Dispute Volume 13—Slavery in the Western Hemisphere Circa 1500-1888*. (Farmington Hills, MI: St. James Press/Gale Group, 2003). In a 2004 interview, Malvasi explained that he had turned his back on the League of the South: "If the best Mike Hill *et al.* can do is mock black people and denounce interracial dating and marriage, then there is no Southern conservative tradition left to preserve" (quoted in Beirich, Heidi, and Potok, Mark. "Little Men," *Intelligence Report*, Southern Poverty Law Center, 116 [2004]: 25). Despite distancing himself from Hill and the LS, Malvasi seems to retain strong links to current neo-Confederacy. At the time of writing, like many current and former LS members, Malvasi is listed on the web site of Donald Livingston's Abbeville Institute as an associated scholar, and he retains connections to the Intercollegiate Studies Institute (ISI). He also recently published *Merigan: A Novel*. (Bangor, ME: Booklocker.com, Inc., 2006).

68. Morecraft, Joseph III. "The Maddest Most Infamous Revolution in History: The Religious Cause of the War Between the States and the Reconstruction of the South," *The Counsel of Chalcedon*, 21.1+2 (1999): 4-11.

69. Anderson, Barry, and Steve Wilkins (in reply). "Letters to the Editor," *Chalcedon Report*, 427 (2001): 24-26.

70. "Declaration of Southern Cultural Independence," *Southern Patriot*, 7.2 (2000): 4. The document, first presented and signed by neo-Confederate activists at the Montgomery, Alabama, state capitol on 4 March 2000, is, at the time of writing, an on-line petition: http://www.petitiononline.com/cripps/petition.html [accessed 1 November 2004].

71. See Scott, Otto J. "Transcendentalism: The New England Heresy," *Southern Partisan*, 2.2 (1982): 16-21; Scott, Otto J. "The Heresy of Violence as Salvation," *Chalcedon News*, (January 1983) 2-3; Scott, Otto J. *The Other End of the Lifeboat*. (Lake

Bluff, IL: Regnery Books, 1985); Scott, Otto J. *The Secret Six: John Brown and the Abolitionist movement.* (Murphy, CA: Uncommon Books, 1993 [1979]).

72. For a review of the theological position of Steve Wilkins and his role in neo-Confederate thought, see Potok, Mark. "Wilkins' World." *Intelligence Report,* Southern Poverty Law Center, 113 (2004): 14-15.

73. Wilkins, Steve. *America: The First 350 Years.* (Monroe, LA: Covenant Publications, 1988): 142.

74. Wilkins, J. Steven. "Theology of the South," *Southern Patriot,* 1.2 (1994) 12.

75. Wilkins, J. Steven. "Southern Culture: Its Rise and Demise—An Interview with Steve Wilkins—Part I," *The Counsel of Chalcedon,* 19.4 (1997): 10-13; "Southern Culture: Its Rise and Demise—An interview with Steve Wilkins—Part II," *The Counsel of Chalcedon,* 19.7 (1997): 10-13. The quotes are from Part I, p. 11.

76. Wilkins, *America,* (1988): 150.

77. Ibid., 148.

78. Wilkins, Steve, and Wilson, Douglas. *Southern Slavery: As It Was.* (Moscow, ID: Canon Press, 1996): 11, 15. The small book by Wilkins and Wilson provoked much debate in Idaho when the authors hosted a discussion evening on the campus of the University of Idaho, Moscow. See Potok, Mark. "Taliban on the Palouse," *Intelligence Report,* Southern Poverty Law Center (113): 9-14. Two local history professors wrote a rebuttal to the claims in Wilkins and Wilson's book: Quinlan, Sean M., and Ramsey, William L. "Southern Slavery as It Wasn't: Coming to Grips with Neo-Confederate Historical Misinformation," *Oklahoma City University Law Review,* 30.1 (2005): 1-17.

79. Wilkins and Wilson, *Southern Slavery,* (1996): 11-12 (original emphasis).

80. Wilkins, *America,* (1988): 138.

81. Wilkins, J. Steven. "R. L. Dabney's 'Defense of Virginia' Revisited," *Chalcedon Reports,* 369 (April 1996): 23-26, and *The Character of Lee and Jackson: A Study in Christian Manhood.* Audio cassette, Lectures on Southern History Series. (Monroe, LA: Covenant Publications, n.d.). On-line: *http://www.gbt.org/wilkins/covenant_publications.htm* [accessed 26 September 2001].

82. Wilkins, J. Steven. "Christianity, the South, and the Culture War," *Chalcedon Reports,* 425 (December 2000): 13.

83. Wilkins, *America,* (1988): 150.

84. "Baptist Convention Rebukes Group on Issue of Confederate Flag," *Citizens Informer,* 28 (Winter 1997-1998): 5.

85. Gaulden, Sid. "Pastors Rally to Support 'Sacred Symbol,'" *Post and Courier,* Charleston, SC (12 December 1996): A1; Young, Bobbie. "Ministers Take on Flag Issue." *Post and Courier,* Charleston, SC (9 January 1997): B1.

86. Fifteen Ministers. "The Moral Defense of the Confederate Flag: A Special Message for Southern Christians," *Southern Partisan,* 16.4 (1996): 1, 16-21. Writing during the Civil War in *The Church and the Rebellion,* (1864), Stanton states this "Address" was signed by ninety-six ministers. The Fifteen Ministers, writing in 1996, state that ninety-eight ministers signed the 1863 "Address."

87. This is how the article by the Fifteen Ministers is described on the contents page of *Southern Partisan,* 16 (4th Quarter 1996): 1. The "editorial staff" state they are "in conjunction with [the] fifteen Christian ministers" who authored the essay.

88. That the Confederate battle flag is a Christian symbol is an argument repeat-

edly made by neo-Confederate activists. In addition to Chapter 6, which discusses this contention, see the following neo-Confederate explanations: Hill, Michael. "The Real Symbolism of the St. Andrews Cross: Christian Liberty vs. the New World Order." On-line: http://www.dixienet.org/dn-gazette/st-andrews-cross.htm [accessed 1 July 2001 and 16 June 2004]; Slimp, Robert L. "Why Christians Should Support the Confederate Flag." *Citizens Informer*, 28.1 (1997): 12; and Jennings, Charles A. *Our Southern Heritage: The Confederate Battle Flag*. (Springdale, AR: Truth in History Publications, 2000).

89. Quoted in Fifteen Ministers. "The Moral Defense of the Confederate Flag," (1996): 18.

90. Ibid., 19, 21.

91. Woods, Thomas E. Jr. "Christendom's Last Stand," *Southern Partisan*, 17.2 (1997): 26.

92. Anderson, Alister C. "Chaplain's Comments," *Confederate Veteran*, 4 (1999): 60. At the time, *Confederate Veteran* published six issues each year, each issue being listed as a volume, e.g., vol. 4, 1999; vol. 6, 1999, etc. No months were given as publication dates. This numbering system has since been revised.

93. Anderson, Alister C. "Chaplain's Comments," *Confederate Veteran*, 6 (1999): 60.

94. Weaver, John. "Chaplain's Comments," *Confederate Veteran*, 6 (2001): 64. See also Weaver, John. "Chaplain's Comments," *Confederate Veteran*, 5 (2000): 60–61 and Chapters 6 and 10.

CHAPTER 3

Gender, Sexuality, and Neo-Confederacy

HEIDI BEIRICH AND KEVIN HICKS

In neo-Confederate ideology, interpretations of gender and sexuality utilize nineteenth-century invocations. When neo-Confederates declare behavior to be "manly" or "womanly," they draw on a legacy of gender relations dating from the antebellum Old South. These are best expressed by what advocates of neo-Confederacy call "Southern patriarchy" or the "culture of honor."[1] Neo-Confederates long to reestablish patriarchy, to bring back a time when men ruled their families, women were subordinate, supposedly lesser races knew their place, and sexual deviants were shunned. Neo-Confederate organizations such as the League of the South (LS) lament the loss of this earlier time—and work to right what they believe are the wrongs created by modern American conceptions of gender. To fully understand neo-Confederate views of gender and sexuality, a tour through the antebellum Southern history that grounds them is required.

The Antebellum Origins of Neo-Confederate Conceptions of Gender

The conception of gender idealized and advocated by neo-Confederate activists has its origins in the nineteenth-century plantation system. Life on the plantation was defined by a complex network of familial relations that provided the basis for social interaction. In this system, each individual played a familial role that was determined by his or her class, gender, and race. Privileges, duties, and obligations were derived from and treated as natural expressions of one's position in the familial hierarchy. Typically portrayed in terms of a human body, this antebellum conceptualization of an organic society served both to delineate and unite members of the plantation world. The head of the body, the top position, was held by the white, male plantation owner, whose superiority stemmed from his supposedly innate ability to protect the organic whole. The toes would symbolize the lowest social positions, where African slaves, given their supposedly lesser natural talents, would most usefully serve the whole, under the guidance and protection of the patriarch. In *The Crucible of Race,* Joel Williamson describes this Southern organicism as "an ideal, unitary order of masters and slaves, whites and blacks . . . an 'organic' society," in which "people would know their own places and functions and those of others around them. They would govern themselves in those places with keen awareness of the approval of others within their circle." Feudal societies, which the antebellum South resembled, were often based on a similar model, a connection Williamson makes explicit: "The head would not want to be the heart, and the hand would not pine to be the head. Rather each would function contentedly in its place according to its nature."[2] Superiority and subordination are the main characteristics of this system, though a sense of community or at least communal equality is derived from membership in the same body.

In many ways, antebellum Southern society could also be viewed as a version of the aristocratic system of Europe. Maintaining a clear class consciousness was central. It consisted of several classes of whites, based on material success, with the exception being that even the lowest white member of white society was inherently superior because the African was enslaved.[3] It is important, though, to note that the South had no titles or hereditary aristocracy in the European sense, and it had institutionalized chattel slavery. Even for plantation magnates, financial success was viewed as having been earned. At the heart of this system was Southern patriarchy; white men, as the leaders of the plantation family, were responsible for the protection of the other people in the system, a social order that contributed to the code of honor Southerners lived under. Strict gender roles, meaning female subordination, were part and parcel of this system, as were unequal racial relations.

Neo-Confederacy, Gender, and the Plantation Household

Today, reactionary neo-Confederates aspire to return to the gender mores of this romanticized version of the antebellum South. Proponents of neo-Confederacy hope to reintroduce into their own families and communities a system modeled on what they consider the organic, plantation-based social system of that time and place, a time that neo-Confederate authors have "transformed into legend and remembered as a Garden of Eden, a noble culture."[4] Some prominent neo-Confederates have gone so far as to literally reestablish the plantation. James Kibler, a leading LS member, renovated a South Carolina plantation home and wrote a paean to it in *Our Fathers' Fields: A Southern Story*.[5] The largest neo-Confederate organization by membership, the Sons of Confederate Veterans (SCV), refurbished a Tennessee plantation, Elms Springs, for its headquarters (see Chapter 10). Thus, at the base of neo-Confederate ideas of gender and sexuality is a sociological vision derived from the fundamentally unequal society of their forebears, a conception that is organic, static, and natural, and structures society on the basis of gender, race, and class hierarchies.

In general, the neo-Confederate worldview, including ideas on gender, consists of a wholesale rejection of modernity. Neo-Confederate ideology is rooted in what proponents consider to be a God-given, unchanging natural order that they believe was uniquely reflected in antebellum Southern culture. Indeed, most neo-Confederates view the antebellum South as having reflected a perfect biblically based society. When neo-Confederates look at rights-based movements of the last two centuries, from abolition to gay rights, each is seen as an unacceptable overturning of this religiously determined natural social order. Franklin Sanders, a neo-Confederate and LS board member, claims that modern American society is abhorrent because its views of equality upset gender relations: "[Today] the ordained social order is overturned, natural hierarchy and patriarchy condemned, and every ignorant and insignificant worm asserts his autonomy and equality with the noblest and wisest."[6] Modernity is more than a simple evil for neo-Confederates. They view current social mores as castrating—specifically targeted to destroy maleness. Chilton Williamson, in a 1994 *Chronicles* article entitled "90's Men: Pushy Queers, Tough Jews, and Sensitized WASPs," proposes withdrawal from modern society, with its "corporate industrialism" and "placed communities," as the only way to save what he views as appropriate gender relations:

> We will breed real men again when we will breed real women to match them, and we will have both when we shall have got rid of the obfuscatory infrastructure of an increasingly obscene syphilization whose unspoken intent is to castrate and humiliate every man, wild or soft, who dares to stand in its way.[7]

Dr. J. Michael Hill, a former Alabama history professor and president of the neo-Confederate LS, provides a succinct version of how neo-Confederates conceive of masculinity and femininity. In men, hypervirility is prized, violence is expected and extolled, and testosterone is lauded as the "politically incorrect hormone" of which "white Southern boys" always feel a "surge" when insulted, in contrast to their "gentler northern brethren." Finding such "real men" to be "sexually alluring," Hill proposes that "the average, red-blooded woman-child" needs male protection and desires "high-testosterone bravado."[8] The family, especially its promise of genetic continuance, is the basis of all society, and the childlike nature of women, which makes them susceptible to male power, is central to continuing the white, Southern male's genetic line. Other, nonreproductive forms of sexuality are deviant.

It is instructive to compare these neo-Confederate views of manhood with those of nineteenth-century authors, a process that emphasizes how past and present are merged in neo-Confederacy. Indeed, the descriptions of Southern manhood by John William DeForest, a late-nineteenth-century Northerner who worked in the South for the Freedmen's Bureau, echo those of Hill and other neo-Confederates:

> It seems to me that the central trait of the "chivalrous Southron" is an in-tense respect for virility. He will forgive almost any vice in a man who is manly; he will admire vices, which are but exaggerations of the masculine. If you will fight, if you are strong and skillful enough to kill your antagonist, if you can govern or influence the common herd, if you can ride a dangerous horse over a rough country, if you are a good shot or an expert swordsman, if you stand by your own opinions unflinchingly, if you do your level best on whiskey, if you are a devil of a fellow with women, if, in short, you show vigorous masculine attributes he will grant you his respect.[9]

DeForest emphasizes many of the same "vigorous masculine attributes" as Hill, even though Hill penned his some 150 years later: exaggerated ma-chismo, fighting, intransigence, and sexual attraction.

The South's "Code of Honor"

This hypervirility was tied to the South's code of honor, which many propo-nents of neo-Confederacy still ascribe to and understand as intimately con-nected with manhood. The code of honor forms the basis, for most neo-Confederates, of civilization itself. The South's honor code, often referred to as an unwritten law, governed relations between Southern men (and some Northerners, lest we forget Aaron Burr and Alexander Hamilton's duel) in the nineteenth century. As historian Bertram Wyatt-Brown notes, honor rep-resents a set of external, ethical principles supported by a collective commu-nity consciousness that establish what actions should be taken under what conditions.[10] In essence, codes of honor replace or supplement the state's responsibility to enforce the rule of law. According to Wyatt-Brown, honor also requires an inner strength and thus not only defines the self-respect and worth of individuals in their own eyes, but also shows the wider society's estimation of a person.

While honor codes have played a role in numerous societies, by the early nineteenth century many Americans saw them as anachronistic as the United States moved toward increasing democracy and social equality, political values that found, and arguably still find, their least acceptance in the South.[11] In the antebellum South, dueling remained a common way to resolve disputes over honor, and South Carolina governor John Lyde Wilson published a book of etiquette for dueling "gentlemen" in 1838, just as the practice was falling out of favor in the rest of the country. Republished in 1858, Wilson wrote in *The Code of Honor; or, Rules for the Government of Principals and Seconds in Duelling*, "If an oppressed nation has a right to appeal to arms in defense of its liberty and the happiness of its people, there can be no argument used in support of such appeal, which will not apply with equal force to individuals."[12] For Southern men, honor was the ultimate sign of their self-worth; individuals either had it or they did not—and if they weren't being given the respect they expected, they had to fight to earn it.

Throughout the nineteenth century, Southerners praised and tried to live by the code of honor. In the words of historian Elliot Gorn, "Piety, hard work, and steady habits had their adherents, but in this society aggressive self assertion and manly pride were the real marks of status."[13] What was most to be feared was not death but public humiliation—betrayal of manhood and honor.[14] As historian James C. Klotter has put it, "Honor required courage; cowardice meant shame; insults could not be tolerated. Action must follow, for only blood could cleanse the stains of honor."[15]

The South's reliance upon honor codes as opposed to the legal system resulted in far higher levels of violence there, particularly in terms of homicide rates, than in the rest of America.[16] Southern violence was higher than the national average in every decade until the 1970s, well after the major changes of the civil rights movement had been legislated and began to be implemented.

. The code of honor gained in prominence in the immediate postbellum period. During Reconstruction, when race relations were shifting against whites and the "aristocratic ideal" was perceived to be under attack, "people held fast to honor as one of the last vestiges of the old antebellum world."[17] The end of slavery, and the insult to Southern honor experienced by defeat in the Civil War, may well have had the perverse effect of heightening the aggressiveness of Southern white males, thus raising levels of violence through-out the region. This loss of honor and attendant sense of emasculation likely contributed to the rise of the Ku Klux Klan and the lynching of African Americans. Arguably, the spike in violence that accompanied the civil rights movement of the 1950s and 1960s stemmed from a similar impulse.[18] According to Amy Karen Phillips, it was during the Reconstruction era (1865–1877) that the stereotype of black men as sexual predators lying in wait for white women developed (though these were somewhat based on antebellum stereotypes as well).[19] Rumors of black rapists became so prevalent, explains Phillips, they became the "folk pornography of the Bible Belt," combining fears of the sullying of white genes with the loss of white male power over white women.[20] She attributes the subsequent postbellum "rise in lynching" to "a volatile mixture of shattered institutions, widespread rumors of rape, claims of racial equality by freed slaves, and the outsized virility of ideal Southern manhood."[21] Both Phillips and Elizabeth Fox-Genovese cite the possibility that Southern white males feared retribution for their frequent sexual liaisons, in essence rapes, of their black female slaves. Fox-Genovese notes this irony because in the antebellum period, "the main interracial sexual threat was that of white predators against black women," yet "the presumed threat of black male sexuality never provoked the wild hysteria and violence in the Old South that it did in the New," when emancipation was met with lynching.[22]

The companion to this overbearing manhood was the absolute subordination of women, who were in essence infantilized in their relationships with men. Again, nineteenth-century chronicler DeForest captures well the Southern beliefs about gender, noting how dated these were for the late nineteenth century: "It may be taken for granted that a people [Southern whites] which so highly prizes virility looks upon man as the lord of creation and has old fashioned ideas as to what is the proper sphere of woman."[23] Women were in a position of complete submission, just above slaves, and were portrayed as enfeebled paragons of virtue needing white men to guide them. George Fitzhugh, an outspoken slavery proponent, said that "in truth, woman, like children, has but one right and that is the right to protection. The right to protection involves the obligation to obey."[24] "Churches, schools, parents, books, magazines, all promulgated the same message," and if a woman violated this submissive gender role she could be "unsexed, rejected, unloved, and . . . [would] probably starve."[25] According to Amy Karen Phillips, this gender hierarchy and particular understanding of women was reflected in etiquette books of the era—mostly written by white men—that instructed Southern women on their proper behavior and "emphasized the purity of white women while denying them intellectual capacity. Southern women were characterized as and encouraged to be 'fickle, capricious, delicate, diffident, and dependent.'"[26]

Masculinity, Race, and Religion

Today's neo-Confederates have created a romanticized vision of antebellum manhood and the civilization they claim it created. This vision of Southern history as an idyll is not supported by the facts. Instead, the prizing of hyper-virility in the late nineteenth century led to a severe outbreak of lawlessness throughout the South, not the stable society in which every element found its perfect place as organic models portend. This violence had much to do with "racism in white Southern culture," as historian Ted Ownby explains:

> Whatever the origins of the fighting element in Southern culture, the presence of blacks was the most influential factor in intensifying and prolonging it. Slavery showed all Southerners the significance of physical force in human relations. The opportunities for cruelty and the need for readiness in the case of slave violence affected the consciousness of almost all Southern whites, and the most extreme forms of violence in the postbellum period—lynching, night riding, and Klan violence—were directed almost exclusively at blacks. Whites' constant need to feel they had physical force superior to that of local blacks left them with a need to prove their fighting abilities both to themselves and to their fellow whites.[27]

By 1920, western rates of violence associated with the expansion into new territories had declined, and the South took the lead as a place of homicide. Statistics published in 1948 showed that every single Southern state's serious crime rate exceeded national figures and usually ranked in the highest percentiles in the United States.[28] Robert Penn Warren, the twentieth-century novelist and Southern Agrarian who contributed to the neo-Confederate bible *I'll Take My Stand* (see Chapter 1), would notice this reality as a child in the 1920s: "There was a world of violence that I grew up in. You accepted violence as a component of life. . . . You heard about violence and you saw terrible fights. . . . There was some threat of being trapped into this whether you wanted to or not."[29]

Much of the intellectual responsibility for pushing these gender ideas into the late nineteenth century rests with Robert Lewis Dabney. As outlined in Chapter 2, Dabney was a Presbyterian minister who served under Stonewall

Jackson during the Civil War and remains a strong intellectual influence on neo-Confederate thought.[30] Dabney's works lay out hierarchal gender and racial relations, and contend that equality in the familial sphere would destroy the South, views that sustain many of today's neo-Confederates. Though Dabney was generally ignored during the Reconstruction period, his views are of prime importance to neo-Confederates who consider him along with the Agrarians as their founding fathers.

The past 150 years have not much altered how neo-Confederates view gender hierarchies or masculinity. Donald Davidson, one of the most racist of the Southern Agrarians, viewed the rejection of change as a fundamental and positive value of Southern culture. LS founding member Thomas E. Woods Jr. explains,

> In *The Attack on Leviathan*,[31] Donald Davidson reflected on the North's social and ideological convulsions: While the North has been changing its apparatus of civilization every ten years or so . . . the South has stood its ground at a fairly safe distance and happily remained some forty or fifty years behind the times. . . . This is one of the principal differences, out of many real differences, between the sections.[32]

Emphasizing and celebrating the rejection of change is unsurprising given the reactionary tendencies of neo-Confederates, who repeatedly tie their fate to that of the past. In LS president Michael Hill's words, "The South stands for—orthodox Christianity, honor, hierarchy, loyalty to place and kin, patriarchy, respect for the rule of law."[33] Hill cites a neo-Confederate icon, the Confederate battle flag, as a symbol opposed to all that followed the Civil War. "It [the Confederate battle flag] says 'NO' to gun control, abortion, Third World immigration, moral deviancy, feminism, paganism, radical environmentalism, exorbitant taxation, globalism, crass consumerism, and big government."[34]

Hill is explicit here about the need for "patriarchy" as a bulwark against modern evils, and advances the notion that patriarchy and civilization are one and the same. In a 1997 *Chronicles* essay, Hill expounded upon this theme, arguing that violence and the honor code are equivalent to civilization. Raging against the "feminist propaganda against the evils of testosterone," Hill extols extreme virility and praises Southerners "who understood the manly arts of self-defense were necessary components of civilization." Even though Hill maintains that the antebellum South was a frontier society that demanded comprehensive knowledge of weapons for survival, he associates the frontier and the honor code specifically with "civilized men," rejecting Northern society as uncivilized.[35] Clearly, the LS president would not share Robert Penn Warren's pessimism over Southern violence.

Further support for neo-Confederate gender beliefs comes from their religious affiliation. As outlined in Chapter 2, many neo-Confederates ascribe to an extreme interpretation of Christianity that proposes a return to biblical law. This religious perspective holds that gender roles are biblically dictated and mandated by natural law. As Michael Lienesch notes in *Redeeming America,* many Christian conservatives see men as "appointed by God to rule."[36] Their theory is simple and straightforward: "Men are to act as authorities, women are to be submissive, and children are to obey. Sexual roles are clear and distinct, and deviations are disapproved, especially in cases such as feminism and homosexuality."[37] Neo-Confederate Robert Salyer, a former JAG officer who was fired by the military for his involvement with the League of the South, makes this notion explicit: "Nations are not unlike families in this sense. They are functions of Natural Law, under the guiding hand of historical Providence."[38] Within this view, modern society is an abomination, violating the Bible and its God-given natural laws, including the proper place of men and women.

Given these beliefs, it is not surprising that neo-Confederates reject notions of equality in gender, race, or any other relationships. It is not just that equality is rejected—the concept is actually seen as destroying the natural, God-given order. When God's gender specifications are violated, all hell breaks loose, literally:

> Convince enough females that they are really "equal" with males in all respects, and convince enough males that their traditional role as protector is biologically aberrant and you have created social chaos and revolution. In the New World Order of Perfect Gender Equity lies the justification for extermination of this biological anomaly. If no testosterone, then no males, no violence, no spouse and child abuse, no rape, no war—the complete triumph of the feminist vision.[39]

In essence, the acceptance of modern society, particularly its gender roles, is a form of genocide as "biologically" aberrant notions and practices are introduced into the society. The most genocidal aspect of modernism, in LS board member Thomas Fleming's view, is that the family is destroyed as men are sapped of their economic means due to competition with women:

> The worst effect of the craze for equal opportunity lies in the curious phenomenon of women's rights. Leaving aside the whole question of inequality

of ability, let us consider equal opportunity's effect on the family, when a
mother decides that the family income and her own "self-fulfillment" take
precedence over her maternal duties. Whatever a woman's reason for going
to work—economic necessity, greed, selfishness—the law guarantees her an
opportunity for employment equal to that of any male head of the house.
The unfairness of an ordinary father with a wife and two children to support
having to compete in the job market with, say, a physician's wife who elects
to enter the work force, is obvious to anyone.[40]

Fleming sees divorce and the growing power of the state over children, as
evidenced in public schools and Head Start programs, as part of a systematic
program to use women's rights to undermine traditional society. In short, neo-
Confederates see feminism, gay rights, and multiculturalism as destructive to
social order and the good life. For this reason, any deviation from a society
based on patriarchy and racial hierarchy is seen as societal suicide, regardless
of how it may or may not positively affect particular individuals.[41] Consequently, neo-Confederate activism intends to repel such versions of society,
perceived as threatening its biblically inspired notions of social welfare:

> Waxing nostalgic for the Founding Fathers' constitutional framework, or
> a time before New Deal economics and federalism, will not suffice. To be
> relevant, the Southern Movement must realize the truth underlying the fight
> against Abolitionism and against Civil-Rights, that inherited order and cul-
> ture do matter, that liberty, equality and fraternity is a mantra of death.[42]

As a result, when neo-Confederates reject notions of equality and practices
of civil and human rights, they view themselves as protecting what they see
as their unique Southern species from genocide.

For proponents of neo-Confederacy, nineteenth-century abolitionism was
simply the first step in undermining a superior social system based on hierarchy and inequality, a historical logic that they often refer to as the coming
of the "New World Order." As Hill has said many times, neo-Confederacy,
"unlike the America of the New World Order, is wedded not to a universal
proposition: equality, democracy, or the rights of man, but to a real past of
place and kin."[43] This emphasis on locality and "kith and kin" is a result of
the antebellum links made in the South between land (i.e., the plantation)
and its inhabitants. For neo-Confederates, the land, its inhabitants, and their
nation are united together by a formula that is not based on legal documents
or state legislation. As Hill summarizes, "Southern identity" is "not dedicated
to any proposition" but rather "bound up in that vast memory of the blood."[44]

This is the ultimate statement of the neo-Confederate organic (and genetic) conception of their society—the Southerners, their land, and their nation are fundamentally bound together in blood, the ultimate binder of any body. Furthermore, this is God-ordained since time immemorial:

> Southern Christians . . . see in Biblical scripture the mandate for a hierarchical society in which modern egalitarian notions have no place, and they view the scattering of the nations at the Tower of Babel as an indictment against the United Nations. The Bible is also one of the sources of the Southern view of the nation as an organic expression of kith and kin.[45]

Southern Masculinity: From Robert E. Lee to Nathan Bedford Forrest

In neo-Confederate literature, history is often taught using hagiographies of the Southern men seen to exemplify manly traits. Most are prominent former Confederate military or political leaders, such as Robert E. Lee, Stonewall Jackson, and Jefferson Davis. For Michael Hill, three men he considers archetypes for Southern manhood are John Smith, Andrew Jackson, and Jim Bowie. Hill lauds Smith for his "self-reliance" and "doings with the sword," citing his long history of military exploits. Jackson is proudly noted for having more interest in dueling than law, often under the pretext of protecting his wife's honor, and Bowie is praised for killing numerous men "in 'nonmilitary' combat" and for becoming rich through "land speculating and slave trading."[46]

The counterpoint to Hill's immense respect for these violent frontiersmen is Confederate general Robert E. Lee. For most of the twentieth century, Lee was most dear to those sympathetic to the Confederate cause. White Southerners created a narrative around Lee as the perfect, chivalrous, Christian Southern gentleman. According to Klotter, "Robert E. Lee represented, to many, the best aspects of southern honor and manhood, in a Christian gentleman. . . . Lee could be shy, was a loving parent, and often preferred the company of women to men."[47] When it was apparent that the Confederacy had lost the Civil War, Lee's ultimate chivalrous act was to accept defeat honorably. Both the LS and SCV suggest that men give their sons the pamphlet *The Maxims of Robert E. Lee for Young Gentlemen,* a short work filled with snippets of Lee's wisdom and instructions on manliness.[48]

And yet, despite the widely held view that Lee exhibited true Southern chivalry, for most neo-Confederates he is not the man they most admire, because he lacked the hypervirility many neo-Confederates revere. Klotter argues that this tension between Lee's version of the Southern gentleman and the type of men extolled by Hill existed throughout the late nineteenth and early twentieth centuries:

> The two very different parts of manhood in Victorian America seemed to be at war with each other—the principle of the Christian Gentleman and the masculine savage ideal. . . . In one sense, the age wanted the myth—the knight of King Arthur, a person of honor, a religious figure, a respecter of women, a man in control of self, yet at the same time a warrior, a fighter, a hero.[49]

For neo-Confederates, the model for today's white Southerners is a different Confederate general, Nathan Bedford Forrest. A successful slave trader before the war, Forrest was more a man of action than Lee. He achieved incredible results on the battlefield, some of which were horrifyingly bloody, most notably a savage massacre of fleeing blacks at Fort Pillow in 1864. Without the highbrow education Lee received at West Point, and renowned, also unlike Lee, for personally leading his men into battle, Forrest survived having some twenty-nine horses shot out from under him, killed around thirty men, and had a bullet removed from his back without pain killers. In a paean published in the glossy neo-Confederate magazine *Southern Partisan*, J. O. Tate can barely find words superlative enough to describe Forrest:

> "Old Bedford" pursued a parabola of heroic individualism that's remarkable not only in the history of the Civil War, and in the history of this country, but also in the history of the world. . . . The point about Forrest—what made him a legendary name—was his matchless courage and energy, his tenacity and imagination, his imposing physical prowess, and, above all, his flinty integrity. Forrest's personal achievement during the War is like no other.[50]

Forrest was also the first Grand Wizard of the Ku Klux Klan just after the Civil War, something not seen as a negative by neo-Confederates who view the early Klan as having been established for self-defense purposes, regardless of the terrible violence perpetrated on blacks. For Tate, modern observers fail to remember "the context in which the first Klan was formed: disorder, violence, 'Union Leagues,' Federal occupation."[51] Forrest was protecting his beloved homeland, not engaging in wanton racial violence. In sum, Forrest is seen as much more representative of the masculinity admired by neo-Confederates than Lee. LS leader Michael Hill has readily acknowledged Forrest as "one of my great heroes,"[52] and he is also a favorite of founding ʟs board member and former University of Alabama history professor Grady McWhiney. By the end of the 1990s, neo-Confederates had clearly chosen the fighter over the statesman, with one of the League of the South's founding board members, Nashville lawyer and longtime segregationist Jack Kershaw, erecting a statue of Forrest near I-65 south of Nashville.[53] Neo-Confederates in Selma, Alabama, placed a bust of Forrest on city property, but after protests the city relocated it to a Confederate cemetery.[54] The ꜱᴄᴠ is also working to restore Forrest's Tennessee boyhood home.

The sum total of this hero worship, honor code, and apologia for violence culminates in a highly romanticized view of the Confederacy that neo-Confederates subsume under the concept of chivalry. Neo-Confederates believe the banner of chivalry belongs solely to real "Southron" men today. Writing for the ʟs, D. Randolph Stoman characterizes chivalry as "bravery, honour, courtesy, respect for women, protection for the weak, generosity and magnanimity to enemies," qualities "passed from generation to generation in the interest of conferring dignity upon one's posterity." Stoman concludes that "a culture of chivalry, or the lack thereof, was the most distinguishing difference between the two peoples [Southerners and Northerners]," a distinction, he believes, that continues.[55]

Femininity and Womanhood

The preoccupation with manhood on the part of neo-Confederates has resulted in a situation where very little is written by neo-Confederates about women in today's South and nearly nothing is written by female neo-Confederates on any subject. When neo-Confederates address the topic of women's roles, the conversation is incredibly reactionary—and usually short. Franklin Sanders, an ʟs board member, penned an essay on "The Southern Household" for the ʟs newsletter, *Southern Patriot*.[56] In it, Sanders suggests that women should attempt to produce as many household goods as possible from scratch, something that will restore to the "housewife" her "artistry." Sanders explains:

> Nor is it too strong to call it artistry, the loving work of wife and mother, who brings both style and perfection to her duty. Every grocery-store frozen dish, every prepared food, every store-bought jam, deprives the mistress of the household of the opportunity to express herself and her love in the artistry of her work. . . . So in all her work of feeding, clothing, and making a

home, those things bought outside the household unnecessarily rob wives and mothers not only of their budgets, but of their lives' artistry.[57]

Though Sanders's essay is ostensibly about the Southern household, he soon changes his topic from women to the evils of paper money. Other neo-Confederates have tangentially addressed the "proper" role of women in off-hand remarks or by referring to female virtue as depicted in novels such as *Gone with the Wind*, voted by *Southern Partisan* as the fifteenth best book of all time. In an aside to a 2004 press release rejecting the reintroduction of the draft, LS board members said, "A country that uses its young women as soldiers, while discouraging wife- and motherhood, is a sick and depraved country sliding towards barbarism and disintegration."[58] Another way in which neo-Confederates address what they view as appropriate female gender roles is by criticizing feminism, as Thomas Fleming did in 2004:

> The problem with feminism had little to do with individual women trying to get better jobs or higher salaries that they do not deserve but with the feminist ideology that denies the reality of what they call "sexual identity" and the special roles that men and women are called upon to play.[59]

Given the neo-Confederate belief in patriarchy, it is not surprising that their writings lack a fuller exploration of the feminine. For them, simplistic and somewhat generic notions such as motherhood suffice. It is consistent, therefore, that neo-Confederates display a fierce hatred for co-educational efforts, which in their view destroy the differences between the sexes. LS member Robert Salyer complained in a 2003 speech that efforts to desegregate military colleges such as the Virginia Military Institute and the Citadel were not "in order to increase the educational opportunities of women." Rather, Salyer argues, these efforts were undertaken "to destroy the concept of the Southern gentleman, the gentleman as distinct from the lady."[60]

Homosexuality and Race in Neo-Confederate Thought

Gender roles also are divided by race in the neo-Confederate worldview, with whites and blacks expected to stay separate in terms of sexual interaction. In neo-Confederate writing, African Americans, both male and female, are clearly as subordinate to whites today as they were in the antebellum period. It is for this reason that there is a preoccupation by neo-Confederate authors with "ethnic and cultural balance" in the South, which leads to staunch positions opposing immigration and interracial marriage.[61] Michael Hill has openly ridiculed notions of racial equality, and in a 2000 web posting mocked his students at the historically black Stillman College:

> "A quote," he [Hill] wrote, "from a recent affirmative action hire: 'Yesta-day I could not spell "secretary." Today I is one.'" He continued: "One of the few benefits I got on a regular basis from having taught for 18 years at Stillman College was reading the class rolls on the first day of class." He went on to list several "humorous" names of his black students, ending, "Where do these people get such names?"[62]

Movements that have led to greater equality for those whose place is below the head in the neo-Confederate imagination of the supposed organic structure of society are disparaged, often vehemently. Feminism is decried, as are multiculturalism and diversity, and the Universal Rights of Man are rejected as "a new brand of politically correct totalitarianism."[63] In addition, the Fourteenth Amendment, which granted voting rights to former slaves, is seen as the evil that led to the current "equality" that has "turned Abraham Lincoln's malignant egalitarianism into rights-based social policies."[64]

For neo-Confederates, homosexuality is absolutely rejected and gay rights are dismissed as "sodomite rights."[65] These gender conceptions make homophobia endemic to neo-Confederate thinking. In the first essay Hill wrote for the LS publication *Southern Patriot,* he attacked former Attorney General Janet Reno, whom he considers to be a lesbian. Commenting on her involvement in a case where two lesbians living in Mississippi were being harassed, Hill said, "In this case the victim group was the cadre of Camp Sister Spirit, a pig farm cum Lesbian retreat. . . . Big Sister Reno informed the good citizens [the local Southerners] . . . that further resistance to the deviants would bring forth the federal hordes."[66] Otto Scott, a founding member of the LS, puts his bigotry this way: "The nature of the homosexual-lesbian defiance of the reality of biology . . . twists the psyche into a dark and dangerous path."[67] Fleming is harsher: "In nearly every known society, some number (often quite small) of human beings chromosomally will fail, for one reason or another, to become fully men."[68] Given these views, it should come as no surprise that Hill fully rejected the 2004 Supreme Court decision that made anti-sodomy laws unconstitutional, stating the decision was an "attempt by Yankee egalitarians to legitimize a perversion that is both an abomination in the eyes of our Creator . . . and a shameful and destructive lifestyle."[69]

This kind of rhetoric is found also in the supposedly more mainstream *Southern Partisan,* which discussed a violent 1993 assault on three gay men:

If you want to know how "Hate Crimes" legislation will work in practice, then here's a good example. Three men from Dundalk were convicted of beating up some homosexuals outside a bar in Baltimore. In Maryland, homosexuals are protected by politicians and coddled by the law. . . . In this case, the punishments were beyond all reason. One man was sentenced to two years in prison. A second received one year in prison. A third 60 days.[70]

Reid Buckley clearly expressed his views in a 1986 article about the death of actor Rock Hudson for the same publication: "The terrible swift sword of the dread AIDS disease is surely what in other ages would be acknowledged as a sign of God's wrath. These are ugly and perverted passions. It is as evil to indulge in illicit sexual cravings as it is to give in to the homicidal passions."[71] Not to be outdone, Michael Hill ties homosexuality and liberal politics to death: "The left-liberals culture, if it can be called such, has the stench of death and destruction all over it (e.g., abortion, AIDS, euthanasia, drugs, crime, sodomy)."[72]

Conclusion: Gender and Neo-Confederacy

Neo-Confederates are not simply willing to sit idly by as gender roles are morphed according to modern ideals. Both the LS and SCV hold summer schools aimed at inculcating young men with what these organizations view as appropriate gender roles. In 2004, the LS hosted a "Summer Institute for Young Men" between the ages of eighteen and twenty-five. The institute combined courses on such things as "what makes Southerners a distinct and unique people" and an "introduction to politically incorrect Southern history" with activities including "woodcraft, swimming, [and] shooting."[73] In the SCV, young men are invited to the Sam Davis Youth Camp, "a wonderful event for our sons and grandsons," a pet project of the group's commander-in-chief from 2002–2004, R. G. "Ronnie" Wilson. The program proposed to tell "the truth about the War for Southern Independence," and counter the supposed "brainwash[ing]" caused by public schools.[74] Part of the Youth Camp curriculum indoctrinated students with paeans to Southern heroes and great men of faith.

These efforts are serious. As neo-Confederates express the anxiety that shifting notions of manhood will undermine their ability to recreate their past, activists relentlessly attack modern culture for castrating men, something that they connect with wiping out their civilization. Roger McGrath, a favorite speaker at both neo-Confederate and overtly white supremacist events, laments that a loss has been sustained just in the course of his lifetime: "Once upon a time, we were a warrior race, honor-bound to stand and fight. . . . Boys knew this was part of their destiny from childhood on—they had an instinct for it, and it was expected of them. Now, we try to feminize our boys, weaken them, even emasculate them."[75] Thomas Fleming is also clear that the reestablishment of Southern patriarchy is hindered by current concepts of manliness:

> Most of the girlie boys on TV (to borrow Ann Coulter's phrase) are not homosexuals, but they present a problem that is far worse. Homosexuals, after a certain number of years, are what they are, and their choice (for most of them) is being "gay" or being celibate. . . . But the epicenes and Ganymedes are self-created out of fear—fear of conflict, fear of social disapproval, fear of women, fear of being men, and fear of having to take the responsibility that men have to take. Perhaps their fathers never took them fishing or gave them a pair of boxing gloves. . . . My own conclusion is that we should leave the "gays" to their own world and save our anger and disgust for the high-voiced, soft-palmed, hair-waved, nonjudgemental, unthreatening unmale nonpersons who will soon be putting the last real men onto tribal homelands.[76]

Clearly, Fleming believes that modern society is engendering in men a preference for female traits, thus destroying any appropriate conception of true manhood. For neo-Confederates, this process has to be stopped before gender roles are completely obscured.

Notes

    1. Hill, Michael. "Honor, Violence, and Civilization," *Chronicles*, 21.8 (1997): 17–19.
    2. Williamson, Joel. *The Crucible of Race: Black-White Relations in the American South since Emancipation.* (New York: Oxford University Press, 1984): 24.
    3. Baughman, Laurence Alan. *Southern Rape Complex: Hundred Year Psychosis.* (Atlanta: Pendulum Books, 1966): 19.
    4. Eckert, Edward K., cited in Britt, Brian. "Neo-Confederate Culture," *Z Magazine*, (December 1996). On-line: *http://www.zmag.org/Zmag/articles/dec96 britt.htm* [accessed 27 January 1999 and 2 December 2004].
    5. Kibler, James Everett Jr. *Our Fathers' Fields: A Southern Story.* (Columbia: University of South Carolina Press, 1998).
    6. Sanders, Franklin. "On Losing Heart," *Southern Patriot,* 7.4 (2000): 3.

7. Williamson, Chilton. "Men Unlimited," *Chronicles*, 18.2 (1994): 14.

8. Hill, Michael. "Honor, Violence, and Civilization," *Chronicles*, 21.8 (1997): 17. Hill's views only apply to *white* men (see Chapters 4 and 5). They are also shared by many pro-Aryan groups, as Kathleen Blee summarizes: "Aryan masculinity is venerated as the bedrock of the white race. . . . Manly traits make the Aryan racial warrior." See her *Inside Organized Racism: Women in the Hate Movement.* (Berkeley: University of California Press, 2002): 112–113. For discussion of gender ideas amongst current white supremacist groups, see Ferber, Abby L., ed. *Home-Grown Hate: Gender and Organized Racism.* (New York: Routledge, 2004), and Schlatter, Evelyn A. *Aryan Cowboys: White Supremacists and the Search for a New Frontier, 1970–2000.* (Austin: University of Texas Press, 2006).

9. DeForest is cited in Scott, Anne F. *The Southern Lady: From Pedestal to Politics 1830–1930.* (Chicago: University of Chicago Press, 1970): 101.

10. Wyatt-Brown, Bertram. *Southern Honor: Ethics and Behavior in the Old South.* (New York: Oxford University Press, 1982): 369; Wyatt-Brown, Bertram. *The House of Percy: Honor, Melancholy, and Imagination in a Southern Family.* (New York: Oxford University Press, 1997): 9. See also Pitt-Rivers, Julian. "Honor," *International Encyclopedia of the Social Sciences*, vol. 7, ed. Edward R. A. Seligman. (New York: Macmillan, 1934): 456–458.

11. American support for equality was historically based on the idea that *whites* were equal—see Baum, Bruce. *The Rise and Fall of the Caucasian Race: A Political History of Racial Identity.* (New York: New York University Press, 2006): 8.

12. Wilson is quoted in Franklin, John Hope. *The Militant South 1800–1861.* (Urbana: University of Illinois Press, 1956): 46. The original citation is from Wilson, John Lyde. *The Code of Honor; or, Rules for the Government of Principals and Seconds in Duelling.* (Charleston, 1838).

13. Gorn, Elliott J. "'Gouge and Bite, Pull Hair and Scratch': The Social Significance of Fighting in the Southern Backcountry," *American Historical Review*, 90.1 (1985): 22, 39–40.

14. This view is also prominent in many Muslim societies, particularly Saudi Arabia, Afghanistan, Pakistan, and Nigeria, where battles over a woman's honor often end in violence usually perpetrated against the woman in question—see Atran, Scott. *In Gods We Trust: The Evolutionary Landscape of Religion.* (New York: Oxford University Press, 2002): 138.

15. Klotter, James C. *Kentucky Justice, Southern Honor, and American Manhood.* (Baton Rouge: Louisiana State University Press, 2003): 49.

16. Ramage, B. J. "Homicide in the Southern States," *Sewanee Review*, 4.2 (1896): 212–214.

17. Klotter, *Kentucky Justice*, (2003): 51.

18. Even neo-Confederates themselves will point to the violence as a result of the loss of white power, but typically excuse the violence because of this, claiming that it was a legitimate response to the Northern assaults brought with Reconstruction. Charles Adams, for example, argues that white supremacy as a reaction to Reconstruction is understandable and excusable—see *When In the Course of Human Events: Arguing the Case for Southern Secession.* (New York: Rowman & Littlefield, 2000): 159–165. Stereotypes of African Americans are discussed at length in Joel Williamson's *The*

Crucible of Race: Black-White Relations in the American South since Emancipation. (New York: Oxford University Press, 1984).

19. Phillips, Amy Karen. "The Southern Rape and Lynching Complex: The Subordination of Southern Women Through a Mechanism of White Supremacy," unpublished paper, Gender and the Law in American History Seminar. (Georgetown University, 29 January 1996). On-line: *http://www.data.law.georgetown. edu/glh/ Phillips.htm* [accessed 2 December 2004]. According to Elizabeth Fox-Genovese, who would become a neo-Confederate after experiencing a religious conversion, there was a stereotype of black men in the antebellum period, often referred to as "Buck," which "encoded white male fears of black sexuality in particular and of virility in general. The convention of the Buck emphasized white views of the single, sexually active black male as . . . [a] perpetual adolescent." Fox-Genovese, Elizabeth. *Within the Plantation Household, Black and White Women of the Old South.* (Chapel Hill: University of North Carolina Press, 1988): 291.

20. Phillips, "The Southern Rape and Lynching Complex," (1996): 9.

21. Ibid., 10.

22. Fox-Genovese, *Within the Plantation Household,* (1988): 291.

23. Quoted in Scott, *The Southern Lady,* (1970): 101.

24. Quoted in ibid., 17.

25. Ibid., 20-21.

26. Phillips, "The Southern Rape and Lynching Complex," (1996): 3-4. Although 1920s Ku Klux Klan groups, like today's neo-Confederates, viewed women as "innocent, virtuous beings," unlike neo-Confederates they relied on women for activism and organizing. The 1920s Klan even published a *Klanswoman's Manual* that described female ideals to be "all that is best, and noblest, and highest in life," and argued that "no race, or society, or country, can rise higher than its womanhood." No comparable neo-Confederate treatise has yet been produced. See Blee, *Women of the Klan,* (1991): 45-57.

27. Ownby, Ted. *Subduing Satan, Religion, Recreation and Manhood in the Rural South, 1865-1920.* (Chapel Hill: University of North Carolina Press, 1990): 16.

28. This data on Southern violence comes from sources cited in Klotter, *Kentucky Justice,* (2003): 132-133, namely Ayers, Edward L. *Vengeance and Justice: Crime and Punishment in the Nineteenth-Century American South.* (Oxford: Oxford University Press, 1985): 266-267, and Potterfield, Austin L. "A Decade of Serious Crime in the United States: Some Trends and Hypotheses," *American Sociological Review,* 13.1 (1948): 49.

29. Klotter, *Kentucky Justice,* (2003): 44.

30. Sebesta, Edward H., and Hague, Euan. "The U.S. Civil War as a Theological War: Confederate Christian Nationalism and the League of the South," *Canadian Review of American Studies,* 32.3 (2002): 253-283.

31. Davidson, Donald. *Attack on the Leviathan: Regionalism and Nationalism in the United States.* (Magnolia, MA: Peter Smith Publishing, 1970). See also Chapter 8.

32. Woods, Thomas E. Jr. "Copperheads," *Southern Patriot,* 2.1 (1995): 3-5.

33. Hill, Michael. "President's Message [The Establishment's Treason]," *Southern Patriot,* 4.2 (1997): 17-18. Also on-line as: "Traitors or Patriots," http://www .leagueofthesouth.com/spatriot/vol4no2/prez16.htm [accessed 2 December 2004].

34. Hill, Michael. "Opportunity Knocks: What We Must Do To Capitalize on

the Mississippi Flag Rally Victory." On-line: http://www.leagueofthesouth.com/
dn-gazette/mississippi.htm [accessed 2 December 2004].

35. Hill, "Honor, Violence, and Civilization," (1997): 17–19.

36. Lienesch, Michael. *Redeeming America: Piety and Politics in the New Christian
Right.* (Chapel Hill: University of North Carolina Press, 1993): 54.

37. Ibid., 53.

38. Salyer, Robert. "A Reply to Jim Langcuster on the Lott Affair." On-line: http://
www.leagueofthesouth.com/dn-gazette/reply-to-langcuster.htm [accessed 2 December 2004].

39. Hill, "Honor, Violence, and Civilization," (1997): 18.

40. Fleming, Thomas. "Old Rights and the New Right," *The New Right Papers,*
ed. Robert W. Whitaker. (New York: St. Martin's Press, 1982): 195.

41. See, for example, Hill, Michael. "Ratification of the 14th Amendment,"
Southern Patriot, 6.6 (1999): 1–3.

42. Salyer, "A Reply to Jim Langcuster."

43. Hill, Michael. "Kith and Kin," *Southern Patriot,* 3.5 (1996): 33.

44. Hill, Michael. "The South and the New Reconstruction," *Chronicles,* 21.3
(1997): 21.

45. Ibid.

46. Hill, "Honor, Violence, and Civilization," (1997): 19.

47. Klotter, *Kentucky Justice,* (2003): 55.

48. Williams, Richard G. Jr. *The Maxims of Robert E. Lee for Young Gentlemen.*
(Fairfax, VA: Xulon Press, 2002): xxi.

49. Klotter, *Kentucky Justice,* (2003): 55.

50. Tate, J. O. "Nathan Bedford Forrest and the Death of Heroes," *So Good a
Cause: A Decade of Southern Partisan,* ed. Oran P. Smith. (Columbia, SC: Foundation
for American Education, 1993): 167–168.

51. Ibid., 168.

52. Hill, Michael. Interview. "The Alan Colmes Show," *NewsTalk* 1050 WEVD
New York (19 August 1999). Transcript on-line: *http://www.templeofdemocracy.com/
WEVD.htm.*

53. Locker, Richard. "Forrest Rides into Skirmish in Nashville," *The Commercial
Appeal,* Memphis, TN (11 July 1998): A1.

54. League of the South, "Forrest Statue to be Erected in Selma," *Southern
Patriot,* 7.2 (2000): 10. For discussion of the controversy surrounding the statue in
Selma, see Alderman, Derek H., and Dwyer, Owen J. "Putting Memory in Its Place:
The Politics of Memory and Commemoration in the American South," *Worldminds:
Geographical Perspectives on 100 Problems,* ed. Donald G. Janelle, Barney Warf, and
Kathy Hansen. (Dordrecht: Kluwer Academic Publishers, 2004): 55–60, and Dwyer,
Owen J. "Symbolic Accretion and Commemoration," *Social and Cultural Geography,*
5.3 (2004): 419–435.

55. Stoman, D. Randolph. "Chivalry: The Defining Element of Southern Culture," *Southern Patriot,* 3.6 (1996): 45.

56. Sanders, Franklin. "The Southern Household," *Southern Patriot,* 4.4 (1997):
27–28.

57. Ibid., 27.

58. League of the South. "League Opposes Reinstitution of the Draft," (2004).

On-line: *http://www.dixienet.org/ls-press-releases/June92004Release2.html* [accessed 2 December 2004].

59. Fleming, Thomas. "Walk Like a Man, Talk Like a Man," *Chronicles*, 28.3 (2004): 11.

60. Salyer, Robert. "Political Correctness." On-line: http://bellsouthpwp.net/m/t/mtuggle/PCSpeech.htm [accessed 9 September 2006].

61. Hill, "Kith and Kin," (1996): 33; Southern Poverty Law Center. "A League of Their Own," *Intelligence Report*, 99 (2000): 15.

62. Southern Poverty Law Center. "The Ideologues," *Intelligence Report*, Southern Poverty Law Center, 116 (2004): 28.

63. Hill, Michael. "The Treason of the Elites." On-line: http://www.dixienet.org/dn-gazette/treason.htm [accessed 30 June 2001], and http://www.leagueofthesouth.com/dn-gazette/treason.htm [accessed 2 December 2004].

64. Hill, "Ratification of the 14th," (1999): 2.

65. Hill, "The Treason of the Elites."

66. Hill, Michael. "President's Message," *Southern Patriot*, 1.1 (1994): 1.

67. Scott, Otto J. "Jonathan Demme's *Philadelphia*," *Otto Scott's Compass*, 4.43 (1994): 4–5.

68. Fleming, "Walk Like a Man," (2004): 10.

69. Hill is quoted in League of the South. "The Latest Battle in the Culture War: Sodomite 'Marriage,'" (2004). On-line: http://www.dixienet.org/ls-pressreleases/May262004Release.html [accessed 26 May 2004 and 15 June 2004].

70. "CSA Today: Maryland," *Southern Partisan*, 13 (3rd Quarter 1993): 17.

71. Buckley, Reid. "Rock Hudson," *Southern Partisan*, 6.1 (1986): 64.

72. Hill, Michael. "The Treason of the Elites."

73. League of the South. Calendar item, (Spring 2004). On-line: *http://www.dixienet.org/ls-homepg/calendar.htm*.

74. Sons of Confederate Veterans. "Summer Institute for Young Men," *Confederate Veteran*, 62.1 (2004): 24.

75. McGrath, Roger D. "Boys Will Be Boys (if given half a chance)," *Chronicles*, 28.3 (2004): 17.

76. Fleming, "Walk Like a Man," (2004): 11.

CHAPTER 4

Neo-Confederacy, Culture, and Ethnicity: A White Anglo-Celtic Southern People

EUAN HAGUE AND EDWARD H. SEBESTA

The concept of ethnicity has been central to social theory for the past thirty or forty years, a period during which global events have changed the ways in which people identify themselves.[1] Processes of decolonization, international migration, economic globalization, and the break-up of the Soviet Bloc have destabilized long-established relationships of political and cultural authority, and, Thomas Hylland Eriksen proposes, these developments continue to provoke both violent and nonviolent "ethnic struggles for recognition, power and autonomy."[2] One central aspect of these reevaluations of ethnicity is the understanding that personal identities are multiple, being constructed and deconstructed in different contexts, enabling people to choose identities to suit their needs. For example, Simon James demonstrates that in Western society, despite the fact that "ethnicities are widely perceived as being 'in the blood'" and "ingrained from birth," they are in reality often selected by people from a multiplicity of possibilities based on differing circumstances.[3] Although this flexibility of ethnicity allows a person to choose to invoke their ethnic identity as, when, and how it is needed, in the United States, as elsewhere, a great deal of determination is still ascribed to one's ethnic identity, as Werner Sollors argues: "Americans are willing to perceive ethnic distinctions—differentiations which they seemingly base exclusively on descent, no matter how far removed and how artificially selected and constructed—as powerful and crucial."[4]

It is within this context that in 1995, neo-Confederate Franklin Sanders told *Southern Patriot* readers that they, like other ethnic nationalists, could pursue secession and gain independence from the United States.[5] In addition, as we explore in Chapter 5, this late-twentieth-century period also saw changing race relations in the Southern states stemming from the civil rights movement and new geographical patterns of immigration, elements that we consider to be important to current neo-Confederate appeals to Southern ethnicity. In this chapter we thus explore how the concepts of ethnicity and, thereafter, culture are utilized to underpin neo-Confederate understandings of their own identities. To examine the conceptualization of Southern ethnic identity that arose with the 1990s iteration of neo-Confederacy, we must again explore its lineaments.

There are two main precedents for neo-Confederate assertions of a distinctive Southern ethnicity. The first is the nineteenth-century belief that the white population of the Southern states was descended from Cavaliers, in contradistinction to those in the Northern states, who were supposedly descendents of Puritans (or Roundheads).[6] Lost Cause authors like Edward A. Pollard argued that these two populations were fundamentally incompatible, producing a profound division that resulted in the Civil War.[7] Similar dichotomies in the early twentieth century informed groups like the United Daughters of the Confederacy (UDC), who promoted the supposedly Anglo-Saxon racial purity of the (white) Southerners in contradistinction to their Northern counterparts.[8] These dualistic constructions of supposed racial and cultural distinctions between Northern and Southern states were efforts to write onto the white populations of the United States differences that could then be used to explain the political divisions of the nineteenth century.

A second series of efforts to explain the (white) Southern population as ethnically different from the North emerged in the 1970s. Arguably energized by the upheavals of the civil rights era, a group of scholars, largely drawing upon each others' contentions and definitions, identified "Southerners" as a distinct ethnic group. Lewis Killian proposed "admittedly a loose definition":

> (1) a white person who has been born and raised at least until young adulthood in the South and who still thinks of himself as a southerner, or (2) a white person who, no matter where he was born and raised, lives in the South and identifies himself as a southerner.[9]

Sociologist John Shelton Reed, who would later write for neo-Confederate publications under his own name and the moniker J. R. Vanover, subsequently classified violence, localism, Christianity, support for Confederate symbols, and opposition to "outside interference" as elements that were strongly held by white Southerners to be aspects that distinguished them from other people in the United States.[10] Reed's assessments, however, were seen by some as fundamentally flawed, forcing homogeneity onto regional populations "to describe southernness as a special case of ethnicity."[11]

Keeping with this tradition, current proponents of neo-Confederacy also understand there to be fundamental differences in the ethnic and cultural composition of the Northern and Southern United States. Neo-Confederates make repeated appeals to "Southerners" and "true Southerners" who are depicted as practicing a distinct culture and identity. Since the mid-1970s neo-Confederate historians have worked to define this Southern identity as ethnically Celtic, in opposition to a supposedly Anglo-Saxon Northern identity. This represents a new attempt to assert an essential ethno-cultural difference between Northern and Southern (white) populations. Here we examine this "Celtic South" thesis and further explore how neo-Confederates understand ethnicities and cultures to be elemental forces that determine behavior transmitted across continents and inherited intact from ancestors. We demonstrate that neo-Confederate authors understand social relations as unequal and hierarchical, and cultures to be "natural" and engaged in a struggle for survival.

Neo-Confederacy and the Identification of Southerners

The determination to distinguish between different sections of the U.S. population as distinctive ethno-racial groups leads neo-Confederates to regularly discuss the need for "Southern people," "Southerners," or "Southrons" to assert their ethnic identity and celebrate their culture. After interviewing League of the South (LS) president Michael Hill, journalist and professor of English Diane Roberts came to the conclusion that when advocates of neo-Confederacy speak of "'southern,' they mean white, they mean British-descended, they mean Confederate."[12] Tara McPherson similarly assesses that neo-Confederate activists "defend . . . a heritage that is undeniably white," but notes that "while 'whiteness' itself is rarely mentioned . . . Celtic, Anglo, and European ancestry often is," concluding that such strategies enable "an exploration of white Southernness" that, when "couched in terms of ethnic identity[,] is less likely to produce an understanding of the privileges whiteness confers," yet "functions as . . . [a] form of covert racism."[13]

Critical race theorists like David Wellman and Richard Dyer maintain that many white people typically do not recognize their own racial identity or their own whiteness.[14] Neo-Confederates, in contrast, do, recognizing race in whatever color it appears, although often implicitly and through reference to ethnicities, peoples, and cultures. Neo-Confederates such as Wayne Carlson repeatedly identify whiteness as a critical component of their own (and the South's) identity, contending that the United States is too "politically correct" to address "the legitimate interests and welfare of the white population of this country."[15] In an editorial excerpted below, LS president Michael Hill refers to Republican voters from Southern states in the 2000 presidential election as "white Southerners," "white Christians," and "white Southrons," in addition to "Southerners," "we," and "us." He thus makes it clear that he envisions himself and his neo-Confederate supporters to be white:

> It is nothing short of amazing how white Southerners continue to let themselves be used by the Republican Party. The ritual is clear: every fourth year some GOP candidate comes South and vows to take seriously our concerns about the country's problems. He presents himself as a "conservative" who, if elected, will divest Washington, DC, of its ill-gotten power and restore the old federated, constitutional republic. But once we entrust him with our votes, he goes away and forgets all his sweet promises.
>
> There is no doubt that the GOP is embarrassed by its white Christian support in Dixie. Sure, they'll take our votes. But once victory is attained, we are asked to keep quiet for the good of the party's image. [George W.] Bush and company have committed the GOP to courting black and Hispanic voters; consequently, if the GOP is seen cavorting with white Southrons it will tarnish their image as the Big Tent Party. . . . We must have another option. . . . We Southerners are a distinct people with a common history and culture. With this in mind, let us be content with nothing less than ruling ourselves.[16]

Here, Hill uses nationalist rhetoric to generate audience empathy and a sense of solidarity with the author. Michael Billig identifies this discursive practice as "deixis," which uses pronouns like "we," "our," and "us" to build a sense of commonality.[17] Using deixis throughout his essay quoted above, Hill's phrases like "we entrust," "our votes," "ruling ourselves," and so on locate both himself and his audience as the "white" Christians and Southerners to whom he refers, a sentiment reinforced by his recognition of contrasting "black and Hispanic voters."

Although neo-Confederate proponents often assert the centrality of whiteness to the people and culture they are concerned about, more commonly the racial adjective is omitted and appeals are made to "Southerners," as at the conclusion of Hill's statement above. In the following excerpt, bestselling neo-Confederate authors James Ronald Kennedy and Walter Donald Kennedy directly identify whom they assert comprises "true Southerners," an appellation that simultaneously implies that other types of Southerners are false. Not only are "true Southerners" people identifying with a "native Southland," but every true Southerner should be an active member of an organization dedi-cated to the preservation and perpetuation of the truth about the Southern cause. The Sons of Confederate Veterans and the United Daughters of the Confederacy are two examples of such organizations.[18]

Kennedy and Kennedy make it very clear that "true Southerners" are de-scended from Confederate soldiers—the criteria needed to join organizations like the SCV and UDC—and therefore are people whose ancestors fought for the Confederate States of America in the 1860s. The overwhelming likelihood is that such a "true Southerner" will be white, a sense reinforced by other appeals made by Michael Hill to "Southern culture" as being "White Anglo-Celtic," in which he invokes a specific type of whiteness, that of the Celts.[19]

Ethnic Southerners and Celtic Ethnicity— Recasting White Identities

In his assessment of the construction of ethnic identities, Eugeen Roosens proposes that "one can make use of any number of signs for differentiation as long as they are credible—that is, as long as they *could* be in line with a particular cultural tradition."[20] Between 1975 and 1988 a series of scholarly studies "ethnicized" white Southern identity past and present as Celtic.[21] This determination underpins contemporary neo-Confederacy. In one of his first published interviews, Michael Hill, for example, told *Southern Partisan* that "when I think of Southerners, I think about our origins in the organic, kin-based societies of Scotland, Ireland and Wales."[22] Such was the attractiveness of equating white Southerners to northwestern European Celts that three years later, at a 1997 LS meeting in Biloxi, Hill could simply identify both himself and his audience as Celtic: "As a Celt myself . . . I know most of you are of Celtic descent as well."[23]

Under such a definition, Celtic Southerners thus become written as ethni-cally and culturally distinct from other whites in the United States, this latter group being identified as "English"[24] or "Anglo-Saxon."[25] "Southern people," therefore, are supposedly distinguishable from other U.S. whites because they exhibit Celtic culture and behavior. Echoing the old assertions of a Puritan North and a Cavalier South, neo-Confederates thus propose that the white population of the United States is fundamentally divided between "Anglo/Saxon (English—and therefore Yankee) [and] . . . Celtic (Welsh, Scottish, and Irish—and therefore Southern)."[26] This division is identified by promi-nent neo-Confederate Clyde Wilson when referring to the Civil War as "the largest ethnic rift in American history."[27]

- Neo-Confederate demands for recognition of the Celtic people of the American South are persistent. When coupled with the elision of slavery and the histories of indigenous peoples of the continent common in neo-Confederate essays and speeches, they underscore the presumption that "Southerners" are white. In a radio interview, moments after he attacked the "flood" of Hispanics arriving in the Southern states, Hill explained that he had "no problem" with "blacks" living in the South, on condition "they . . . come down here and live as Southerners."[28] Hill thus suggests that one can be "Southern" and not white, on condition that nonwhites abide by rules of behavior and "Southernness" delineated by neo-Confederates. Such assertions of tolerance, the occasional nonwhite supporter, and neo-Confederate web sites that "decry any . . . hate-mongering, or Klan or neo-Nazi activity" enable neo-Confederate proclamations that their beliefs are not racist.[29] Yet proponents of neo-Confederacy repeatedly conflate Southerners with whites and appeal to "European" and "Anglo-Celtic" culture and ancestry as the basis of Southernness.

• Historically, explains Richard Dyer, Western whiteness has been far from monolithic. Some ethnicities within whiteness have been envisioned as "whiter than others," and Noel Ignatiev demonstrates how Celtic ethnicity in the nineteenth-century United States was popularly perceived to be non-white, as cartoonists depicted simian Irish immigrants as belonging "if not to the black race, then to an intermediate race located socially between black and white."[30] Times have changed, however, and Pittock argues that at the end of the twentieth century, Celtic ethnicity enjoyed a revival in popularity that saw it equated "with simple pleasures, rural pursuits and a certain primitive addiction to partying," all of which, he mused, "provides an undeniable appeal."[31]

The Celtic ethnicity forwarded in neo-Confederate venues comprises what Herbert J. Gans calls a "symbolic ethnicity" in which the complexities of life as experienced by the original ethnic migrant community are erased by those claiming to inherit the ethnicity who then subsequently demand a return to traditions such as "the cohesive extended immigrant family . . . or the unambiguous orthodoxy of immigrant religion."[32] The result, perhaps curiously, is that current displays of ethnic and cultural identities by these descendents of immigrants are often more explicit than those of their forebears. Motivated by a perceived "cultural homogenization" in the United States, contends Gans, "they are constantly looking for new ways to establish their differences."[33]

Despite growing recognition amongst social theorists of the symbolic performance of ethnicities, the multiplicity of individual identities, and their contextual constructions, ethnic identities remain popularly considered as "part of our essential natures."[34] Yet people are not born with an ethnic or cultural identity imprinted into their genes; rather, ethnicities are acquired over time and through experiences, and are being continuously reshaped by everyday practices and interactions with others. Despite this, ethnic identities are typically portrayed as timeless, primordial, and inviolable, innately causing specific attitudes, beliefs, and behaviors. For many politicians and activists, these inherited ethnic characteristics also form the basis for a homogenous national culture, and a belief that everyone sharing an ethnic identity belongs "to the same great national family."[35] Enhancing the metaphorical association of an identity rooted in biology and family, blood and kin are commonly invoked as bases for ethnic and, from there, national belonging. Since World War II and Nazi insistence on the racial purity of German nationality, direct appeals to biology as the basis for national identity have been discredited. Yet in contemporary politics and popular culture they have been "replaced by *cultural* definitions of race," according to Stuart Hall.[36] This enables discussions of race that are euphemistically articulated in terms of culture and community, precisely the strategy that neo-Confederate activists utilize. Sidestepping direct appeals to racial white superiority, neo-Confederates exalt whiteness as the essence of Southernness by utilizing an appeal to Celtic culture, ethnicity, ancestry, and national belonging.

Neo-Confederate Assertions of Celtic Ethnicity

Neo-Confederates, such as Barry Reid McCain, have asserted that "in the South the Anglo-Celts . . . are numerically and culturally dominant, and other groups that have moved into the South have adopted their culture and have become Anglo-Celts by assimilation." In McCain's reasoning, "the Anglo prefix merely signifies use of the English language," and the Anglo-Celt is in fact "a Celt who speaks English, yet retains Celtic cultural characteristics." Not only is this population supposedly "numerically and culturally dominant" in the U.S. South, it is only in this region where some type of authentic and untarnished Celtic culture seems to persist: "While Anglo-Celt can apply to many people in the British Isles and large parts of the population of various ex-British colonies, it is the South where Anglo-Celts established a homeland and have retained many of their core cultural traits."[37]

Such assertions of Celtic dominance and the centrality of Celtic culture to the U.S. South are the result of concerted efforts since the mid-1970s by proponents of neo-Confederate thought to generate a historical-theoretical outline around which to base demands for secession from the United States and establishment of an independent Confederacy. This has been primarily based on the supposed binary between Celtic Southern states and English Northern states. The proposal that division between Celtic and English ethnic groups is central to the ethnic structure of the United States has been legitimated by its presence in prominent and reputable scholarly publications, even making it to the pages of the mass-market weekly magazine *Newsweek*, where "the controversial notion" was reported "that the Civil War was a continuation, on new turf, of the ancient struggle by the Anglo-Saxons to subdue the wild Celtic tribes of Scotland, Ireland and Wales."[38]

⟡ The Celtic South thesis was initially developed by Grady McWhiney and his colleagues Forrest McDonald and Ellen Shapiro McDonald.[39] Their articles and books, particularly McWhiney's *Cracker Culture* (1988)—"a central text for the Southern League [LS]"—have become the foundation for neo-Confederate understandings about the ethnic division of the United States between Celtic and English cultural groups.[40] The Celtic South thesis proposes that the antebellum U.S. South was culturally different from the North because each area attracted different immigrant groups from the British Isles, with Celts settling in the South and the English in the North.

⟡ Almost everything about the South supposedly came from these Celtic origins, from farming techniques to cooking, eating habits, courtship, dancing, music, and educational styles.[41] If residents in the antebellum South were not immigrants from Celtic areas of the British Isles, McWhiney asserts they became "Celticized" regardless of their racial or ethnic background. People resident in Northern states were similarly "Anglicized" by the dominance of English residents and culture in that region.[42] McWhiney proposes:

> Celts brought their traditional ways and values with them to the Old South and . . . they not only continued to practice them but were so successful in imposing their ways upon most of the ethnic minorities they settled among that a list of southern traits most observed by contemporaries reads like an inventory of traditional Scottish, Irish, and Welsh cultural characteristics.[43]

Purported to have been conveyed across centuries and oceans, and transmitted to and imposed upon other residents of the U.S. South, being Celtic, as neo-Confederates understand it, determines every aspect of behavior for "Southerners." One's Celtic culture can be traced through genealogy and is, McDonald and McWhiney argue, unchanging:

> The sociological/geographical accounts of Celtic peoples by the Greeks Strabo and Diodorus [are] for all the world like a caricature of our rural

neighbors in modern Alabama. In other words, except for variations in technology and dress, description of Celtic social norms spanning two thousand years and more are entirely interchangeable.[44]

Such efforts to establish a two-thousand-year genealogy for Celtic culture in the American South confers both longevity to the culture and legitimacy to the ethnic group that exhibits it. Identifying today's Southerners as descendents of ancient ancestors implicitly validates neo-Confederate claims to primary residence in the South (the supposed "homeland" of Celtic "core cultural traits"). Despite centuries of struggle against erosion, Celts and Celtic culture, it seems, survive as Southern. "The original settlers of the South," argues Michael W. Masters in *Southern Patriot,* migrated from "Scotland, Wales, Cornwall, Northern Ireland (the 'Scotch-Irish' or 'Ulster Scots'), and Ireland itself." He continues:

> We share not only a common blood line but common culture, temperament, moral values, work ethic, folk ways and a bond to the land and to our own people that distinguishes us from other "peoples" in other lands. . . . Two thousand years ago the Roman historian Tacitus, writing in *De Germania* about the Germanic tribes that are the common ancestors of most Western Europeans today, in all their scattered homelands around the world, said that they possessed a fondness for personal freedom, an independence of spirit, an unusually high status accorded women, and a deep affection for the land. These traits, distinctly Southern, have survived twenty centuries.
>
> These are our heritage and our right by birth. No man on earth—and no law made by man—has the right to take them away from us.[45]

Masters, who has also written for the Council of Conservative Citizens and Jared Taylor's *American Renaissance,* explains that the longevity of Celtic culture can be traced back over two thousand years to central Europe.[46] The transmission, intact, of supposedly consistent Celtic behaviors to (white) Southerners throughout history implies they must comprise the basis for current cultural practices and cannot be altered. Yet much of the evidence for the survival of these unchanging beliefs and behaviors is somewhat unlikely. McDonald and McWhiney, for example, have proposed that the Celtic ethnicity of the South can be heard musically as "the similarity between the sound of a bagpipe and that of Southern country fiddlers is almost eerie."[47] Elsewhere McWhiney has suggested that because people in both the Southern United States and Ireland drink illegally distilled liquor, both are Celtic: "Even today southerners and Irishmen are partial to what they both call moonshine."[48]

Equally, when assessing the apparently Celtic tradition of livestock farming, McWhiney proposes that this Celtic practice has been unchanged for centuries: "Livestock still run free in parts of Scotland and Ireland. In 1981 and 1983 I observed free-ranging cattle and sheep in the Scottish Highlands and in the north and west of Ireland."[49] This point is also made by James Catron in the League of the South's *Southern Patriot* column, "from our members," in which he asserts that Celtic peoples "invented" cattle farming: "The very words *range, ranch, rancho, rancher,* and *ranchero* are of Gaelic origin."[50]

Catron's discussion of language is typical of neo-Confederate efforts to display the Celtic aspects of speech that are supposedly distinctive to (white) Southerners. Michael Hill advised supporters at the 1997 Biloxi conference in which he identified himself and his audience as Celtic that they should cry out the Gaelic word *buaidh* (victory) at rallies and meetings.[51] In addition, neo-Confederate authors typically inform others of their Celtic ancestry, or familiarity with Celtic areas and peoples. This is critical to establishing neo-Confederate identity and credibility. LS member Barry Reid McCain, for example, explains in a biographical note that he "has travelled extensively in the Celtic-fringe, and speaks Gaelic." Elsewhere, Grady McWhiney, Thomas Fleming, Michael Hill, and other leading neo-Confederates have mentioned their visits to Scotland and Ireland, their Celtic ancestry, or use Gaelic terms in their writings and speeches.[52]

In addition to their construction of a Celtic South, neo-Confederates consistently assume that the Celts they describe are men. Whether a "kinsman,"[53] "Welshmen,"[54] or "herdsmen,"[55] neo-Confederate authors constantly refer to Celts using masculine pronouns. For example, McCain explains that Southerners and Celts prefer rural lifestyles because "the Celt always has needed his space," and lauds the patriarchal structure of the Celtic family which he identifies as the "*derbfine,* or four generations in a family; son, father, grandfather, and great-grandfather."[56] In the following excerpt, neo-Confederate theorist Grady McWhiney separates "Celts" from "women," "animals," and "slaves," the latter all equitable as property of the male actor, making the association between masculinity, Celts, and Southerners explicit:

> Celts and Southerners . . . believing it foolish to engage in work unnecessarily . . . much preferred to enjoy life while their animals, their women, or their slaves made a living for them.[57]

When coupled with the construction of "Southerners" as white, it becomes apparent that the ethnic distinction that is perceived to be the foundation of the putative Confederacy proposed by neo-Confederate activists is that of white men of northwestern European descent.

This belief in a distinctive Celtic ethno-cultural group in the U.S. South now enjoys popular currency amongst neo-Confederates and other proponents of Confederate heritage. For example, the League of the South hosted a "Southern Celtic conference" in Biloxi on 6 April 1996, and Pulitzer Prize winner Tony Horwitz, describing the beliefs of the neo-Confederate "romantics" and battle reenactors he met in the U.S. South, explains:

> The South they revered was hot-blooded, Celtic, heedlessly courageous; their poster boy was the Scottish clansman played by Mel Gibson in the splatterfest *Braveheart*. In their view, rationalism and technological efficiency were suspect Yankee traits, derived from a mercantile English empire that had put down the Scots and Irish.[58]

Recommending *Braveheart* to readers of *Southern Patriot,* the neo-Confederate LS told members that "unreconstructed Southerners will find it difficult to miss the parallels between the Scots and our Confederate forebears."[59] In turn, neo-Confederate Clyde Wilson called on his audience at the 1996 LS annual conference to "imagine the film of our *Braveheart: The Life of General Nathan Bedford Forrest.*"[60] *Southern Partisan* also pursued an examination of the "Scottish-Southern connection,"[61] and Tommy Stringer observed that "both the Confederate Battle Flag and Confederate uniforms are common sights at Highland Games [in Southern U.S. states]."[62] That Celtic culture and the Confederacy became intertwined and often conflated in neo-Confederate venues is typified in a *Southern Patriot* essay by Grady McWhiney, which explains that the Confederate president's "appeal for orators and poets to preserve the deeds of heroic Southerners reveals that [Jefferson] Davis understood the South's heritage. Southerners, like their Celtic ancestors, were oral and aural people who perpetuated much of their past in stories and songs."[63]

There are many more examples of what neo-Confederates identify as culturally Celtic behaviors that now compose "southern traits," too many to examine in detail. We focus here on one of the most important: a supposed propensity for violence.

Celtic Violence

> The South was and still is a violent society because violence is one of the cultural traditions that Southerners brought with them to America. Their Celtic ancestors were, authorities agree, characteristically violent.[64]
> GRADY MCWHINEY, 1988

In neo-Confederate constructions of Celtic identity, the propensity for violence is never far from the surface. Valorization of violent behavior and equally violent punitive discipline is welcomed enthusiastically, not just as a historical precedent for contemporary Southern society, as McWhiney presents it, but also as a central part of the future, as stated by LS president Michael Hill:

> A reputation for toughness was, and still is, the best keeper of the peace, and this is why the South (or at least the small towns and rural areas) remains an oasis of civilization. We can only hope that coming generations of white Southern men will carry on this tradition of honorable self-defense. . . . Should this life-sustaining pugnacity disappear, so too will the South. And with the South will go the last remnant of a vigorous, self-confident, and manly Western civilization.[65]

Violence and the proclivity of men to react to insults and disputes by resorting to fighting is explained as a consequence of a traditional Celtic culture. McWhiney contends that "people of Celtic culture [have] exhibited an abiding love of combat" that can be traced back to early Europe and "have fought much the same way for more than two thousand years."[66]

Within the holistic worldview of neo-Confederacy, the Civil War can be explained by reference to Celtic culture. Neo-Confederates maintain that due to the Celtic ethnicity of its troops, the Confederate army fought battles using tactics and strategies that were inherited as part of their Celtic culture. These were, in short, charging heroically at a better armed and organized enemy. "Southerners lost the Civil War," McWhiney and Jamieson lament, "because they were too Celtic and their opponents were too English."[67]

Examining these contentions further reveals that Celtic culture and ethnicity are invoked by neo-Confederates to justify gun ownership and vigilantism. Hill, for example, argues that "the Celts realized that the true foundation of independence was that every man be armed," and extends this to maintain that Celtic cultural norms legitimate the right of Southerners to administer "private justice." Hill supports these contentions by reviewing "the violence of a warrior society" from twelfth-century Wales, via the historical

Scottish clan system, to the Irish Republican Army, explaining that "justice administered by private organizations . . . is a long-standing tradition in the Celtic world."[68]

The League of the South's web site in 2004 featured a picture of a young white man, posed with his fists seemingly clenched, and an accompanying statement that "honor, violence and civilization" compose "a proud Southern tradition that still endures. . . . Young Southerners still reflect the toughness of their Southern and Anglo-Celtic forbears. . . . Should this life-sustaining pugnacity disappear, so too will the South." It was a message Hill had initially outlined in *Chronicles* seven years earlier.[69]

Neo-Confederates assert that it is the descendants of Celts who migrated to the American South in the pre–Civil War era who are responsible for much of the violence in the United States, both past and present. These contentions are problematic, presenting an understanding that violent behavior is innate and acquired from distant ancestors. It rationalizes that violent actions are inherited cultural practices transmitted across generations and that one's ethnicity determines one's contemporary character and behavior. Concomitant with these beliefs is the way that Scottish, Irish, and more generally Celtic propensity for violent behavior is considered laudatory. Indeed, neo-Confederate arguments about violence inherent in Celtic culture have been cited to exonerate the high rates of homicide amongst white men in the American South as being "natural."[70] This can subsequently be utilized to justify any violent action, absolving practitioners from responsibility and explaining it as merely an accident of ancestry.

Who Were the Celts?

Before challenging the neo-Confederate construction of the Celtic South directly, it should be noted that the very idea of a historical Celtic people is rather dubious. Neo-Confederate activists have drawn upon Greek and Roman records for their historical connection,[71] though Malcolm Chapman argues that the term "Celt" in classical texts does not refer to a particular tribe or people.[72] Rather, it was used as a more generic term meaning "foreigner." Other scholars argue that the popular contention of Scotland as populated by Celts is "an ethnological fiction" from the eighteenth century.[73] Indeed, the idea of Scotland, Wales, and Ireland being a Celtic fringe of the British Isles is a relatively recent construction and, Simon James emphasizes, "No one in Britain or Ireland called themselves a 'Celt' or 'Celtic' before 1700."[74] Rather, "Celtic" was a politically expedient description of Gaelic languages in the eighteenth century, and thereafter became ascribed to cultural traits, racial types, and national groups, as was common throughout this period. By the nineteenth century, "Celtic" had come to describe, however inaccurately, the non-English people and regions of the United Kingdom.

. With the term in common usage by the nineteenth century, eminent authors such as Matthew Arnold and Ernest Renan attached to it certain behaviors and values.[75] These contentions received much coverage on both sides of the Atlantic, prompting many, amongst them John Fiske, to examine whether the United States could be considered to have a racially Celtic population.[76] Historian Murray Pittock contends that W. F. Skene's 1880 book *Celtic Scotland* "put forward a vision of Celtic agrarian society as a kind of golden age on which Anglo-Saxon ideas of private ownership and landlord rights had been imposed."[77] An antithesis to modern industrial capitalism, this idealized Celtic society valorized "the virtues of primitive simplicity, unimproved rurality, bravery, loyalty, elemental courtesy and honour."[78] With Irish republican writers like W. B. Yeats (1865–1939) drawing on this interpretation of Celts as heroic men fighting to protect their communities against the modern industrial state, the image of a "masculinized, revivified Celt" fighting for Celtic liberation soon encompassed Celticness as a whole.[79] It is this imagery that forms the basis of the Celtic identity revered in neo-Confederate discourse, yet archaeologist John Collis maintains that "the ancient Celts are depicted as child-like but easy to rouse, bold in battle, drunken and boastful. These are the racial stereotypes which are transformed into the 'Celtic Spirit' of the modern Celt."[80]

Discussing Southern Agrarian Frank Owsley's (1949) *Plain Folk of the Old South*, for example, Kennedy and Kennedy note that for these "white Southerners who were not a part of the plantation system . . . contempt for materialism was a natural part of the cultural heritage of the Celtic people from which the majority of them sprang."[81] In turn, the League of the South's Barry Reid McCain remarks that "Celtic traits live in the South . . . [sporting] elements of a cultural continuum that reaches back to ancient Europe." One such trait is supposedly a "warrior culture" in which "the normal Southern male (and female) equat[e] being armed to being free." "Southern food, music, art, political concepts, values—even the way we look," concludes McCain, "are all linked inseparably with the Celtic-fringe of the British Isles."[82] Making what could be interpreted as a racial argument, McCain asserts that a person's visual appearances—"even the way we look"—is indicative of their culture, ancestry, and ethnic identity. One could identify a "normal Southern male (and female)," it seems, just by looking at them—just as Clyde Wilson proposes that a citizen in a revived Confederacy could be easily recognized and distinguished from an immigrant by their appearance (see Chapter 5).

As noted, throughout neo-Confederate writing on the importance of Celtic culture and the cultural distinctiveness of the South runs an assumption that Celtic practices have remained unchanged for centuries. These practices, therefore, must be evident in the South, a region supposedly distinct from the rest of the country ethnically, culturally, socially, and politically. In the New Dixie Manifesto, Hill and Fleming underscore the differences they perceive between "Southerners" and "Americans" and argue for the preservation of such distinctions: "Southerners respect the rights of all Americans in every region to preserve their authentic cultural traditions and demand the same respect from others."[83] If "authentic cultural traditions" deserve protection and respect, then neo-Confederacy's Celtic culture, a tradition that can supposedly be traced to antiquity, is seemingly more fundamental to human existence than an implicitly inauthentic U.S. culture that has, according to the LS, "lowered standards of morality and debased human dignity [and] . . . appealed to mankind's worst impulses through profanity and obscenity in the arts and literature; . . . depict[ing] decadence and debauchery as normal and desirable."[84]

With these notions deeply embedded in their self-image, neo-Confederates have constructed binaries, similar to nineteenth- and early-twentieth-century articulations of a Cavalier South and Puritan North, in which white and native-born Southerners are considered virtuous and innately engender more positive behaviors than are evident elsewhere in the United States. Though based on simplistic categories of Celtic versus English as a model for the South versus the rest of the country, this assertion of Celtic culture allows neo-Confederates to proclaim their ethnic distinctiveness. As commonly accepted principles of self-determination in international politics center upon allowing self-rule for distinct ethno-national and cultural groups, the neo-Confederate articulation of their distinct Celtic culture provides supporters with an argument for secession and the establishment of an independent nation-state. In turn, claiming Celtic ethnicity and culture is a way to be distinct from the U.S. mainstream while retaining precisely the privileges of whiteness currently evident in Western society—even when alleging that Southern Celtic culture is being persecuted. Such manipulations are masked by assertions that Celtic culture has persisted unchanged for centuries and that today's Southerners are acting on the beliefs of their ancestors and embodying their cultural practices and behaviors.

Critique of Neo-Confederate Celtic Contentions

It is generally held that the antebellum Southern states did have a considerable population who migrated from Scotland and Ireland, but these people were neither monolithically Celtic nor regionally concentrated.[85] Furthermore, historian David Moltke-Hansen contends that the Celtic South thesis is flawed because its proponents "have placed the beginning of British settlement of the South fully a century and more later than it occurred."[86] In addition, the origins of these Celtic immigrants to the antebellum South are inconsistently defined in the Celtic South thesis. In an early essay on the subject, McDonald and McWhiney argued that the Celtic residents of the British Isles who moved to the area that became the U.S. South were typically from "the southwestern, western, and northern parts of England, the Scottish Lowlands and Highlands, and most especially the 'Scotch-Irish' plantations in Ulster, northern Ireland."[87] Elsewhere, as Berthoff indicates, the neo-Confederate definition of Celtic territories stretches to include Wales, Cornwall, and an ever-growing list of English counties: "Cumberland, Westmoreland, Durham, Northumberland, Lancashire, Cheshire, Shropshire, Hereford."[88] Elsewhere, McDonald and McWhiney expand the extent of Celtic areas in the British Isles to include Devon, Somerset, Dorset, and Wiltshire as Celtic counties of England.[89] This is an expansive definition that leaves only southern and eastern England as non-Celtic areas of the British Isles. Consequently, historian Rowland Berthoff states that this identification of Celtic areas "follows no known usage."[90] To complicate the issue further, McWhiney expands his definition of Celtic, moving beyond the British Isles to include Normandy and Brittany in France, and McDonald includes most of northern and central Europe, including the entire Alpine mountain range.[91] Such pan-European definitions of Celtic culture and peoples developed in the eighteenth century and have been bolstered in the late twentieth century by European Union exhibitions.[92] They are, however, highly problematic, founded on numerous questionable assumptions, and have been the matter of contentious debate amongst archaeologists—to the point where the idea of a pan-European Celtic civilization and culture has been largely discredited.[93]

Not only is the definition of Celtic culture and ethnicity utilized by neo-Confederate theorists inaccurate, critics have also contested neo-Confederate assumptions of how Celtic culture and ethnicity operate. Historian Ned Landsman, for example, argues that the understandings of culture and ethnicity utilized in developing the Celtic South thesis "differ little from racial type."[94] Michael P. Johnson, in turn, has attacked the "rigidly genealogical concept of southern culture" utilized in McWhiney's book *Cracker Culture*, which "makes clear that real southern Crackers were white men."[95] Anthony J. Sheehan has also argued that Hill's academic publication on the Celtic origins of the South "smacks strongly of pseudo-scientific Victorian notions of 'races' and 'racial characteristics.'"[96]

When answering their critics, McDonald and McWhiney have utilized rather than rejected antiquated notions of biological racial groups, with references to Celtic "stock," "genetic mixtures," and "bloodlines."[97] Discussing this type of narrative, which articulates the genetic transmission of culture, Dyer notes: "In these discourses, all blood and genes carry mental properties, but, invisibly, white blood and genes carry more intelligence, more spirit of enterprise, more moral refinement. Thus our bodily blood or genes give us that extra-bodily edge."[98]

Much of the neo-Confederate argument for a distinctive Celtic culture in the South is made by elision and circularity. The term "Celtic" is itself useful, as it comes replete with popular imagery, and the components of Celtic culture are available for reinterpretation and appropriation based on whatever meaning is useful to proponents. Elements that do not meet the required vision of Celtic culture can be omitted, whereas others—such as the propensity for violence—can be heralded. That a certain behavior (e.g., violence) is taken as evidence of an individual acting on their Celtic culture thus becomes self-fulfilling: a person exhibiting Celtic behavior is Celtic because the behavior they are exhibiting is Celtic. Not only does this assume a homogeneous Celtic culture, but it also suggests that individuals are beholden to their culture when acting in the world. This is a highly problematic and simplistic conceptualization of culture, a term cultural theorist Raymond Williams identifies as "one of the two or three most complicated words in the English language."[99]

Challenging the Neo-Confederate Concept of Culture

In their assessments of Celtic culture, neo-Confederate activists assume that "culture" comprises a fixed set of behaviors transmissible across generations that determine a person's actions. This is a super-organic understanding of culture, one in which human will is submerged beneath a greater cultural imperative.

In his assessment of "culture," Williams shows the close relationship between "culture" and the idea of "natural growth."[100] Such a connection enables some to contend that "culture" comprises the "natural" essence of a person or group. According to cultural geographer Don Mitchell, however, merely determining that something is a result of "culture" obscures the dynamic processes of power relations and individual decision making that shape behaviors and beliefs. Although attributing practices to culture is common, Mitchell argues that "the power of 'culture' resides in its ability to be used to describe, label or carve out activities into stable entities, so that they can be named an attribute of a people."[101] "Cultures are not simply systems of meaning and value carried around in the head" or benign sets of customs and traditions, explains Peter Jackson, but "*processes* through which meanings are constructed, negotiated, and experienced."[102] The equation of culture to behavior, custom, and tradition typifies the problematic "super-organic approach" to the understanding of culture, which "adopts the view that culture is an entity at a higher level than the individual, that it is governed by a logic of its own, and that it actively constrains human behaviour."[103] In such a conceptualization, culture determines behavior, reducing people to vessels carrying their culture across generations. This culture then supposedly instills certain values and characteristics that all recipients of the culture exhibit: "When culture is defined as the active force and the individual the passive recipient, homogeneity will be assumed, for individuals must be blank pages upon which the culture pattern is imprinted."[104] The super-organic idea of culture assumes what James Duncan terms a "Pavlovian conditioning." Because people are members of a certain culture, and all members exhibiting this culture are homogeneous, they all react to it in the same way, exhibiting the same beliefs and behaviors. In sum, the neo-Confederate understanding of Celtic culture is super-organic.

Rather than being the explanation for behavior, however, appeals to culture should be interrogated to expose what their proponents hope to gain from such an assertion. The critical question, therefore, is this: What does the identification of a Celtic culture gain for neo-Confederates?

There are at least four intersecting and mutually reinforcing reasons for advocating a distinctive Celtic culture of the "Southern people." First, this justifies the argument that the South is a culturally and ethnically distinctive area within the United States and is thus worthy of status as an independent nation-state. Neo-Confederates can point to other ethnic cultures that are striving for autonomy, in particular the Celtic nationalisms of Wales, Ireland, Scotland, and even the Lega Nord in Italy, where Celtic identity has similarly been drawn upon to form an ethno-racial basis for separatist demands.[105] Second, the types of behavior neo-Confederate leaders associate with Celtic culture align with their more general views about masculine valor and martial spirit. Third, since the mid-1970s and in particular following the release of the film *Braveheart* in 1995, there has been a rapid growth in interest in Celtic heritage and ancestry in the United States.[106] This suggests that neo-Confederates have been able to align their proposals regarding Celtic cultural distinction with this increased popularity and thus potential source of supporters. Fourth, Reginald Byron argues that claiming Celtic culture and ancestry in the United States has "a powerful effect in shaping a sense of self" and enables connection to "a history and a biography that is simultaneously defined by having one's origins in the British Isles but being emphatically not Anglo-Saxon but rather a member of a different, purer, nobler, and more primordial 'race,' the Celts."[107]

The neo-Confederate appeal to Celticness is also a politically expedient conduit through which to appeal to whiteness, albeit without articulating this directly. This does not mean that all people who respect and/or celebrate their Celtic ancestry are somehow laboring under a false consciousness or are inherently racist; rather, neo-Confederates utilize appeals to Celtic ancestry and culture in much the same way as Mitch Berbrier describes "new racists" in the late-twentieth-century United States appealing to European ancestry to recast white supremacist ideology as ethnic "pride."[108]

Self-determination for an ethnically Celtic South would produce an independent nation-state with the ability to make legislation and enable structures to be put in place to protect, in neo-Confederate terms, the Celtic culture and Southern people or, rather, the native-born, white, Confederate-descended population. Secession is necessary because, as John Vinson outlined in *Southern Patriot*, there is a "plot to submerge Southern Anglo-Celts in a tidal wave of Third World immigration,"[109] and a failure to achieve self-determination will result in "ethnocide," as William L. Cawthon explained using the language of racial purity:

> With the failure of the U.S. Congress to restrict immigration, with low white birthrates, and with the rapid rise of mixed race marriages, the white population of the United States in a hundred years could easily be no more than 10–25% of the total, and dropping every year, so that eventually few whites would be left here. The traditions of the Anglo-Celtic South would then be alien, and to many, a hated memory. This future is not fantasy. It is the logical outcome of the present policy and trends.[110]

Neo-Confederate Appeals to a "Natural Hierarchy" and Social Order

The identification of what is natural (and therefore good) as opposed to unnatural (and thus bad) is "an essential ingredient of nationalist ideology."[111] They are also central to neo-Confederacy. Rather than constructing the common dichotomy of nature versus culture, neo-Confederates argue that ethnic cultures are natural and that the natural social order that once existed has been detrimentally disrupted by modern society and needs to be restored.

The idea that natural is the antithesis of man-made emerged during the eighteenth and nineteenth centuries when Romanticism, the Enlightenment, and the Industrial Revolution were reshaping social relationships and political ideas in Europe. As a result of these dramatic societal changes, Raymond Williams explains, a state of nature could "be contrasted—sometimes pessimistically but more often optimistically and even programmatically— with an existing state of society."[112] Such an understanding meant that calls for a return to "natural" social relationships could be used in appeals against the transformation of society. Such contentions implied that contemporary social aspects, such as life in modern industrial cities, were unnatural, having moved away from a prior state of nature that was understood as the rightful condition of life. Appeals to nature, therefore, "played critical roles in arguments about, first, an obsolete or corrupt society, needing redemption and renewal, and, second, an 'artificial' or 'mechanical' society, which learning from Nature must cure."[113] The natural state of affairs was, therefore, proposed to be the way things were before their corruption by the modern industrial nation-state, and opponents to such development could thus argue for a return to nature.

The implication in such conceptualizations is that nature constitutes what is normal, indeed God-given, and that human alterations to these relationships are necessarily artificial and detrimental. Appealing to nature is therefore a powerful way to legitimate one's worldview, rendering it beyond challenge because that is just how things should be. The artificial structures of modern society should be overthrown, enabling nature to return the human social condition to its supposedly elemental situation. An appeal to something as being natural could, Williams maintains, be utilized to support any number of social issues, from justifying property rights to violence and war. For neo-Confederates, the appeal to nature is a way to assert a hierarchical, anti-democratic society.

"The South," explained Hill in an interview, "has always preferred a *natural hierarchy*. You're always going to have some violations of people's rights, for whatever reason, but we just believe that a *natural social order* left to *evolve organically* on its own would be better for everyone."[114] For Hill and other neo-Confederates, however, this natural, organic condition has not been left to evolve of its own accord. Rather, and as we discuss more fully in Chapter 5, for neo-Confederates the natural state of affairs has been challenged by policies such as racial desegregation and multiculturalism. Such policies are dismissed as "social engineering" by neo-Confederate authors like William Cawthon Jr. and are thus understood to be artificial impositions that alter the supposedly "natural social order."[115] Social equality is, for neo-Confederates, unnatural and must be overturned to restore the inequitable natural state of affairs, which John Vinson described in *Southern Patriot:* "The simple truth is that all men are not equal in morality and talents. Honest theology and biology decree it so. In a free society, men will *naturally* reap different status and rewards. . . . Those who promote total equality rebel against God and the *natural* order."[116] The "natural order" of human life is thus one of disparity and, consequently, a society that is not free is one that exhibits or advances human equality. For neo-Confederates, a free and natural society is one "composed of superiors, equals and inferiors," a state of affairs that Michael Hill notes, drawing on nineteenth-century theologian Robert Lewis Dabney, is evident in "the teachings of Holy Scripture." "The social theory of equality" is dismissed as a "pernicious" eighteenth-century invention that has subsequently, and artificially, been imposed on the natural, God-given, unequal social order.[117]

These sentiments have a long history in the philosophical tradition that informs current neo-Confederacy. In *The Unregenerate South,* a book that has become an important part of the current neo-Confederate canon, Mark Malvasi describes Richard M. Weaver's argument that "aristocracy and patriarchy, which placed some men in the service and under the protection of others," were critically necessary to maintain "social order."[118] Experiences like racial discrimination and segregation, Malvasi continues, "did not denote some unnatural pattern in human affairs. . . . Instead they constituted an intuitive process of discretion, refinement and taste" that, for Weaver, rightly led to a hierarchical society.[119]

This supposedly natural state of social inequality and hierarchy is also understood to shape relationships between distinctive groups of people. Thus, society is understood as a competitive arena in which different "cultural groups" are engaged in a struggle for survival, as Michael Hill writes:

> Competition among cultural groups seeking the resources to survive and prosper is natural and proper. To deny this by asserting the silly slogan, "the

brotherhood of man," is cultural suicide; it will not eliminate the competition, but will lull us into acquiescing in our own destruction.[120]

That rivalry between "cultural groups" is, for Hill, "natural and proper," and echoes a "further powerful personification" of nature described by Raymond Williams:

> Nature the selective breeder: natural selection, and the "ruthless" competition apparently inherent within it, were made the basis for seeing nature as both historical and active. Nature still indeed had laws, but they were laws of survival and extinction: species rose and flourished, decayed and died.[121]

Hill evidently believes that "cultural groups" are separate and identifiable entities, that they are in constant competition, and that a failure to participate in such struggles results in the demise of one culture and the endurance of another. Any effort to alter the supposedly natural and unequal social order artificially disrupts this struggle for survival among "cultural groups." Recall that, as outlined above, the Celtic South thesis championed by advocates of neo-Confederacy purports that today's white Southern residents are members of a Celtic cultural group, with beliefs and behaviors transmitted via bloodlines unchanged for two thousand years. Further, this Celtic culture is embodied, shaping people's attitudes, actions, and appearances. For proponents of neo-Confederacy, Celtic culture, like any other culture, is natural in that it is evident in human biology and promulgated through reproduction. It is passed across generations as part of someone's genetic heritage and is in their blood. If Celtic culture has survived and endured centuries of this supposedly natural competition among cultural groups, it must be a strong and powerful culture, one that would rise to the top of the natural social order and claim the resources that it merits.

Neo-Confederacy and Social Darwinism

The invocation of social inequality as God-given in "Holy Scripture," coupled with the belief that there are distinct cultures battling each other for resources, that the strongest culture will supersede others and come to dominate a hierarchical social system, and that all this is "natural" is social Darwinism. It is this set of beliefs that underpins neo-Confederacy.

Social Darwinism developed at the end of the nineteenth century when theorists like Herbert Spencer transferred Darwin's biological theories of evolution and natural selection to people and nations.[122] Social Darwinism proposed that people (both as individuals and as national or cultural groups) were equitable to species in that they evolve and compete for territory and resources in much the same way as animals and plants. A failure to compete successfully, within this social Darwinist understanding of society, results in individual, ethnic, and cultural extinction. In a call to his neo-Confederate supporters in 2002, Michael Hill was explicit about who he thought was most threatened by current U.S. society: "To put it bluntly, young white males are now an endangered species."[123]

Such nineteenth-century reasoning is consistent with other neo-Confederate perspectives on religion and gender roles, which form the basis for a patriarchal white (Anglo-Celtic) supremacist vision as the desired structural and social order. In sum, neo-Confederacy asserts that Celtic culture has been conveyed across generations to today's white Southerners, that this culture shapes behavior in the present, and that social inequality is the "natural order" — a way of life that federal authorities are intent on destroying in their pursuit of equal rights.

Conclusion: Neo-Confederacy's Celtic Culture

The late twentieth century saw a "return of ethnicity" to politics, typically in the guise of appeals to culture and as a synonym for race.[124] Within this context, the construction of a Southern Celtic cultural and ethnic identity is a critical plank of the neo-Confederate agenda and the latest in a long tradition of trying to construct the white South as an ethno-racial-cultural group. Claims to a distinctive Southern culture and ethnicity, evident in the nineteenth century and reinvigorated in the 1970s, give neo-Confederate activists the basis to argue that their ethnic group — white Anglo-Celtic Southern people — deserves an independent state in which, Hill explains, "a European population, especially Anglo-Celts, . . . must be preserved as the dominant majority."[125]

The Celtic South thesis utilized within the neo-Confederate movement to explain the ethnic distinctiveness of the Southern United States is, however, untenable on a number of fronts — from its expansive definition of Celtic to its assumptions that culture is unchanged over distance and time and super-organically determines behavior. Yet Celtic ethnicity is repeatedly asserted by proponents of neo-Confederacy such as Barry Reid McCain as the fundamental basis of the U.S. South, both past and future:

Celts have defined the South and will continue to do so. If the South had been settled predominantly by Norwegians or perhaps Chinese, then there would not have been the Confederacy, a Dixie, and those peculiar Southerners with all their unique virtues and vices.[126]

Although neo-Confederates such as McCain purport to speak for and about "Southerners," their vision of the membership of a Southern ethnic group is one of white Confederate sympathizers, with a twist of Celtic nationalism. When examined in detail, therefore, neo-Confederate understandings of their own ethnicity and culture reveal a vision of a hierarchical society where ethnic distinction and white privilege are intertwined as supposedly "natural" structures essential to the maintenance of an unequal social order. A social order without such arrangements is ascertained to be fundamentally flawed, antithetical to both nature and God. As such, serious questions must be raised about neo-Confederacy. The repeated assertions by neo-Confederate proponents such as Michael Hill that neo-Confederacy comprises "mainstream, middle-class goals," and not the advocacy of hierarchies encompassing superiority and inferiority in racial, gender, class, or other social relations, must be challenged.[127]

Notes

1. A full theoretical engagement with the literature exploring contemporary ethnicity is beyond the scope of this book. Werner Sollors provides an etymology of the term in *Beyond Ethnicity: Consent and Descent in American Culture.* (Oxford and New York: Oxford University Press, 1986). See also Sollors's *The Invention of Ethnicity.* (Oxford: Oxford University Press, 1989). Anthropological studies are at the forefront of such examinations—see, *inter alia,* Thomas Hylland Eriksen, *Ethnicity and Nationalism: Anthropological Perspectives,* 2nd ed. (London: Pluto Press, 2002), Marcus Banks, *Ethnicity: Anthropological Constructions.* (London: Routledge, 1996), and Eugeen E. Roosens, *Creating Ethnicity: The Process of Ethnogenesis.* (Newbury Park, CA: Sage, 1989). Both Roosens and Sollors suggest that in the 1960s "ethnicity" took on new meanings and popular currency in the United States, primarily through the work of Frederick Barth, for example his collection *Ethnic Groups and Boundaries* (Boston: Little and Brown, 1969) and pioneering studies by Nathan Glazer and future U.S. senator Daniel Patrick Moynihan (*Beyond the Melting Pot* and *Ethnicity: Theory and Experience*). For a general collection that compiles a range of understandings and essays about the concept, see Hutchinson, John, and Smith, Anthony D., eds. *Ethnicity.* (Oxford: Oxford University Press, 1996).
2. Eriksen, *Ethnicity and Nationalism,* (2002): 2.
3. James, Simon. *The Atlantic Celts: Ancient People or Modern Invention?* (London: British Museum Press, 1999): 72. See also Waters, Mary C. *Ethnic Options: Choosing Identities in America.* (Berkeley: University of California Press, 1990).

4. Sollors, *Beyond Ethnicity*, (1986): 13.

5. Sanders, Franklin. "The Global Rise of Ethnic Nationalism," *Southern Patriot*, 2.2 (1995): 11–13.

6. Dawson, Jan C. "The Puritan and the Cavalier: The South's Perception of Contrasting Traditions," *Journal of Southern History*, 44.4 (1978): 597–614. See also Taylor, William R. *Cavalier and Yankee: The Old South and American National Character*. (New York: George Braziller, 1961).

7. Pollard, Edward A. *The Lost Cause: A New Southern History of the War of the Confederates*. (New York: E. B. Treat & Co., 1866): 49.

8. See, for example, Rutherford, Mildred Lewis. *Address Delivered by Miss Mildred Lewis Rutherford: The Civilization of the Old South: What Made It: What Destroyed It: What Has Replaced It*. (Athens, GA: McGregor Co. Printers, 1916).

9. Killian, Lewis M. *White Southerners*. (New York: Random House, 1970): 10–11. Another significant contribution to this debate was George Brown Tindall's essay "Beyond the Mainstream: The Ethnic Southerners," published in *Journal of Southern History* in 1974. It is reprinted in his *The Ethnic Southerners*. (Baton Rouge: Louisiana State University Press, 1976).

10. Reed, John Shelton. *Southerners: The Social Psychology of Sectionalism*. (Chapel Hill: University of North Carolina Press, 1983): 120, and *The Enduring South: Subcultural Persistence in Mass Society*. (Chapel Hill: University of North Carolina Press, 1986 [1972]). Reed based his findings on surveys largely carried out in the 1950s and 1960s, with the most recent being 1971. Questions from the latter are reproduced in an appendix to *Southerners*. Thus, "outside interference" could be understood by white respondents as a synonym for desegregation. See also Reed's *One South: An Ethnic Approach to Regional Culture*. (Baton Rouge: Louisiana State University Press, 1982); "Southerners," *Harvard Encyclopedia of American Ethnic Groups*, ed. Stephan Thernstrom, Ann Orlov, and Oscar Handlin. (Cambridge, MA: Belknap Press of Harvard University Press, 1980): 944–948.

11. Sollors, *Beyond Ethnicity*, (1986): 176–177.

12. Roberts, Diane. "The New Dixie Manifesto," *Utne Reader* (January–February 1998): 69.

13. McPherson, Tara. "I'll Take My Stand in Dixienet—White Guys, the South and Cyberspace." *Race in Cyberspace*, ed. Beth E. Kolko, Lisa Nakamura, and Gilbert B. Rodman. (New York and London: Routledge, 2000): 126.

14. Wellman, David. *Portraits of White Racism*, 2nd ed. (Cambridge: Cambridge University Press, 1993); Dyer, Richard. *White*. (London: Routledge, 1997).

15. Carlson, Wayne. "Suicide of the West." *Southern Events*, 7.4 (2002): 10. Reproduced on the League of the South's Web site: *http://www.leagueofthe south.com/ dn-gazette/suicide-west.htm* [accessed 10 June 2004].

16. Hill, Michael. "The South and the G.O.P." On-line: *http://www.leagueofthe south.com/dn-gazette/south-gop.htm* [accessed 19 January 2001 and 2 December 2004].

17. Billig, Michael. *Banal Nationalism*. (London: Sage, 1995).

18. Kennedy, James Ronald, and Kennedy, Walter Donald. *The South Was Right!*, 2nd ed. (Gretna, LA: Pelican Publishing, 1994 [1991]): 307.

19. Roberts, Diane, and Hill, Michael. "Interview: The Southern League—Hoping the South Will Rise Again." Weekend Edition, National Public Radio, (5 May 1996).

20. Roosens, *Creating Ethnicity*, (1989): 18 (original emphasis).

21. The dates selected refer to the first and last major works identifying what came to be known as the Celtic South thesis. These were Forrest McDonald and Grady McWhiney's "The Antebellum Southern Herdsman: A Reinterpretation," *Journal of Southern History*, 41.2 (1975): 147–166, and Grady McWhiney's *Cracker Culture: Celtic Ways in the Old South*. (Tuscaloosa: University of Alabama Press, 1988). Thanks to the anonymous reviewer for suggesting the term "ethnicize" to describe this process.

22. "Partisan Conversation—Michael Hill: The Southern League," *Southern Partisan*, 14 (4th quarter 1994): 36–37.

23. Hill, Michael. Fourth Annual League of the South National Conference, Biloxi, MS. (All Points South, 1997). Transcribed from videotape. Such ascription of Celtic identity to supporters of neo-Confederacy has not been welcomed by all in the Southern United States who identify themselves as having Celtic ancestry. The Alabama Celtic Association (ACA) decided to boycott the April 2003 Southern Heritage Celtic Festival. ACA president Major Randall Massey "said the organization is concerned that the mix of Scottish clans with other heritage groups bothered the association. 'What if a photographer catches someone with a Confederate flag around a clan tent. . . . How can you guarantee this will not happen?'" Cargile, John W. "Southern Heritage Celtic Festival Boycotted," *Society of Southern Celts*, (August 2002): 1.

24. McWhiney, Grady, and Jamieson, Perry. *Attack and Die: Civil War Military Tactics and the Southern Heritage*. (Tuscaloosa: University of Alabama Press, 1982): 180.

25. Hill, James Michael. *Celtic Warfare 1595–1763*. (Edinburgh: Donald, 1986): 173.

26. Kennedy and Kennedy, *The South Was Right!* (1994): 249. The work of Grady McWhiney, some of which will be discussed here, was central to this redefinition of Southernness as a Celtic ethnicity—see Hague, Euan. "Texts as Flags: The League of the South and the Development of a Nationalist Intelligentsia in the United States 1975–2001," *Hagar: International Social Science Review*, 3.2 (2002): 299–339.

27. Wilson, Clyde. "Crackers and Roundheads," *Chronicles*, 12.10 (1988): 23.

28. Hill, Michael. Interview. "The Alan Colmes Show," *NewsTalk* 1050, WEVD, New York (19 August 1999). Transcript on-line: http://www.templeofdemocracy.com/WEVD.htm.

29. McPherson, "I'll Take My Stand in Dixienet," (2000): 124. The neo-Confederate relationship with, and opinions about, the Ku Klux Klan and other explicitly white supremacist groups treads a fine line. Empathetic with some of their white supremacist aims, but wary of being seen to associate too closely with avowed racists, neo-Confederates often publicly reject the Klan and associated groups but applaud their historical activities. For example, neo-Confederate John Chodes defends the Ku Klux Klan, claiming it has been blamed for crimes that it did not commit, because African Americans were attacked by other blacks and federal Union League members wearing Ku Klux Klan costumes. "The legend of the Klan and its alleged 'invisible empire,'" Chodes maintains, "has provided the Federal government with a golden opportunity to greatly expand its size and scope as it endlessly ferrets out real or imagined racists, not only in the South but in every corner of the United States." See his essay "The Union League: Washington's Klan," *The League of the South Papers*, No. 3 (Tuscaloosa: League of the South, 1999): 1. Another historical white suprema-

cist group active during the Reconstruction era following the Civil War was the Red Shirts. These were rifle clubs and cavalry groups which, through a campaign of intimidation and violence, restored white supremacy to South Carolina in 1876. Since 2001, LS neo-Confederate separatists have taken the name and uniform of the Red Shirts as their own—see "New League Redshirts," *Southern Patriot*, 8.4 (2001): 16; "League Redshirts A Hit," *Southern Patriot*, 8.5 (2001): 12.

30. Ignatiev, Noel. *How The Irish Became White*. (New York: Routledge, 1995): 76. See also Jacobson, Matthew Frye. *Whiteness of a Different Color: European Immigrants and the Alchemy of Race*. (Cambridge, MA: Harvard University Press, 1998).

31. Pittock, Murray H. *Celtic Identity and the British Image*. (Manchester: University of Manchester Press, 1999): 3.

32. Gans, Herbert J. "Symbolic Ethnicity: The Future of Ethnic Groups and Cultures in America," *Ethnic and Racial Studies*, 2.1 (1979): 9.

33. Ibid., 15–16.

34. Hall, Stuart. "The Question of Cultural Identity," *Modernity and Its Futures*, ed. Stuart Hall, David Held, and Tony McGrew. (Oxford: Blackwell, 1994): 291.

35. Ibid., 296.

36. Ibid., 298. (original emphasis). See also Gilroy, Paul. *There Ain't No Black in the Union Jack'—The Cultural Politics of Race and Nation*. (Chicago: University of Chicago Press, 1991 [1987]).

37. McCain, Barry Reid. "From Our Members: The Anglo-Celts," *Southern Patriot*, 3.5 (1996): 35.

38. Adler, Jerry, and Morris, Holly. "Celts vs. Anglo-Saxons," *Newsweek*, (10 August 1981): 70.

39. There is an extensive series of academic articles and monographs that together compose the Celtic South thesis. The first such article was McDonald, Forrest, and McWhiney, Grady. "The Antebellum Southern Herdsman: A Reinterpretation," *Journal of Southern History*, 41.2 (1975): 147–166. Thereafter McDonald and McWhiney collaborated regularly; see "In Search of Southern Roots," *Reviews in American History*, 5.4 (1977): 453–457; "The Celtic South," *History Today*, 30.7 (1980): 11–15; "The South from Self-sufficiency to Peonage: An Interpretation," *American Historical Review*, 85.5 (1980): 1095–1118; "Communication Regarding 'The South from Self-sufficiency to Peonage: An Interpretation,'" *American Historical Review*, 86.1 (1981): 243–244; "AHR Forum: Comparative History in Theory and Practice: A Discussion," *American Historical Review*, 87.1 (1982): 123–143; "A Response to Rowland Berthoff 'Celtic Mist over the South,'" *Journal of Southern History*, 52.4 (1986): 547–548; "Celtic South," *Encyclopedia of Southern Culture*, ed. Charles Reagan Wilson and William Ferris. (Chapel Hill: University of North Carolina Press, 1989): 1131–1132; "The Ethnic Factor in Alabama History: A Neglected Dimension," *Alabama Review*, 31.4 (1978): 256–265; "Prologue," *Cracker Culture: Celtic Ways in the Old South* by Grady McWhiney. (Tuscaloosa: University of Alabama Press, 1988): xxi–xliii; McDonald, Forrest, and McDonald, Ellen Shapiro. "The Ethnic Origins of the American People, 1790," *William and Mary Quarterly (Third Series)*, 37.2 (1980): 179–199; "Communications regarding 'The Ethnic Origins of the American People, 1790,'" *William and Mary Quarterly (Third Series)*, 37.4 (1980): 702–703; "Commentary regarding 'The Ethnic Origins of the American People, 1790,'" *William and Mary Quarterly (Third Series)*, 41.1 (1984): 129–135; "Communications Regarding 'The Ethnic Origins of the American People,

1790,'" *William and Mary Quarterly (Third Series)*, 41.4 (1984): 682–683. McWhiney, Grady. "The Revolution in Nineteenth Century Alabama Agriculture," *Alabama Review*, 31.1 (1978): 3–32; "Saving the Best from the Past," *Alabama Review*, 32.4 (1979): 243–272; "Continuity in Celtic Warfare," *Continuity*, 2 (1981): 1–18; "Education in the Old South: A Reexamination," *The Southern Enigma: Essays on Race, Class, and Folk Culture*, ed. Walter J. Fraser Jr. and Winfred B. Moore Jr. (Westport, CT: Greenwood Press, 1983): 169–188; "Ethnic Roots of Southern Violence," *A Master's Due: Essays in Honor of David Herbert Donald*, ed. William J. Cooper Jr., Michael F. Holt, and John McCardell. (Baton Rouge: Louisiana State University Press, 1985): 112–137; "Antebellum Piney Woods Culture: Continuity over Time and Place," *Mississippi's Piney Woods: A Human Perspective*, ed. Noel Polk. (Jackson: University Press of Mississippi, 1986): 40–58; *Cracker Culture: Celtic Ways in the Old South*. (Tuscaloosa: University of Alabama Press, 1988); "Celtic Roots in an 'English' Nation: Cultural Patterns for the Genealogist." Paper presented at the National Genealogical Society 8th Annual Conference. (Biloxi, MS: 1988); "The Celtic Heritage of the Old South," *Chronicles*, 13.3 (1989): 12–15; *Confederate Crackers and Cavaliers*. (Abilene, TX: McWhiney Foundation Press, 2002); McWhiney and Jamieson, *Attack and Die*, (1982); McWhiney, Grady, and McDonald, Forrest. "Celtic Names in the Antebellum Southern United States," *Names: Journal of the American Name Society*, 31.2 (1983): 89–102; McWhiney, Grady, and McDonald, Forrest. "Celtic Origins of Southern Herding Practices," *Journal of Southern History*, 51.2 (1985): 165–182; McWhiney, Grady, and Mills, Gary B. "Jimmie Davis and His Music: An Interpretation," *Journal of American Culture*, 6.2 (1983): 54–57.

40. Roberts, Diane. "The New Dixie Manifesto," *Utne Reader* (January–February 1998): 69. McWhiney's *Cracker Culture* was reviewed by David R. Wade, "The Celt as Southron," in *Southern Partisan*, 11 (3rd Quarter 1991): 50–52.

41. McDonald, "The Ethnic Factor in Alabama History," (1978): 256–265; McWhiney, *Cracker Culture*, (1988) and "The Celtic Heritage of the Old South," *Chronicles*, 13.3 (1989): 12–15.

42. McWhiney, *Cracker Culture*, (1988): 22.

43. Ibid., 38.

44. McDonald and McWhiney, "In Search of Southern Roots," (1977): 456. McDonald and McWhiney are reviewing George Brown Tindall's *The Ethnic Southerners* here, and contend that "Tindall's search for the origins of southernism, like the searches of all his predecessors, fails in the end" because of his ascription of Southerners as WASPs (white, Anglo-Saxon Protestants) and not as Celts.

45. Masters, Michael W. "We Are a People," *Southern Patriot*, 2.4 (1995): 27–28.

46. Jared Taylor (or Samuel Jared Taylor) is associated with white nationalism and publishes *American Renaissance* (Oakton, VA: The New Century Foundation, monthly). See Nieli, Russ. "Jared Taylor," *Contemporary Voices of White Nationalism in America*, ed. Carol M. Swain and Russ Nieli. (Cambridge: Cambridge University Press, 2003): 87–113; Anti-Defamation League. "American Renaissance." On-line: http://www.adl.org/learn/ext_us/amren.asp?xpicked=5&item=amren [accessed 11 September 2006].

47. McDonald and McWhiney, "The Celtic South," (1980): 15.

48. McWhiney, "Ethnic Roots of Southern Violence," (1985): 134. This assertion that Southerners are apparently drunkards because of their Celtic heritage contrasts starkly with Aspinwall's recognition of the connections, both political and theological,

between the temperance movements in Scotland and the United States in the early twentieth century. See Aspinwall, Bernard. *Portable Utopia: Glasgow and the United States, 1820–1920*. (Aberdeen: Aberdeen University Press, 1984).

49. McWhiney, *Cracker Culture*, (1988): 83.

50. Catron, James. "New Druids?" *Southern Patriot*, 4.5 (1997): 36.

51. Hill, Michael. Fourth Annual League of the South National Conference, Biloxi, MS. (All Points South, 1997). Transcribed from videotape.

52. Sebesta, Edward H. "The Confederate Memorial Tartan: Officially Approved by the Scottish Tartan Authority," *Scottish Affairs*, 31 (2000): 55–84. The connection between Scotland and the U.S. South needs more investigation. The Scottish Romantic novelist Sir Walter Scott was widely revered in the South in the nineteenth century and an influence on authors such as Thomas Dixon, who wrote *The Clansman: An Historical Romance of the Ku Klux Klan* (1905), which was the basis of D. W. Griffith's film *The Birth of a Nation*—see Chandler, James. "The Historical Novel Goes to Hollywood: Scott, Griffith and Film Epic Today," *The Birth of a Nation*, ed. Robert Lang. (New Brunswick, NJ: Rutgers University Press, 1994): 225–249. Southern Agrarian John Crowe Ransom also made a curious appeal for the Southern U.S. states to pursue a "Scottish analogue" in *I'll Take My Stand*. Arguing for a Southern nationalism that would lead not to secession but to a situation like the United Kingdom and "the position of Scotland under the British crown," Ransom suggested that this would enable "a section with a very local and peculiar culture . . . [to] be secure and respected." He continued, "And Southern traditionalists may take courage from the fact that it was Scottish stubbornness which obtained this position for Scotland; it did not come gratuitously; it was the consequence of an intense sectionalism that for fought many years before its fight was won" (p. 24). Ransom, John Crowe. "Reconstructed but Unregenerate," *I'll Take My Stand: The South and the Agrarian Tradition*, Twelve Southerners. (New York: Harper Torchbooks, Harper and Row, 1962 [1930]): 1–27. Thanks to David Stenhouse for alerting us to Ransom's essay.

53. Hill, Michael. "Celtic Justice," *Chronicles*, 22.1 (1998): 14.

54. McDonald, "The Ethnic Factor in Alabama History," (1978).

55. McDonald and McWhiney, "The Antebellum Southern Herdsman," (1975).

56. McCain, "From Our Members: The Anglo-Celts," (1996): 36 (original emphasis).

57. McWhiney, *Cracker Culture*, (1988): 41.

58. Horwitz, Tony. *Confederates in the Attic: Dispatches from the Unfinished Civil War.* (New York: Vintage, 1998): 290.

59. *Braveheart*. Review in *Southern Patriot*, 2.3 (1995): 18. See also Hague, Euan. "Scotland on Film: Attitudes and Opinions about *Braveheart*." *Études Écossaises*, 6 (1999–2000): 75–89.

60. Wilson, Clyde. "After Independence," *Southern Patriot*, 3.4 (1996): 30.

61. Cook, Mary Alice. "The Scottish-Southern Connection," *Southern Partisan*, 15 (2nd Quarter 1995): 42–43, 54; DuRocher, Steve. "The Scottish-Southern Connection, Part II," *Southern Partisan*, 15 (2nd Quarter 1995): 44–45.

62. Stringer, Tommy. "The Original Southrons," *Southern Partisan*, 19 (4th Quarter 1999): 44. Stringer had visited the Grandfather Mountain Scottish Highland Games in North Carolina, the topic of a book by Celeste Ray, *Highland Heritage: Scottish Americans in the American South*. (Chapel Hill: University of North Carolina Press, 2001). See also Ray's essay, "Scottish Heritage Southern Style," *Southern Cul-*

tures, 4.2 (1998): 28–45. For further discussion of the connection of the Celtic-South to Scotland see Hague, Euan. "Haggis and Heritage—Representing Scotland in the United States," *Culture, Consumption and Commodification,* ed. John Horne. (Eastbourne: Leisure Studies Association, 2001): 107–130.

63. McWhiney, Grady. "Jefferson Davis: Our Greatest Hero," *Southern Patriot,* 2.3 (1995): 22.

64. McWhiney, *Cracker Culture,* (1988): 149.

65. Hill, Michael. "Honor, Violence, and Civilization," *Chronicles,* 21.8 (1997): 19.

66. McWhiney, "Continuity in Celtic Warfare," (1981): 1.

67. McWhiney and Jamieson, *Attack and Die,* (1982): 180.

68. Hill, Michael. "Celtic Justice," *Chronicles,* 22.1 (1998): 13–15. In a subsequent exchange "On Celtic Culture," *Chronicles,* 22.4 (1998): 4–5, Hill's article was dismissed as "pure fantasy" by Patrick Walsh. Given the right of reply, Hill reiterated his proposal that "Celtic peoples have developed and administered their own system of private justice. . . . When our luxurious style of living inevitably gives way to the hard realities of life as our ancestors knew it, men such as these will be indispensable."

69. Hill, Michael. "Honor, Violence, and Civilization," *Chronicles,* 21.8 (1997): 17–19.

70. See, for example, Nisbett, Richard E. "Violence and U.S. Regional Culture," *American Psychologist,* 48.4 (1993): 442. See also Cohen, Dov; Nisbett, Richard E.; Bowdle, Brian F.; and Schwarz, Norbert. "Insult, Aggression, and the Southern Culture of Honor: An 'Experimental Ethnography,'" *Journal of Personality and Social Psychology,* 70.5 (1996): 945–960; Cohen, Dov. "Law, Social Policy, and Violence: The Impact of Regional Cultures," *Journal of Personality & Social Psychology,* 70.5 (1996) 961–978; Nisbett, Richard E., and Cohen, Dov. *Culture of Honor: The Psychology of Violence in the South.* (Boulder, CO: Westview Press, 1996).

71. Neo-Confederate authors that make this direct connection include McDonald, "The Ethnic Factor in Alabama History," (1978) and his "Prologue" to McWhiney's *Cracker Culture,* (1988); McWhiney and Jamieson, *Attack and Die,* (1982); Hill, *Celtic Warfare 1595–1763,* (1986); Masters, "We Are a People," (1995); and Busbice, Roger. "The Confederate Nation and Our Celtic Cousins," *Southern Events,* 4.3 (1999): 1, 19–20.

72. Chapman, Malcolm. *The Gaelic Vision in Scottish Culture.* (London: Croom Helm, 1978); *The Celts: The Construction of a Myth.* (London: Macmillan, 1992).

73. McCrone, David; Morris, Angela; and Kiely, Richard. *Scotland—The Brand: The Making of Scottish Heritage.* (Edinburgh: Edinburgh University Press, 1995): 57.

74. James, *The Atlantic Celts,* (1999): 17.

75. Arnold, Matthew. *On the Study of Celtic Literature and Other Essays.* (New York: E. P. Dutton and Co., 1919 [1867]); Renan, Ernest. *The Poetry of the Celtic Races and Other Studies.* Translated by William G. Hutchison. (London: Walter Scott Ltd., n.d. [1860]).

76. Fiske, John. "Are We Celts or Teutons? Part 1," *Appletons' Journal,* 2.28 (1869): 243–245; Part 2 in *Appletons' Journal,* 2.29 (1869): 278–279; Part 3 in *Appletons' Journal,* 2.31 (1869): 336–338; Part 4 in *Appletons' Journal,* 2.36 (1869): 499–501; Part 5 in *Appletons' Journal,* 3.41 (1870): 42–43; and Part 6 in *Appletons' Journal,* 3.44 (1870): 129–131.

77. Pittock, *Celtic Identity*, (1999): 75.

78. Ibid., 4. See also Trumpener, Katie. *Bardic Nationalism: The Romantic Novel and the British Empire.* (Princeton, NJ: Princeton University Press, 1997).

79. Pittock, *Celtic Identity*, (1999): 77.

80. Collis, John. "Celts and Politics," *Cultural Identity and Archaeology: The Construction of European Communities*, ed. Paul Graves-Brown, Siân Jones, and Clive Gamble. (London: Routledge, 1996): 172.

81. Kennedy and Kennedy, *The South Was Right!* (1994): 21.

82. McCain, "From Our Members: The Anglo-Celts," (1996): 36.

83. Hill, Michael, and Fleming, Thomas. "New Dixie Manifesto: States' Rights Will Rise Again," *Washington Post*, (29 October 1995): C03.

84. League of the South. "Declaration of Southern Cultural Independence," *Southern Patriot*, 7.2 (2000): 4. On-line: *http://www.petitionOn-line.com/cripps/petition.html* [accessed 1 November 2004].

85. See, *inter alia*, Erickson, Charlotte. *Invisible Immigrants: The Adaptation of English and Scottish Immigrants in Nineteenth-Century America.* (Coral Gables, FL: University of Miami Press, 1972); Aspinwall, *Portable Utopia*, (1984); Aspinwall, Bernard. "The Scots in the United States," *The Scots Abroad: Labour, Capital, Enterprise, 1750-1914*, ed. R. A. Cage. (London: Croom Helm, 1985): 80–110; Karras, Alan L. *Sojourners in the Sun: Scottish Migrants in Jamaica and the Chesapeake, 1740-1800.* (Ithaca: Cornell University Press, 1992); Hewitson, Jim. *Tam Blake and Co. — The Story of the Scots in America.* (Edinburgh: Canongate Books, 1993); Dobson, David. *Scottish Emigration to Colonial America, 1607-1785.* (Athens: University of Georgia Press, 1994); Hunter, James. *A Dance Called America: The Scottish Highlands, the United States, and Canada.* (Edinburgh: Mainstream Press, 1994).

86. Moltke-Hansen, David. Contribution to "AHR Forum: Comparative History in Theory and Practice: A Discussion," *American Historical Review*, 87.1 (1982): 133. In addition to this chapter, for a fuller discussion of the academic debates over the Celtic South thesis, see Hague, "Texts as Flags," (2002). The utilization of cultural geographers' work by proponents of the Celtic South thesis is examined by Edwards, Tracy. "An Analysis of the Celtic Thesis: A Re-interpretation of the American South and the Associated Argument," unpublished paper. (Syracuse, NY: Syracuse University, Department of Geography, 2000).

87. McDonald and McWhiney, "The Antebellum Southern Herdsman," (1975): 156.

88. McDonald and McDonald, "The Ethnic Origins," (1980): 195. Rowland Berthoff's review of the fallacies of the Celtic South thesis are most extensively outlined in "Celtic Mist over the South," *Journal of Southern History*, 52.4 (1986): 523-546. Berthoff was a consistent critic of the Celtic South thesis: see also his contributions to "Communications regarding 'The Ethnic Origins of the American People, 1790,'" *William and Mary Quarterly (Third Series)*, 37.4 (1980): 701-702; "AHR Forum: Comparative History in Theory and Practice: A Discussion," *American Historical Review*, 87.1 (1982): 123-143; "'A Rejoinder' to Forrest McDonald and Grady McWhiney 'A Response' to 'Celtic Mist over the South,'" *Journal of Southern History*, 52.4 (1986): 548-550.

89. McDonald and McWhiney, "The South from Self-sufficiency," (1980): 1108.

90. Berthoff, "Celtic Mist over the South," (1986): 525.

91. These expansions are in the authors' contributions to *Cracker Culture* (1988). Forrest McDonald is another prominent historian with close ties to neo-Confederacy. In addition to being a major advocate of the Celtic South thesis, he has contributed to *Southern Partisan*. For example, "Why Yankees Won't (and Can't) Leave the South Alone," *Southern Partisan*, 5.1 (1985): 15–19; "The Achievement of M. E. Bradford, Part I," *Southern Partisan*, 2.4 (1982): 34–35. His book, *A Constitutional History of the United States* (Malabar, FL: Robert E. Krieger Publishing, 1982), argues that the landmark Supreme Court desegregation ruling *Brown v. Board of Education* "rested upon a racist assumption" because although segregated schooling was evidently deleterious to African Americans, "it was not disadvantageous to whites to be deprived of blacks in their classrooms" (p. 224). McDonald also argues that in its civil rights rulings, "the Supreme Court substituted its own notions of social justice for those of the Constitution and the laws." As such, McDonald's assessments are often invoked by advocates of neo-Confederacy.

92. McCarthy, James, and Hague, Euan. "Race, Nation, and Nature: The Cultural Politics of 'Celtic' Identification in the American West," *Annals of the Association of American Geographers*, 94.2 (2004): 378–408.

93. This archaeological debate includes assessments by Megaw, Ruth, and Megaw, Vincent. "The Atlantic Celts: Ancient People or Modern Invention?" *Antiquity*, 73.282 (1999): 961–962; James, Simon. "Celts, Politics and Motivation in Archaeology," *Antiquity*, 72.275 (1998): 200–209; Cunliffe, Barry. *The Ancient Celts*. (Oxford: Oxford University Press, 1997); Collis, John. "Celtic Myths," *Antiquity*, 71.271 (1997): 195–201; Collis, "Celts and Politics," (1996).

94. Landsman, Ned. "Communications," *William and Mary Quarterly (Third Series)*, 41.4 (1984): 680–683. Landsman's attack (pp. 680–681) is directed at Forrest McDonald and Ellen Shapiro McDonald.

95. Johnson, Michael P. Review of *Cracker Culture: Celtic Ways in the Old South*, by Grady McWhiney. *Journal of Southern History*, 55.3 (1989): 490. Johnson also identifies McWhiney's eighteenth- and nineteenth-century Celtic "crackers" as "the cultural progenitors of the Agrarians," adding that this link, implicit throughout McWhiney's text, is "a somewhat implausible line of descent" (p. 490).

96. Sheehan, Anthony J. Review of *Celtic Warfare 1595–1763* by James Michael Hill. *Irish Historical Studies*, 27.105 (1990): 93.

97. McDonald and McWhiney, "The South from Self-sufficiency," (1980): 1108.

98. Dyer, *White*, (1997): 24.

99. Williams, Raymond. *Keywords: A Vocabulary of Culture and Society*. (New York: Oxford University Press, 1976): 76. Nature, which we will discuss below, is noted by Williams as "perhaps the most complex" (p. 184).

100. Ibid., 77.

101. Mitchell, Don. "There's No Such Thing as Culture: Towards a Reconceptualization of the Idea of Culture in Geography," *Transactions of the Institute of British Geographers (New Series)*, 20.1 (1995): 112–113.

102. Jackson, Peter. *Maps of Meaning: An Introduction to Cultural Geography*. (London: Unwin Hyman, 1989): 2, 180 (original emphasis).

103. Ibid., 18.

104. Duncan, James. "The Superorganic in American Cultural Geography," *Annals of the Association of American Geographers*, 70.2 (1980): 194.

105. Curiously, even though neo-Confederate activists and members of the Lega Nord have worked together, the behaviors that both associate with Celtic identity are actually quite different. Advocates of neo-Confederacy cite drunkenness, laziness, boisterousness, and commitments to family and religion as behaviors of Celtic Southerners. In contrast, the Lega Nord suggests these are the attitudes of un-Celtic southern Italians, and prefer to advocate that their constituents, the supposedly Celtic people of northern Italy, are law-abiding, hard-working, and entrepreneurial. Such an inversion of what it means to be Celtic further demonstrates how claims to ethnic identity can be manipulated, although both the Lega Nord and neo-Confederates do propound the superiority of Celtic warriors. See Hague, Euan; Giordano, Benito; and Sebesta, Edward H. "Whiteness, Multiculturalism and Nationalist Appropriation of Celtic Culture: The Case of the League of the South and the Lega Nord," *Cultural Geographies*, 12.2 (2005): 151–173; Giordano, Benito; Hague, Euan; and Sebesta, Edward H. "Asserting Celtic Roots—The Use of Celtic Culture in the Nationalist Campaigns of the Lega Nord and the League of the South," *Canadian Review of Studies in Nationalism*, 31.1–2 (2004): 23–36.

106. Hague, "Haggis and Heritage," (2001); Hague, Euan. "The Scottish Diaspora: Tartan Day and the Appropriation of Scottish Identities in the United States," *Celtic Geographies: Old Culture, New Times*, ed. David C. Harvey, Rhys Jones, Neil McInroy, and Christine Milligan. (London: Routledge, 2002): 139–156.

107. Byron, Reginald. *Irish America*. (Oxford: Clarendon Press, 1999): 261.

108. Berbrier, Mitch. "White Supremacists and the (Pan-)Ethnic Imperative: On 'European-Americans' and 'White Student Unions,'" *Sociological Inquiry*, 68.4 (1998): 498–499.

109. Vinson, John. "Reject the Yankee Creed," *Southern Patriot*, 5.5 (1998): 11.

110. Cawthon, William Lamar Jr. "George Wallace and the South, Part II," *Southern Patriot*, 6.1 (1999): 6.

111. Breuilly, John. *Nationalism and the State*, 2nd ed. (Chicago: University of Chicago Press, 1993 [1982]): 61.

112. Williams, *Keywords*, (1976): 188.

113. Ibid.

114. Michael Hill, interview with Diane Roberts, National Public Radio (5 May 1996) (emphasis added).

115. Cawthon, William Lamar Jr. "George Wallace and the South," *Southern Patriot*, 5.6 (1998): 6.

116. Vinson, John. "Know Your Mission," *Southern Patriot*, 3.1 (1996): 5 (emphasis added).

117. Hill, Michael. "A Righteous Anger," *Southern Patriot*, 5.3 (1998): 2.

118. Malvasi, Mark G. *The Unregenerate South: The Agrarian Thought of John Crowe Ransom, Allen Tate, and Donald Davidson*. (Baton Rouge: Louisiana State University Press, 1997): 227.

119. Ibid. Malvasi's connections to neo-Confederacy are discussed in Chapter 2, note 67.

120. Hill, Michael. "A People without History," *Southern Patriot*, 2.1 (1995): 2.

121. Williams, *Keywords*, (1976): 188–189.

122. See Williams, Raymond. "Social Darwinism," *The Limits of Human Nature*, ed. Jonathan Benthall. (London: Allen Lane, 1973): 115–130, and Hawkins, Mike.

Social Darwinism in European and American Thought, 1860–1945: Nature as Model and Nature as Threat. (Cambridge: Cambridge University Press, 1997). Charles Darwin had little to do with the development of social Darwinism, initially opposing its contentions. Toward the end of his career, however, Darwin began to ascribe to Spencer's theories of social Darwinism, human competition, and survival of the fittest.

123. Hill, Michael. "A Vital Economic Issue," *Southern Patriot*, 9.2 (2002): 2.

124. Hall, Stuart. "The Question of Cultural Identity," *Modernity and Its Futures,* ed. Stuart Hall, David Held, and Tony McGrew. (Oxford: Blackwell, 1994): 304.

125. Hill, Michael. "Kith and Kin," *Southern Patriot*, 3.5 (1996): 34.

126. McCain, "From Our Members: The Anglo-Celts," (1996): 36.

127. Hill, Michael. "Letters to the Editor: A Scavenger Hunt for Villains," *Wall Street Journal*, (5 June 1995): A15.

CHAPTER 5

Neo-Confederacy and the Understanding of Race

EUAN HAGUE AND EDWARD H. SEBESTA

The previous chapters have demonstrated that neo-Confederacy comprises a comprehensive worldview and consistent ideological belief system. Having examined neo-Confederate understandings of religion, gender, and Southern ethnicity, our contributors have established that proponents of neo-Confederacy envision a white, Anglo-Celtic ethnicity, a belief in patriarchy, so-called "orthodox" Christianity, and social arrangements that are hierarchical and perceived through the lens of social Darwinism. In this chapter we turn to explore how understandings of race are central to neo-Confederacy.

In his analysis of racist discourses, Teun van Dijk argues that in the United States, "specific buzz words, such as *busing* and *quota*, are used to prevent the civil rights of minorities from 'going too far.'"[1] Many neo-Confederate publications, including *Southern Partisan, Southern Patriot,* and *Chronicles,* regularly use such language in their frequent discussions of race, immigration, and associated legislation. Neo-Confederates also propose that cultures and ethno-racial characteristics are inherited, that behaviors are innate and immutable, and that it is unnatural and thus impossible for two or more ethno-racial groups to co-exist in the same space on equal terms. Racial integration is rejected, and programs such as affirmative action are dismissed as unnatural strategies of social engineering, doomed to failure and vindictively imposed on white Southerners to increase the power of central government by gaining the sanction of nonwhite groups. Furthermore, neo-Confederates systematically attack civil rights and challenge egalitarianism, democracy, and social equality. The alternative, for advocates of neo-Confederacy, is to pursue the formation of small, mono-ethnic states with localized legislative powers in which, given the analyses presented thus far, inequality and hierarchy would exist as results of supposedly natural processes.

In sum, the neo-Confederate perspective is that equal rights for all racial and ethnic groups are a foolhardy idea, advocated and promoted by malicious politicians eager to increase their own power and that of the federal government in general. As a result, the whole direction of U.S. society following the Civil War has been wrong because, beginning with Reconstruction, according to P. J. Byrnes in *Southern Partisan,* "the federal government assumed a role in the lives of citizens that the Founding Fathers never intended; and the results have been a growing usurpation of local sovereignty, the rise of moral anarchy, and political absolutism."[2]

The Southern Poverty Law Center has argued that the "neo-Confederate movement [is] increasingly rife with white supremacists and racist ideology."[3] Yet despite this evaluation, prominent neo-Confederates insist that their ideology is not racist and justify this contention in at least five different ways. First, they point to their few African American supporters, such as H. K. Edgerton and *Southern Partisan* columnist Walter Williams.[4] Second, neo-Confederate writers question the very concept of racism or define it either so narrowly or so broadly as to render it useless. For example, the League of the South (LS) has asked rhetorically: "We'd like to know where 'racism' or 'segregation' is condemned as sin in the Bible," implying that in the absence of such a condemnation, racist beliefs are morally justified.[5] Similarly, by using quotation marks and sarcastically saying that this "sin" is "modern," William L. Cawthon Jr. intimates a failure to understand what racism actually entails and suggests that the concept was recently invented and thus has little legitimacy.[6] In turn, Wayne Carlson, writing in the neo-Confederate publication *Southern Events,* proposes that the "only legitimate meaning" of racism is one that sees the practice "as stemming from the deliberate attack upon someone, or some group, seeking to do them harm solely because of their race."[7] This narrow definition, in which only premeditated assault is considered racism, is highly problematic and dismisses commonly accepted examples of racism such as offensive depictions of African Americans in nineteenth-century cartoons and literature. Limiting the definition of racism to calculated violence serves to displace its practice onto extremists such as neo-Nazis, abrogating racism that exists in other sections of society.[8] At the opposite end of the scale, Thomas Fleming in *Chronicles* has contended that "if racism means nothing more than naïve ethnic prejudice, then virtually everyone in this world is either a racist or a hypocrite."[9]

Third, advocates of neo-Confederacy preempt accusations of racism by claiming from the outset that they are not racist. This practice is typical of what critical race theorist Teun van Dijk calls "disclaimers" that seek to maintain a veneer of tolerance while preserving white dominance.[10] For example, the LS has a statement on its web site to the effect that the organization is inclusive and will seek legal recourse against those who claim otherwise. Similarly, neo-Confederates regularly feel the need to stress, as Barry Reid McCain, notable proponent of the Celtic South thesis, does in *Southern Partisan*, "the obligatory statement of the Southern male before he is allowed to comment on race. . . . I AM NOT A RACIST, nor have I ever been one, etc., etc.," before proceeding to claim that "race is a primary factor in the survival and definition of our Southern culture. . . . It is not a racist act to defend one's race, and this needs to be done. This is basic to our survival."[11]

A fourth strategy is to dismiss the allegation and turn the issue back onto those who raise it, as the League of the South's Michael Hill has advised followers: "Let us not flinch when our enemies call us racists. . . . Rather, just reply with, 'So, what's your point?'"[12] This is accompanied by a fifth tactic, a deliberate avoidance of the topic. The neo-Confederate LS, for example, neatly elides the issue of race by articulating a commitment to colorblindness: "When we send out a membership application, we don't know to whom we are sending it, and we don't have any category marked 'race.' So when people ask me how many black members we have, I tell them honestly I don't know."[13] Despite these strategies, there is no doubt that supporters of neo-Confederacy see their struggle as one in which race is fundamental, and this leads proponents to regularly comment upon the practice of race relations in the United States.

Racial Segregation

At the conference which founded the League of the South in 1994, Thomas Fleming, a subsequent director of the organization, angrily declared:

> The national government has been using armed force to suppress the South ever since the 1950s. They have beaten us black and blue with their civil rights legislation that has nothing to do with the rights of black Americans and everything to do with the imposing of the tyranny of Federal judges.[14]

Such a position is typical of neo-Confederate activists. The central assertion is that the speaker's position is one of opposition to federal government activity. The implication is, however, fundamentally about race. As Halberstam and others make clear, the presence of federal troops ensuring the safety of African Americans in the South was critical to the success of the civil rights movement.[15] Here Fleming utilizes deixis, the rhetorical technique (outlined in Chapter 4) that enables a speaker to generate a dichotomy of oppositional perspectives.[16] Eliding the issue of race, Fleming recasts the civil rights movement as a power struggle between the local residents who opposed it ("us") and a tyrannical "national government" and "Federal" authorities ("they"/ "their"). Hill similarly argues:

> The latest stage in the nationalization of government and the destruction of our original confederal system occurred in the 1950s and 1960s. During these decades the government moved into the South under judicial decree and destroyed the social fabric of communities in the name of civil rights. By taking control of school and voting districts and by making private property (lunch counters and other so-called "public accommodations") subject to federal regulation, Washington forced the retreat of many Southerners from their public duties and responsibilities.[17]

Both Fleming and Hill were addressing supporters: Fleming at a conference, Hill in an essay that appeared in the LS publication *Southern Patriot*. Hill envisions civil rights as an imposition on unwilling "Southerners" by a wanton federal government, and federal authorities are seen as destructive, dismantling the "social fabric of communities." In the 1950s and 1960s, writes Hill, vindictive U.S. authorities were involved in an unjustifiable invasion of the South—"the government *moved into* the South" and did so not by congressional, presidential, or constitutional authority, but merely on the whims of "judicial decree," implying an undemocratic process. Control over schools, for example, was taken away, again insinuating that it was illegitimate. In this passage Hill does not specifically mention race or desegregation, but the period he discusses (1950s and 1960s) and the assertion of "civil rights" suggests that changing race relations are at the core of his account. Of course, the lunch counters and "so-called 'public accommodations'" that Hill bewails ("so-called" and in quotation marks to imply these public areas are not really public and should be operated as private owners see fit) were racially segregated before federal intervention. Despite this reality, Hill avoids the issue of racial desegregation, dwelling on the issue of the expansion of federal power that is supposedly the cause of the destruction he describes. Indeed, Hill suggests that African American constitutional rights were *not* the rationale for federal action—these seemingly damaging processes were carried out "*in the name of* civil rights," implying that the federal government acted to accrue power for itself, not to genuinely ensure rights for all citizens.

Hill and Fleming, co-authors of the New Dixie Manifesto, interpret the 1950s and 1960s as the beginning of the end of the type of society their supporters favored. It was during this period that the civil rights movement empowered African Americans, and immigration from Latin America increased following the passage of the 1965 Immigration Act (or Hart-Celler Act), which also ended the national origins quota system that had largely limited immigration to Europeans. Comparing 1960s civil rights legislation and its subsequent impact with federal efforts to rebuild the South after the Civil War and the abolition of slavery, neo-Confederates such as Fleming argue that civil rights were imposed on the South by malicious federal authorities, repeating the experiences of Reconstruction (1865–1877) for another generation:

> The fruits of the first Reconstruction of the 1860's and 1870's were Jim Crow laws, the Ku Klux Klan, and a corrosive legacy of bitterness that still lingers on the tongue as a sour aftertaste. The second Reconstruction of the 1960's and 1970's is only now abating, and what splendid triumphs we can record for it; the shambles, literally, we have made of our urban school systems, a black population that is not only reduced to what could be permanent peonage to the federal government but is also subject to high rates of violent crime (as perpetrators and victims), drug abuse, bastardy, and AIDS. The triumph is even greater, if we take into consideration the increased racial polarization that has afflicted the nation. Don't be fooled by polls or pieties. Racial attitudes are harder and meaner than they ever were.[18]

Here Fleming argues that the African American population has actually suffered as a result of civil rights legislation. Rather than liberated, Fleming contends that African Americans find themselves in "permanent peonage to the federal government," and at risk of crime, AIDS, and a series of other social ills that disproportionately affect the African American community. This represents a common strategy in neo-Confederate writing on race, namely to argue that civil rights legislation has failed the African Americans, primarily because it was federally mandated. Fleming even suggests that the United States would be better off had nineteenth-century Reconstruction and 1960s civil rights legislation not occurred, and that racial antagonisms are now at an all-time high: "Racial attitudes are harder and meaner than they ever were." What is absent from Fleming's statement is revealing. If these are the most "polariz[ed]" racial relations "ever," then race relations were somehow less antagonistic in the periods of slavery, the Black Codes, and Jim Crow segregation. This contention is also made in a *Southern Patriot* article in which an anonymous essayist argues that the "racial harmony" of the "Christian Old South" was destroyed by vindictive U.S. authorities during Reconstruction, and the federal government fomented racial antagonisms in the South that persist to this day.[19] To restore "racial harmony," according to this *Southern Patriot* contributor, requires a return to the paternalism of the nineteenth century, an era when assumedly benevolent whites brought African Americans to Christianity, before Union troops and subsequent legislation tore apart these agreeable arrangements and initiated the processes that have led to today's racial hostilities. The belief that the racial arrangements existing before the civil rights legislation of the 1960's generated a harmonious society is reasserted elsewhere by Fleming, who states that during the twentieth century, racial segregation enabled African Americans to flourish: "Looking back at the 1940's and 50's," he suggests, "it is hard for an honest man not to regard those decades as the highwater mark of black life in these United States."[20] To suggest that race relations were better under slavery and segregation, given the brutalities of both periods, must be taken to represent a white supremacist perspective.

Advancing a similar argument in *Southern Patriot*, William L. Cawthon has claimed that the practice of racial "segregation is not evil or wrong. It is simply a policy to promote the integrity of a group." Racial integration, on the other hand, is immoral and has harmed every aspect of U.S. society because it promulgates "the merger and therefore the ultimate extinction of two separate peoples." "The segregated society of the South," Cawthon concludes, "was far, far more moral than is modern American society."[21] For Cawthon, the "merger . . . of two separate peoples" is unconscionable; racial groups must be kept apart to avoid mutual "extinction." How this "extinction" is a consequence of desegregation is unstated, although *Southern Partisan* readers were warned by Robert Whitaker in 1986 that miscegenation is "the final solution to the white problem."[22] Almost twenty years later, Samuel Francis, writing in *Chronicles*, saw the election of Barack Obama as a senator from Illinois in 2004 as indicative of a concerning trend toward "multiracial persons." With a white American mother and a black African father, Obama was identified as the type of person whose very being is a result of "the multiracial and multicultural mess toward which mass immigration and the dwindling birth-rates of white Americans are leading [and] . . . the homogenization of race, culture, region, class, religion, and nation into the same stew."[23] Francis's fear of racial mixing and miscegenation is evident in his concern over the falling birthrate among whites, as well as his belief that "the rulers of the New America will have to be people largely indistinguishable from him [Obama]." Perhaps this is what Cawthon also fears when claiming that racial "extinction" will occur unless group "integrity" is preserved.

Reconstruction

Given the invocation of Reconstruction as a period during which federal authorities provoked racial animosity between whites and blacks, it is instructive to understand how neo-Confederate ideologues envision this era. Frank Conner's *The South Under Siege,* for example, contends that congressional proposals for Reconstruction comprised a "long-range master plan for impoverishing, subjugating, dominating, and humiliating the Southerners, while destroying their culture and brainwashing them into third-rate copies of Northerners." The result was that "the South lost its manhood during Reconstruction—and never regained it."[24] To make his evaluations, Conner draws upon brothers Walter Donald Kennedy and James Ronald Kennedy, leading neo-Confederate authors who argue that Reconstruction was an "evil scheme" that accomplished "evil goals" and destroyed the Constitution.[25] In addition, Conner identifies as one of his main sources a *Southern Partisan* special issue in which Reconstruction was called "the Southern holocaust,"[26] and self-identified paleoconservative Paul Gottfried rejected current historical interpretations of Reconstruction as "leftwing elitist," "hateful," and "ranting."[27] Gottfried proposed instead a return to texts like *The Tragic Era* by Claude G. Bowers that describes African Americans as lazy, predatory, "primitive and ignorant," a "Congo crowd," "living in idleness and squalor," who while enslaved were, in contrast, "fat and contended . . . warmly attached to an indulgent master" and "naturally kindly and trustful," but, following emancipation, raped white women insatiably.[28]

Michael Andrew Grissom, author of the important neo-Confederate text *Southern by the Grace of God,* maintains that "in the mild form of slavery practiced in the South [African Americans] would more fittingly have been called servants."[29] Describing Reconstruction as "wicked" and a "nightmare," Grissom cites as an authority the early-twentieth-century novelist Thomas Dixon.[30] Dixon was an "obsessed racist," and his novels celebrate the Ku Klux Klan and portray African Americans as lascivious, wild, and ignorant (see Chapter 8).[31] For Grissom, however, Dixon is to be applauded: "For a true sampling of the tenor of the times, it is highly recommended that the reader obtain a copy of Dixon's 1905 classic, *The Clansman.*" Dixon's text, explains Grissom, "is a revelation to most Americans who are never exposed to the truth," and its grotesque racist caricatures, although fictional, "are mirror images of people he knew."[32]

By describing Dixon's novels as a "true sampling" of the Reconstruction era, Grissom is implying that other assessments of the period are false. Similarly, *Southern Partisan* applauds Bowers's "traditional view" of Reconstruction for its "accuracy," in "stark contrast" to recent examinations of the period by historians Eric Foner and Richard Nelson Current.[33] The implication is, of course, that the "traditional view" is "accura[te]" and that recent historical scholarship on Reconstruction is erroneous because it highlights the racism of authors such as Bowers and Dixon. Praising texts written before World War II and encouraging sympathizers to refer to them for definitive descriptions of U.S. history is a common neo-Confederate strategy, as is republishing these old texts and recommending them to the growing number of families who homeschool their children (see Chapter 7).[34]

Martin Luther King

Neo-Confederates identify the post–World War II civil rights era and associated federal legislation outlawing racial segregation as the moment when the moral and cultural decline of the United States accelerated and harmonious race relations were destroyed. It is useful, therefore, to investigate neo-Confederate hostility toward the civil rights leader Martin Luther King Jr., whose "dream" of racial integration and equality, Joseph Sobran told *Southern Partisan* readers, has become "America's nightmare" because civil rights have "spawned" violent African American criminals who target whites. "Whatever King and his ilk intended," Sobran avers, "black thugs across the country got the message that they could murder, rape and rob with some covert sympathy from black leaders and white liberals."[35]

Thomas Fleming has called King an "intemperate and vicious revolutionar[y]," who, like other African American leaders Jesse Jackson and Stokely Carmichael, is "the very model of a degraded demagogue who addicts his followers to the stimulating but debilitating fix of greed and envy."[36] One of the most outrageous neo-Confederate rejections of King appears in Frank Conner's *The South under Siege*. In an anti-Semitic tirade, Conner maintains that other than in oratory skills, King was largely inept and merely a puppet controlled by Jews whose efforts to impose diversity and multiculturalism on the United States, advance liberalism, and disrupt Christianity are ongoing. Conner maintains that "Jewish activists" provided the financing and manpower for the civil rights movement. "The Jewish-influenced national news media," explains Conner, largely coordinated King's campaign, and without the support of Jews in government and academic positions, "there would have been no 1960s Southern black-civil-rights movement." For Conner, the civil rights movement was a period when "Northern Jews wage[d] all-out ideological war against the White South" in an effort to "destroy the white Southern culture and bring the white Southerners under complete control of the federal government, in order to create an unforgettable object lesson for the rest of the Gentiles in the U.S."[37]

Given this animosity toward King, the federal holiday in his honor is greeted with annual outrage by neo-Confederates, who regularly try to prevent its observance.[38] When Congress created the King holiday in 1983, the *Southern Partisan*'s Richard Quinn lamented that "many other Americans lived lives more deserving of honor" and suggested the "sponsors of King Day chose a symbol that presses salt in the wounds of those old enough to remember and lies to those too young to understand." The holiday should not have been established because

> its purpose is vitriolic and profane. . . . King's memory represents, more than anything else, the idea that institutional arrangements—laws, ordinances and traditions—should be subordinated to the individual's conscience. . . . The blacks have chosen a man who represents not their emancipation. . . . Rather, they have chosen a man whose role in history was to lead his people into a perpetual dependence on the welfare state, a terrible bondage of body and soul.[39]

The tenor of Quinn's essay suggests that politicians only honored King because it was politically correct to do so. They neither know who King really was nor realize that the very civil rights legislation King pushed for has actually harmed African Americans. For Quinn, King is not worthy of veneration because he refused to abide by the laws of the day (viz., racial segregation), disrupting the social order in a manner that was both self-serving and illegitimate. *Southern Partisan* essayists typically propose that they know the truth about King, which is supposedly hidden from the general public.[40] Defending his vote against the King federal holiday, North Carolina senator Jesse Helms told *Southern Partisan* that on Capitol Hill he had merely made "a matter of record some of the facts that were acknowledged to be true and accurate by those who criticized me," and stated that opposition to his stance against the King holiday was representative of "efforts over the past quarter century to reshape American society to a secular and materialist mold."[41] In a subsequent *Southern Partisan* interview, Mississippi senator Trent Lott echoed Helms, claiming the King holiday was "basically wrong" and that many people were "more deserving" of recognition than the civil rights leader.[42] Other contributors to magazines promoting neo-Confederacy also fulminated against the King holiday. In February 1984, after Virginia's legislature established a King holiday and simultaneously discontinued the state's Confederate Memorial Day, John Hurley subsequently explained in *Southern Partisan* that the motivation of state officials was not to honor King, but to avoid charges of racism:

> With this bold stroke they are telling us that the greatest army that ever took the field is to be forgotten. Our brave ancestors, who defended home and hearth and in the face of overwhelming odds refused to accept the premise that it was better to be Fed than dead, are to be excised from the pages of history. . . . Forget the veteran. Forget heritage. Forget the dead. Forget the past. All must go: Constitution, family, gender distinction, heritage and Christian culture itself. The important thing is that no one level the finger of accusation at the legislature and make the dreaded charge of "racist."[43]

Michael Hill has also suggested that the Martin Luther King holiday is illegitimate. Using quotation marks to implicitly question King's credentials, Hill states that "The 'Reverend' 'Dr.' Martin Luther King, Jr., far from being the saint of recent liberal myth, was nothing but a philandering, plagiarizing, left-wing agitator." It is fear of being accused of racism that means the place of King cannot be challenged. Just as Hurley proposed that Virginia's inauguration of a King holiday would somehow precipitate the end of civilization, so too does Hill, who says that "only a sick and reprobate society" would honor King rather than nineteenth-century Confederate leaders like Robert E. Lee or Stonewall Jackson, who were "paragons of Christian manhood."[44] Continuing his commentary, Hill insists that the King holiday legitimates "every leftist perversity—hate crimes legislation, legalized infanticide, feminist and sodomite rights, gun control, unchecked Third World immigration, radical environmentalism, racial quotas, forced busing, reparations for slavery, etc.," and that the African American civil rights leader has become "the secular messiah of liberaldom" that prioritizes "the belief that 'all men are created equal.'" "If you want a multicultural, de-Christianized America in which our European Christian heritage will be obliterated," Hill tells supporters via the LS web site, "then by all means honor Martin Luther King, Jr."[45]

The civil rights era and its most prominent leader are thus touchstones for advocates of neo-Confederacy, whose intense focus on this period, and despite appeals to the contrary, demonstrate that changing race relations are a fundamental factor informing neo-Confederacy. To the authors quoted here, Martin Luther King is a liar and adulterer, a false idol in whose name federal authorities and liberal activists (and in Conner's case, Jews) are trying to erase Christianity from the American landscape and impose an egalitarianism that will erode the very foundations of the United States. The civil rights movement that King led in the 1960s is interpreted as a catalyst for such evils, and, as a result, officially honoring King is tantamount to approving this supposedly detrimental transformation of American society.

The Civil Rights Legacy: School Desegregation and Affirmative Action

Leading neo-Confederate venues such as *Southern Partisan* and *Chronicles* consistently attack policies like affirmative action and school desegregation with broadsides that range from fears of miscegenation to assertions that jobs are allocated on a quota basis and that all people suffer as a result.[46] Kennedy and Kennedy, for example, locate the demise of livable society in the civil rights era and derisively refer to desegregation and other civil rights legislation as "schemes" and "experiments" employed by "liberals" working toward the "goal of human equality." Implying that these policies constitute a test that in their opinion has failed, Kennedy and Kennedy utilize the linguistic techniques of deixis and the buzz words of racist discourse to claim that they, like other "Southern people . . . have been forced to endure such insults as busing, racial quotas, minority set-asides, affirmative action plans, reverse discrimination, and a discriminatory South-only Voting Rights Act."[47] These civil rights legacies, and their ongoing practice, regularly animate neo-Confederates.

Regarding school desegregation, which was initiated by the 1954 Supreme Court decision *Brown v. Board of Education of Topeka, Kansas,* we turn to the words of leading proponent of neo-Confederacy Michael Andrew Grissom:

It has been said, and truthfully so, that the white man liked the negro, who was jolly, light-hearted, good-natured, and trustworthy—all of which are admirable traits in any man. It must also be recognized, however, and with no unkind intention, that never in the wildest imagination of the southern white man did he ever, when purchasing black workers from Yankee slave traders, intend for descendents of Africans to become marriage prospects for his sons and daughters.

And thus it was, when the order of the Supreme Court fell like an atomic bomb on the civilization of the South. On May 17, 1954, the highest court of the land decreed that all schools would be required to integrate, forcing the white southerner to send his children into a school, the traditional institution which produces boyfriend-girlfriend relationships, now burdened with the added complication of the black factor. The counsel of generations was dissolved in an instant. . . . The political machinery was in place for forcing wholesale integration upon the peaceful people of the South. It was inevitable. The two races were going to be rammed into one another head-on. . . . There was but one solitary aim: *Mix the races.*[48]

For Grissom, school desegregation was not about providing equal educational opportunities for African Americans, nor was it a rejection of the "separate but equal" understandings of provisions for African Americans and whites established by the 1896 *Plessy v. Ferguson* Supreme Court decision. It was a federal effort to "mix the races," the consequence of which would be that African Americans would "become marriage prospects" for the children of white Southern men. Grissom's basic concern, despite his disclaimer that he means no ill intent, is about the reproductive sexuality of future generations and miscegenation. Describing desegregation as "social engineering" that is "forced" and "always artificial,"[49] Grissom proceeds to complain that following the 1954 *Brown v. Board of Education* decision, "every legal barrier to inter-racial marriage has been nullified," and that television programs "promote, through implausibly hypothetical scenarios, black and white togetherness." Echoing Kennedy and Kennedy in his use of deixis and racist discourse, Grissom bemoans "quotas," "integrated schools, and blacks at the *front* of the bus!" The consequence is that "we've been bussed, cussed, and thrust into close encounters of all kinds . . . in an effort to merge the black and white races of the South into one swirling mass of amalgamated humanity."[50]

After echoing the same fears about racial integration that William Cawthon perceived as causing the "extinction of two separate peoples," and that Samuel Francis envisioned as a "stew" in which racial identities are homogenized, Grissom, like other neo-Confederates, proposes that desegregation resulted in the loss of African American jobs, communities, and facilities such as schools. For Grissom, racial segregation meant "blacks and whites dwelt in harmony" and "racial trouble was minimal."[51] Alongside the erasure of racial distinction resulting from interracial marriage, Grissom's assessment proposes that desegregation actually worsens conditions for African Americans as well as the white community.

Published by the Rockford Institute based in Rockford, Illinois, a city that in the 1990s was mandated to desegregate its schools (see Introduction), *Chronicles* has regularly featured writers who argue that school desegregation has done anything but raise the educational levels of African Americans. Court desegregation orders are presented to readers as "exorbitantly expensive social engineering schemes."[52] According to Fleming, desegregation spending is used to "boost the morale of minority students and their parents" through practices like "weekend trips to expensive resorts," and "no matter how they rig the tests or dumb them down, the gap between rich and poor, black and white stays the same."[53] Similarly, in a review of desegregation cases throughout the United States that discusses their numerous shortcomings, Joyce Haws notes efforts in Delaware where, "over the 19 years of the scheme's implementation, the 'achievement gap' between black and white students has *widened*—not an uncommon occurrence in desegregation cases."[54] Grissom concludes that such evidence is exoneration. Racially segregated schooling, he maintains, "is vindicated with every passing day" because "public, integrated schools are in a state of unparalleled deterioration and are unable to serve the educational needs of black students. . . . Schools that have the extra burden of mixing black and white students are not serving either race well."[55] One result of such attitudes toward racially integrated education is the increasing practice of home schooling among neo-Confederates (see Chapter 7). Much like other neo-Confederate arguments about late-twentieth-century society, therefore, assessments of school desegregation generate a sense that federal civil rights programs are at best inappropriate and at worst malignant.

The supposedly anti-white implementation of affirmative action measures also animates neo-Confederates. Documenting the decline in wages in real terms under policies enacted since the 1970s, Michael Hill has informed readers of *Southern Patriot* that this is not a result of "deregulation, corporate downsizing, the decline of union membership, and a static minimum wage," nor of outsourcing or immigration. Rather, "the cause of the disparity is quite simple: a politically correct corporate culture of institutionalized race and sex quotas that discriminates against our young white males," that is, affirmative action.[56]

To believers in neo-Confederacy, African Americans as well as whites have been negatively impacted by affirmative action. Because "blacks have been encouraged to blame all their miseries on racism" and "look to the government and the judiciary to solve their problems," former *Southern Partisan* editor Warren Leamon explained, affirmative action policies that federal authorities have implemented mean that "competent and incompetent blacks are lumped together as receivers of special favors." When coupled with school desegregation, the result is "that black political power decreases daily." The way out of this situation, be it pursued by the African American community or others, is to react against school busing and affirmative action: "What seems inevitable," Leamon concludes, "is some form of segregation." Admitting that "to some, such a view will seem realistic and commonsensical; to others, cynical and racist," Leamon proposes that racial segregation was "simultaneously an attempt to produce harmony between the races and to suppress a race, [and] was defended by good men and used by evil ones."[57]

If the outcomes of the civil rights movement served neither the white community, who neo-Confederates argue now face discrimination as a result of affirmative action policies, nor the African American community, who have lost power and see no educational gains as a result, and the solution to this state of affairs is a proposed return to some form of racial segregation, then who did gain from the civil rights movement and its subsequent legislation? The answer is provided for *Chronicles* readers by Thomas Fleming:

> Not only did the civil rights movement succeed in thrusting a tyrannical national government upon school districts, business, and local governments, it also deliberately destroyed the then-existing networks of power in the black community. . . . Our experiment in government-imposed civil rights has been an unmitigated disaster for everyone except the bureaucrats, social workers, and affirmative action appointees who are its principal beneficiaries.[58]

Nation, Ethnicity, and Multiculturalism

Critical race theorists Michael Omi and Howard Winant argue that "the racial order anchored by the state [has] destabilized" as a result of the civil rights movement, and racial politics in the United States has been rewritten by initiatives such as affirmative action and school desegregation.[59] The current incarnation of neo-Confederacy has developed in this late-twentieth- and early-twenty-first-century political context. Another legacy of the civil rights movement is the concept of multiculturalism, the meaning and import of which continues to be debated. For some, multiculturalism promises greater equality, while for others it is merely a conduit for maintaining the status quo (i.e., white privilege), albeit with a surface-level recognition of a multiracial society. Still others have concluded in the wake of multiculturalism and its attendant politics that supposedly homogeneous national communities and cultural traditions no longer exist — if they ever did. In part this idea has emerged as an antiracist discourse that advocates "equality among multiple cultures"; indeed, Avery Gordon and Christopher Newfield contend that some invocations of multiculturalism purposely bypass the issue of race, referring instead to America's "cultural pluralism."[60] Yet one consequence of this, Omi notes, is actually a "racialization of politics," albeit one where race is typically implied rather than explicitly outlined.[61] Whatever its guise, the concept of multiculturalism is taken by many on the political right to be a denigration of U.S. traditions, and Newfield and Gordon see amongst conservative populists like Rush Limbaugh "a dread of *cultural* coexistence with the different, even when the different ones could still be *economically and politically* subordinated."[62]

In neo-Confederate publications, the United States is often portrayed as a "multicultural empire," and as such is presumed to be invalid as a nation.[63] For those espousing neo-Confederacy, the base unit for a nation is ethnicity, and the preferred national form is a "homogeneous republic"—an ideal that neo-Confederates often trace to the founding of the United States.[64] Although neo-Confederate documents never quite specify how a "homogeneous republic" is to be attained or its degree of homogeneity evaluated, we propose that race and ethnicity are central to the ideology. For proponents of neo-Confederacy, ethnic distinctions are fundamental. An ethnically heterogeneous national population is considered a contradiction in terms, evidence of an imperial United States that, according to Michael Hill,

> will necessarily be hostile towards the interests of the founding stock of the country (historically-speaking, that would be white, Western European, Christian folks) who might wish to preserve their own power base grounded in the founding principles of America.[65]

Examining the worldwide increase of separatist nationalist movements in the 1990s in *Southern Partisan,* William Lamar Cawthon Jr. argues that the central meaning of the word "nation" is that it identifies "a people with common attributes" and "thus blood, kin, family past, tradition, and the culture accompanying them are all bound up in what it means to be a nation."[66] Cawthon proceeds to identify the South as "a classic nation" worthy of independence. This identification is because, as we explored in previous chapters, a key element in neo-Confederacy is its explicit identification of whiteness, European and Christian identities, and recognition of the "Anglo-Celtic" ethnicity of the Southern United States. Having such a strong ethnicity merits recognition as a "nation," a political concept that *Chronicles* editor Thomas Fleming explains:

> The Latin *natio,* derived from the verb *nascor* ("to be born"), originally signified birth and then came also to mean people connected by blood: a tribe or race. If *patria* is primarily a social and cultural concept, *natio* is essentially biological and racial.[67]

The implication of such a definition is that multiracial nations, such as the United States, are fundamentally artificial. A nation is, within the neo-

Confederate imagination, necessarily founded upon ethnicity which is, in turn, incontestable biological and racial reality. League of the South board member Franklin Sanders understands a world where "ethnic separatism is now the global political norm," the consequence of which is that "ethnic realities have already dismembered World War I gerrymanders like Czechoslovakia and Yugoslavia, and the Great Eater of Nationalities, the USSR, has vomited up its captive nations."[68] Ethnicity is reality, while multiethnic nations are considered to be gerrymandered constructs that cannot hold. Similarly, nations built on ideologies such as Communism are destined to collapse because "ideological identity has wilted while ethnic identity (always as deeply rooted as life itself) has blossomed." "For Southern patriots, the outlook couldn't offer more hope," according to Sanders, because, given these definitions, it is reasonable to assume that the United States as a multiethnic nation-state sustained by ideologies of capitalism and democracy will inevitably fragment along ethnic lines. As the Confederacy is one of the "captive nations" within the gerrymandered United States and because its (white) population supposedly exhibits a strong Anglo-Celtic "Southern identity" which "over 125 years of Reconstruction have failed to erase," an independent Confederacy is preordained.[69]

Precisely because numerous "sectional (not to mention racial and ethnic) cultures" coexist within the United States, leaving it without a unified national identity, explains Michael Washburn in *Chronicles*, the country was "never really legitimate" and does not, therefore, constitute a "true" nation.[70] For neo-Confederate authors, the idea of a multiethnic or multiracial nation is a contradiction in terms. Genuine nations are ethnically distinct. Ethnoracial distinction means that each ethnic group needs its own discrete territory and, when added to the social Darwinism evident in neo-Confederacy, the result is a belief that ethnic groups fight for the space in which to establish their nations:

> Whether the differences are purely ethnic, purely economic, or a mixture of the two, it is hard for two peoples to inhabit the same space at the same time. Nations and peoples are families, if only in myth, and families must look out for their own interests. In the subhuman world, the law that goes by the name of Gause's principle of competitive exclusion stipulates that two species cannot occupy the same ecological niche, and a similar principle applies to subspecies and social groups in direct proportion to the strength of their identity. . . . It is the war of families and kindreds and gene pools that dominates human existence.[71]

Here Fleming's sociobiological reasoning proposes that different "peoples" cannot cohabit and that "families" and "gene pools" are engaged in constant warfare in an effort to survive. When mapped onto other neo-Confederate understandings of race and ethnicity, this suggests the need for mono-ethnic territories where each ethno-national group has its own land. Fleming elsewhere explains that the inevitable result of spatial cohabitation by different groups is repression of the weak by the powerful. Citing historical examples, he proposes three possible outcomes for multiethnic territories. The first is the achievement of mono-ethnic populations "by practicing a mixture of genocide and expulsion." The second is "fusion." If cohabiting ethnic groups "are sufficiently similar in race and culture, they can assimilate and merge," as Fleming supposes Scandinavians and Germans did in the British Isles. The third possibility, if neither of the other solutions is "practical," is ethnic domination and subordination. Historically these have been reinforced by "legal, political, and social codes that discouraged intermarriage and reduced the less advanced and less powerful ethnic group to a subservient position."[72] Racial groups, it seems, cannot mix or integrate if they are not "sufficiently similar." If they do, as Cawthon noted above, the result is "extinction" of both. Dissimilar ethno-racial-cultural groups, given Fleming's sociobiological and social Darwinist rationales, are naturally given to struggle for supremacy, and the losers in this struggle will be the "less advanced" who will subsequently be institutionally discriminated against. To avoid such an outcome, therefore, dissimilar racial and cultural groups should, it seems, be allowed to demarcate their own living spaces and be left alone to develop themselves and their families in "their own interests."

Given the assertions that cultural and ethnic groups are fundamentally different, we now turn to examine how leading proponents of neo-Confederacy and neo-Confederate venues understand nonwhite peoples. Teun van Dijk argues that racist discourse is often constructed through a dichotomy of "positive self-presentations" and "negative other-presentations."[73] This positive self-presentation generates a self-image of virtue, value, and, of course, tolerance. To neo-Confederates, these are attributes of the Anglo-Celtic white Southerners, as described in Chapter 4. The "negative other-presentation" is typically applied to "immigrants ('illegals') or other minorities ('associated with drugs,' 'not motivated to work')."[74] This dualistic presentation of the positive self and negative other means that the beliefs and practices of others are not explicitly dismissed; rather, they are presented as abnormal and different, the insinuation being that they are inferior. Resultantly, argues van Dijk, racist discourse does not have to be blatant:

The white group is generally presented in neutral or favorable terms, especially in the domain of ethnic affairs, whereas immigrants, foreigners, refugees, or resident minorities are portrayed as the source of problems, conflicts, and threats.[75]

One subtext, of course, is that "we" are superior and threats to our normality are caused by those who are not like us. To neo-Confederates like Michael Hill, nonwhites are understood to be irreconcilably different from white people:

> Most "dark skinned" people have shown little aversion to the various forms
> of totalitarian government in our modern age. In fact, "big government"
> poses as a friend and protector of the "dark skinned" masses everywhere. No-
> where is this more evident than in America's current immigration policy and
> Washington's firm commitment to multiculturalism and diversity (the new
> civic religion). The resulting "browning of America" is seen as a good thing
> by white liberals, big business (cheap labour, you understand), and "dark
> skinned" folks themselves, who see more power accompanying their growing
> numbers. Clearly, the chief enemies of these interests are the descendents of
> the white Christian founding stock of America. . . . As long as a completely
> politicized law enforcement and legal establishment favors the interests of
> the "dark skinned" people (including Arab Muslims and the black Nation
> of Islam) over those of white men, then we can expect more terrorism and
> chaos on the streets of America.[76]

The "interests" of "white men," it seems, are now ignored by a multicultural United States that is making every effort to accommodate nonwhite people who are the source of disruption and crime on American streets. Echoing such themes, neo-Confederate publications commonly contain narratives of authors, presumably white men, visiting U.S. cities from their homes in the suburbs or rural areas, cities described in publications such as *Southern Partisan* as dangerous places:

> You will never find a specific acknowledgement of racism unique to the
> urban blight of big city life, where blacks and other dark-skinned minorities
> are starving in ghettos, where murder and brutality are too commonplace
> even to investigate, where drugs and gang violence are a way of life and
> where dangerous children stare with hardened eyes.
>
> Those millions of ghetto dwellers are segregated more totally than under
> any system the South ever conceived.[77]

In these visits, authors recount the threat of encountering a diverse, multicultural population, often giving the impression that a multiracial nation and national culture are untenable as nonwhite ethno-racial groups maintain their own distinctiveness, their failure to assimilate with the white population seemingly supported by federal authorities. Nonwhite ethno-racial groups including "Latino, black, and Asian nationalist gangs" are supposedly "seeking the racial dismemberment of the United States," which, Fleming suggests, is actively encouraged by U.S. authorities because "in refusing to control immigration, the Federal Government is writing a script for ethnic civil war."[78]

Southern Partisan contributor Patrick Brophy identifies himself as a member of the "'Old Stock': the racial group that's been in America since before the Revolution: English leavened with some Scottish, Welsh, Scotch-Irish, French, Dutch, and German," presumably nationalities that are, in Fleming's words, "sufficiently similar in race and culture" to "assimilate and merge." Hailing from the small town of Nevada, Missouri, Brophy describes a visit to New York City where he encountered "only Italians, Jews, Puerto Ricans." This leads him to wonder: "Where are the Americans?"[79] Upon further reflection, Brophy's "Americans" turn out to be suburban commuters. This leads him to ponder the state of American culture, something he suggests is being "intrud[ed] into and dilut[ed]" by "alien 'cultures'" and their attendant "unmowed lawns and unsavory cooking odors." Echoing Fleming, Brophy believes that federal authorities in service to ethnic minority groups are deliberately creating a multicultural United States to usurp the rights of the native white population. As we have demonstrated above, advocates of neo-Confederacy understand a multiethnic nationality to be untenable, a notion with which Brophy concurs. He proposes that "a society can have only one real, live 'culture' at a time," meaning that multiculturalism results in cultural "stultification," "antiquarianism," or "divisiveness and bitterness." In his assessment, Brophy implies that the "Americans" he discusses are white members of the "Old Stock," and that other American residents are aliens who are not only impossible to assimilate but are also "diluting" American culture rather than, say, enriching it. Back in his hometown, and in a manner reminiscent of the name analysis used by McWhiney and colleagues to formulate the Celtic South thesis, Brophy examines surnames in his local telephone book. He calculates that 95 percent of residents are "Old Stock" and laments that although this group founded the United States, their "culture," a term that in Brophy's article is used in a manner synonymous with ethnicity, is ignored.

Another author, Paul Kirchner, wrote of his bold visit to an unnamed U.S. city in *Chronicles*. In urban areas, Kirchner explains, "the lawless . . .

thrive" because the welfare state panders to them. Indeed, without such state support, "they would starve to death or be exterminated by the law-abiding majority." Kirchner tantalizes readers with a tale of sharing an elevator with three "youths" who have "droopy posture, droopy eyes and lower lips" while he carries a concealed "Smith & Wesson airweight 'Bodyguard' model .38 Special" in his pocket.[80] The "youths" appear to Kirchner to be aliens. He is unable to understand what they say and notes that the city is "their world" and "foreign" to him. These three residents of urban America are out of the ordinary to Kirchner, a self-identified "middle-class white" man. They look, speak, and behave differently than he does. Yet that is not all; Kirchner's essay supposes that these unsettling urban U.S. residents are inveterate criminals who, if only federal authorities allowed it, would be actively "exterminated" by the "law-abiding majority," namely non-urban, white, middle-class U.S. residents like himself. Like much neo-Confederate writing, therefore, Kirchner's article presupposes irreconcilable ethnic differences and the fundamental incapability of members of different ethnic groups to occupy the same territory without coming into conflict.

To further evidence the failure of racial integration and the impossibility of cohabitation by different ethnic groups, neo-Confederate publications regularly offer stories of crime to their readers in which the criminals are, invariably, nonwhite. *Southern Patriot*, for example, noted the "predictable destruction of private property," primarily "white-owned businesses," caused by African American students on vacation in Mississippi and Florida in 2000.[81] Although accounts were "too barbaric to print," *Southern Patriot* utilized tired white supremacist stereotypes about the inability of African American men to control themselves, particularly in the presence of "white women." Such behavior by African Americans, *Southern Patriot* implied, was inevitable but could not be stopped by local police officers because federal officials intervened on behalf of the students. In making a distinction between "young blacks" and "law-abiding citizens," and emphasizing that the victims of the violence were "whites," the anonymous *Southern Patriot* contributor infers that "citizens" and "blacks" are distinct groups and that a fundamental condition of U.S. society is the inability of different ethnic groups to occupy the same location without resorting to violence. Similar examples abound in the neo-Confederate literature. Justin Raimondo in *Chronicles*, for example, describes the "militant black racists" who force Vietnamese residents to leave their public housing residences in San Francisco.[82] Reconfirming the intractability of ethnic animosity, Raimondo concludes that "black hatred of whites, and of Asians of all denominations, is the grisly and frightening secret at the heart of American race relations."[83] *Southern Patriot* has also advised readers that "Blacks are 250 times more likely to commit criminal violence to whites than vice versa [and] Blacks commit violent crimes at four to eight times the white crime rate."[84] In *Chronicles*, sociologist Steven Goldberg wrote, "The blunt truth is that a disproportionate rate of murder by a small number of young black men (whatever *its* causes) counts for the shocking level of violent crime."[85] He suggests that the "black homicide rate" has numerous causal factors, including "family instability (particularly illegitimacy and the absence of a father); educational deprivation, . . . joblessness, prejudice, and drugs." Recall, however, that advocates of neo-Confederacy typically conceive of cultures and ethnicities (such as Celticness) to be transmitted over time and space, such that people exhibiting their Celtic culture today behave in much the same manner as their ancestors did two thousand years ago. If we take neo-Confederacy to be consistent in its understandings of ethnicity and culture, therefore, the behaviors of nonwhites will be similarly perdurable and unchanging. The violent and destructive behavior of African Americans is, it seems, almost innate, but unlike Celtic violence, which advocates of neo-Confederacy celebrate as honorable and even life-sustaining, violent behavior when committed by African Americans is regularly condemned.

Chronicles contributor Kevin Lamb has proposed that "by focusing upon social forces alone" as causes of criminal behavior, "critics continue to ignore other important factors that contribute to violent crime." The most important factor that mainstream critics ignore, Lamb believes, is "behavioral genetics" and "individual differences in personality, intelligence, and temperament." Unfortunately, due to "political correctness" among "social scientists" with "deeply held egalitarian beliefs," these connections between genes, intelligence, and violence are not being studied.[86] Lamb's essay was applauded in *Chronicles* by J. Philippe Rushton, who explained that his own studies demonstrate that the connection between testosterone and aggression means that "general misbehavior for men is 75 percent heritable and that violence is 50 percent heritable." Furthering his claim that hormones determine the propensity for violence, Rushton maintained that race can be used to understand the crime statistics because "blacks (on average) have more testosterone than whites, who have more than Asians."[87] It is not just the relationship between race and crime that Rushton has told *Chronicles* readers is a result of biology. He has also explored "racial differences in brain size and intelligence, sexual habits and fertility, personality and temperament, and speed of maturation and longevity," concluding that people cannot be treated equally as racial differences are incontrovertible. Replicating his equation of testosterone to violence, crime, and racial group, Rushton assesses the proclivity for sexual activity amongst different peoples. He believes that "people of African ancestry are more sexually active than Europeans, who are more sexually active than Asians," and that sexual behavior and promiscuity are little affected by cultural practices such as marriage. Proposing that "black samples are found to have intercourse earlier, with a greater number of casual partners and with a more positive attitude to sexual display than either white or Asian samples," Rushton's assessments could be read as repeating the long-discredited concepts of the inherent differences between Caucasoid ("white," "European"), Mongoloid ("Asian"), and Negroid ("black," "African") races.[88] These essential racial differences mean that nonwhite groups will never exhibit the behavior of whites because races are just irreconcilably different. This leads Thomas Fleming to suggest the following:

> Whatever trust we are to put in race and IQ correlations, black achievements both in Africa and North America give little indication that black people, taken statistically *en masse*, possess the kinds of abilities that are required for success in the modern world.[89]

The belief circulating in neo-Confederate venues such as *Chronicles, Southern Partisan*, and *Southern Patriot* is that nation-states should be formed on a mono-ethnic basis. When coupled with a recognition that contemporary U.S. society is multicultural, and that different ethno-racial cultures are irreconcilable, perhaps even at a genetic level, this leads neo-Confederate publications to assert the need for a revocation of policies that create multicultural nations, envisioned as artificially imposed on people who do not want to share "their own interests" (their everyday lives and, arguably, their power) with other ethno-racial groups. Multiculturalism is envisioned by neo-Confederates to be a fundamentally unnatural state of affairs that threatens the distinctive cultural practices and group identity of Anglo-Celtic Southerners. If "all souls are equal," John Vinson opines, then "distinctions of flesh and blood such as ethnicity are meaningless."[90] Patently for Vinson and other neo-Confederates, all souls are not equal, and distinct ethnic groups should not, therefore, have to share communities. The League of the South thus demands "the right of free association" because "peoples of different cultures" need to be able to "pursue their own interests without interference from bureaucrats and social engineers who push such enormities as global democracy and multiculturalism."[91]

Such assertions propose, albeit indirectly, a return to prior structural conditions in which each "culture" (ethno-racial group) had their own self-contained communities. It is an understanding of mono-ethnic territories and racial segregation. This is not, however, a segregation of equals. With ethnic groups continuously engaged in a struggle for supremacy, the future status of the white, Anglo-Celtic people of the South, with whom neo-Confederates identify, is crucial. It is this determination to ensure the survival and primacy of the Anglo-Celtic Southerners that motivates people like Michael Hill:

> For our progeny to enjoy the benefits of liberty and self-government, we must make sure that they, and not the descendents of immigrants from third world cultures, dominate the south. It is imperative then that we gain control over the borders of Dixie as soon as possible in order to stop the influx of immigrants who neither care for nor understand the things that make liberty and prosperity possible. . . . Let us then reassert with pride our Anglo-Celtic heritage as a barrier to the looming multicultural tidal wave that is set to sweep over this country.[92]

Immigration

In the speech above, Michael Hill adds another dimension to the doctrine of neo-Confederacy: immigration. Making it clear that culture, ethnic group, and nation are synonyms by stating that the immigrants that threaten the Anglo-Celtic South come from "third world cultures," Hill asserts that it is imperative that his descendents and their ethno-cultural kin, presumably all white, hold power over decision making in the future Confederacy. If neo-Confederates are unsuccessful in their quest for independence and institutional control, "our descendents will live as a hated and persecuted minority in a land settled and civilized by their ancestors."[93] Recall that advocates of neo-Confederacy understand that different ethnic groups cannot share territory on equal terms and are engaged in a constant Darwinistic struggle for power. The white (Anglo-Celtic) population of the Southern states, should it be outcompeted by other ethno-cultural groups, will necessarily be repressed and subordinated by the victors. This will result, in neo-Confederate logic, in being "pushed off our lands" and ultimately extinction, because "we will cease to exist as a people." Hill is afraid that whites in the Southern United States will be forced to cede territory and, by implication, authority, given the sheer number of nonwhite people. This situation is growing ever more likely as immigration and federal commitments to "radical egalitarianism," "multiculturalism," "diversity," and "tolerance" coalesce to "tell us clearly that we are the intended targets of continued reconstruction and ultimate dispossession."[94] The way to avoid such a life-threatening eventuality is for neo-Confederates to secede. After independence, Clyde Wilson of the University of South Carolina explains, a Confederation of Southern States could establish legislation that will ensure future territorial control:

> In the new Confederacy, unlike the U.S., we wont [*sic*] have a bit of difficulty telling the difference between a citizen and an illegal alien. We can hope that the problem will be easily solved and that Smyrna, Georgia, and Siler City, North Carolina, will no longer be outposts of Mexico.[95]

Wilson's subtext here is clear: citizenship can be visually evaluated and people who do not look like Confederate Americans (i.e., are not visibly white) will not be legal citizens of an independent Confederacy. Echoing the *Southern Patriot*'s division of U.S. residents into "citizens" and "blacks" when discussing vacationing African Americans, Wilson's allusion is that legitimate citizens are white and illegitimate ones are not. Identifying cities that have seen increased Hispanic populations in recent decades, Wilson refers to these as "outposts of Mexico" and intimates that all Hispanic residents are illegal immigrants.[96] Indeed, he suggests that in accepting immigrants and being a multicultural nation, the United States has caused a "problem" for itself—a "difficulty" that would be erased when identification of citizens by racial and ethnic group follows Confederate independence.

An independent Confederation of Southern States would be able to set its own immigration policies and thus its "borders [will be] sealed against massive Third World immigration." Such an approach would ensure that "the interests of the core population of Anglo-Celts is protected from the ravages of so-called multi-culturalism and diversity" and that a "European majority" would only "welcome . . . productive and sympathetic members of other nations and cultures" if they accepted the terms of residence laid down by the "European majority" (i.e., whites) in power.[97] Until this is achieved, however, neo-Confederate activists have called for supporters to take a "more aggressive direction" and organize anti-immigrant rallies across the South.[98]

In such discussions about immigration, as with much neo-Confederate rhetoric, race is rarely referred to explicitly; rather, difference is explained in terms of belonging to the other "nations" and "cultures" that are manifestly distinct from the South's "core population" of Anglo-Celts, a shorthand for native whites. Although advocates of neo-Confederacy regularly decry immigration, there is no similar antagonism toward European immigrants, those from the "First World." Although immigration from Europe is much reduced from its peaks in the late nineteenth and early twentieth centuries, nativist sentiment of neo-Confederacy is not against all immigrants, just those deemed to be from the "Third World"—clearly referring to nonwhites. Indeed, Hill laments that following the 1965 Hart-Celler Act's reform of immigration, federal authorities have been complicit in encouraging "millions of non-Europeans" to come to the United States and "maintain their own culture and language." [99] These ethnic groups are considered fundamentally "unassimilable" with white, European-descended Americans, and as such constitute an irreconcilable challenge to the very existence of the United States: they either "lack the understanding to preserve our vital institutions" or "are overtly hostile to our civilization." In the struggle for survival and demographic superiority, continued non-European immigration will result in "numerical dominance by aliens" and white minority status. [100] Writing in *Southern Partisan*, Samuel Francis believes that these developments will promulgate the "decay of the West." [101] This view was encapsulated in the statement of *Southern Partisan* contributor Tom Landess, who, when he learned that the Statue of Liberty was in need of structural repairs in the mid-1980s, reported that he was "glad." He "hate[s]" the principles the statue stands for, namely the acceptance of immigrants into the United States whose presence supposedly causes "most of the problems we face today." Returning the Statue of Liberty to France and, by association, reversing U.S. immigration policy would mean that "crime in the streets would disappear, we'd have a surplus in the federal treasury, and teenage pregnancies would be a thing of the past." [102]

In neo-Confederate rhetoric and in Western political discourse more generally, "immigration is often described in the military metaphor of an invasion. Similarly, large groups of immigrants . . . are described . . . in terms of threatening amounts of water or snow in which *We* may drown: waves, floods, avalanches, etc." [103] Describing the numbers of immigrants as "massive," "enormous," and "huge" exacerbates this sentiment. In his appeal for Southern secession published in *Southern Partisan*, Cawthon decries that since 1965, federal policy has "opened the floodgates to massive Third World immigration," which "has the power to transform the South and the United States fundamentally and unalterably." [104] Such scaremongering is typical, seen also in Wayne Carlson's claims that "the influx of tens of millions of legal and illegal immigrants" who have "birth rates two to three times that of other racial or ethnic groups . . . will soon control the destiny of [California], and every other State they choose to come to." [105] Michael Hill employs similar rhetoric to assert that the

> massive influx of Muslims, Latinos, and other non-Western peoples [that] poses a threat to the racial, ethnic, and cultural balance of our country . . . will eventually weaken and destroy our civilization. . . . More importantly,

they will physically displace the descendants of the founding stock and we will cease to control the homeland bequeathed us by generations of noble and honorable men and women—our ancestors.[106]

In their examination of Austrian politics and the campaign rhetoric of far-right politician Jörg Haider, Martin Reisigl and Ruth Wodak demonstrate that Haider and his supporters often repeated the assertion that immigrants would "flood" into Austria, a metaphor implying that existing residents are imperiled. "The conclusion goes as follows," they explain: "one should prevent a flood from inundating the endangered area. To be precise: one should take measures in order to prevent the immigrants from becoming too many."[107] Similarly, in neo-Confederate writing, the South is the "endangered area" under threat from nonwhite immigrants. There is consistent comment in neo-Confederate publications that nonwhite immigrants have the "power to transform," "weaken," and "destroy" the Southern states. Cawthon warns that such change would be "fundamental" and "unalterable," while Hill suggests that demographic structures of "our country" will be threatened with imbalance. The loss of "control" over "the homeland" is, we suggest, a euphemism for the loss of political, propertied, and economic power that has previously accrued to the white status quo, a contention that Hill affirms with his utilization of deixis:

> Each passing day brings new evidence that we Southerners are being dispossessed of our land, culture, and inheritance. . . . We are also being deluged by millions of Third World immigrants who refuse to be assimilated, are settling our lands, carrying strange diseases, using up scarce natural resources, and otherwise eating up our financial substance.[108]

The changing demographic composition of the Southern states will result in different social, cultural, and political structures and distributions of power. This, neo-Confederates demand, must be prevented.

The discussions of birth rates, of being "flooded" or "deluged," of displacement from "our lands" and of others using up our limited "resources"—these are all shorthand for the fear of being outnumbered. The relative proportion of native-born whites as a percentage of the population will decline as immigration continues. In a democratic society where, at least in theory, all citizens have equal access to power and policy because we each have one vote, a fear of being outnumbered is a fear of being outvoted. The distribution of political power will inevitably change as the U.S. population changes. The neo-Confederate fear of immigrants is therefore a fear that white privileges will be eroded and that the ability of whites to define legislation will be reduced. When an immigrant becomes a U.S. citizen, she or he can effect change as easily as an existing resident can by voting for it. For neo-Confederates, therefore, the democratic process is actually unfair in that it balances opportunities rather than privileging those with prior residency. It is consistent with other neo-Confederate beliefs, therefore, that proponents oppose the very philosophy of democracy and challenge the existing system of voting in the United States.

Opposition to Equality

Describing the growth of the Hispanic population in North Carolina since 1990 as "a cultural blitzkrieg" that has resulted in "smoldering ruins of institutions felled by the incursion," Charles Davenport Jr. argues that immigration to the United States "represent[s] the overthrow of one culture by another."[109] He claims that U.S. political leaders exhibit a "diversity fetish" which presupposes that "all cultures are equal," and he laments that the commitment to multicultural equality is a "perversion." As is common in neo-Confederacy circles, these modern ills are seen to stem from the Civil War, which is considered to have been a fundamental break with the founding principles of the United States. As such, political commitments to equality and egalitarianism are traced to the supposedly nefarious impacts of amendments to the U.S. Constitution in the Civil War era. Most neo-Confederate ire is directed toward the Fourteenth and Fifteenth Amendments, ratified in 1868 and 1870, respectively, which guaranteed African Americans the rights to citizenship and its benefits. Thomas E. Woods Jr., for example, argues that "the principle behind [the Fourteenth] amendment is wholly incompatible with a federal system." Eliding an argument about race and rewriting it as opposition to the expansion of federal authority, Woods maintains that the amendment resulted from "militant egalitarians" in the federal government who "managed to gain control over the affairs of every neighborhood and school system in America."[110] Michael Hill also denounces the Fourteenth Amendment and envisions a direct link between it and civil rights legislation, both of which serve to undermine society: "The 14th Amendment to the Constitution," he wrote in 1999, "has been the fulcrum for most of the dubious decisions of the courts this century." This is because

> wrong-headed liberal interpretations of the 14th Amendment have turned
> Abraham Lincoln's malignant egalitarianism into rights-based social poli-

cies. And the evil genie of universal "human rights," once loosed from its bottle, can never be restrained because "rights"—for women, racial and ethnic minorities, homosexuals, pedophiles, etc.—can be manufactured endlessly.[111]

Kennedy and Kennedy also challenge these amendments, further arguing that equal enfranchisement was illegally imposed on the Southern states by federal authorities through the 1965 Voting Rights Act. A correct interpretation of the Constitution, they maintain, would mean that the state rather than the federal government would decide who has the right to vote. In this manner, Kennedy and Kennedy appeal to a pre–civil rights era when enfranchisement in the South was basically limited to middle- and upper-income white citizens through the imposition of poll taxes, eligibility restrictions, and other discriminatory legislation. They argue that the right to vote should only be extended to those citizens who can pass tests on reading, writing, history, geography, and mathematics.[112] Second, Kennedy and Kennedy propose that citizens should pay to vote, and voters can neither be on welfare nor have been previously declared bankrupt. The result, of course, would be a vast reduction in the electoral rolls, with those who pay the poll tax controlling the ballot box. "The liberal concept of one man–one vote, or universal franchise," Kennedy and Kennedy maintain,

> is so deeply entrenched in the liberal dogma of the Yankee government that very few are willing to challenge its legitimacy. This is especially true in the South. Here we are faced with the danger of being labeled as a society attempting to deny the franchise permanently on the basis of race. Where will anyone find a popular politician who is willing to confront charges of racism and bigotry just to promote an improvement of the quality of the electorate.[113]

Like the other neo-Confederate activists discussed above, Kennedy and Kennedy preempt charges of racism, maintaining their efforts are not to reduce the participation of racial and ethnic minorities in elections, but to "improve" the electorate. Their position could appear to be merely in favor of producing better-informed voters, but envisioning an electoral process that restricts decision-making power to elites (who happen to be predominantly white), with others only receiving the benefit of their wisdom, is entirely consistent with their neo-Confederate worldview.

Opposition to equality, whether in the franchise or other aspects of U.S.

society, is a central plank of neo-Confederacy. In his speech at the foundation of the League of the South, Hill stated that "rampant egalitarianism" is one of the most "corrosive agents of modernity."[114] Fleming condemns the concept of equal rights as fallacious and that as a result "real rights—to maintain a family, practice religion, and hold property—are destroyed."[115]

Conclusion: Neo-Confederacy and Race

In this chapter we have demonstrated that race is central to the neo-Confederate imagination. Although the language employed by neo-Confederate authors typically elides the issue of race, sympathetic audiences can be assumed to recognize "cultures," "Americans," "youths," and "citizens" as euphemisms for ethno-racial groups, and interpret the deictic references to "we," "us," and "our" accordingly. Within neo-Confederate texts, race (and, synonymously, culture and ethnicity) is assumed to be a fundamental aspect of the human condition, rooted in biology. Ethno-racial groups are determined to be irreconcilably different and continuously engaged in struggles for mastery. This means that current practices of multiculturalism and policies of immigration are, to neo-Confederates, antithetical to the very existence of peoples and nations. They will also eventually lead to the eradication of a distinctive white population in the Southern states by creating opportunities for miscegenation, opportunities that malignant federal authorities have encouraged through legislation mandating racial desegregation.

Much neo-Confederate writing identifies the 1950s and 1960s as the onset of a problematic and ongoing societal transformation, which implies that African American and white communities should have remained segregated. Equal and civil rights are dismissed as fundamentally artificial, and legislation desegregating schools and promoting affirmative action are derided as experiments in social engineering. Martin Luther King is scorned as, amongst other things, a liar and adulterer, and the federal holiday in King's name symbolizes a threat to American institutions. Immigrants from non-Western nations are rebuked as impossible to assimilate, causing irreversible damage to life in the Southern United States and Western civilization itself.

Neo-Confederacy recognizes race and ethnicity as enduring components of human identity that should always define people and determine their access to power and territory. Human social arrangements, neo-Confederates maintain, should center upon ethno-racial identity; structures and institutions challenging such arrangements are manufactured to artificially engineer society. Consequently, current U.S. multicultural society and equal voting rights for all citizens are dismissed as fundamentally unnatural and forcibly imposed by the state.

To build empathy with a receptive audience, and to meet the necessity in current U.S. politics of avoiding charges of racism, advocates of neo-Confederacy keep explicitly disagreeable historical narratives and comments about race largely off stage. Yet from these examples, it is clear that neo-Confederacy is replete with assumptions about the detrimental presence in the United States of people who are not white. Despite repeated appeals by its articulators as to its nonracist content, there is clearly a "negative other-presentation" of nonwhite peoples in neo-Confederate venues and by leading advocates of neo-Confederacy.

Notes

1. van Dijk, Teun A. "Elite Discourse and the Reproduction of Racism," *Hate Speech*, ed. Rita Kirk Whillock and David Slayden. (Thousand Oaks, CA: Sage, 1995): 22. Commentator on Southern ethnicity Lewis Killian notes that by the 1980s, when racial integration was advancing and overt racism was denounced, white Americans began to use "code phrases such as 'welfare fraud' and 'crime in the streets'" to direct blame for the state of affairs following desegregation toward African Americans, and the "term *special interests* . . . constituted a veiled reference to—and protest against—the growing credibility of the concept of ethnic group rights." Killian, Lewis M. *White Southerners*, rev. ed. (Amherst: University of Massachusetts Press, 1985): 167–168 (original emphasis).

2. Byrnes, P. J. "The Roots of the Verdict in L.A.," *Southern Partisan*, 13 (1st Quarter 1993): 6.

3. Southern Poverty Law Center. "Rebels with a Cause," *Intelligence Report*, 99 (2000): 6.

4. See, for example, Southern Poverty Law Center. "Confederates in Black," *Intelligence Report*, 99 (2000): 24–25, and Williams, Walter. "Phony Diversity," *Southern Partisan*, 22.5 (2002): 39. In *The Last Rebel Yell* (Nashville: Rebel Press, 1991), Michael Andrew Grissom draws on conservative African Americans and racial separatists like Nation of Islam leader Louis Farrakhan to justify his arguments opposing interracial marriage and school desegregation. The role of conservative African Americans in current U.S. politics and their beliefs about civil rights, affirmative action, multiculturalism, and religion, amongst other things, is examined by Angela D. Dillard, *Guess Who's Coming to Dinner Now? Multicultural Conservatism in America*, (New York: New York University Press, 2001).

5. "Remembering . . . : George Corley Wallace (1919–1998)," *Southern Patriot*, 5.5 (1998): 8.

6. Cawthon, William Lamar Jr. "George Wallace and the South," *Southern Patriot*, 5.6 (1998): 7. Cawthon's essay contained a second part, published in *Southern Patriot*, 6.1 (1999): 6, 10.

7. Carlson, Wayne. "The Suicide of the West," *Southern Events*, 7.4 (2002): 10.

8. Whillock, Rita Kirk, and Slayden, David, ed. *Hate Speech*. (Thousand Oaks, CA: Sage, 1995). See also, Wellman, David. *Portraits of White Racism*, 2nd ed. (Cambridge: Cambridge University Press, 1993).

9. Fleming, Thomas. "The Illusions of Democracy," *Chronicles*, 20.1 (1996): 9. See also Robert Whitaker's entries for "racist," "bigot," and "race question" in his "Partisan Dictionary" series, respectively *Southern Partisan*, 5.2 (1985): 65, *Southern Partisan*, 5.1 (1985): 14, and *Southern Partisan*, 3.3 (1983): 9. His definition of "freedom" as the "right to exercise one's prejudices" appears in "Partisan Dictionary," *Southern Partisan*, 4.1 (1984): 49.

10. League of the South. "Copyrights, Credits, Disclaimers and Warnings," (1995–1999). On-line: http://www.leagueofthesouth.com/ls-homepg/legal_notices .html [accessed 10 June 2004]; van Dijk, "Elite Discourse," (1995): 9.

11. McCain, Barry Reid. "Letter to the Editor: Ready . . . Fire . . . Aim," *Southern Partisan*, 14.4 (1994): 2.

12. Quoted in Pinzur, Matthew I. "League of the South Pushes Separatist Views," *Florida Times-Union*, Jacksonville (10 September 2001): A-1. On-line: http://jacksonville.com/tu-On-line/stories/091001/met_7240080.html [accessed 20 October 2004]. The quote comes from an email listserv and was intercepted by the Southern Poverty Law Center. In another email, Hill "condemns interracial marriage, saying Southerners should 'intermarry with their own kind.'" Pinzur verified that Michael Hill had written these emails: "Hill confirmed writing the messages, but said the SPLC was 'not honorable' when it copied them from a private mailing list."

13. "Partisan Conversation—Michael Hill: The Southern League," *Southern Partisan*, 14 (4th quarter 1994): 35.

14. Fleming, Thomas. League of the South National Conference, Charleston, South Carolina (1994). Transcribed from videotape. Available from Southern League, P.O. Box 40910, Tuscaloosa, AL 35404-0910.

15. Halberstam, David. *The Children*. (New York: Fawcett Books, 1999).

16. See Billig, Michael. *Banal Nationalism*. (London: Sage, 1995).

17. Hill, Michael. "A People without History," *Southern Patriot*, 2.1 (1995): 2.

18. Fleming, Thomas. "Government of the People," *Chronicles*, 14.3 (1990): 12.

19. "In Defence of the League of the South," *Southern Patriot*, 7.5 (2000): 14.

20. Fleming, Thomas. "Equality or Privilege: Gored on the horns of the American dilemma," *Chronicles*, 18.8 (1994): 12.

21. Cawthon, "George Wallace and the South," (1998): 7.

22. Whitaker, Robert W. "Partisan Dictionary," *Southern Partisan*, 6.4 & 7.1 (1986–87): 9.

23. Francis, Samuel. "Perfect for This Moment," *Chronicles*, 29.3 (2005): 39.

24. Conner, Frank. *The South under Siege (1830–2000): A History of the Relations between North and South*. (Newnan, GA: Collards Publishing Company, 2002): 195, 206.

25. Kennedy, James Ronald, and Kennedy, Walter Donald. *The South Was Right!*, 2nd ed. (Gretna, LA: Pelican Publishing, 1994 [1991]): 168, 180.

26. "Reconstruction: The Tragic Era," *Southern Partisan*, 8.3 (1988): 16.

27. Gottfried, Paul. "Revisiting a Dark and Bloody Ground: Two New Books on Reconstruction," *Southern Partisan*, 8.3 (1988): 18–19. Gottfried discusses Current,

Richard Nelson. *Those Terrible Carpetbaggers*. (New York: Oxford University Press, 1988), and Foner, Eric. *Reconstruction: America's Unfinished Revolution, 1863–1877*, (New York: Harper and Row, 1988). Foner is the subject of Gottfried's most vitriolic attack.

28. Bowers, Claude G. *The Tragic Era: The Revolution after Lincoln*. (Cambridge, MA: Riverside Press, 1929): 56, 57, 58, 307, 508–509.

29. Grissom, Michael Andrew. *Southern by the Grace of God*. (Gretna, LA: Pelican Books, 1989 [1988]): 128.

30. Ibid., 147.

31. Lang, Robert, ed. *The Birth of a Nation*. (New Brunswick, NJ: Rutgers University Press, 1994): 7.

32. Grissom, *Southern by the Grace*, (1989 [1988]): 180, 533.

33. "Reconstruction: The Tragic Era," *Southern Partisan*, 8.3 (1988): 16.

34. Sebesta, Edward H., and Hague, Euan. "The U.S. Civil War as a Theological Struggle: Confederate Christian Nationalism and the League of the South," *Canadian Review of American Studies*, 32.3 (2002): 253–283.

35. Sobran, Joseph. "The Liberal Theory of Causation," *Southern Partisan*, 18 (3rd Quarter 1998): 50.

36. Fleming, Thomas. "Middle American Helots," *Chronicles*, 17.6 (1993): 14.

37. Conner, Frank. *The South under Siege (1830–2000): A History of the Relations between North and South*. (Newnan, GA: Collards Publishing Company, 2002): 397–400. Conner also explains that most of these "Jews" were Communists.

38. "In South Carolina, the League helped to block a M. L. King Jr. holiday in Greenville County, and we have become a political force of some note in the Palmetto State because of the efforts of State Chairman James Layden and State Director Robert Hayes." Hill, Michael. "A Realistic Assessment," *Southern Patriot*, 10.5 (2003): 1–2. This County Council decision was also heralded in "Double Secret Boycott," *Southern Partisan*, 23.1 (2003): 10.

39. Quinn, Richard. "Martin Luther King Day," *Southern Partisan*, 3.4 (1983): 4. Quinn's black heroes listed as more deserving than King are George Washington Carver, Booker T. Washington, and General Chappie James.

40. See, for example, "The Dream, Part III," *Southern Partisan*, 3.4 (1983): 7.

41. Baldwin, Donald. "A *Partisan* Conversation—Jesse Helms," *Southern Partisan*, 4.2 (1984): 36.

42. Quoted in Hines, Richard T. "A *Partisan* Conversation with Trent Lott," *Southern Partisan*, 4.4 (Fall 1984): 47.

43. Hurley, John. "Notes from Confederate Memorial Hall," *Southern Partisan*, 4.2 (Spring 1984): 67. The column ends with a call for donations and support for a petition to "restore Lee-Jackson Day" and the "Virginia Heritage Victory Fund."

44. Hill, Michael. "Worshipping at the Altar of St. Martin the Immaculate," On-line: *http://www.leagueofthesouth.com/dn-gazette/altar-st-martin.htm* [accessed 24 June 2004].

45. Ibid.

46. The literature on these topics is, of course, extensive. Amongst others, see Patterson, James T. *Brown v. Board of Education: A Civil Rights Milestone and Its Troubled Legacy*. (Oxford: Oxford University Press, 2001); Orfield, Gary. *The Reconstruction of Southern Education—The Schools and the 1964 Civil Rights Act*. (New

York: Wiley-Interscience, 1969); Bell, Derrick, ed. *Shades of Brown: New Perspectives on School Desegregation.* (New York: Columbia University Press, 1980); Wells, Amy Stuart, and Crain, Robert L. *Stepping over the Color Line: African-American Students in White Suburban Schools.* (New Haven: Yale University Press, 1997). Thanks to Pauline Lipman for suggesting these titles. A good place to start an examination of affirmative action is Kranz, Rachel. *Affirmative Action.* (New York: Facts on File, 2002), which provides an overview and annotated bibliography of further reading.

47. Kennedy and Kennedy, *The South Was Right!* (1994 [1991]): 249.

48. Grissom, *The Last Rebel Yell,* (1991): 411, 419, 420 (original emphasis).

49. Ibid., 401, 421.

50. Ibid., 433.

51. Ibid., 410.

52. Haws, Joyce B. "What Are We Willing to Settle For?" *Chronicles,* 23.9 (1999): 22.

53. Fleming, Thomas. "It Takes a Village," *Chronicles,* 22.9 (1998): 11.

54. Haws, Joyce B. "The Takeover of Our Schools," *Chronicles,* 22.9 (1998): 15 (original emphasis).

55. Grissom, *The Last Rebel Yell,* (1991): 428.

56. Hill, Michael. "A Vital Economic Issue," *Southern Patriot,* 9.2 (2002): 2.

57. Leamon, Warren. "The Long Guilt Trip," *Southern Partisan,* 6:3 (Summer 1986): 15, 17–18.

58. Fleming, Thomas. "Government of the People," *Chronicles,* 14.3 (1990): 12.

59. Omi, Michael, and Winant, Howard. *Racial Formation in the United States: From the 1960s to the 1990s,* 2nd ed. (New York: Routledge, 1994 [1986]): 88.

60. Gordon, Avery F., and Newfield, Christopher. "Introduction," *Mapping Multiculturalism,* ed. Avery F. Gordon and Christopher Newfield. (Minneapolis: University of Minnesota Press, 1996): 4; Newfield, Christopher, and Gordon, Avery F. "Multiculturalism's Unfinished Business," *Mapping Multiculturalism,* ed. Avery F. Gordon and Christopher Newfield. (Minneapolis: University of Minnesota Press, 1996): 80.

61. Omi, Michael. "Racialization in the Post–Civil Rights Era," *Mapping Multiculturalism,* (1996): 184.

62. Newfield and Gordon, "Multiculturalism's Unfinished Business," (1996): 103–104 (original emphasis).

63. The identification of the United States as a "multicultural empire" is also made by Clyde Wilson. "Vive Quebec Libre," *Southern Patriot,* 4.1 (1997): 2, and Michael Hill, "Worshipping at the Altar."

64. Hill, Michael. "Pax Americana," *Southern Patriot,* 9.3 (2002): 1.

65. Ibid. The most extensive and erudite articulation of the neo-Confederate belief in small, homogeneous states is by Donald W. Livingston. *Philosophical Melancholy and Delirium: Hume's Pathology of Philosophy.* (Chicago: University of Chicago Press, 1998).

66. Cawthon, William Lamar Jr. "The South as an Independent Nation," *Southern Partisan,* 17 (3rd Quarter 1997): 20. In the same issue, Cawthon is described as "active in the League of the South" (p. 24).

67. Fleming, Thomas. "In the Time of the Breaking of Nations," *Chronicles,* 24.1 (2000): 11.

68. Sanders, Franklin. "The Global Rise of Ethnic Nationalism," *Southern*

Patriot, 2.2 (1995): 11. Along similar lines, prominent neo-Confederate activist Donald Livingston argues in his 1998 book *Philosophical Melancholy and Delirium* that the United States after the Civil War can be equated with Bismark's unification of Germany and Lenin's of the USSR, namely as a centralization of power and the imposition of unitary authority to hold smaller nationalities within a larger state.

69. Sanders, "The Global Rise," (1995): 11.

70. Washburn, Michael. "Southern League," *Chronicles*, 19.6 (1995): 7.

71. Fleming, Thomas. "Middle American Helots," *Chronicles*, 17.6 (1993): 13–15.

72. Ibid., 13.

73. van Dijk, "Elite discourse," (1995).

74. Ibid., 22.

75. Ibid., 10.

76. Hill, Michael. "Angry White Men (With Guns)," *Southern Patriot*, 9.6 (2002): 6. Hill's spelling of "labour" is deliberate. Neo-Confederate authors reject U.S. spellings and propose a return to British English, albeit applying this belief inconsistently in their writing.

77. "Spike Lee," *Southern Partisan*, 9 (3rd Quarter 1989): 12.

78. Fleming, Thomas. "America's Crackup," *National Review*, 49.14 (1997): 64.

79. Brophy, Patrick. "Outside the Melting Pot," *Southern Partisan* 11 (2nd Quarter 1991): 34–35.

80. Kirchner, Paul. "Trespassing in the City," *Chronicles*, 19.12 (1995): 45. We suggest that the people Kirchner encountered were African American, as later in his essay he notes the stereotyping of "poor black youths."

81. "Black Spring Break," *Southern Patriot*, 7.2 (2000): 10.

82. Raimondo, Justin. "Letter from San Francisco," *Chronicles*, 21.11 (1997): 34. Raimondo also authored an essay in *Southern Partisan*, 17 (1st Quarter 1997): 32–33, entitled "The Mugging of Texaco," which purported to explain "the tragedy and danger of so-called civil-rights legislation."

83. Raimondo, "Letter from San Francisco," (1997): 35.

84. "Crime Report," *Southern Patriot*, 6.5 (1999): 6. The neo-Confederate press is here reporting on a study conducted by the New Century Foundation, which it claims "the state-controlled media [have] refused to cover." The New Century Foundation (publishers of *American Renaissance*) is a white supremacist group led by Jared Taylor; see Beirich, Heidi, and Potok, Mark. "Irreconcilable Differences," *Intelligence Report*, 122 (2006): 24–27, and Southern Poverty Law Center. "The Groups," *Intelligence Report*, 122 (2006): 28–33. Taylor's essays have appeared in *Southern Patriot* (e.g., 2.4 (1995): 29; 3.2 (1996): 13) and a sidebar in the League of the South publication listed *American Renaissance* as one of the recommended "noteworthy publications" because it "provides hard-hitting analysis of largely ignored racial issues [and] pulls no punches in its discussions of black-on-white crime, racial IQ differences, the ills of affirmative action, and current immigration policies." It is not, the League of the South warns, "for the timid or faint-hearted"—see "Noteworthy Publications," *Southern Patriot*, 2.4 (1995): 32. Another study by Jared Taylor is approvingly discussed by Samuel Francis in "The Truth about Guns and Race," *Southern Partisan*, 14 (2nd Quarter 1994): 48. Francis argues that Taylor's research evidences that U.S. crime rates are higher than those in Western Europe solely due to the behavior of African Americans: "white Americans have no serious problem with guns that gun control laws would solve; it's

mainly black Americans who have problems with guns and cause problems for others." Taylor's views on race and crime are challenged in Southern Poverty Law Center. "Coloring Crime," *Intelligence Report*, 99 (2000): 37–39.

85. Goldberg, Steven. "Black Murder," *Chronicles*, 19.1 (1995): 20 (original emphasis).

86. Lamb, Kevin. "Crime Genes and Other Delusions," *Chronicles*, 20.12 (1996): 45–46.

87. Rushton, J. Philippe. "On Crime Genes," *Chronicles*, 21.3 (1997): 5. Rushton is a eugenicist whom Heidi Beirich and Mark Potok identify as "the most important race scientist at work today." His work correlates intelligence, criminality, and sexuality (see "40 To Watch," *Intelligence Report*, Southern Poverty Law Center, 111 [2003]: 37–38).

88. Rushton, J. Philippe. "Race, Aids, and Sexual Behavior," *Chronicles*, 20.1 (1996): 39–40. Rushton advises readers to examine his book, *Race, Evolution and Behavior* (New Brunswick, NJ: Transaction, 1995). He also states that as a result of his findings, he has been subjected to "ferocious attacks," criticism by Canadian authorities and his employer, the University of Western Ontario.

89. Fleming, Thomas. "The Illusions of Democracy," *Chronicles*, 20.1 (1996): 9.

90. Vinson, John. "Reject the Yankee Creed," *Southern Patriot*, 5.5 (1998): 10–11. Here, Vinson also identifies Martin Luther King Jr. as the "apostle of equality" and the "arch-partisan of Big Government and socialist redistribution."

91. League of the South. "The League of South Position: Our Statement of Purpose," (1995–1999) On-line: http://www.dixienet.org/positions/lsposition.htm [accessed 23 October 2003 and 15 June 2004].

92. Hill, Michael. Fourth Annual League of the South National Conference, Biloxi, MS. (All Points South, 1997). Transcribed from videotape.

93. Hill, Michael. "A New Direction for the League," *Southern Patriot*, 10.4 (2003): 1.

94. Ibid.

95. Wilson, Clyde. "After Independence," *Southern Patriot*, 3.4 (1996): 27. Many neo-Confederate activists have adopted their own orthographic rules; thus "wont" is purposely spelled without an apostrophe.

96. Examining Siler City, Barry Yeoman makes clear that many Hispanic residents are U.S.-born citizens and legal immigrants from El Salvador, Guatemala, and Mexico. See "Hispanic Diaspora," *Mother Jones*, 25.4 (2000): 35–42, 76–77.

97. Hill, Michael. "Kith and Kin," *Southern Patriot*, 3.5 (1996): 34.

98. Hill, Michael. "A New Direction for the League," *Southern Patriot*, 10.4 (2003): 1. The plans for anti-immigrant rallies are in Hill, Michael. "A Realistic Assessment," *Southern Patriot*, 10.5 (2003): 1–2.

99. Hill, Michael. "Kith and Kin," *Southern Patriot*, 3.5 (1996): 33–34.

100. Ibid.

101. Francis, Samuel T. "The Huddled Masses," *Southern Partisan*, 3–4 (1981): 31.

102. Landess, Thomas. "The Statue of Liberty Is Falling to Pieces, and I'm Glad," *Southern Partisan*, 4.3 (1984): 8.

103. van Dijk, Teun A. "Racist Discourse," *Routledge Encyclopedia of Race and Ethnic Studies*, ed Ellis Cashmore. (London: Routledge, 2004): 353 (original emphasis). See also Jackson, Peter. *Maps of Meaning: An Introduction to Cultural Geography*

(London: Unwin Hyman, 1989), which examines the language of "floods" of immigrants (pp. 140–145).

104. Cawthon, William Lamar Jr. "The South as an Independent Nation," *Southern Partisan*, 17 (3rd Quarter 1997): 22.

105. Carlson, "The Suicide of the West," (2002): 10.

106. Hill, Michael. "Kith and Kin? Or a 'Proposition Nation?'" On-line: http://www.dixienet.org/dn-gazette/kith.htm [accessed 2 January 2004].

107. Reisigl, Martin, and Wodak, Ruth. *Discourse and Discrimination: Rhetorics of Racism and Anti-Semitism.* (London: Routledge, 2001): 76.

108. Hill, "A Realistic Assessment," (2003): 1.

109. Davenport, Charles Jr. "Towards a Common Culture," *Southern Partisan*, 22.4 (July/August 2002): 21. This article was published in the *Southern Partisan* issue between volumes 22.3 and 22.5, although there is no issue number on the magazine itself.

110. Woods, Thomas E. Jr. "Copperheads," *Southern Patriot*, 2.1 (1995): 5.

111. Hill, Michael. "Ratification of the 14th Amendment," *Southern Patriot*, 6.6 (1999): 1–2.

112. Prior to the 1965 Voting Rights Act, reading and writing tests for voters had been notoriously applied in the Southern United States in an effort to deny the vote to African Americans; see Kousser, J. Morgan. *The Shaping of Southern Politics: Suffrage Restriction and the Establishment of the One-Party South, 1880–1910.* (New Haven: Yale University Press, 1974), and Perman, Michael. *Struggle for Mastery: Disenfranchisement in the South, 1888–1908.* (Chapel Hill: University of North Carolina Press, 2001).

113. Kennedy and Kennedy, *The South Was Right!* (1994 [1991]): 251.

114. Hill, Michael. League of the South National Conference, Charleston, South Carolina (1994). Transcribed from videotape. Details for ordering this videotape are in *Southern Patriot*, 2.1 (1995): 8, which advises readers to request the video from Southern League, P.O. Box 40910, Tuscaloosa, AL 35404-0910.

115. Fleming, Thomas. "On Liberty," *Southern Partisan*, 2.3 (1982): 4.

PART II

PRACTICING NEO-CONFEDERACY

CHAPTER 6

Fighting for the Lost Cause: The Confederate Battle Flag and Neo-Confederacy

GERALD R. WEBSTER AND JONATHAN I. LEIB

During the past decade the American South has witnessed dozens of controversies over the appropriate display of symbols, the celebration of historical events, and the memorialization of individuals associated with the short-lived Confederate States of America (1861–1865). These controversies have surrounded school dress codes that ban clothing with Confederate symbols in Alabama,[1] the naming of public schools after Confederate military figures in Virginia,[2] the display of the Confederate battle flag on specialty license plates in Tennessee[3] and on a city logo in Florida,[4] litigation over a barbecue sauce boycott stemming from the producer's support for Confederate symbols in South Carolina,[5] and the chief justice of the U.S. Supreme Court leading a sing-along including the song "Dixie" at a gathering of lawyers from Maryland, Virginia, West Virginia, North Carolina, and South Carolina.[6] While the most widely publicized of such controversies have occurred in the Deep South states of Mississippi, Alabama, Georgia, and South Carolina,[7] at times these debates have spilled beyond the region's boundaries to states such as Maryland,[8] Texas,[9] Kansas,[10] and Massachusetts,[11] and even to the chambers of the U.S. Senate in Washington.[12]

These debates are almost universally over the meaning of Confederate symbols, past and present. Many of the region's white residents view the Confederate battle flag, for example, as symbolic of the bravery and sacrifice of their ancestors during the Civil War. To these citizens the battle flag is emblematic of the honor and integrity of the struggle for Southern independence as embodied in the myth of the "Lost Cause." In contrast, other residents of the region interpret the battle flag as symbolic of the South's political and military efforts to preserve slavery within its boundaries. These residents, including most of the region's African American population, also associate the battle flag with the violent activities of racist hate groups during the Massive

Resistance to desegregation in the 1950s and 1960s.[13] Thus, while many if not a majority of the South's native white residents view symbols associated with the Confederate States of America in terms of heritage, most of the region's black residents view the same symbols as emblematic of hate and racism.[14]

It is not coincidental that strident debates over the meaning of Confederate symbols have risen significantly in number in the past decade. Simultaneous with the increase in such controversies has been the growing size and militancy of the neo-Confederate movement across the South.[15] While today there are several dozen active neo-Confederate organizations, the formation of the Council of Conservative Citizens (ccc) in 1985 and the League of the South (ls) in 1994 provided aggressive leadership and direction to the movement.[16] Confederate battle flags and discussions of neo-Confederate beliefs are prominent on the web sites of both groups. The ccc is more directly racist in its appeals for support than the ls, and is the larger of the two groups in terms of total membership.[17] But the less racial and strident appeals of the ls have been more successful in attracting a broad membership with many professionals, including academics.[18] The ls has also been a participant in multiple battles over the public display of the battle flag in such states as Alabama, Georgia, and South Carolina.[19] And the neo-Confederate movement generally has been highly effective in attracting support by appeals that are nationalist in character about defending "Southern heritage."[20] These groups have also been supported by the publication and wide distribution of a large number of "call to arms" books, including Grissom's *Southern By the Grace of God* (1988), Kennedy and Kennedy's *The South Was Right!* (1994), Hinkle's *Embattled Banner* (1997), Thornton's *The Southern Nation: The New Rise of the Old South* (2000), and Kennedy's *Myths of American Slavery* (2003), among many others.[21]

Emphasizing the flags of the Confederacy, their use and meaning, this chapter has three purposes. First, we provide an overview of the history of development, use, and display of the various Confederate flags, especially the battle flag. Second, we discuss the myth of the Lost Cause and why a vigorous defense of the battle flag is viewed as so central to the neo-Confederate movement's efforts. Finally, we provide three examples of the neo-Confederate movement's use and defense of the battle flag.

Confederate Flag History

Jefferson Davis was inaugurated as president of the provisional government of the Confederate States of America (csa) on 18 February 1861 on the steps

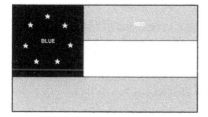

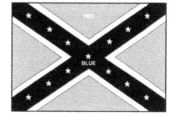

Figure 6.1. The four primary flags of the Confederacy: First Flag of the Confederacy, 4 March 1861 ("Stars and Bars," *top left*); Second Flag of the Confederacy, 1 May 1863 ("Stainless Banner," *bottom left*); Third Flag of the Confederacy, 4 March 1865 ("Final Edition," *top right*); Confederate Battle Flag ("Starry Cross" or "Southern Cross," *bottom right*).

of the Alabama statehouse in Montgomery. At the time no official flag of the csa had been adopted and the state flag of Alabama flew over the new Confederate capital. But the provisional government formed a "Committee on Flag and Seal" to develop a national flag for the seceding slave states. The committee reviewed hundreds of proposed flags, many bearing a strong resemblance to the national flag of the United States. The committee's chair, Confederate congressman William Porcher Miles, proposed an alternative design for the csa's national flag based upon the flag of South Carolina's Secession Convention, which provided the model for the later Confederate battle flag.[22] Miles's flag was not adopted, however, and the first flag of the Confederacy, similar to the national flag of the United States, was divided into three equal-width stripes, with red stripes at the top and bottom and a white stripe in the center (Figure 6.1, *top left*). The upper stripes were broken on one side by a blue canton, including a star for each state joining the csa.[23]

The similarity of the new Confederate flag to the national flag of the United States soon proved problematic. First, the Stars and Bars and the

Stars and Stripes were easily confused for one another on Civil War battle-fields. For example, Confederate general P.G.T. Beauregard nearly fired upon reinforcements moving to join him at the Battle of Bull Run in July 1861, thinking they were carrying the U.S. national flag. Later that same day Confederate troops did fire upon another Confederate regiment, again based on confusion over the flags. These events led Beauregard to press for a change.[24] Second, as the war progressed and became more violent, the Stars and Stripes became viewed more critically as "vile, odious and execrable."[25] As a result, the similar design of the Stars and Bars became a liability, leading to calls for "a true replacement" flag to be developed.[26]

Due to these complaints, on 1 May 1863 the Confederate Congress passed a bill to create a new national flag, subsequently referred to as the "Stainless Banner" (Figure 6.1, *bottom left*).[27] The bulk of the flag was white with the familiar Confederate battle emblem placed on the flag's canton. Some discussions of the flag suggested its white field was "emblematic of the purity of the Cause which it represented."[28] But other contemporaneous comments indicated the flag's white field was a statement about race. The *Savannah Morning News*, for example, argued that the flag's white field indicated that "we are fighting to maintain the Heaven-ordained supremacy of the white man over the inferior colored race" and that the new flag would be "hailed as the WHITE MAN'S FLAG."[29] Bonner also points out with regard to this interpretation that Confederate racism "hardly needed overt expression" and that the "flag's whiteness and 'purity' . . . [also reflected] . . . religious rather than explicitly racial themes" to many.[30] Religious fervor and racism were commonly mixed in the region during this period, and arguments that slavery was part of God's plan to Christianize Africa were prevalent.[31] Some clergy argued that slavery reflected a biblical hierarchy of God, men, women, children, and slaves, with objections to this structure being dismissive of God's will.[32] Thus, claims of racial and religious purity were frequently conflated, and arguments that the flag represented one or the other are not mutually exclusive but are arguably reflective of overlapping worldviews during the period.

Problems with the Stainless Banner emerged soon after its introduction. Most important, the flag was too easily mistaken for a flag of truce on a wind-less day. After several months of debate, the Confederate Congress adopted the "final edition" of the national Confederate flag on 4 March 1865. This version reduced the size of the Stainless Banner and added a red vertical strip to the fly end (Figure 6.1, *top right*).[33] Thus, it was only a variation of the previous national flag and arguably continued to reflect the Stainless Banner's emphasis upon the "purity" of the Confederacy's cause and/or the superiority of the white race.[34]

⸗ As noted above, the Confederate battle flag was proposed as the national flag in early March 1861 by William Porcher Miles. The design of Miles's flag included the blue saltire (or Saint Andrew's Cross), borrowed from the flag of Scotland and was similar to South Carolina's Secession Convention flag.[35] After the Battle of Bull Run, General Beauregard requested that Miles pursue a change in national flags through the Confederate Congress. Miles suggested this effort was unlikely to be successful and proposed that his earlier design for the Confederate national flag was sufficiently distinctive to be used as a battle flag. Beauregard and others concurred and a square design for the Confederate battle flag was developed (Figure 6.1, *bottom right*).[36] Notably, Miles favored the battle flag design because "it avoided the *religious* objections about the cross (from the Jews and many Protestant sects), because it did not stand out *so conspicuously* as if the cross had been placed upright."[37] Frequently referred to as the "Southern Cross" or "Starry Cross," the Confederate battle flag was in regular use from late 1861 throughout the remainder of the Civil War. It has arguably become more associated with the Confederacy than any of the three short-lived Confederate national flags.[38]

During Reconstruction the battle flag was sometimes treated as "contraband" and its display was forbidden.[39] While some Southerners did fly the battle flag at their residences to demonstrate their defiance of federal authority during Reconstruction,[40] the flag's display appears to have been limited until the departure of federal troops in 1877. Subsequently the flag was a common icon at Confederate soldier reunions and celebrations promoting the memory of the "Lost Cause" throughout the latter portion of the nineteenth century.[41] Such celebrations were most common during the "Confederate memorial period" between 1890 and 1915, with a decline in their frequency as the number of surviving Confederate veterans declined. Due in part to the successful meshing of soldiers from both the North and South in the Spanish-American War, relations between the two sections improved after 1900. In 1905 and 1906 Congress voted to return battle flags captured during the Civil War to the Confederate Museum in Richmond.[42]

⸗ The visibility and notoriety of the battle flag also increased after 1900 due to the development of motion pictures and a fascination with Civil War themes by several film directors. A steady flow of such films began in 1908 with the release of *Days of '61*.[43] Many of these films were dismissive of African Americans and portrayed a "moonlight and magnolias" image of the white Antebellum South.[44] Clearly the most successful and damaging of the approximately 500 silent films released about the Civil War era in the first two decades of the twentieth century was D. W. Griffith's *The Birth of a Nation* (1915), based upon Thomas Dixon's 1905 novel *The Clansman*.[45] This movie portrayed African Americans as "savages" and the Ku Klux Klan as heroic protectors of Southern society.[46] Griffith's movie may have had more influence upon elevating the image of the South and the use of its symbols than any other except David O. Selznick's *Gone with the Wind* (1939). These two movies, and dozens of other lesser-known films, facilitated an image of a chivalrous and honorable Confederacy, furthered the development of the myth of the Lost Cause, and at least indirectly increased the acceptability of the Confederate battle flag.

The battle flag became increasingly prevalent during World War II when a number of regiments from the South capitalized on its growing notoriety and flew it over their quarters and battlefields.[47] The dispersion of the American armed forces around the globe during the war also made the battle flag a recognizable international symbol.[48] After the war public recognition of the battle flag increased dramatically as a result of its use at the Democratic Party's 1948 national convention. The convention adopted various civil rights proposals for its party platform, enraging the delegations of several Southern states. In response, the delegations walked out of the convention waving the battle flag.[49] Delegates from these states subsequently met in Birmingham in July 1948 as the States' Rights Party, nominating rabid segregationist Strom Thurmond as their presidential candidate. The so-called "Dixiecrat" convention opened with students from the University of Mississippi and Birmingham Southern University entering the auditorium waving battle flags.[50] Given that the States' Rights Party's platform was dominated by the issue of racial segregation, the Dixiecrat movement greatly increased the flag's association as the preeminent symbol of those opposing civil rights for the nation's black citizens.

The use of the battle flag as a symbol of such opposition increased dramatically after the 1954 Supreme Court's decision *Brown v. the Board of Education* and its rejection of "separate but equal" educational facilities for black and white students. The flag was also appropriated by hate groups such as the Ku Klux Klan and increasingly became an icon associated with strident if not violent racism. Some government entities in the South also provided sanction for its use in this manner. In 1956 the Georgia state legislature added the Confederate battle emblem to its state flag. Supporters of the change have suggested its timing was due to the approaching Civil War centenary, but flag opponents have argued the change was "to underscore the state's resolve to defy the federal government's attempts to integrate the state and destroy the 'Jim Crow' system of segregation."[51] In 1962, South Carolina raised the battle flag over the dome of its state capitol. As in Georgia, while some have suggested that this action was undertaken to commemorate the Civil War centenary, recent research has indicated the flag's placement was also to underscore resistance to the civil rights movement.[52] And in 1963 the fiery segregationist governor of Alabama, George Wallace, raised the battle flag above the state capitol dome in Montgomery just prior to a visit by U.S. Attorney General Robert F. Kennedy to discuss the desegregation of the University of Alabama.[53] The fact that Montgomery served as the first capital of the Confederacy was surely not lost on observers of Wallace's actions.

The Myth of the Lost Cause and the Battle Flag

The debate revolving around the meaning of the Confederate battle flag is both passionate and at times vitriolic. To understand the reasons for the stridency of the controversy, one must appreciate the flag's centrality to the myth of the Lost Cause, and the centrality of the myth to the South's regional identity, at least as defined by the neo-Confederate movement. The myth of the Lost Cause was initiated in the wake of the Confederacy's defeat in 1865, and has been progressively enlarged and modified for over a century.[54] The South was both physically and emotionally devastated by the Civil War. As David Goldfield notes:

> Union armies had destroyed two-thirds of the South's assessed wealth, two-fifths of the livestock, and one-quarter of the white men between the ages of twenty and forty. The invasion ruined half the South's farm machinery, destroyed many of its railroads, and shattered its industry. . . . In 1860 the southern states possessed slightly less than one-third of the nation's wealth; by 1870 that share had declined to 12 percent.[55]

Southerners had viewed themselves and their cause as religiously correct if not theologically inspired.[56] Charles Reagan Wilson writes, "Ministers and churches . . . insisted that the Confederacy was a crusade against the evil empire of the Yankee. It was a holy war."[57] Thus, "their defeat was more than a lost war; they had evidently fallen out of favor with God."[58] In response, the region sought an explanation for their defeat and found it in the developing rationalizations of the Lost Cause. Using "mental alchemy" on the results of the war itself, white Southerners "spun the straw of defeat into a golden mantle of victory. . . . They rejected the idea of defeat and the guilt such a result implied."[59]

The rejection of the idea of defeat was cumbersome to perpetuate, and the effort became highly intertwined with the region's aggressive religiosity.[60] This perspective aided in the elevation of the "righteousness of the Lost Cause to build a South united against" the perceived Godlessness of the North. Because the Lost Cause was not only the "defining element of white southern life," but also inextricably tied to slavery, the region's leaders could not promote a "reconciliation between the races" because it would implicitly admit Southern guilt.[61] As part of the myth, Southerners celebrated and revered the South's prewar conditions, structures, and viewpoints. As a result, "little reform was possible when the most Christian of acts was to try to live up to the standards of a slave society in the name and memory of the pure white soldiers who had died."[62] This mythologizing and rationalization created a "religion of the Lost Cause," or a "southern civil religion."[63] Wilson notes that "the history of the attitude known as the Lost Cause was the story of the use of the past as the basis for a Southern religious-moral identity, an identity as a chosen people."[64]

The elements of the myth of the Lost Cause are variable by time period and observer. But Mark Perry succinctly states that the "liturgy of the Lost Cause" included

that the South's cause was just, had nothing to do with slavery, that the southern armies had never been defeated but were simply overwhelmed by sheer numbers, that southern men were brave and true crusaders, [and] that Robert E. Lee could make no mistakes.[65]

J. Michael Martinez and Robert M. Harris explain that the myth was maintained by the

idea that by honoring and commemorating the personal sacrifice of Southerners as well as championing the social and political values of the antebellum South, the region could assuage the guilt and anxieties that many Confederates felt after Appomattox, and if not recapture the glory of the past, perhaps build a future from the ashes. . . . If the South was a defeated region, at least the former states of the Confederacy held one advantage over the North: In the South, "old times there are not forgotten."[66]

To ensure the past would not be forgotten, organizations were formed across the South to keep the CSA's progressively embellished memory alive. Such groups as the Sons of Confederate Veterans (SCV), United Daughters of the Confederacy (UDC), and Ladies' Memorial Associations (LMAs) actively promoted the "sacralization" of the antebellum South "by elevating the symbols of the Confederacy to sacred status." These symbols, including the battle flag, "functioned not as mere emblems but as *religious* symbols, as collective representations of the Southern historical experience" to ensure the Confederacy was both "Sacred" and "Immortal."[67] The LMAs and UDC also actively promoted the construction of monuments to memorialize the region's failed efforts in the Civil War. While the LMAs built hundreds of monuments in Southern cemeteries soon after the conflict's end, the UDC later pursued the erection of statues and plaques in the region's public spaces.[68] Flags, particularly the battle flag, were central elements in the process of the CSA's memorialization. As stated by Coski, "While the national flags of the Confederacy were not forgotten or forsaken, memorial organizations further elevated the status and visibility of the St. Andrew's cross pattern." The selection of the battle flag was largely because many veterans "testified that the battle flag was the only flag that meant anything to them."[69]

With the foregoing in mind, the roles of race and religion must be reiterated. The champions of the Lost Cause define Southern culture as white Southern culture and rarely allow for the contributions of black Southerners, many with lineages in the region equal to or longer than their white neighbors. Edward Ayers states that "the Confederate flag is a topic of such debate and divisiveness in the South today because it denies all that black and white Southerners share, because it reduces the South to a one-time and one-sided political identity."[70] The "nation" over which the battle flag flew between 1861 and 1865 plainly did not recognize its black residents as citizens or deserving of the freedoms conceived in the Declaration of Independence or Constitution.[71] These racist opinions and perspectives were cloaked and rationalized by the deeply religious fashion in which they were supported and promoted in Southern society. The battle flag is thus viewed by many white Southerners as a religious symbol of the fight to maintain the South as a bastion of Christianity, with its defense understood as an element of Christian duty. Yet given the plantation system defended by the Confederacy, Christian or not, the battle flag is understood as an emblem of the racism and violence of human chattel slavery by most of the region's black residents.[72] Equally true is the reality that some people, many of whom are active in the neo-Confederate movement, do not concede that the "Lost Cause" is lost, and would like to structure U.S. society and politics in the image of the pre–Civil War South.[73]

Neo-Confederate Groups and the Battle Flag

As noted above, there are now a long list of active neo-Confederate groups operating both in and out of the South, including the Confederate Society of America, the Council of Conservative Citizens, the Heritage Preservation

Association, the League of the South, the Southern Legal Resources Center, and the Southern Party. K. Michael Prince suggests that neo-Confederate groups can be differentiated from heritage organizations based upon the causes they pursue. While both neo-Confederate and Southern heritage groups such as the UDC and SCV attempt to defend Confederate history and symbols, "neo-Confederates view themselves as political separatists and southern nationalists and tend to take the idea of southern secession more seriously than heritage groups do."[74] In spite of this effort to distinguish between the two types of organizations, Prince concedes that distinctions between the two types of groups often "break down, with influences, positions, and even personnel flowing back and forth."[75] Thus, the Southern Poverty Law Center includes both the UDC and the SCV on their list of neo-Confederate groups.[76] But clearly neo-Confederate groups do have a more prominent political agenda, and frequently are more overtly racist.

It is also important to note that the development of the Internet has provided a vehicle for neo-Confederate groups to disseminate their messages as well as increase their memberships. The Internet allows such groups to interact with far larger numbers of individuals at far lower cost than the traditional means of using the mail or meeting halls.[77]

The remainder of this chapter provides examples of the neo-Confederate movement's use and defense of the Confederate battle flag. The first two examples examine the Council of Conservative Citizens and the League of the South. The third example centers around the use and defense of the Confederate battle flag by a private business, Maurice Bessinger's chain of barbecue restaurants in central South Carolina. Since 2000, Bessinger has become a *cause célèbre* of the neo-Confederate movement.[78] Not surprisingly, all three of the examples examined below have effectively employed the Internet to their benefit. We begin with the Council of Conservative Citizens.

Council of Conservative Citizens

The Council of Conservative Citizens (CCC) was founded in 1985, but traces its roots to the "Citizens' Councils" first created in Mississippi in the mid-1950s. Also called "White Citizens' Councils," these groups were formed to oppose integration in the wake of the Supreme Court's 1954 decision in *Brown v. Board of Education*.[79] In the Massive Resistance to the Court's order, these organizations spread rapidly from Mississippi to Alabama, Louisiana, South Carolina, Florida, Texas, Virginia, Arkansas, and Tennessee. By 1957 there were approximately 250,000 members of these Citizens' Councils.[80]

The White Citizens' Councils have been referred to as the "uptown Klan" or "country club Klan" because of their efforts to avoid the "cruder forms of lawlessness perpetrated by the Klan" and efforts to develop more "prestigious membership rosters."[81] In spite of enrolling politicians, doctors, and business leaders, the goals of the Councils were not fundamentally unlike those of the Klan. They embraced virulent racism to defend the "Southern way of life," using economic pressure instead of physical violence to pursue their goals. Among these were the preservation of "the 'natural rights' of racial separation and 'the maintenance of our States' Rights to regulate public health, morals, marriage, education, peace and good order in the States under the Constitution of the United States.'"[82] The Councils were openly racist and argued that African Americans were "indolent" and had an "inherent deficiency in mental ability."[83] Their literature railed against integration, egalitarianism, and liberalism, and accused the NAACP of being "controlled by Communists intent on destroying America."[84]

The White Citizens' Councils declined in membership and importance as black Southerners progressively gained their constitutional civil rights in the 1960s and 1970s. But in 1985 the organization was reborn as the Council of Conservative Citizens (CCC). Meeting in Atlanta, the thirty "founders" included several former members of the White Citizens' Councils who came together due to their "frustration with government 'giveaway programs, special preferences and quotas, crack-related crime and single mothers and third generation welfare mothers dependent on government checks and food stamps.'"[85] Using the membership base of the earlier White Citizens' Councils, the CCC was successful in attracting converts and had a membership of approximately 15,000 in 1999.[86] Today the organization focuses on such issues as the New World Order, states' rights, interracial marriage, black-on-white crime, the destruction of Southern culture, and the defense of the Confederate battle flag. The racism that permeated the Citizens' Councils in the 1950s and 1960s was only slightly less blatant than that characterizing the CCC's current techniques and agenda.[87]

A visit to the CCC's web site quickly confirms the group's racially based message.[88] In mid-June 2004, their home page prominently displayed a Confederate battle flag without explanation, which suggests that the flag is a general symbol of the group's worldview. The same page also included a battle flag as an icon that provided a link to "Confederate Wave," a project to erect 1,000 flag poles for flying the battle flag across Georgia. At the time Georgia was involved in a protracted controversy over efforts to alter its state flag, which included the battle emblem.[89] The web site proclaimed that "the anti-Southern cartel can be defeated. The purpose of this website is to provide information on how to do so and make the . . . tools available to you. You too can Stand Up and Defend Southern Heritage." Confederate Wave was successful in Georgia and then expanded to Alabama.

The opening page of the CCC's web site also includes advertisements for books and videotapes, links to articles and editorials espousing the group's point of view, and links to CCC state chapters. When examined for this essay, the main page included a note about the passing of ninety-seven-year-old Alberta Martin, the last living widow of a Confederate soldier. As a human connection to the Confederacy, Mrs. Martin was referred to as the "'first lady' of Confederate heritage groups late in her life."[90] In June 2004, a visitor to the site could order a supply of Maurice Bessinger's mustard-based barbecue sauce. Bessinger has become an active participant in the neo-Confederate movement and is discussed in more detail below. Visitors could also order a book entitled *The King Holiday and Its Meaning*, purporting to explain "the Truth about Martin Luther King and why he does not deserve a national holiday in his honor."

The CCC web site also typically includes articles on subjects of interest to its members. In June 2004, the web site provided articles on integration ("Brown vs. The Bored"), gays and lesbians ("'Homo' Depo Supports Queer Agenda"), slavery ("Republican Apologies for Slavery"), Jews ("Celebrities Embrace Jewish Sorcery"), immigration ("Immigration's Silent Invasion"), and states' rights ("Separation, Secularism, or States' Rights?"). A perusal of these articles clearly indicates the CCC's affinity with its more aggressive anti-Semitic and racist precursor.

As noted, the CCC's web site provides links to its chapters around the United States. In June 2004 there were thirteen such links to chapters in Arkansas, Georgia, Indiana, New York, Mississippi, and South Carolina, among others. From the East Central Tennessee chapter's page one may find a "Frequently Asked Questions" section, discussing a number of the organization's views. For example, one learns that the CCC differs from other conservative groups because it is "not afraid to speak out on racial problems and other taboo subjects." The discussion goes on to say that the CCC speaks "out for white European-Americans, their civilization, faith and form of government. . . . The CCC recognizes that European Christian heritage is essential for the survival of our standard of living and way of life." Though admitting that the Southern Poverty Law Center, Anti-Defamation League, and National Association for the Advancement of Colored People have "branded the CCC as a racist hate group," the web site argues that this is "not true." Rather, the site claims that the "word *racism* was concocted by a communist ideologue in the 1920s . . . to instill guilt and shame in the minds of white people and to inflame racial hostility among blacks." The discussion concludes with the contention that "it is normal for white people to be proud of their race and heritage."[91]

The CCC's site also includes nearly two dozen links to the sites of other organizations, many with racist or Confederate themes. Thus, one can connect with "Eurocentric," the "Order of St. Andrew," or "Civil War Two," find a copy of the Confederate Constitution, and order a flag from the Ruffin Flag Company. One of the most disturbing links is to a site entitled "KPS Reports," which states it is directed at German Americans. This site claims that Germany was "The Noblest Nation of the Twentieth Century." While not all linked sites are as directly racist or anti-Semitic, thematically they are almost uniformly extremist.

The CCC has also generated a fair measure of press attention in recent years due to its interactions with notable politicians. For example, in 1999 among its estimated 15,000 members were thirty-four members of the Mississippi state legislature, including a mix of both Democrats and Republicans.[92] A number of notable political figures have attended CCC meetings, including former Mississippi governor Kirk Fordice, former Alabama governor Guy Hunt, former North Carolina senator Jesse Helms, and former Alabama public service commissioner George C. Wallace Jr. The CCC received its most substantial national attention when it was revealed that Republican congressman Bob Barr of Georgia and Senate Majority Leader Trent Lott, Republican of Mississippi, had delivered speeches to the group. Lott's involvement with the CCC was apparently more substantial than Barr's, and he was reportedly an "honorary member." *The Citizens Informer,* a CCC publication, reported that Lott stated in his speech to the group "that the people in this room stand for the right principles and the right philosophy." Unlike Barr, Lott "never condemned the group's racist ideology explicitly and unequivocally."[93]

The League of the South

The League of the South (LS), formerly the Southern League, was founded in June 1994, in Tuscaloosa, Alabama. Its founder, Dr. Michael Hill, was at the time a part-time history instructor at the University of Alabama who argued that the federal government had unconstitutionally usurped the power of the states. In response, the purpose of Hill's organization was to reestablish the constitutional balance of authority between the states and the federal government, even if such an effort required secession. Also central to the purpose of the LS was to increase public awareness of the history and culture of the South and to improve reverence for the South's symbols, including the Confederate battle flag (Figure 6.2).[94]

Figure 6.2. Dr. Michael Hill speaking at a Confederate Memorial Day Parade, Northport, Alabama, 26 April 1997. (Photograph by Gerald R. Webster)

The LS grew throughout the late 1990s, and by 2000 the Southern Poverty Law Center estimated the group had 9,000 members spread across ninety-eight chapters in twenty states.[95] In 2003, Hill stated the LS had 15,000 members.[96] In spite of a number of controversies, the leaders of the LS were less strident than those of many other neo-Confederates, at least in its early years. This may have been due in part to the sophistication of members of the LS leadership, which included a number of PhDs teaching at prominent universities in the South, including the University of South Carolina, the University of Georgia, the University of Virginia, and Emory University.[97] As the organization's membership grew, however, so too did the number of members with associations to hate groups. The group's increasing extremism led the Southern Poverty Law Center to classify the LS as a hate group in 2000. As Mark Potok, editor of the Center's *Intelligence Report*, stated, "Where the League's leaders once emphasized the culture and history of the South, today they are publicly hostile to blacks and other minorities."[98] After noting LS efforts at promoting historical revisionism, such as their contention that the "Civil War had almost nothing to do with slavery," Potok goes on to state that "the danger is that the toxic views of Michael Hill and his co-religionists, increasingly public as the neo-Confederate movement grows, will come to be seen as just another interpretation of history."

A visit to the LS web site (formerly http://www.dixienet.org, and, at the time of writing, http://www.leagueofthesouth.net) quickly indicates the group's allegiances and points of view. At the top of the site is a collage of rally or march scenes displaying numerous battle flags. Below this opening panel is the statement that "We Seek to Advance the Cultural, Social, Economic, and Political Well Being and Independence of the Southern People by all Honourable Means." Of course, "Southern People" is implicitly if not explicitly defined as those of "Anglo-Celtic" heritage. An LS posting pertaining to "freedom of expression" argues that the Scots, Irish, Welsh, and English gave the South its "core culture" and "Dixie its unique institutions and civilisation. . . . We must maintain this all-important link to our European heritage from which we have drawn inspiration."[99] Though Hill suggests that black Southerners should be treated with "Christian charity," he argues that this does not mean LS members must accept "egalitarianism" if it means "that white Southerners should give control over their civilisation and its institutions to another race, whether it be native blacks, or Hispanic immigrants." Hill continues:

> Today's white Christian Southerners are the blood descendants of the men and women who settled this country and gave us the blessings of freedom and prosperity. To give away this inheritance in the name of "equality" or

"fairness" would be unconscionable. As the progeny of Lee, Jackson, Forrest, and Davis, let us summon the courage to defend what the God of the ages has given us.[100]

Thus, the contributions of the South's black residents, many with family histories of regional residence longer than their white neighbors, are largely dismissed. They are not viewed as part of the "nation," and thus not included fully in the LS's vision of the South's future.

The League of the South's hostility to non-Southerners is also made clear in its rhetoric about Yankees and immigrants. On 17 June 2004, the web site targeted immigrants with a picture of a woman, most likely Latina, standing behind a dozen small children between two shack-like structures with the words "America's Third World Future." Yankees, on the other hand, are charged with defaming Confederate symbols. Hill is quoted in a 13 January 2003 article as saying that "Yankee politicians Richard Gephardt (Missouri) and Joe Lieberman (Connecticut)" should "go home and leave Southerners and their symbols alone. This kind of Yankee meddling is not welcome in the South." Hill claims that such attitudes "point up a deep-seated hatred and a desire to whitewash what the War for Southern Independence was all about." To Hill, "liberal Yankee politicians" are "telling us we must furl the flag and commit cultural suicide."[101] He suggests that the flag debate "is a war for the South's very survival. We ask no quarter and shall give none."[102]

Southern symbols including the battle flag receive a great deal of attention on the LS web site. Hill provides an impassioned defense of the battle flag in "The Real Symbolism of the St. Andrews Cross."[103] He quotes Dr. Clyde Wilson, a member of the LS Board of Directors, as stating that the Confederate battle flag is "the most potent symbol in all the world today of a spirit of resistance to all that is summed up by the label 'New World Order.'" While agreeing with Wilson, Hill suggests "we would do better to frame the debate in terms of what our noble flag stands for and that is Christian liberty." As he argues, the New World Order is a "state of open rebellion against God," and "Christians must stand against the new pagan order." He concludes: "Wherever and whenever our starry St. Andrews cross waves, let it be in defense of . . . [the] . . . vital truth" that humanity has a "subordinate standing to Him." Thus, the battle flag becomes not only a symbol of the Confederacy and the Lost Cause, but also of Christian duty to oppose the demise of Southern culture by outside forces, particularly globalists and Yankees.

The LS web site also provides substantial links to other groups providing Southern news and views and companies selling Southern or Confederate items. Among these are C.S.A. Today ("Dixie's News Source for Christian

Southerners"), Dixie Broadcasting ("The Powerful New Voice of Today's Southern Movement"), Southern Outlet.com (flags, books, and music), Little River Trading Company (flags, music, clothing), the Rebel Store (flags, bumper stickers, collectibles), the Y'all Come Back Music Center (Southern and Scottish music), and numerous books with Southern themes. All of these advertisers use the battle flag as part of their displays.

The League of the South has arguably become the preeminent Southern nationalist group among the many now active, and a full accounting of its positions and activities is beyond the scope of this chapter. But as should be clear from the discussion above, its membership is passionate, frequently sophisticated, and substantial. At the time of writing there are at least nineteen state or multi-state LS chapters, with most located in the southeastern portion of the United States. The LS views the antebellum South as having been proper, heroic, and Christian, and a goal of the group is to re-create its values and circumstances while championing secession.[104] Although the LS provides explicit discussions of religion, with only a few exceptions, its discussions of race are more coded. Thus, Hill argues that the passage of the Fourteenth Amendment led to the "most far-reaching and nefarious consequences of Reconstruction,"[105] and Hill and Fleming suggest in the "New Dixie Manifesto" that "States' Rights Will Rise Again."[106] Recent press releases rail against immigration,[107] "Sodomite 'Marriage,'"[108] the Georgia flag debate,[109] and court decisions regarding the separation of church and state.[110] The LS also is increasingly becoming active in politics and was instrumental in the formation of the Southern Party. It endorsed John Thomas Cripps, pastor of the Confederate Presbyterian Church in Lumberton, Mississippi, in the 2003 gubernatorial election in Mississippi, citing his support for the preservation of the battle flag within the Mississippi state flag, his opposition to the "cultural Marxism" of "globalist institutions," his support for states' rights, and his standing as a "man who understands that God's law, as found in the Bible, is the basis for all legitimate man-made law."[111]

Maurice Bessinger, Barbecue, and the Flag

Our final example pertains to Maurice Bessinger, the owner of South Carolina's largest chain of barbecue restaurants, and his activist defense of the battle flag. In the summer of 2000, Bessinger protested the removal of the Confederate battle flag from atop the South Carolina state capitol by removing the American flags flying over his restaurants and replacing them with both the South Carolina state and Confederate battle flags.[112] In addition to unsuccessful efforts to force Bessinger to remove the battle flag from atop his restaurants, the controversy led at least nine large supermarket chains in the South to remove his signature mustard barbecue sauce from their shelves (Figure 6.3). The controversy also led a South Carolina utility company to disallow its employees from parking company vehicles at any of Bessinger's restaurants while on their lunch breaks, leading to harsh threats by members of the South Carolina legislature against the company.

Bessinger has been embroiled in controversies associated with race, religion, and aspects of the myth of the Lost Cause for several decades. For example, subsequent to the passage of the Civil Rights Act of 1964, activists attempted to integrate Bessinger's Columbia barbecue restaurant, one of the city's remaining holdouts against segregation. At the time Bessinger was a leading supporter of segregation in Columbia and actively fought against desegregation as president of the National Association for the Preservation of White People.[113] Due to his refusal to allow black patrons to eat in his restaurant, a lawsuit was filed and eventually resulted in a landmark decision by the U.S. Supreme Court.[114] Though unsuccessful, Bessinger defended his right to maintain a segregated restaurant by invoking the First Amendment and claiming he could not be forced to serve black patrons because his religious beliefs "compel[ed] him to oppose integration of the races whatsoever."[115] Suggesting that his white customers wanted to be served in a segregated environment, Bessinger argued in 2001 that the 1964 Civil Rights Act was "unconstitutional" because "it takes away our freedom to serve customers in the way they prefer."[116] Using a religious allusion, Bessinger argued that *the logic of private property rights includes the God-given right to run a segregated business if that is your choice, and your customers have indicated their approval of your choice by continuing to do business with you.*[117]

Bessinger also believes that the civil rights movement was forced on the South by "left-liberals" and that "segregation existed because both races wanted it and believed they were better off with it."[118] He argues that there is a direct link between the civil rights movement, the 1964 Civil Rights Act, and a developing world government controlled by global elites. To Bessinger these developments are apocalyptic in character, with the arrival of the "globalists" being a forerunner of the arrival of the Antichrist.[119] Indeed, he concludes that "the civil rights movement is a Satanic attempt to make it easier for a global elite, a group of extremely wealthy men with no Constitutional or national or cultural loyalties, working at an international level, to eventually seize power in this country."[120]

The preservation of the Confederate battle flag is central to Bessinger's fight against the Antichrist and global government because he sees it as a symbol of "God Almighty" that predates Christianity by at least 2,000

Figure 6.3. Maurice Bessinger's gourmet mustard barbecue sauce.
(Photograph by Jonathan Leib)

years.[121] He argues that "the X-Cross . . . has been God's battle-axe against Satan, against tyrants who would build global empires, and therefore against evil, tyrannical, centralized government."[122] Railing against efforts to remove the battle flag from public places in the South, he states that "God cannot be happy about this!"[123]

As noted, Bessinger was catapulted into the news in 2000 while the South Carolina legislature debated whether to remove the Confederate battle flag from the top of the state's capitol dome. During the debate, Bessinger issued a press release and sent a videotape to legislators urging them to keep the flag on top of the capitol, arguing that removing it would result in a loss of heritage, tourist dollars, and property values.[124] In July 2000 the battle flag was moved from the capitol dome to a Confederate soldiers' monument on the state capitol's grounds.[125] In response, Bessinger lowered the American flags that flew over his restaurants and raised battle flags in their place (Figure 6.4).[126] In August 2000 officials in the Columbia suburb of Lexington fined Bessinger for violating the town's zoning ordinance, which prohibited flying banners other than the U.S. or South Carolina flags without a permit.[127] Although Lexington officials offered to sell Bessinger such a permit, he refused, claiming that flying the flag was his constitutional right and that doing so was "not a racial statement but an exercise in personal liberty."[128]

Shortly after the controversy erupted, the Lexington town council altered their ordinance to permit Bessinger to fly the Confederate battle flag above his restaurant.[129] But by the time this accommodation had been completed, two columnists for *The State* in Columbia, South Carolina, had published articles detailing Bessinger's segregationist past.[130] John Monk's column was based upon an interview with Bessinger in which he detailed his attitudes on race, slavery, the Civil War, and the meaning of the battle flag. Echoing several aspects of the myth of the Lost Cause, Bessinger argued that the Civil War was not fought over the issue of slavery and that the battle flag "is a real Christian symbol. . . . It means freedom and liberty." In the interview, Bessinger made a distinction between "biblical slavery and heathen slavery." He stated that one must believe in "biblical" slavery because "if the Bible teaches that there is biblical slavery, then one must accept that or be against God." He argued that slavery in South Carolina was largely "biblical slavery," and that "most of the Southern slaves were treated well. They were members of the family."[131]

Monk's column also generated substantial interest because he revealed that Bessinger sold in his restaurant tapes and tracts on a variety of topics including slavery. Monk quotes one of these, "A Biblical View of Slavery," as stating that "slavery is not in and of itself sinful. The Bible allows slavery"

Figure 6.4. South Carolina state and Confederate battle flags flying outside Maurice Bessinger's barbecue restaurant, Lexington, South Carolina, October 2001. (Photograph by Jonathan Leib)

and "Many of those African slaves blessed the Lord for allowing them to be enslaved and sent to America. Because what they had over here was far better than what they had over there."[132] The author of the tract, Pastor John Weaver, is a Bob Jones University graduate and has authored other such tracts that can be accessed via Bessinger's web site, including "The Truth About the Confederate Battle Flag."[133] The controversy revolving around "A Biblical View of Slavery" helped to trigger the boycott of Bessinger's products and was subsequently pulled from his restaurants; it is not currently available on his web site, though discussion of it remains there.[134] It is also notable that the Southern Poverty Law Center reported that Weaver was appointed as Chaplain-in-Chief of the Sons of Confederate Veterans in 2000, a post he occupied until July 2004.[135]

In September 2000, Sam's Club, a division of Wal-Mart, removed Maurice's BBQ Sauce from their shelves throughout the Carolinas after a customer complained about the battle flag flying over Bessinger's restaurant.[136] Wal-Mart quickly followed suit, removing the products from their shelves throughout the South. Before making the decision, Wal-Mart employees visited Bessinger's West Columbia flagship restaurant, with a Wal-Mart vice president subsequently stating that the company was "not comfortable with some of the things we saw in there."[137]

Bessinger did receive support in his fight against the boycott from several quarters, including Reform Party presidential candidate Pat Buchanan (Bessinger's West Columbia operations had served as South Carolina headquarters for Buchanan's 1996 presidential run), the League of the South (which called for a boycott of those supermarkets that refused to carry Bessinger's sauce), and the National Association for the Advancement of White People (which on its web site called for a phone, email, and letter writing campaign against Wal-Mart).[138]

The grocery store boycott of Bessinger's products had substantial negative financial implications for his business. By the end of 2000, Bessinger estimated that his total revenues were down by 55 percent, with his wholesale business down by 98 percent.[139] As a result, Bessinger filed suit in state court against the nine grocery chains claiming the companies had withdrawn his products due to his personal political and religious views, which "had violated the state's unfair trade practices act." Two courts dismissed Bessinger's suits in October 2003 and March 2004, stating that there was no evidence that the grocery chains were "contractually bound to conduct business with Bessinger."[140] Bessinger responded that "state law is on my side without a doubt, but it's being interpreted in favor of the big chains. . . . Justice will be served. I have been terribly wronged." Though the court ruled that the legal system "cannot force a grocery store to sell a vendor's product," Bessinger appealed the decision to the U.S. 4th Circuit Court of Appeals.[141] In November 2004, the Circuit Court of Appeals affirmed the lower courts' decisions.[142] In May 2005, the U.S. Supreme Court refused to hear Bessinger's final appeal.[143]

The statewide controversy over Maurice Bessinger and the Confederate flag reemerged in August 2002 when SCANA, South Carolina's only Fortune 500 corporation and the parent company of the state's largest electric utility (SCE&G), announced that it was banning Confederate flag decals on private employee cars in its parking lots. Furthermore, employees could no longer park its company vehicles in Bessinger's parking lots during their lunch breaks. A SCANA spokeswoman stated that "both the flag and Maurice Bessinger are divisive issues. . . . For us to continue to be successful, we must have healthy, collaborative relationships with customers and co-workers. Divisive activities that disrupt harmony in the workplace are bad for business."[144] Bessinger denounced the company's decision, noting that "if the people of South Carolina cannot have freedom to honor one's heritage, then we are not free but are in fact slaves of these powerful groups and their lackeys in the government."[145] SCANA's policies led to protests as well as sharp criticism from Republican state senate president Glenn McConnell, who "threatened to wipe away SCANA's state-sanctioned monopoly, a move that could have crippled a publicly traded company with more than $3 billion a year in revenue,"[146] while two other pro-flag state senators threatened to block the utility's proposed rate hike before the state's public service commission.[147] Following the protests and threats, SCANA "clarified" its position, stating that it had not imposed an outright ban on Confederate flag stickers in its parking lots, but that they would maintain their policy that company vehicles were not to be parked in Bessinger's lots.[148] In response, Bessinger offered free meals to SCANA employees willing to park their company trucks in his lots. He also allowed SCANA employees driving their personal vehicles to his restaurants 50 percent discounts with proof of their employment. These discounts reportedly cost his business $3,000 a week.[149]

Conclusion: Neo-Confederacy and the Confederate Battle Flag

The Lost Cause presents a mythologized past that many in the neo-Confederate movement wish to use as a blueprint for the South's social, economic, and political future, whether or not the region remains part of the United States. Today the battle flag has been appropriated to be representative of all things neo-Confederate, a symbol of an idealized future for the region or even a new nation. As is clear from the three examples presented in this chapter, this vision is of a South that is strongly conservative, white, fundamentalist Christian, xenophobic, homophobic, self-reliant, and parochial.

The tainted character of the symbols of the Confederacy must be viewed through the lens of their racialized history.[150] During the Civil War, the battle flag represented the common soldier's efforts on behalf of the Confederacy's elite to maintain the plantation-slave-cotton complex and was arguably representative of the Confederacy generally and slavery especially. After Appomattox the battle flag increasingly became representative of the mythologized biblical righteousness of the CSA in its battle against the "Godless" Union, increasing its association with a strain of racially tainted Christian theology. After the Supreme Court's 1954 decision in the *Brown* case, the battle flag rapidly became the chosen symbol of the South's frequently violent Massive Resistance to the dismantling of the Jim Crow system of segregation, and became associated with the virulent racism of the 1950s, 1960s, and 1970s. Developing in the 1980s and 1990s, the neo-Confederate movement has used the battle flag as emblematic of its battles against the New World Order, globalists, multiculturalists, egalitarians, Marxists, and immigrants, in addition to those traditional targets for derision, such as racial minorities, nonfundamentalist Christians, and non-Southerners. While the battle flag's meaning has arguably been expanded, at the heart of its symbolism remains the perceived ongoing battle in a South set upon by nonwhite and non-Christian outside forces. The neo-Confederate movement cannot concede that the Confederate battle flag is racially tainted; such a concession would be paramount to conceding that the Lost Cause is racially tainted. As is clear from our discussion of the Council of Conservative Citizens, the League of the South, and Maurice Bessinger, to do the latter would negate the very reasons for the movement's existence.

Notes

1. Kampis, Johnny. "School Board Maintains Ban on Confederate Flag," *Tuscaloosa News,* (10 October 2000): 1A, 5A.

2. Szkotak, Steve. "Schools Fighting to Remove Confederate Namesakes," *Tuscaloosa News,* (21 December 2003): 7B.

3. Fly, Colin. "Tennessee Plate Includes Battle Flag," *Tuscaloosa News,* (28 January 2004): 3B.

4. Andio, Alliniece T. "Lake City Clash Over Flag Coincides with Olustee Fest," *Florida Times-Union,* Jacksonville (15 February 2001). On-line: *http://www.jacksonville.com/tu-On-line/stories/02150/met_5404429.html* [accessed 15 February 2001].

5. LeBlanc, Cliff. "Judge Drops One Suit Brought by Bessinger," *The State,* Columbia, SC (21 October 2003): A1.

6. Timberg, Craig. "'Dixie' Sing-a-long Led by Rehnquist Hits a Sour Note," *Birmingham News,* (22 July 1999): 8A.

7. Leib, Jonathan I., and Webster, Gerald R. "The Confederate Flag Debate in the American South: Theoretical and Conceptual Perspectives," *Beyond the Color Line? Race, Representation, and Community in the New Century,* ed. A. Willingham. (New York: Brennan Center for Justice at NYU School of Law, 2002): 221–242.

8. Associated Press. "Confederate Flag Supporters Rally Outside NAACP Meeting," *Tuscaloosa News,* (10 July 2000): 5A.

9. Vertuno, Jim. "Confederate Plaques Pulled at Courthouse," *Birmingham News,* (13 June 2000): 6A.

10. Asseo, Laurie. "Boy Loses Confederate Flag Fight," *Tuscaloosa News,* (3 October 2000): 4A.

11. Hentoff, Nat. "Stars and Bars at Harvard," *Washington Post,* (13 July 1991): A19.

12. Webster, Gerald R. and Webster, Roberta H. "The Power of an Icon," *Geographical Review,* 84.2 (1994): 131–143.

13. Bartley, Numan V. *The Rise of the Massive Resistance: Race and Politics in the South during the 1950's.* (Baton Rouge: Louisiana State University Press, 1969); Wilhoit, Francis M. *The Politics of Massive Resistance.* (New York: George Braziller, 1973).

14. Leib, Jonathan I. "Teaching Controversial Topics: Iconography and the Confederate Battle Flag in the South," *Journal of Geography,* 97.4–5 (1998): 234. See also Leib, Jonathan I. "Heritage versus Hate: A Geographical Analysis of Georgia's Confederate Battle Flag Debate," *Southeastern Geographer,* 35.1 (1995): 37–57, and Leib, Jonathan I. and Webster, Gerald R. "Rebel With(out) a Cause? The Contested Meanings of the Confederate Battle Flag in the American South," *Flag, Nation, and Symbolism in Europe and America,* ed. Thomas Hylland Eriksen and Richard Jenkins. (New York: Routledge, 2007): 31–52.

15. Southern Poverty Law Center. "Rebels with a Cause," *Intelligence Report,* 99 (2000): 6–12.

16. Southern Poverty Law Center. "A League of Their Own," *Intelligence Report,* 99 (2000): 13–17; Anti-Defamation League. "The Council of Conservative Citizens," *ADL: Law Enforcement Agency Resource Network: Extremism in America* (2004). On-line: *http://www.adl.org/learn/ext_us/CCCitizens.asp?xpicked=3&itme=12* [accessed 4 April 2004]; Webster, Gerald R. "If First You Don't Secede, Try, Try Again: Secession, Hate and the League of the South," *Spaces of Hate: Geographies of Discrimination and Intolerance in the U.S.A.,* ed. Colin Flint. (New York: Routledge, 2004): 137–164.

17. Allen, Colin. "Neo-Confederate Watch: Colin Allen Interviews Edward Sebesta," *The Touchstone,* 9.1 (March 1999). On-line: http://www.rtis.com/reg/bcs/pol/touchstone/february99/neoconf.html [accessed 8 April 2004].

18. Hague, Euan. "Texts as Flags: The League of the South and the Development of a Nationalist Intelligentsia in the United States 1975–2001," *Hagar: International Social Science Review,* 3.2 (2002): 299–339.

19. Webster, "If First You Don't Secede," (2004): 137–164.

20. See, for example, Kay, Greg. "Southerners and Nationalism," *New Nation* (2003). On-line: http://www.newnation.org/Archives/NNN-Guest-Column-29.htm[accessed 30 March 2004].

21. Grissom, Michael Andrew. *Southern by the Grace of God.* (Gretna, LA: Peli-

can Books, 1989 [1988]); Kennedy, James Ronald, and Kennedy, Walter Donald. *The South Was Right!* 2nd ed. (Gretna, LA: Pelican Publishing, 1994 [1991]); Hinkle, Don. *Embattled Banner: A Reasonable Defense of the Confederate Battle Flag.* (Paducah, KY: Turner Publishing Company, 1997); Thornton, R. Gordon. *The Southern Nation: The New Rise of the Old South.* (Gretna, LA: Pelican Publishing Company, 2000); and Kennedy, Walter Donald. *Myths of American Slavery.* (Gretna, LA: Pelican Publishing, 2003).

22. Cannon, Devereaux D. *The Flags of the Confederacy: An Illustrated History.* (Memphis: St. Lukes Press, 1988): 7–13; Prince, K. Michael. *Rally 'Round the Flag, Boys: South Carolina and the Confederate Flag.* (Columbia: University of South Carolina Press, 2004): 12

23. Bonner, Robert E. *Colors & Blood: Flag Passions of the Confederate South.* (Princeton, NJ: Princeton University Press, 2002): 39–66

24. McElroy, Patrick M. "The Confederate Battle Flag: Social History and Cultural Contestation." Unpublished thesis. (Tuscaloosa: University of Alabama, Department of Anthropology, 1995): 34–35.

25. Quoted in Bonner, *Colors & Blood,* (2002): 103.

26. Ibid., 104.

27. Cannon, *The Flags of the Confederacy,* (1988): 14–21.

28. Ibid., 19.

29. Quoted in Bonner, *Colors & Blood,* (2002): 115; See also Gordon, Asa. "Confederate Battle Flag Link to White Supremacy Well Documented!" *Atlanta Daily World,* (3 December 2000). On-line: http://www.members.aol.com/neoconfeds/adwdec3.htm [accessed 30 March 2004]; Sebesta, Edward H. "The White Supremacist Design Ideas in the 2nd and 3rd National Confederate Flags." On-line: http://www.templeofdemocracy.com/2ndnat.htm [accessed 30 March 2004].

30. Bonner, *Colors & Blood,* (2002): 116.

31. Sebesta, Edward H., and Hague, Euan. "The U.S. Civil War as a Theological War: Confederate Christian Nationalism and the League of the South," *Canadian Review of American Studies,* 32.3 (2002): 253–283.

32. Webster, Gerald R. "Religion and Politics in the American South," *The Pennsylvania Geographer,* 35.2 (1997): 155–158.

33. Cannon, *The Flags of the Confederacy,* (1988): 22–24.

34. Sebesta, "The White Supremacist Design Ideas."

35. Hague, Euan. "The Scottish Diaspora: Tartan Day and the Appropriation of Scottish Identities in the United States," *Celtic Geographies: Old Culture, New Times,* ed. David C. Harvey, Rhys Jones, Neil McInroy, and Christine Milligan. (London: Routledge, 2002): 139–156.

36. Cannon, *The Flags of the Confederacy,* (1988): 51–54.

37. This point is made by William Porcher Miles. Letter to General G. T. Beauregard (21 August 1861). *The Southern Magazine,* 3.4 (1872): 308.

38. Webster, Gerald R., and Leib, Jonathan I. "Whose South Is It Anyway? Race and the Confederate Battle Flag in South Carolina," *Political Geography,* 20.3 (2001): 271–299.

39. Coski, John M. "The Confederate Battle Flag in Historical Perspective," *Confederate Symbols in the Contemporary South,* ed. J. Michael Martinez, William D. Richardson, and Ron McNinch-Su. (Gainesville: University Press of Florida, 2000): 100.

40. McElroy, "The Confederate Battle Flag: Social History and Cultural Contestation," (1995): 40.

41. Foster, Gaines M. *Ghosts of the Confederacy: Defeat, the Lost Cause, and the Emergence of the New South, 1865–1913.* (New York: Oxford University Press, 1987).

42. Coski, "The Confederate Battle Flag," (2000): 195.

43. Chadwick, Bruce. *The Reel Civil War: Mythmaking in American Film.* (New York: Alfred A. Knopf, 2001): 40–44.

44. Ibid., 6.

45. Thomas Dixon is discussed in Chapter 8.

46. Chadwick, *The Reel Civil War,* (2001): 96–106.

47. Springer, Chris. "The Troubled Resurgence of the Confederate Flag," *History Today,* 43.6 (1993): 7–9.

48. Coski, "The Confederate Battle Flag," (2000): 108.

49. Barnard, W. D. *Dixiecrats and Democrats.* (Tuscaloosa: University of Alabama Press, 1985).

50. Coski, "The Confederate Battle Flag," (2000): 109.

51. Leib, Jonathan I., Webster, Gerald R., and Webster, Roberta H. "Rebel with a Cause?: Iconography and Public Memory in the Southern United States," *GeoJournal,* 52.4 (2001): 306. See also Leib, Jonathan I. "Heritage versus Hate: A Geographical Analysis of Georgia's Confederate Battle Flag Debate," *Southeastern Geographer,* 35.1 (1995): 37–57, and Davis, John Walker. "An Air of Defiance: Georgia's State Flag Change of 1956," *Georgia Historical Quarterly,* 82.2 (1998): 305–330.

52. Webster and Leib, "Whose South Is It anyway?" (2001): 271–299; Prince, *Rally 'Round the Flag,* (2004).

53. Webster, Gerald R., and Leib, Jonathan I. "Political Culture, Religion and the Confederate Battle Flag Debate in Alabama," *Journal of Cultural Geography,* 20.1 (2002): 1–26.

54. Nolan, Alan T. "The Anatomy of the Myth," *The Myth of the Lost Cause and Civil War History,* ed. Gary W. Gallagher and Alan T. Nolan. (Bloomington: Indiana University Press, 2000): 11.

55. Goldfield, David. *Still Fighting the Civil War: The American South and the Southern History.* (Baton Rouge: Louisiana State University Press, 2002): 18.

56. Miller, Randall M., Stout, Harry S., and Wilson, Charles Reagan, eds. *Religion and the American Civil War.* (New York: Oxford University Press, 1998).

57. Wilson, Charles Reagan. *Judgment and Grace in Dixie: Southern Faiths from Faulkner to Elvis.* (Athens: University of Georgia Press, 1995): 19.

58. Goldfield, *Still Fighting the Civil War,* (2002): 18.

59. Ibid., 19.

60. Hunter, Lloyd A. "The Immortal Confederacy: Another Look at Lost Cause Religion," *The Myth of the Lost Cause and Civil War History,* ed. Gary W. Gallagher and Alan T. Nolan. (Bloomington: University of Indiana Press, 2000): 185–218.

61. Paludan, Phillip Shaw. "Religion and the American Civil War," *Religion and the American Civil War,* ed. Randall M. Miller, Harry S. Stout, and Charles Reagan Wilson. (New York: Oxford University Press, 1998): 33.

62. Ibid.

63. Stout, Harry S., and Grasso, Christopher. "Civil War, Religion, and Communications: The Case of Richmond," *Religion and the American Civil War,* (1998): 347. See also Hunter, "The Immortal Confederacy," (2000): 185–218.

64. Wilson, Charles Reagan. *Baptized in Blood: The Religion of the Lost Cause, 1865–1920.* (Athens: University of Georgia Press, 1980): 1.

65. Perry, Mark. *Conceived in Liberty: Joshua Chamberlain, William Oates, and the American Civil War.* (New York: Penguin Books, 1997): 368.

66. Martinez, J. Michael, and Harris, Robert M. "Graves, Worms, and Epitaphs: Confederate Monuments in the South Landscape," *Confederate Symbols in the Contemporary South,* (2000): 144.

67. Hunter, "The Immortal Confederacy," (2000): 187, 193 (original emphasis).

68. Martinez and Harris, "Graves, Worms, and Epitaphs," (2000): 130–192; see also Gulley, H. E. "Women and the Lost Cause: Preserving a Confederate Identity in the American Deep South," *Journal of Historical Geography,* 19.2 (1993): 125–141. This process of memorializing the Lost Cause in the South's public spaces has been challenged (and controversial) for over a decade. For example, in Richmond, Virginia, the former capital of the Confederacy, vitriolic debate surrounded the 1995 erection of a statue to African American tennis star, human-rights activist, and Virginia native Arthur Ashe on Monument Avenue, which includes five statues to Confederate heroes and is considered to be one of the South's leading Confederate memorial sites. See Leib, Jonathan I. "Separate Times, Share Spaces: Arthur Ashe, Monument Avenue and the Politics of Richmond, Virginia's Symbolic Landscape," *Cultural Geographies,* 9.3 (2002): 286–312. Controversy also surrounded the 1999 unveiling of a large mural of Robert E. Lee as part of a larger historical display on Richmond's Canal Walk redevelopment project. See Leib, Jonathan I. "Robert E. Lee, 'Race,' Representation and Redevelopment along Richmond, Virginia's Canal Walk," *Southeastern Geographer,* 44.2 (2004): 236–262.

69. Coski, "The Confederate Battle Flag," (2000): 101, 102.

70. Ayers, Edward L. "What We Talk about When We Talk about the South," *All Over the Map: Rethinking American Regions,* ed. Edward L. Ayers, Patricia Nelson Limerick, Stephen Nissenbaum, and Peter S. Onuf. (Baltimore: Johns Hopkins University Press, 1996): 79.

71. Foner, Eric. *Who Owns History?* (New York: Hill and Wang, 2002): 167–204.

72. Webster and Leib, "Political Culture, " (2002): 1–26.

73. See, for example, Southern Caucus. "Why the South's 'Lost Cause' Isn't Lost!" On-line: http://www.southerncaucus.org/archives.htm [accessed 16 June 2004].

74. Prince, *Rally 'Round the Flag,* (2004): 55.

75. Ibid.

76. Southern Poverty Law Center. "The Neo-Confederates," *Intelligence Report,* 99 (2000): 28–31.

77. Warf, Barney, and Grimes, John. "Counterhegemonic Discourses and the Internet," *Geographical Review,* 87.2 (1997): 259–274; Webster, Gerald R., and Kidd, Timothy. "Globalization and the Balkanization of States: The Myth of American Exceptionalism," *Journal of Geography,* 101.2 (2002): 73–80.

78. See, for example, League of the South. "Wal-Mart and Sam's Heritage Violation," (2000). On-line: http://www.dixienet.org/hv/wal-mart.htm [accessed 11 May 2004]; Bessinger, Maurice. *Defending My Heritage: The Maurice Bessinger Story.* (West Columbia, SC: LMBONE-LEHONE Publishing, 2001); and Ford, Omar. "Locals Gather for Confederate Flag Rally at Waterfront Park," *Beaufort (SC)*

Gazette, (27 April 2003). On-line: http://www.beaufortgazette.com/local_news/ story/2492239p-2316384c.html [accessed 11 May 2004].

79. Bartley, *The Rise of the Massive Resistance*, (1969): 82–107.

80. Wilhoit, *The Politics of Massive Resistance*, (1973): 112.

81. Ibid., 111.

82. Anti-Defamation League. "The Council of Conservative Citizens," *ADL: Law Enforcement Agency Resource Network: Extremism in America* (2004). On-line: http:// www.adl.org/learn/ext_us/CCCitizens.asp?xpicked=3&itme=12 [accessed 4 April 2004].

83. Ibid.

84. Anti-Defamation League. "The Council of Conservative Citizens," *ADL Backgrounder* (1998). On-line: http://www.adl.org/backgrounder/ccc.asp [accessed 12 June 2004].

85. Anti-Defamation League. "The Council of Conservative Citizens," *ADL: Law Enforcement Agency*, (2004).

86. Southern Poverty Law Center. "The Neo-Confederates," (2000): 28–31.

87. Anti-Defamation League. "The Council of Conservative Citizens," *ADL: Law Enforcement Agency*, (2004).

88. See the Council of Conservative Citizens, National web site. On-line: *http:// www.cofcc.org/index.htm* [accessed 12 June 2004].

89. Leib, Webster, and Webster, "Rebel with a Cause?" (2001): 303–310.

90. In mid-June 2004 another "last Civil War widow" was uncovered in Arkansas named Maudie Hopkins. In 1934 at the age of 19 Ms. Hopkins married William M. Cantrell, then 86. Mr. Cantrell died in 1937, but supported the two of them on his Civil War pension during their three-year marriage. The pension brought "$25 every two or three months" into the household. See Nelson, Melissa. "Arkansas Woman Also Confederate War Widow," *Birmingham News*, (6 June 2004): 3B.

91. Council of Conservative Citizens, East Central Tennessee Chapter. "Frequently Asked Questions about the Council of Conservative Citizens." On-line: http://www.cofcc.org/ page12.htm [accessed 13 June 2004].

92. Edsall, Thomas. "Controversial Group Has Strong Ties to Both Parties in South," *Washington Post*, (13 January 1999): A2.

93. Anti-Defamation League. "The Council of Conservative Citizens," *ADL: Law Enforcement Agency*, (2004). See also Anti-Defamation League. "The Council of Conservative Citizens 'in the News': A Chronology of Events," *The Militia Watchdog* (1999). On-line: http://militia-watchdog.org/ccc.htm [accessed 12 June 2004].

94. Jones, Cinterro. "Professor Forms Southern League," *Crimson White*, (3 October 1994): 1, 5; Webster, "If First You Don't Secede," (2004): 137–164.

95. Southern Poverty Law Center. "A League of Their Own," *Intelligence Report*, 99 (2000): 13–17.

96. Beirich, Heidi, and Potok, Mark. "40 To Watch," *Intelligence Report*, Southern Poverty Law Center, 111 (2003): 27.

97. Hague, Euan. "Texts as Flags: The League of the South and the Development of a Nationalist Intelligentsia in the United States 1975–2001," *Hagar: International Social Science Review*, 3.2 (2002): 299–339.

98. Potok, Mark. "Of Hate and Heritage," *Intelligence Report*, Southern Poverty Law Center, 99 (2000): n.p.

99. League of the South. "Freedom of Association and Preserving the South's Core Anglo-Celtic Culture," (1995–2002). On-line: http://www.dixienet.org/positions/free-ac.htm [accessed 16 June 2004].

100. Hill, Michael. "The Issue of Race in the Southern Independence Debate: A Call for Proportionality, Honesty, Integrity, Morality and an End to Demagoguery," League of the South Position Paper, (2000). On-line: *http://www.dixienet.org/positions/race.htm* [accessed 15 June 2004 and 2 December 2004].

101. League of the South. "Yankee Politicians and Confederate Symbols," (2003). On-line: http://www.dixienet.org/ls-press-releases/yankee-polit.htm [accessed 16 June 2004].

102. League of the South. "No Compromise in Georgia or Elsewhere," (2003) On-line: http://www.dixienet.org/ls-press-releases/no-comp.htm [accessed 16 June 2004].

103. Hill, Michael. "The Real Symbolism of the St. Andrews Cross: Christian Liberty vs. the New World Order." On-line: http://www.dixienet.org/dn-gazette/st-andrews-cross.htm [accessed 1 July 2001 and 16 June 2004].

104. Webster and Kidd, "Globalization and the Balkanization," (2002): 73–80.

105. Hill, Michael. "Ratification of the 14th Amendment," *Southern Patriot*, 6.6 (1999): 1.

106. Hill, Michael, and Fleming, Thomas. "New Dixie Manifesto: States' Rights Will Rise Again," *Washington Post*, (29 October 1995): C03.

107. League of the South. "Flawed Immigration Policy Must Be Changed," (2003). On-line: http://www.dixienet.org/ls-press-releases/illegals.htm [accessed 14 June 2004].

108. League of the South. "The Latest Battle in the Culture War: Sodomite 'Marriage,'" (2004). On-line: http://www.dixienet.org/ls-pressreleases/May262004 Release.html [accessed 26 May 2004 and 15 June 2004].

109. League of the South. "RE: Georgia State Flag," (2003). On-line: http://www.dixienet.org/ls-press-releases/georgia-state.htm [accessed 16 June 2004].

110. League of the South. "Special Statement from the League of the South on the Ten Commandments Monument Removal," (2003). On-line: http://www.dixienet.org/ls-press-releases/10ComSpecial.htm [accessed 14 June 2004].

111. League of the South. "League of the South Endorses John Cripps in Mississippi Governor's Race," (2003). On-line: http://www.dixienet.org/ls-press-releases/Cripps.htm [accessed 15 June 2004].

112. Webster and Leib, "Whose South Is It anyway?" (2001): 271–299.

113. Cox, Maxie Myron Jr. "1963—The Year of Decision: Desegregation in South Carolina." Unpublished Ph.D. Dissertation. (Columbia: University of South Carolina, Department of History, 1996); Southern Regional Council. "Will the Circle Be Unbroken? Episode 4: Hey, Hey, Ho, Ho, Segregation's Got to Go—Columbia, South Carolina," (1997). Script on-line: http://www.unbroken.org/scripts04.htm [accessed 21 May 2004].

114. *Newman v. Piggy Park Enterprises, Inc.* 390 U.S. 400 (1968).

115. *Newman v. Piggy Park Enterprises, Inc.* 256 F. Supp. 941 (1966) at 954.

116. Bessinger, Maurice. *Defending My Heritage: The Maurice Bessinger Story.* (West Columbia, SC: LMBONE-LEHONE Publishing, 2001): 78.

117. Ibid., 82 (original emphasis).

118. Ibid., 74.

119. Ibid., 73–75.

120. Ibid., 70.

121. Ibid., xxi.

122. Ibid., 151.

123. Ibid., xxi.

124. Associated Press. "Bessinger Says Flag Should Stay," *The State*, Columbia, SC (6 January 2000): A6.

125. Webster and Leib, "Whose South Is It anyway?" (2001): 271–299.

126. Associated Press. "Maurice Raises Confederate Flag at Restaurants," *The State*, Columbia, SC (23 August 2000): B1.

127. Hines, Lora, and Flach, Tim. "Piggie Park Owner Faces Daily Fine for Flying Flag," *The State*, Columbia, SC (24 August 2000): B1.

128. Wilkinson, Jeff, Burris, Roddie, and Flach, Tim. "Bessinger Defends His Flag; Lexington Issues Second $500 Fine," *The State*, Columbia, SC (25 August 2000): A1.

129. Flach, Tim. "Lexington Finalizes Flag-Display Controls," *The State*, Columbia, SC (6 September 2000): B3.

130. Monk, John. "God, Barbecue, Slavery Meet at Maurice's," *The State*, Columbia, SC (27 August 2000): B1; Bolton, Warren. "Bessinger's BBQ not Sweet Enough to Erase Bitterness of Past, Present," *The State*, Columbia, SC (29 August 2000): A8; Firestone, David. "Sauce Is Boycotted, and Slavery Is the Issue," *New York Times*, 29 (September 2000): A14.

131. Monk, "God, Barbecue, Slavery," (27 August 2000): B1.

132. Similar attitudes caused a controversy in the Alabama state legislature in 1996 when Representative Charles Davidson used biblical passages in a speech that justified slavery. Davidson argued that those who disagreed with him "are obviously bitter and hateful against God and his word, because they reject what God says and embrace what mere humans say concerning slavery." He also suggested that the descendants of those Africans enslaved who embraced Christianity "are most grateful today." See Webster, "Religion and Politics," (1997): 151–172.

133. Weaver, John. "The Truth about the Confederate Battle Flag." On-line: http://www.mauricesbbq.itgo.com/truth.html [accessed 11 May 2004].

134. Weaver, John. "Pastor John Weaver Demands Explanation," (2000). On-line: http://www.mauricesbbq.itgo.com/politics/pastor-john-weaver.htm [accessed 30 June 2004].

135. Southern Poverty Law Center. "Racist Lawyer Joins SCV Leadership," *Intelligence Report*, 101 (2001): 3.

136. Thomas, Maurice. "Sam's Club Pulls Maurice's Sauce," *The State*, Columbia, SC (12 September 2000). On-line: http://www.dixienet.org/hv/wal-mart.htm [accessed 11 May 2004].

137. Thomas, Maurice. "Wal-Mart Takes Sauce off Shelves," *The State*, Columbia, SC (13 September 2000). On-line: http://www.dixienet.org/hv/wal-mart.htm [accessed 11 May 2004].

138. Davenport, Jim. "Buchanan Joins Fight over Barbecue Sauce," *Associated Press*, (16 September 2000). On-line: http://www.dixienet.org/hv/wal-mart.htm [accessed 11 May 2004]; Hill, Michael. "Retail Establishments Single Out Southern Patriot for

Discrimination," League of the South Press Release, (29 September 2000). On-line: http://www.dixienet.org/ls-press-releases/maurice.htm [accessed 11 May 2004 and 16 June 2004]; National Association for the Advancement of White People. "Freedom of Expression? NOT According to Sam's and Wal-Mart!" (2000). On-line: http://www.naawp.com/news/freedom-of-expression-walmart.htm [accessed 11 May 2004].

139. Dietrich, R. Kevin. "Stores Stand Firm on Sauce's Ban," *The State*, Columbia, SC (26 December 2000): A7.

140. Williams, Charles. "State Judge Dismisses Bessinger BBQ Suit," *Post and Courier*, Charleston, SC (17 March 2004). On-line: http://www.charleston.net/stories/031704/sta_17bess.html [accessed 11 May 2004]. See also Associated Press. "Bessinger Says He Has Sued Nine Grocery Chains," *The State*, Columbia, SC (16 August 2003): B2; LeBlanc, Cliff. "Judge Drops One Suit Brought by Bessinger," *The State*, Columbia, SC (21 October 2003): A1.

141. Williams, "State Judge Dismisses Bessinger," (2004).

142. See *Bessinger v. Food Lion, Winn Dixie, Sam's Club, Wal-Mart Stores, and Harris Teeter*, U.S. Court of Appeals No. 04-1067 through 04-1071. On-line: http://pacer.ca4.uscourts.gov/opinion.pdf/041067.U.pdf.

143. See U.S. Supreme Court No. 04-1246. On-line: http://www.supremecourtus.gov/orders/courtorders/051605pzor.pdf.

144. Quoted in Monk, John. "Confederate Flag Banned in SCANA Parking Lot," *The State*, Columbia, SC (15 August 2002). On-line: http://www.thestate.com/mld/thestate/3867128.htm [accessed 11 May 2004].

145. Quoted in Monk, John. "Sen. Glenn McConnell Wants Legislature to Punish the Company," *The State*, Columbia, SC (17 August 2002). On-line: http://www.thestate.com/mld/thestate/3882143.htm [accessed 11 May 2004]. Given the controversial nature of his comments on slavery in 2000 that helped spark the supermarket boycott of his products, it is interesting to note Bessinger's assumption of the mantle of slavery vis-à-vis his perceived relationship with the government. He has also suggested that the 1964 Civil Rights Act *"makes us slaves"* because the government is telling him whom he must serve and whom to hire (i.e., African Americans). Indeed, he asserted that *"this is involuntary servitude"* (original emphasis). Thus, having to serve and hire the descendants of slaves makes Bessinger a slave. See Bessinger, *Defending My Heritage*, (2001): 78.

146. Roig-Franzia, Manuel. "In S.C. Flag Dispute Enters Private Sector," *Washington Post*, (1 September 2002). On-line: http://www.washingtonpost.com/ac2/wp-dyn?pagename=article&contentId=A21133-2002Aug31&notFound=true [accessed 6 May 2004]; See McConnell, Glenn. "Editor's Note: The Following Letter Was Written by State Senator Glenn McConnell, R-Charleston, to William Timmerman, the Chief Executive Officer of SCANA," *The State*, Columbia, SC (17 August 2002). On-line: http://www.thestate.com/mld/thestate/news/local/3882087.htm [accessed 12 May 2004].

147. Monk, John. "SCANA Reverses Flag Policy," *The State*, Columbia, SC (21 August 2002). On-line: http://www.thestate.com/mld/thestate/3906200.htm [accessed 11 May 2004]. Widely considered to be South Carolina's most influential state senator and leading legislative battle flag defender, McConnell owns a Civil War memorabilia store in North Charleston that sells Maurice's BBQ Sauce—though McConnell has stated that he disagrees with Bessinger's views on slavery (see Kropf, Schuyler. "Mc-

Connell Selling Bessinger's Sauce," *Charleston Post & Courier*, (27 February 2001). On-line: http://www.mauricesbbq.com/politics.mcconell-selling-sauce.htm [accessed 23 June 2004], and Monk, John. "Sen. Glenn McConnell Wants Legislature to Punish the Company," *The State*, Columbia, SC (17 August 2002). On-line: http://www .thestate.com/mld/thestate/3882143.htm [accessed 11 May 2004]).

148. SCANA. "SCANA Clarifies Position on Controversial Issues," Press Release (21 August 2002). On-line: http://www.scana.com [accessed 11 May 2004]; Monk, John. "SCANA Reverses Flag Policy," *The State*, Columbia, SC (21 August 2002). On-line: http://www.thestate.com/mld/thestate/3906200.htm [accessed 11 May 2004].

149. Roig-Franzia, "In S.C. Flag Dispute," (2002).

150. This point is well made by Halton, Mark R. "Time to Furl the Confederate Flag," *Christian Century*, 105.17 (May 1988): 494–496.

CHAPTER 7

Neo-Confederacy and Education

EUAN HAGUE

Neo-Confederacy has long counted numerous academic professionals amongst its proponents, including current and former university and college faculty members as well as church ministers and other educators. As a result, strategies that encompass education form a central plank of the neo-Confederate program. Many neo-Confederates argue the educational system in the United States is prejudicial and discriminates against what they identify as Southern culture and heritage. The League of the South (LS), for example, has developed curricula for all ages that challenge established U.S. views of religion, history, and the Civil War, and promotes these curricula to home-schooling families. Other neo-Confederates such as Emory University philosophy professor Donald W. Livingston have argued that those who support such alternative historical interpretations need to help finance their dissemination and thus "should consider diverting some of the funds they unthinkingly give to mainstream colleges and universities to an institute of their choice."[1] Livingston himself helped to establish the League of the South Institute for the Study of Southern Culture and History (LSI) and subsequently founded the Abbeville Institute, which includes neo-Confederates like Thomas Fleming and Clyde Wilson amongst its faculty.[2] Similarly, the Stephen D. Lee Institute, closely aligned with the Sons of Confederate Veterans (SCV), promotes education about the South to those attending its events.[3] Many other comparable institutes were founded in the 1990s and 2000s, often counting the same individuals in their faculties.[4] In addition, summer 2006 saw the SCV operate its fourth annual Sam Davis Youth Camp for boys and girls ages twelve to seventeen, which taught attendees

> the truths about the War for Southern Independence . . . [and] thoughtful
> instruction in Southern history, the War Between the States, the theology

of the South during the War, lessons on Southern heroes, examples of great men of the Faith, and for the first year, special programs and sessions for our Southern ladies![5]

In this chapter, I focus on one of these neo-Confederate institutes, the League of the South Institute (LSI), which has developed a series of educational strategies for members and supporters to pursue. These include peer-to-peer teach-ins called "hedge school" seminars (a title chosen by the LS leadership because it refers to a system of education amongst Irish nationalists in the eighteenth century that was illegal under British law), an annual "Summer Institute" where LS officials deliver academic talks, and advocacy of home schooling.[6] The LS also publishes position papers, records lectures sold as teaching materials, and hosts national conferences where organization leaders lecture on numerous topics. Neo-Confederates maintain that it is the patriotic duty of peers to teach each other, and that of parents to educate their children, so that all may then defend the "truth" about the South and the Confederacy from the alleged misrepresentations forwarded by mainstream academic institutions.

Although the LSI and the other neo-Confederate educational venues do not award recognized academic qualifications, attract funding from government sources, or force their adherents to choose between them and other educational outlets, they do challenge the legitimacy of the U.S. educational system and question the teaching of U.S. history and other subjects in public and, to a lesser extent, private schools. This stance was brought into sharp perspective in August 2001, when the serving attorney for the Nassau County School Board since 1997, Richard Withers, was asked to resign from the body because he was a member of the League of the South. The rationale behind the move was that someone who belongs to an organization that rejects public schooling and actively promotes home schooling could not represent the best interests of a county school board. Entering the debate in Florida, LS president Michael Hill was quoted as saying, "Education, in the great Christian tradition, has always been the role of parents. Public schools, which were foisted upon the South during Reconstruction, have become propaganda factories and are not really educating people in the true sense of the word."[7] Although Withers claimed that he was unaware of the LS policy on schooling, and argued that it was not a conflict of interest, he resigned his membership in the League of the South.[8]

This chapter explores the development and operation of an educational program amongst neo-Confederate activists that proponents envisage as an alternative to the supposedly indoctrinating processes of public schooling and the academic mainstream. Despite the U.S. educational system being highly diffuse, with locally elected school boards, curricula often varying by state, and largely autonomous school districts, neo-Confederates picture the U.S. educational system as a top-down, government-designated process of indoctrination that ideologically conditions children. Such a stance is analogous to wider neo-Confederate beliefs regarding state authority and reflects beliefs about mass schooling in Western industrialized nations that have long been assessed by theorists of nationalism and nation-state formation.

Education and Nationalist Politics

In the nineteenth century, newly industrializing nation-states needed a literate, numerate workforce and had the power to produce one through a system of mass, standardized education. In this provision of an education for all by the modern nation-state, trained experts (teachers) rather than families or local communities were the educators, and schooling took place on a national scale. The costs of providing education for all citizens meant that mass schooling could only be provided by the state.[9] Not only did schools teach literacy and numeracy, they also inculcated patriotism and a standard national language. In the United States, for example, a sense of U.S. identity continues to be instilled into schoolchildren through rituals like the daily Pledge of Allegiance to the national flag.[10] Such processes of inculcation have been termed "banal nationalism" by Michael Billig, as they make the consumption and reproduction of the nation-state an ordinary, everyday experience.[11] Ernest Gellner, a leading analyst of nationalism, maintains that for the modern nation-state the "monopoly of legitimate education" is more important than the "monopoly of legitimate violence."[12] French thinker Louis Althusser adds that within the modern (Western) nation-state, schooling is more important to the maintenance of the nation-state than either parliamentary democracy or universal suffrage. Whereas everyone has to attend school, a stipulation enforced by state law, not everyone has to vote or even has the right to vote, and there have been times in the twentieth century when nation-states have abandoned parliamentary democracy but retained mass schooling. No state institution or corporate body other than schools has an audience of children guaranteed for "eight hours a day for five or six days out of seven."[13] Schooling thus becomes a critical component in inculcating nationalism. For neo-Confederates, one purpose of educating future generations is to pass on understanding and support of their beliefs in Southern nationalist causes, as Al Benson Jr. explains in *Southern Events:*

If we are to be able to affect the thinking and worldview of our grandchildren, we must work to develop a curriculum that will give them the essentials. . . . This struggle is multi-generational. It will not be won in a year, or in ten years, and if we fail to attempt to provide our children with decent educational material it will never be won. We must educate enough of our children via home schooling so that the day will come when they will stand up and present an accurate Southern viewpoint.[14]

Inculcation of young people into support for the Confederacy has long been a strategy of groups like the United Daughters of the Confederacy (UDC), whose members have actively joined school boards and vetted textbooks to ensure that mass education in the United States is provided with a pro-Confederate view of U.S. history.[15] Historian James McPherson, for example, explains that in the late nineteenth and early twentieth centuries, Confederate sympathizers and heritage organizations felt it was essential for the descendents of Confederate veterans to be inculcated into Southern nationalism and, as a result, "the Lost Cause triumphed in the curriculum, if not on the battlefield."[16] One strategy utilized by the UDC was to form chapters of "Children of the Confederacy." The constitution of these children's chapters, as outlined at the 1938 UDC annual convention, mandated that

the children of the South shall be taught the true history of the South; to honor and perpetuate the memories and the deeds and high principles of their Confederate ancestors; to assist in protecting and marking historical places of the Southern Confederacy.[17]

Descendents of Confederate veterans were supposed to participate in such groups until the age of eighteen, thereafter joining either the UDC or SCV. The UDC also produced texts to try and inculcate children into a pro-Confederate understanding of U.S. history, such as Decca Lamar West's *Catechism on the History of the Confederate States of America* (1934). A resident of Waco, Texas, West was an active figure in the UDC between World War I and World War II. In the *Catechism*, the issues of slavery and states' rights shape the history to be memorized by children:

Q: What causes led to the war between the States, from 1861 to 1865?
A: The disregard of those in power for the rights of the Southern States.
Q: How was this shown?
A: By the passage of laws annulling the rights of the people of the South.
. . .

Q: What were these rights?

A: The right to regulate their own affairs, one of which was to hold slaves as property.

. . .

Q: How were the slaves treated?

A: With great kindness and care in nearly all cases, a cruel master being rare, and lost the respect of his neighbors if he treated his slaves badly. Self-interest would have prompted good treatment if a higher feeling of humanity did not.

Q: What was the feeling of slaves towards their masters?

A: They were faithful and devoted and were always ready and willing to serve them.[18]

The *Catechism* was targeted not only at those who joined Children of the Confederacy chapters. It was also promoted as a book for all schoolchildren and the UDC hoped that it would be adopted throughout the United States. In its opening pages, Hope Harrison Turner, president of the Texas UDC, declares: "Because it is accurate, true and concise we recommend it most highly to all State Text Book Boards and to all teachers in all schools as supplementary material in the study of the history of America."[19] Efforts by Confederate sympathizers to propagate their version of the Civil War and the Confederacy by teaching it to children are, therefore, long-standing. Current neo-Confederates are continuing these efforts, although for them the issue of the site of schooling as well as the content of the material disseminated is of particular importance.

Louis Althusser, further developing his thesis that education is central to instilling nationalist sympathies in children, argues that the schools are where national ideologies are taught and contested. A national school system may be public and/or private, but these sectors are reliant on centralized, agreed-upon standards to confer legitimacy, and thus it was into schools that the UDC tried to place texts like the *Catechism*. More recently, however, proponents of neo-Confederacy have developed a strategy that proposes local-scale schooling that is outside the existing national system. Neo-Confederate activists have adopted a strategy of using parents and peers to develop and teach curricula, building up numbers of adherents to the neo-Confederate worldview from the grassroots. Rather than control schooling and curricula in a top-down manner, the LS, for example, suggests that its members teach their peers and their children using texts and topics approved by neo-Confederate institutions such as the LSI. Michael Hill has demanded that neo-Confederate parents should "refuse . . . to send their children to the government's schools; to stand for and sing the national anthem or pledge allegiance to the banner of Yankee occupation."[20] This local-scale educational strategy may be intended in the long term to produce enough like-minded individuals to generate popular support for national secession and, thereafter, instigation of an independent Confederacy. Consistent with their separatist nationalism, therefore, the neo-Confederate challenge to the U.S. national system of education simultaneously questions the authority of the U.S. nation-state.

Neo-Confederate Opposition to Public Education

From the outset of the neo-Confederate movement, and likely due in part to educational precedents pursued by groups like the UDC and the presence of numerous educators amongst its proponents, the issue of education has been central to its mission. Utilizing education to promulgate neo-Confederacy is clearly an attempt to instill support for its positions in future generations. According to Paul Gottfried and Thomas Fleming's sympathetic review of the conservatism within which contemporary neo-Confederacy developed, campus activism in the 1960s was seen by scholars such as Russell Kirk and Richard M. Weaver as evidence of the "disintegration of academic order and intellectual integrity."[21] Universities were increasingly becoming the sites of liberal viewpoints, and new curricula were replacing traditional educational strategies based on the classic texts of philosophy and literature. Many conservative professors believed mainstream scholarly opinion now disregarded their ideas and thus decided, according to Gottfried and Fleming, to drop out of the academy and into journalism and policy institutes. Those who stayed felt isolated, reducing their interaction with peers and students to the point when, by the late 1970s, conservative scholars had withdrawn "from the mainstream of academic debate," becoming "an embittered and marginalized minority" on U.S. university campuses.[22]

It was following this period of supposed conservative academic retreat that future neo-Confederates like Clyde Wilson and Thomas Fleming began contributing essays to collections that have since become part of the neo-Confederate canon. Fleming's description of his own career mirrors those of the conservative academics he discusses. He taught Greek and Latin at Miami University in Oxford, Ohio, and at the College of Charleston before his full-time involvement in the Rockford Institute; he has also been a private school head teacher, board member of a Lutheran school, and a home-schooling parent.[23] Public education, for Fleming, is just one part of a century-long process "in the subjugation of the family" that has included "giving rights to married women, delinquency and child protection statutes, women's suffrage, compulsory school attendance, Social Security, and no-fault divorce laws."[24] Echoing Althusser's critique of the French education system, Fleming laments that "compulsory attendance laws require children to be sent to *a* school. High taxes—federal, state, and local—combined with the high tuition of most private schools ensure that most children will be sent to public schools where they will be taught how to become good Americans." This "indoctrination" into U.S. society Fleming attacks as fundamentally flawed. He dismisses public schooling as akin to "experiments" with "rats" in "laboratories." Repeating the language that neo-Confederates utilize to describe multiculturalism, equal opportunities, and human and civil rights, Fleming argues that public schooling is "social engineering," and he is particularly critical of the provision of sex education.[25] Fleming also condemns the separation of church and state, which prevents the practice of Christianity in public schools.

The issue of schooling regularly animates authors in *Chronicles*, who criticize schools in the United States as "government factories of mediocrity." Their proposed alternatives typically include descriptions of their experiences homeschooling their own children.[26] Similarly, a series of hostile articles in the bimonthly neo-Confederate magazine *Southern Patriot* has opposed public schooling. In a lecture delivered at the LS national convention and reproduced in *Southern Patriot*, Steve Wilkins argues that neo-Confederates cannot "expect children who are bold, courageous, faithful, diligent, respectful of tradition, honouring their heritage, when you send them to be educated by those who have no respect for any of these things."[27] Schools in the United States are decried as "atheistic" and "secular" and those working within them are "unbelievers and barbarians." Wilkins, an LS director who has homeschooled six children, advocates the same for every likeminded parent: "It is time that we remove our children from the unholy influence of government schools." Public schools in the United States, he maintains, are involved in "bald-faced, secular indoctrination" such that "education of our children" is something that Southerners "must reclaim." Neo-Confederates who are not homeschooling their children "have entrusted their [children's] education to those who by and large hate what you love." In his tirade, Wilkins envisions home schooling as part of a wider campaign of Christian education and Christian nationalism that understands the Civil War as a theological struggle over the direction of the United States (see Chapter 2). Home schooling is understood to be, as Michael Hill has stated, a Christian tradition. LS member Scott Williams, citing biblical passages and theologians to support his contentions, argues that the separation of church and state and the failure of teachers to deliver a curriculum centered on Christianity are problematic. For Williams, good practice requires that parents educate their children, whereas public education, by contrast, produces antisocial atheists because of the "entire mind-set of the anti-Christian government establishment."[28]

A similar argument, namely that the education system in the United States is part of a plot to expunge Christianity, has been made in *Southern Patriot* by Leslie Riley, identified as the Mississippi state chairman of the Constitution Party. Maintaining that "theft-funded, God-hating, South-hating, Leviathan/New-World-Order-promoting government schools are our enemies' greatest weapon against us," Riley draws on Robert Lewis Dabney's dismissal of public schooling to argue that:

> Government schools were conceived, planned and implemented by atheistic, Marxist/Communist subversives in the 1800s, whose openly stated goal was to undermine Christianity and the family and to reduce the influence of the church and parents on children and culture. They did this in hopes of training generations who would more readily accept their anti-Christian socialist ideals and policies. With this in mind, modern "publik" schools are not an abysmal failure in need of reform or repair. They have been extremely successful for what they were designed to do.

Riley urges parents to "PULL YOUR CHILDREN OUT OF THESE SCHOOLS — WHATEVER THE COST" and begin homeschooling and thus cause the "collapse" of "these illegitimate, unbiblical, unconstitutional 'Communist training centers.'"[29] John Altman, identified by *Southern Patriot* as a retired public high school teacher of government and history, also sees U.S. public education to be "in shambles," and as a result, "the social and moral fabric of America has begun to unravel." To explain why this is the case, and why for "nearly two generations of American youth" education has been "severely impaired," Altman cites the impact of the "infamous" 1954 Supreme Court decision *Brown v. Board of Education*, which mandated racial desegregation in public schools. This decision, for Altman, was part of "the Court's attempt to impose a detested social (Marxist) revolution on the South and the rest of the nation."[30]

As with other neo-Confederate opinions, even when arguments seem to be about judicial power or federal authority, the underlying issue is the changing state of race relations in the United States in the wake of the civil rights era. Thomas Fleming, for example, mocks the operation of busing children to generate racially integrated schools as "some vision of social harmony."[31] In 1981, he dismissed "twenty-five years of unsuccessful experimentation" in Southern schools, implying that a better education was provided by the segregated schools of the pre–civil rights era.[32] In a British newspaper, Hill was forthright in his condemnation of "state-enforced integration" and complained that having no choice between segregated and nonsegregated facilities was "not freedom."[33]

It is not only the desegregation of students that is blamed for failing schools. Neo-Confederate Roger Busbice has praised segregated teachers' unions in *Chronicles.* "Until the mid-1970's," he explained, "public education in Louisiana, like that in much of rural America, was solidly and successfully based on traditional methodology." Teachers and their labor unions, Busbice continued, "reflected the legacy of racial segregation" with two unions, one white and the other African American. When these two unions merged in 1976, a result of "Machiavellian manipulation" by state and union officials, the outcome was resistance by some of the white teachers to the new unified body. Busbice proceeds to laud the holdouts as protecting "traditional values" and "true professionalism," implying that those who agreed to the racial integration of teachers' unions were discreditable.[34]

As is often the case within the movement, neo-Confederacy advocates frequently invoke pre–Civil War models as solutions for current educational ills. Arguing that "for Southerners, there is only one sound standard with which to compare modern education: the fully developed model of, say, 1860,"[35] Fleming applauds Robert Louis Dabney's hostility to mass public schooling and calls for a return to a period when in the South it was primarily only the sons of the white elites who received schooling. Reiterating neo-Confederate beliefs about gender, Fleming proposes that an early-nineteenth-century curriculum would graduate "tough and resolute men who create, sustain and defend civilization" and who are "aggressively virile."[36] The implication is that Fleming supports an exclusivist educational system for today that produces self-chosen male leaders. Echoing the views of the antebellum period when a patriarchal aristocracy controlled the South, Fleming argues that the United States has failed in the "important—indeed, the primary—task of education, which is to form the mind and character of an intellectual, moral, and social aristocracy." In contrast to the American public school system, which, Fleming laments, "grinds out year after year . . . post-human androids," schooling by neo-Confederate activists would produce a generation of aristocratic, elite men able to lead a new Confederacy.[37]

Although Fleming supports a traditional curriculum based on classical Greek and Roman texts and controversial writings (such as Dabney's theological treatises), other neo-Confederates provide a different interpretation of educational values. Historian Grady McWhiney, a well-known scholar of the

American South and the Civil War who taught at the University of British Columbia, the University of Alabama, and Texas Christian University, and who was a founding director of the League of the South before his death in April 2006, was the most prominent proponent of the neo-Confederate Celtic South thesis.[38] Drawing again on the supposedly Celtic origins of American Southerners, McWhiney argued that people in the South were, and by implication are, distrustful of formal, professionalized education. This hostility is seen as inherent to Celts who, McWhiney comments, were "not merely unschooled but uninterested in being schooled."[39] The result is a supposed Southern preference for teaching only what a student wants to know, knowledge beyond that being described by McWhiney as resulting in "weakened or destroyed . . . native values and traditions."[40] For example, schooling Southerners in the nineteenth century, he interprets, produced "brainwashed youngsters" who supported abolition and opposed slavery.[41]

Neo-Confederate beliefs about education, as articulated by many of their leading activists, envision an elite group of young white men being schooled in Greek, Latin, Renaissance French and Italian, and English literature.[42] This archaic and exclusionary vision of education as a resource for a privileged few stands in contrast to the mass-schooling operations of the contemporary nation-state, itself largely a product of the nineteenth century. Indeed, it is the pre-industrial model to which neo-Confederates wish to return.

The League of the South Institute for the Study of Southern Culture and History

Education, argues Ernest Gellner, is critical in shaping individual identities, and if that education can be controlled, so can the identities of future generations.[43] The LS began its educational program with a summer school in South Carolina in 1995. Planning to teach "every aspect of the Southern tradition," in 1996 the League of the South Institute for the Study of Southern Culture and History (LSI) was formed.[44] Emory's Donald Livingston played a major role in creating the LSI, which he envisaged as a response to the "suppression" of the Southern point of view by "American nationalism" which has "demonized" the Southern states. Drawing upon over fifty LS members who are, or were, accredited academics as the faculty of the Institute, the LSI would, "through research, publication, and teaching . . . provide a sound scholarly understanding of the Southern Tradition and the permanent truths contained within it." The Institute aims to educate high school, university, and adult students who will defend these Southern truths within the American academy, thus "taking back our colleges and universities from the politically correct."[45]

Registered as a 501(c)(3) tax-exempt nonprofit body, the LSI is part of the Mary Noel Kershaw Foundation, a charity established by LS director Jack Kershaw for "general cultural and educational activities of significance to the Southern people."[46] At the time of writing, the LSI director is Mark Winchell, a professor of American literature at Clemson University. An expert on Southern Agrarians, Winchell has authored numerous biographies, including a recent assessment of Donald Davidson.[47]

Academics such as Winchell are typical LSI members, many of whom envision themselves as inheritors of a Southern nationalist literary and philosophical lineage dating back at least to the Southern Agrarians. Indeed, nationalist political movements such as neo-Confederacy are often developed and led by academics. Professional historians, for example, reinterpret history from a nationalist perspective, and literature experts become engaged in writing a nascent national literary canon or arguing which texts should be included in one.

Both academic and non-academic LSI members articulate the belief that they are engaged in a struggle to reassert Southern cultural and, thereafter, political identity:

> As the intellectual leaders of the Southern movement, LSI members and associates seek to restore a solid cultural foundation which will nourish and sustain a free and prosperous people. Without such a foundation, all other facets of the Southern movement—political, social, and economic—will not flourish.[48]

The LSI project is thus a starting point for a wider political nationalism, with its members composing a nationalist intelligentsia.[49] Given the concentration of academics in their ranks, the Institute is well positioned to achieve its goal of educating both LS members and non-members.[50]

The League of the South and Home Schooling

With many neo-Confederates homeschooling their children, the LS appointed Katherine Dalton Boyer as its director for the Home Schooling and Secondary Education Program at the end of 2001. The program sets out curricula for middle and high school students, primarily in topics regarding U.S. national and state histories, literature, the Constitution and governance, and

Latin (at the time of writing, the syllabus, along with home-schooling strategies, was available at http://www.lsinstitute.org/Homeschool.htm).[51]

The League's home-schooling program curriculum suggests a range of
conservative authors, such as Confederate president Jefferson Davis and neo-
Confederate originator M. E. Bradford. Favored novelists include Nobel
Prize winner William Faulkner and pro-Confederate Civil War historian
Shelby Foote. Other recommended writers are controversial figures: Booker T.
Washington's interpretation of the role of African Americans in U.S. society,
for example, has been challenged for favoring financial self-sufficiency over
political equality and supporting racial segregation. As Table 7.1 shows, many
of the books recommended for teaching U.S. history predate the civil rights
era, the more recent titles dating from the late-twentieth-century period of
neo-Confederacy. Robert Selph Henry's work, written in the 1930s, is representative of the League's positions on the Civil War and Reconstruction.
Henry argued that the abolition of slavery was "not the cause for which the
soldiers . . . fought"; rather, the issues were the right of secession and states'
rights versus those of the centralized government—positions that neo-
Confederates regularly reiterate.[52] In turn, Rod Gragg, a *Southern Partisan*
advisor and contributor, produced a source book of original documents that
selectively outline slavery and the Civil War for children. For example, five
pages recount unrepresentative excerpts from the 1936–38 Federal Writers'
Project, presenting stories of slaves' loyalty to and love of their owners:

> Many Southern officers and some enlisted men went to war accompanied
> by their body servants, and in several cases slaves picked up weapons and
> fought alongside their masters in combat. Most slaves remained at home,
> however, and freedom, when it came, was generally celebrated. Still, many
> slaves were fearful and suspicious of Yankee troops; many looked indignantly
> upon the thieving and destruction committed by the invaders, and many
> remained loyal to their owners—especially those who had treated their slaves
> humanely.[53]

The LSI also recommends work by its own faculty members Steve Wilkins
and James McClellan, and a study of the Civil War by Ludwell Johnson. Johnson avowedly takes the perspective of "Southerners" in response to perceived
"political correctness" in historical scholarship, which he blames for misrep-
resenting the Confederacy. Amongst other things, he claims that "slaves were
sometimes loved and cherished by their masters as if they were members of
the family," arguing this is typically omitted in favor of a monolithic view of
slavery's brutality.[54] Of the older texts mentioned, Albert Taylor Bledsoe's

Table 7.1. The League of the South's List of Recommended Texts on U.S. History for Homeschoolers

Author/Editor	Publication Date	Title
Bledsoe, Albert Taylor	1866	Is Davis a Traitor? or, Was secession a constitutional right previous to the war of 1861?
Smith, Charles Henry	1861–1903	"Bill Arp" Stories and Sketches
Taylor, Richard	1879	Destruction and Reconstruction
Harris, Joel Chandler	1876–1908	Tales of Uncle Remus
Washington, Booker T.	1901	Up from Slavery
Wister, Owen	1906	Lady Baltimore
Pringle, Elizabeth Alston	1913	A Woman Rice Planter
Thompson, Waddy	1920	History of the People of the United States
Latané, John Holladay	1921	History of the United States
Thompson, Waddy	1921	The First Book of United States History
Henry, Robert Selph	1931	Story of the Confederacy
Henry, Robert Selph	1938	The Story of Reconstruction
Foote, Shelby	1958–1974	The Civil War: A Narrative
Genovese, Eugene D.	1974	Roll, Jordan, Roll: The World the Slaves Made
Bradford, M. E.	1981	Founding Fathers: Brief Lives of the Framers of the Constitution
Wilkins, Steve	1988	America: The First 350 Years
Gragg, Rod	1989	The Illustrated Confederate Reader
Harwell, Richard B.	1989	The Confederate Reader: How the South Saw the War
McClellan, James	1989	Liberty, Order and Justice: An Introduction to the Constitutional Principles of American Government
Barrows, C. K., et al.	1995	Black Confederates (Forgotten Confederates: An Anthology about Black Southerners)
Johnson, Ludwell	1995	North Against South: The American Iliad, 1848–1877
Sullivan, Walter	1995	The War the Women Lived: Female Voices from the Confederate South
Barrows, C. K., et al.	2001	Black Southerners in Confederate Armies: A Collection of Historical Accounts

7.2. The League of the South's List of Recommended "Southern Family Movies" for Homeschoolers

Title	Date	Director
The General	1927	Clyde Bruckman and Buster Keaton
Judge Priest	1934	John Ford
The Little Colonel	1935	David Butler
The Littlest Rebel	1935	David Butler
Jezebel	1938	William Wyler
Gone with the Wind	1939	Victor Fleming
Santa Fe Trail	1940	Michael Curtiz
Colonel Effingham's Raid	1946	Irving Pichel
Song of the South	1946	Harve Foster and Wilfred Jackson
Intruder in the Dust	1949	Clarence Brown
Drums in the Deep South	1951	William Cameron Menzies
I'd Climb the Highest Mountain	1951	Henry King
Good-bye, My Lady	1956	William A. Wellman
The Searchers	1956	John Ford
The Proud Rebel	1958	Michael Curtiz
Escort West	1959	Francis D. Lyon
The Alamo	1960	John Wayne
True Grit	1969	Henry Hathaway
Tomorrow	1972	Joseph Anthony
The River	1984	Mark Rydell
The Trip to Bountiful	1985	Peter Masterson
Stars Fell on Henrietta	1995	James Keach
Old Man	1997	John Kent Harrison
The Hunley	1999	John Gray

1866 treatise aims to "wipe off the charges of treason and rebellion" from Confederate leaders and show that secession was legal under the 1787 U.S. Constitution.[55] In turn, both Charles Henry Smith and Joel Chandler Harris, through their respective characters Bill Arp and Uncle Remus, romantically recollect the plantation South, and as a result have repeatedly incurred accusations of racism.[56]

Table 7.2 lists "Southern family movies" recommended by the LS homeschooling program. All include positive portrayals of heroic Confederate troops outsmarting their Union opponents or the importance of family relations. They include Buster Keaton's *The General* (1927), about a Confederate engineer who loses his twin loves (his train and his girl) to Union soldiers, pre–World War II Hollywood epics of the plantation-house South such as *Gone with the Wind* (1939) and *Jezebel* (1938), more recent adaptations of novels by Faulkner, and a series of westerns starring John Wayne. Walt Disney's *Song of the South* (1946), which animates Harris's Uncle Remus stories, is also recommended but is unavailable in the United States because it has been "suppressed by the PC crowd."[57] *The Santa Fe Trail* (1940) stars Errol Flynn as Confederate hero Jeb Stuart outwitting General Custer, played by none other than Ronald Reagan. Alongside these, the LS recommends lectures on audiocassette by many leading neo-Confederates, including LS directors Steve Wilkins and Clyde Wilson.

This selection of materials sheds light on the neo-Confederate vision of Southern history and culture. The LSI recommends books published before the 1950s because they supposedly offer "solid and unbiased presentations" of U.S. history, whereas more recent texts, which attempt to overturn the ethnocentrism and racism of the past, are considered skewed and thus illegitimate.[58] The utilization of outdated source materials also speaks to the fact that there are, as advocates of neo-Confederacy repeatedly assert, "permanent truths" in Southern culture and history—implying that interpretations of the South dating from the post–civil rights era are just that, interpretations, and not the "permanent truths" presented in the older texts to be used by "families wishing to give their children more than . . . bland and inaccurate history."[59]

The teaching of "permanent truths" about the South to children at home evidences that neo-Confederate activists are challenging not just curricula, but the location where schooling occurs. If education is an exclusively parental affair, Gutmann explains, parents can "predispose their children, through education, to choose a way of life consistent with their familial heritage."[60] In turn, this enables the removal of the state from a critical aspect of national socialization and enables neo-Confederate sympathizers to fill that gap with teachings about what they envision as their own nation: the Confederation of Southern States. With such beliefs, neo-Confederates argue that the only way to ensure that a child's education is consistent with their interpretations of U.S. history and Confederate heritage is to take responsibility for that education themselves.[61]

Much like the insistence by neo-Confederates on the distinctive Celtic culture of the South, home schooling is part of the effort by neo-Confederate activists to generate a sense of cultural difference between themselves and the rest of the United States. By proposing that LS members who homeschool their children utilize titles long out of print, the LS hopes to produce cohorts who learn, feel, and believe they are culturally and historically different from others in the United States. As the LSI makes clear: "Unless we pass on our traditions to the young, the hope of restoring our ancient Christian liberties will die with us." Inculcating future generations in "Southern-positive" history and culture is central to the home-schooling strategies and curricula forwarded by proponents of neo-Confederacy.[62] Further, the fact that some of the texts recommended by the LSI are now frowned upon for their racist portrayals and dubious historical assessments enhances the sense that people are learning about a culture that mainstream educators are supposedly suppressing. Children who learn from late-nineteenth-century texts such as Bledsoe's may be able to make reasoned arguments for secession both in the past and in the future. The home-schooling strategies employed by proponents of neo-Confederacy, therefore, aim to propagate Confederate nationalism and inculcate future generations to continue to actively support neo-Confederacy.

"Hedge Schools" and League of the South Schooling

For neo-Confederates, secession is both a political and an educational trend, aimed at undermining the nation-state status quo and producing a new series of local-scale political and educational associations and thus a new social order. Consequently, neo-Confederate activists argue for secession from established educational institutions, as well as for "new venues for learning."[63] One such venue, in addition to home schooling, is what the LS terms "hedge schools." These are seminars where LSI faculty members provide reading material to interested individuals, who then assemble for discussion "anywhere that space permits."[64] LSI hedge schools have explored topics including Southern efforts to abolish slavery, the writings of John C. Calhoun and other nineteenth-century politicians, theology, Constitutional law, and the Civil War. Donald W. Livingston lauds hedge schools as giving students the opportunity to "meet scholars of national and international reputation who open them to avenues of learning they are not likely to find in their normal course of study." He notes that they are "funded and arranged at low cost by local sponsors," but he nevertheless requests that "civic-minded" individuals who in the past were "literally funding their own cultural destruction" by donating money to other educational institutions instead fund operations such as LSI hedge schools.[65]

The LS envisions hedge schools as a response to the centralizing, homogenizing tendencies of the U.S. educational system. The term "hedge schools" dates from the seventeenth and eighteenth centuries, when Ireland was under British rule. Then as now, according to neo-Confederate logic, Celtic traditions faced persecution and were threatened with extinction by powerful centralized states that illegally occupied the territory of the Celts. The LSI depicts the lecturers in the original Irish hedge schools, and by association their own seminar leaders, as chivalrous defenders of their "true, good and noble" culture.[66] Mainstream American academia and mass schooling seek to erase Southern history and identity, and as a result "Southerners today face a greater threat to their identity than that confronting the Irish three centuries ago."[67]

Drawing romantic parallels with Irish hedge schools, Livingston praises LSI seminars "held in church buildings, homes, the backrooms of a barbecue shack and of a supermarket . . . and even in the open air under a palmetto grove." The hedge schools are aimed at students in high school to adults of all ages, providing individuals "who reject the demonization of the South and of their tradition," in the words of Livingston, with an antidote to the "smog of political correctness" that has dominated U.S. education for "two generations" or "less than forty years."[68] This timing echoes the chronology forwarded by other neo-Confederates, referring again to the 1960s—the era of racial deseg-regation in U.S. education. Since this time, argues Livingston, education has become politicized, implying that prior to this period education was apolitical and that the peer-group-organized, local-scale hedge schools provided by the neo-Confederates are similarly free from ideology.

As with the home-schooling initiative, the neo-Confederate hedge schools represent a particular nationalist strategy. Unable to take over the direction of education on a national scale, and without the means to seize the state and impose its own educational agenda and curricula, proponents of neo-Confederacy promote the hedge schools in an attempt to build up a base of support for their nationalist program centered on individual and local associations. Indeed, describing the role of hedge schools, Livingston concludes that "it is only from the bonds of friendship, community, and learning formed in these small independent gatherings that cultural renewal is likely to arise."[69] "Cultural renewal" to neo-Confederates would be a rejection of the current U.S. nation-state and its education system, and its replacement with an independent Confederacy in which local decision making is dominant, authority is in the hands of patriarchs, and education is exclusive. Neo-Confederates thus appear to accept Althusser's contention that to contest the existing nation-state necessitates contesting the political meanings of what he terms the "ideological state apparatus," namely culture, church, family, and education.[70] It is these institutions, maintains Althusser, rather than the administrative state, the military, or elected government, that are most criti-cal in contests over ideology. It is locations like homes, schools, and churches where the practical implementation of political wills is most apparent on a daily basis. With their secessionist beliefs and strategies, neo-Confederate activists assert that local communities and families have the authority to resist the centralized state and suggest that the starting point for such a struggle is education.

Conclusion: Neo-Confederacy, Nationalism, and Education

In "A Message to the Southern Poverty Law Center and Its Leftist Allies," the LS issued a statement that read in part:

> That our story does not get heard, much less debated, can be attributed largely to the success of government schooling. Government schools have perverted or ignored the truth for generations and have contributed mightily to the "dumbing down" of the population so that clear thinking and logical argumentation on important issues has become impossible.[71]

Theorists of nationalism and the state have consistently argued that mass education and schools are critical to the socialization (or indoctrination to some) of children into national citizens, and nationalists have long paid attention to education as a means through which to achieve their political goals. Indeed, analyzing educational reform in the United States and Canada, Sarah Riegel reminds us that "education itself is inherently political."[72] Most commonly, the institution promoting national socialization has been the nation-state, and its continuing development of a system of mass education fosters a sense of national attachment and commonality amongst a population. Education as such is provided on a national scale and practiced through national agencies, examination boards, and standardized certification processes. In the first half of the twentieth century, pro-Confederate groups such as the UDC attempted to instill Confederate sympathies in children through strategies that ranged from nationally promoting textbooks and curricula they considered appropriate to establishing chapters of Children of the Confederacy. Today's neo-Confederates, however, envision the construction of a nation through the process of education, both at a wholly different spatial level and in different geographic locations. Focusing on the local scale and the home, they propose that a population of Southern nationalists can be built up from the grassroots by educating colleagues, peers, and their own children with neo-Confederate ideology. Instead of education being imposed from above, neo-Confederates promote and actively pursue education from below. Their aim is to first educate individuals and from this socio-cultural base build political demand for secession.[73] It is the family, then, as both educators and the basic unit of allegiance to the putative Confederation of Southern States that becomes the critical institution in this project. There are also many similarities with the wider Christian-centered home-schooling movement in the United States.[74] Yet despite its many supporters, Gutmann argues that home schooling is inherently elitist and can lead to children being taught "religious and racial intolerance" by their parents.[75] If education is carried out wholly in private rather than public and thus is centered only on the family, the opportunities to meet others, witness diversity, and debate different perspectives are greatly reduced.

The neo-Confederates' fundamental critique of the U.S. educational system, namely that there is no local control over schooling and the federal influence on curricula is entrenched, is of course erroneous, given the decentralized nature of schooling and the process of electing local school boards. Realistically, therefore, it is unlikely that home and hedge schooling will achieve the ultimate neo-Confederate aim of secession. Through their educational strategies, however, groups like the League of the South are intent on producing cohorts of activists invested and engaged in neo-Confederacy and are thus generating a solid base for future political activity.

Notes

1. Livingston, Donald W. "Barbecue Shacks, Palmetto Groves, and Other Schools," *Chronicles*, 24.9 (2000): 18–19.

2. Advertisement for the Abbeville Institute in *Southern Partisan*, 24.6 (2004/2006): n.p. See also, Erath, Clara. "The Value of Southern Tradition," *UDC Magazine*, 68.7 (2005): 17; "A Report on the Abbeville Institute," *Southern Partisan*, 24.6 (2004): 24–27. Other Abbeville Institute scholars include Marshall DeRosa, Thomas DiLorenzo, Paul Gottfried, James Kibler, Mark Malvasi, Mark Winchell, and Thomas Woods—see http://www.abbevilleinstitute.org/Scholars.htm [accessed 25 September 2006].

3. Sullivan, Christopher M. "The Stephen D. Lee Institute," *Confederate Veteran*, 64.1 (2006): 8–9.

4. See "Confederate Education," *Southern Partisan*, 24.6 (2004): 24–26.

5. Sam Davis Youth Camp. On-line: http://www.samdavis.scv.org [accessed 15 October 2006]. Sam Davis (1842–1863) was a Confederate soldier who was caught operating behind enemy lines by Union troops, tried by court martial, and executed as a spy.

6. Robert Kee explains that under British rule in eighteenth-century Ireland, "the only education for Catholic children which did not involve their exposure to Protestant proselytism was in illicit schools in hedgerows and byways." These institutions became known as "hedge schools." Kee, Robert. *The Green Flag: A History of Irish Nationalism.* (London: Weidenfeld and Nicolson, 1972). For further historical

review of Irish hedge schools see Dowling P. J. *A History of Irish Education: A Study in Conflicting Loyalties.* (Cork: Mercier Press, 1971), and Boyce, D. George. *Nationalism in Ireland.* (London: Croom Helm, 1982).

7. Hill, quoted in Pinzur, Matthew I. "League of the South Pushes Separatist Views," *Florida Times-Union,* Jacksonville (10 September 2001): A-1. On-line: *http:// jacksonville.com/tu-On-line/stories/091001/met_7240080.html* [accessed 20 October 2004].

8. This story was extensively covered by journalists Allison Schaefers and Matthew I. Pinzur in the *Florida Times-Union* of Jacksonville. See Schaefers, Allison, and Pinzur, Matthew I. "Lawyer Leaves League of the South," *Florida Times-Union,* (8 September 2001). On-line: *http://jacksonville.com/tu-On-line/stories/090801/met_7229306.html* [accessed 20 October 2004]; Schaefers, Allison. "NAACP Says Board Attorney Should Quit," *Florida Times-Union,* (6 September 2001). On-line: *http:// jacksonville.com/tu-On-line/stories/090601/met_7207653.html* [accessed 20 October 2004]; Schaefers, Allison. "NAACP Still Wants Schools Attorney Out," *Florida Times-Union,* (15 September 2001). On-line: *http://jacksonville.com/tu-On-line/stories/091501/ met_7291766.html* [accessed 20 October 2004]; Schaefers, Allison. "School Board Attorney Says 'Confidence Vote' Is Violation," *Florida Times-Union,* (19 September 2001). On-line: *http://jacksonville.com/tu-On-line/stories/090601/met_7207653 .html* [accessed 20 October 2004]. The incident is also reviewed in Southern Poverty Law Center. "League of the South Loses Members and Momentum," *Intelligence Report,* 104 (2001): 4.

9. This argument is made by, amongst others, Ernest Gellner in *Thought and Change.* (Chicago: University of Chicago Press, 1964), and in *Nations and Nationalism.* (Ithaca: Cornell University Press, 1983).

10. Pledging allegiance is discussed by Coles, Robert. *The Political Life of Children.* (Boston: Atlantic Monthly Press, Little, Brown, 1986).

11. Billig, Michael. *Banal Nationalism.* (London: Sage, 1995).

12. Gellner, *Nations and Nationalism,* (1983): 34.

13. Althusser, Louis. *Lenin and Philosophy and Other Essays.* (New York: Monthly Review Press, 1971): 156.

14. Benson, Al Jr. "Southerners and Home Schooling," *Southern Events,* (Fall 1998): 11.

15. See, Cox, Karen L. *Dixie's Daughters: The United Daughters of the Confederacy and the Preservation of Confederate Culture.* (Gainesville: University Press of Florida, 2003).

16. McPherson, James M. "Long-Legged Yankee Lies: The Southern Textbook Crusade," *The Memory of the Civil War in American Culture,* ed. Alice Fahs and Joan Waugh. (Chapel Hill: University of North Carolina Press, 2004): 75.

17. United Daughters of the Confederacy. *Minutes of the Forty-Fifth Annual Convention.* (1938): 380–382.

18. West, Decca Lamar. *Catechism on the History of the Confederate States of America, 1861–1865.* (Austin: Texas Division United Daughters of the Confederacy, 1934): 9–12.

19. Turner, Hope Harrison. "Presentation," *Catechism on the History of the Confederate States of America, 1861–1865,* by Decca Lamar West. (Austin: Texas Division United Daughters of the Confederacy, 1934): n.p.

20. Hill, Michael. "President's Message [Cultural Secession: Abjuring the Realm]," *Southern Patriot*, 1.2 (1994): 1.

21. Gottfried, Paul, and Fleming, Thomas. *The Conservative Movement*. (Boston: Twayne Publishers, 1988): 40.

22. Ibid., 58.

23. The information about Fleming's educational career comes from the preface of Gottfried and Fleming, *The Conservative Movement*, (1988), and Fleming, Thomas. "It Takes a Village," *Chronicles*, 22.9 (1998): 10–13.

24. Fleming, "It takes a village," (1998): 11.

25. Fleming, Thomas. "Old Rights and the New Right," *The New Right Papers*, ed. Robert W. Whitaker. (New York: St. Martin's Press, 1982): 192–193.

26. Humpty Dumpty. "Learning, Larning, and Schooling," *Chronicles*, 23.9 (1999): 12. A regular contributor to *Chronicles'* discussions of education is Mary Pride, who has homeschooled her nine children. See, for example, "*Star Trek* or *Star Wars*? Two Futures for American Education," *Chronicles*, 23.9 (1999): 13–15; "Going the Distance—How Homeschoolers Will Change College," *Chronicles*, 24.9 (2000): 16–17. Other homeschoolers writing in *Chronicles* include Andrei Navrozov. "My Son, the Sociopath: The Education of a No-man," *Chronicles*, 23.9 (1999): 16–18, and Scott P. Richert. "Magistrate Mahoney, or: How I Learned to Stop Worrying and Started Homeschooling," *Chronicles*, 23.9 (1999): 19–21, and "Just Another Tequila Sunrise," *Chronicles*, 25.11 (2001): 33.

27. Wilkins, Steve. "The Foundations of Cultural Restoration," *Southern Patriot*, 8.5 (2001): 7.

28. Williams, Scott Whitten. "Seven Reasons to Home School," *Southern Patriot*, 5.4 (1998): 11.

29. Riley, Leslie. "Save the Children (and the South): Dont [*sic*] Send Them to Marx's Schools," *Southern Patriot*, 8.1 (2001): 14.

30. Altman, John W. "From Our Members [Taking Back the Schools]," *Southern Patriot*, 5.4 (1998): 10, 8.

31. Fleming, "Old Rights," (1982): 192.

32. Fleming, Thomas. "Southern Schooling and the Ancient Wisdom," *Why the South will Survive*. Fifteen Southerners. (Athens: University of Georgia Press, 1981): 107. Much like other neo-Confederates, Fleming offsets accusations of racism immediately after criticizing school integration and busing as key factors impacting upon what he regards as scholastic decline: "It would be a mistake to attach too much importance to problems engendered by integration and forced busing. Questions of race were simply a wedge to be inserted by the reformers into the cracks of social and intellectual divisions, a handy tool for demolishing the structure of society" (p. 118).

33. Gallagher, Paul. "Far-right Group's Leader Defends Use of Saltire," *The Scotsman*, (30 September 2002).

34. Busbice, Roger. "Letter from Louisiana: Putting Children First," *Chronicles*, 26.9 (2002): 31–32.

35. Fleming, "Southern Schooling," (1981): 108. On p. 109, when offering a Southern example of a model education, Fleming says, "No better representative of the South could be chosen than the Confederacy's president [Jefferson Davis]."

36. Fleming, Thomas. "Burn This Book," *Chronicles*, 24.9 (2000): 11.

37. Fleming, Thomas. "Grow Old along with Me," *Chronicles*, 23.9 (1999): 11.

38. Hague, Euan. "Texts as Flags: The League of the South and the Development of a Nationalist Intelligentsia in the United States 1975–2001," *Hagar: International Social Science Review*, 3.2 (2002): 299–339.

39. McWhiney, Grady. "Education in the Old South: A Reexamination," *The Southern Enigma: Essays on Race, Class, and Folk Culture*, ed. Walter J. Fraser Jr. and Winfred B. Moore Jr. (Westport, CT: Greenwood Press, 1983): 181.

40. Ibid., 183.

41. Ibid., 174.

42. Fleming, "Burn This Book," (2000): 10–12.

43. Gellner, *Nations and Nationalism*, (1983).

44. Livingston, Donald W. "Barbecue Shacks, Palmetto Groves, and Other Schools," *Chronicles*, 24.9 (2000): 19.

45. Until late 2001 the LSI was headed by Livingston. His statements about the establishment and aims of the LSI are from "League of the South Institute for the Study of Southern Culture and History—A Message from the Director." On-line: http://www.dixienet.org/ls-institute/los-institute.htm [accessed 25 August 1999].

46. "The Mary Noel Kershaw Foundation." On-line: http://www.dixienet.org/ls-homepg/marynoel.html [accessed 1 November 2004].

47. Winchell typically publishes under his full name, Mark Royden Winchell, for example, *Where No Flag Flies: Donald Davidson and the Southern Resistance*. (Columbia: University of Missouri Press, 2000).

48. Statement on the home page of the League of the South Institute for the Study of Southern Culture and History (LSI). On-line: http://www.lsinstitute.org [accessed 1 November 2004].

49. For discussions of the theory and historical role of the intelligentsia in nationalism see, *inter alia*, Smith, Anthony D. *Theories of Nationalism*. (London: Duckworth, 1971), *The Ethnic Revival in the Modern World*. (Cambridge: Cambridge University Press, 1981), *National Identity*. (London: Penguin, 1991), "Nationalism and the Historians," *Ethnicity and Nationalism*, ed. Anthony D. Smith. (Leiden: E. J. Brill, 1992): 58–80; Nairn, Tom. *The Break-up of Britain*. (London: New Left Books, 1977); Gouldner, A. W. *The Future of Intellectuals and the Rise of the New Class: A Frame of Reference, Theses, Conjectures, Arguments, and an Historical Perspective on the Role of Intellectuals and Intelligentsia in the International Class Context of the Modern Era*. (New York: Seabury Press, 1979), *Against Fragmentation: The Origins of Marxism and the Sociology of Intellectuals*. (New York: Oxford University Press, 1985). In relation to neo-Confederacy, see Hague, "Texts as Flags," (2002).

50. At the time of writing LSI faculty members included David Aiken, professor of English at the College of Charleston, South Carolina; Marshall DeRosa, professor in the division of social science at Florida Atlantic University; and Thomas DiLorenzo, professor of economics at Loyola College in Maryland.

51. Kathryn Dalton Boyer recommends numerous Latin textbooks, although she notes that some of the more recent editions may be unsuitable because "politically correct and unbalanced discussions of the position of women and slavery" have been added. See "Guide to Latin instruction for Homeschoolers." On-line: http://www.lsinstitute.org/Latin.htm [accessed 29 October 2004]. In their article "The Future of

Home Schooling," *Peabody Journal of Education,* 75.1–2 (2000): 233–255, Michael P. Farris and Scott A. Woodruff argue that classics are of increasing importance to homeschoolers.

52. Henry, Robert Selph. *The Story of the Confederacy,* rev. ed. (New York: Bobbs-Merrill Company, 1936 [1931]): n.p. In his later book *The Story of Reconstruction* (New York: Bobbs-Merrill Company, 1938), Henry (p. 233) argues that the Ku Klux Klan was formed for "the protection of the ex-Confederate element of the population" and that "imitators, whether white or black," disguised themselves as Klan members for "plunder or private vengeance," spoiling the organization's "good name." Henry also compares the Civil War and Reconstruction to Homer's *Iliad,* a stance reiterated by neo-Confederate and regular *Southern Partisan* contributor Ludwell H. Johnson in his *North against South: The American Iliad 1848–1877,* 2nd ed. (Columbia: Foundation for American Education, 1995), originally published under the title *Division and Reunion: America 1848–1877.* (New York: John Wiley and Sons, 1978).

53. Gragg, Rod. *The Illustrated Confederate Reader.* (New York: Harper and Row, 1989): 84. Other interviews with former slaves from the Federal Writers' Project of the Works Progress Administration (1936–38) demonstrate the brutalities of slavery—see, *inter alia,* Yetman, Norman R., ed. *When I Was a Slave: Memoirs from the Slave Narrative Collection.* (Mineola, NY: Dover Publications, 2002).

54. Johnson, *North Against South,* (1995): vii, 1. This second edition was published and promoted by the Foundation for American Education, the group that publishes *Southern Partisan.*

55. Bledsoe, Albert Taylor. *Is Davis a Traitor; or, Was Secession a Constitutional Right Previous to the War of 1861?* (Baltimore: Innes and Company, 1866): v. For discussion of the neo-Confederate practice of reprinting nineteenth-century texts, see Sebesta, Edward H., and Hague, Euan. "The U.S. Civil War as a Theological War: Confederate Christian Nationalism and the League of the South," *Canadian Review of American Studies,* 32.3 (2002): 253–283.

56. Smith (1826–1903) was a staunch supporter of the Confederacy, fought in the Civil War, and was elected to the Georgia state senate in 1865. Harris (1848–1908) grew up on and around plantations in pre–Civil War Georgia. Poor, he regularly interacted with slaves and drew upon African American folklore and dialect for his writing in the *Atlanta Constitution.* There remains debate about whether Harris's characters are crude derogatory stereotypes or satirical and subversive portrayals of slavery—see, for example, Parker, David B. *Alias Bill Arp: Charles Henry Smith and the South's Goodly Heritage.* (Athens: University of Georgia Press, 1991), Walker, Alice. "Uncle Remus: No Friend of Mine," *Southern Exposure,* 21.1–2 (1993): 36–37 and Chapter 8.

57. League of the South Institute web site for homeschoolers. On-line: http://www.lsinstitute.org/Homeschool.htm [accessed 1 November 2004].

58. Ibid.

59. Ibid.

60. Gutmann, Amy. *Democratic Education,* rev. ed. (Princeton, NJ: Princeton University Press, 1999): 28.

61. Thomas Fleming, for example, does not believe everyone should homeschool. Many parents "born since 1940," he asserts, are "ignorant," "self-indulgent," and "muddleheaded," lacking self-discipline and unable to adequately control their children. Fleming, Thomas. "Grow Old along with Me," *Chronicles,* 23.9 (1999): 12.

62. League of the South Institute web site for homeschoolers.

63. Livingston, Donald W. "Barbecue Shacks, Palmetto Groves, and Other Schools," *Chronicles*, 24.9 (2000): 18.

64. Ibid., 19. See also Livingston, Donald W. "Irish 'Hedge' Schools—A Model to Rebuild Southern Culture," *Southern Events*, 4 3 (1999): 1, 17–18, and League of the South. "What Is a Hedge School Seminar?" On-line: http://www. dixienet.org/ ls-institute/los-institute.htm#school [accessed 25 August 1999].

65. Livingston, "Barbecue Shacks," (2000): 18–19. This is ironic as neo-Confederate leaders in the late-1990s, such as Michael Hill, Donald W. Livingston, Clyde Wilson, and Grady McWhiney held tenured teaching positions and pursued successful careers teaching at Southern universities, including Stillman College, the University of Alabama, Emory University, Texas Christian University, and the University of South Carolina.

66. Livingston, "Barbecue Shacks," (2000): 18.

67. League of the South. "What Is a Hedge School Seminar?"

68. Livingston, "Barbecue Shacks," (2000): 18–19.

69. Ibid., 19.

70. Althusser, *Lenin and Philosophy*, (1971): 157.

71. League of the South. "A Message to the Southern Poverty Law Center and Its Leftist Allies." On-line: http://www.dixienet.org/ls-press-releases/LS-special-reports/splc.htm [accessed 15 September 2000 and 3 February 2002].

72. Riegel, Sarah. "The Home Schooling Movement and the Struggle for Democratic Education," *Studies in Political Economy*, 65 (2001): 93.

73. Many nationalist movements begin with a cultural revival—see, for example, the Scottish and Irish nationalisms of the late eighteenth century reviewed in Trumpener, Katie. *Bardic Nationalism: The Romantic Novel and the British Empire*. (Princeton, NJ: Princeton University Press, 1997).

74. See the explanations for home schooling in Stevens, Mitchell L. *Kingdom of Children: Culture and Controversy in the Homeschooling Movement*. (Princeton, NJ: Princeton University Press, 2001).

75. Gutmann, *Democratic Education*, (1999): 30.

CHAPTER 8

Literature and Neo-Confederacy

KEVIN HICKS

From the early 1600s several different cultures developed in America. The South-
ern culture, I think, in many ways was the strongest and the most enduring. We
have our own speech and our own manners, among other things. We have our
own music and our own literature which can be recognized. America as it is now
doesn't have any culture.[1]
—CLYDE WILSON, 1999

Works of fiction—novels and poetry—can mean more to a people than all the
political manifestoes and reports from all the think tanks and foundations ever
established by misguided philanthropy. A people's character, at its best and worst,
can be read from its novels.[2]
—THOMAS FLEMING, 1982

Introduction

For neo-Confederates like Clyde Wilson and Thomas Fleming, the idea of
true Southern culture and identity is most clearly expressed through the region's narrative traditions: song lyrics, historical accounts, or, as examined
here, fictional literary works. Organizations like the League of the South (LS)
and the Sons of Confederate Veterans (SCV) have established literary boards,
produced seminars on Southern artists and writers, sponsored music festivals,
and printed lists of "essential reading for educated Southerners" in magazines,
including *Southern Partisan*.[3] Leaders of the LS, many of whom have PhDs
in history and literature, have stressed cultural issues by producing sixty-five
videotapes in a series entitled "The History and Literature of the South" and
have also established an educational arm, the League of the South Insti-

tute (see Chapter 7). These efforts assert the neo-Confederate belief that the South is the true inheritor of classical Greek and Roman cultural traditions and that the South constitutes a distinct society that can lay claim to what Eugene Genovese calls "alternative visions of social order" from those of the supposedly Northern, "bourgeois world view."[4]

That neo-Confederates, like any nationalist movement, would view narratives as essential to defining Southern identity is not unusual. Most literary critics and historians agree that storytelling constructs meaning out of particular cultural and historical circumstances, but what makes the neo-Confederates different is that this process is not one of invention but of revelation. For them, true Southern literature is not so much the product of individual experience and imagination as it is the effect of an unchangeable and "constant southern identity."[5] For today's neo-Confederates, the South is a fixed, known entity with an essential Southern culture that is not open to interpretation. As Michael Kreyling notes, from such a vantage point "southern literature will always be recognizable by a formula as constant as the thing itself, for the South and its history are 'facts' and 'entities' that remain intact and impervious to literary representation."[6]

The key to understanding how neo-Confederates define what constitutes authentic Southern narratives and consequently true Southern identity lies in recognizing the "facts," "entities," and the "formula" that convey their fixed conception of the South. In fiction, this means investigating such matters as character types, plots, and settings that express "Southerness." Images of the young cavalier, plantation belle, and loyal house slave, for example, can be seen as not just the stereotypes of a bygone world captured in Southern novels, but as reflections of neo-Confederate conceptions of what the real South is and what it should look like again. While Southern literature does take on new forms over time — antebellum historical romances giving way to Reconstruction-era "Lost Cause" melodramas that were supplanted in the early twentieth century by the anti-modern works of the Southern Agrarians — the neo-Confederate "formula" for what constitutes real Southern works remains strikingly consistent: they are novels that authenticate, celebrate, or mourn the loss of a world that is 'naturally' hierarchical, patriarchal, racially determined, and far superior to the present. In this world, men rule, women inspire, and blacks know their place.

Of course, such stark "facts" belie the complexity of neo-Confederate conceptions of Southern literature. For example, patriarchy finds itself manifested in various male characters, ranging from a cultured member of the elite to a simple backwoodsman, a chivalrous Revolutionary, or Confederate leader, protective father, or husband. Female characters appear as stately matrons, sacrificial frontierswomen, impulsive young ladies, and angelic children. Likewise, hierarchy exists as the natural organizing principle in descriptions of military commands, political organizations, social interactions, and familial relations. Finally, the issue of race is linked to both patriarchy and hierarchy, as African Americans are presented as both children of the master and natural workers in the cotton fields in demeaning characterizations, including the happy, loyal slave, the comedic Sambo, and the highly sexualized, animalistic freedman.

What unites all these various characters is that together they establish the mythic structure of the neo-Confederate's South. As critic Rollin G. Osterweis explained, popular literature has often been the vehicle to both situate and perpetuate "social myths."[7] For neo-Confederates, such myths revolve around the idea that the true South embodies and reflects natural laws and moral principles that have their foundation in divine truth. Explaining this in *Southern Partisan*, Mark Malvasi, author of the important neo-Confederate text *The Unregenerate South*, argues that the South has long sought to preserve a "Christian social order" in the face of the destabilizing forces of capitalism and democracy. Consequently, traditional Southern conservatives like the neo-Confederates are wont to "accept the conditions and limitations that God has imposed upon them" and reject "all schemes to liberate human beings from history, society, family, and self."[8] Whether it is in narratives that celebrate the Old South, that bemoan Reconstruction, or that justify slavery and segregation, the mythic South to neo-Confederates is a fundamentally moral civilization whose members are guided by the highest Christian principles of honor, duty, loyalty, faith, and integrity. Arrayed against it are forces that threaten this mythical world with upheaval: savage natives, meddling Abolitionists, ruthless capitalists, self-serving liberals, and power-hungry blacks. This struggle for the South pits the traditional against the modern, rural against urban, agrarian against industrial, Christian against heathen, and neo-Confederacy against democracy and civil rights.

Pre-Civil War Literature and William Gilmore Simms

Of the fiction produced in the South before the Civil War, neo-Confederates praise two literary traditions: Southern historical romances, exemplified by William Gilmore Simms, and Southwestern humor, a genre associated with Augustus Baldwin Longstreet. As the critic Richard Gray has noted, both Simms and Longstreet played an integral role in helping to shape the "South's own image of itself."[9] Prominent LS member James Meriwether, a professor emeritus of English at the University of South Carolina, has edited several official editions of Simms's work; his wife, Anne, heads the William Gilmore Simms Society in Aiken, South Carolina; and another neo-Confederate, James E. Kibler, an English professor at the University of Georgia, edits *The Simms Review*. In addition, LS faculty member David Aiken stars in a video-tape on Longstreet created for the organization's "History and Literature of the South" series.

In the antebellum period, Southern writers like Simms and Longstreet were engaged in an imaginative struggle to determine the essential character of the South. Although, as Gray points out, their efforts were hardly success-ful and represented only a limited conception of the Southern experience, the imagery and the vocabulary they employed, particularly that of the noble "feudal plantation and the simple self-subsistent farm," echoed that used by political pamphleteers of the era.[10] If not actually propaganda pieces in their own right, such works dovetailed with the political goals of defending the idea that the South was a distinct cultural region and justifying its "peculiar" institutions. Tellingly, Simms, Longstreet, and their principal literary genres are prominent in neo-Confederate Clyde Wilson's "The South and Southern History," a list of texts that reveal the South's "separate historical experience and culture."[11]

During his long career, William Gilmore Simms published over eighty books, including works of fiction, drama, poetry, biography, history, and geography. He is best known for a series of historical romances based on the South from settlement to the early nineteenth century. Commonly referred to as the Colonial, Revolutionary, and Border Romances, these represent Simms's effort to promote a specifically Southern identity. Although born of modest means, Simms was an ardent supporter of the Southern ruling class and felt that Southern society was inherently superior, a fact he strove to con-vey through his fiction. Consequently, his romances were designed not only to "correspond with general exactions of the truth," but also to capture "the best essentials of human society—such as constitute the moving impulses of men to action." He hoped his romances would minister "to morals, to mankind, and to society" by showing the "fierce courage—tenacious patriotism . . . [and] struggling virtue" of his decidedly Southern heroes.[12] In fact, Gray con-tends, Simms's "overriding thesis" was "his belief in the patriarchal model, a hierarchical system that found its summit and embodiment in what he called 'the Southern aristocrat—the true nobleman of that region.'"[13]

The clearest expression of Simms's Southern aristocrat is in the seven books comprising his Revolutionary Romance series. Recalling the efforts of parti-san American forces to overcome their loyalist and English adversaries, these romances focus on a group of Revolutionary officers, who with few exceptions are young Carolinian cavaliers. In *The Partisan* (1835), the impression conveyed by Major Singleton's entrance into a tavern is typical of such men: "His person was symmetry itself, and the ease with which he managed his steed, the unhesitating boldness with which he kept on his way and gazed around him at a period and in a place where all were timid and suspicious, could not fail to fix attention."[14] Confident, authoritative, and honorable to a fault, these are men who inspire others not so much because of their noble birth (although most can trace their ancestry back to either Scottish or English royalty) but because of what their bloodlines have imbued them with—natural leadership skills. Without even knowing him, the good men under Singleton's command immediately recognize this inherent quality: "His frank, fearless manner, fine eye, and manly, though smooth and youthful face, took admirably with them, and at once spoke favorably to their minds in support of his pretensions to govern them."[15]

Regularly described by Simms as "gallant" and "chivalric," these gentlemen soldiers are often compared to medieval knights, an analogy that helps to explain Simms's view of Southern society. Like a feudal estate, the world of Simms's romances conforms to rigid notions of patriarchy and hierarchy. Its leaders, such as Major Singleton, uphold a chivalric code by placing duty before desire, valor before fear, and honor before all else. As leaders, they are responsible for protecting those who occupy the social ranks beneath them, most centrally the main female character. Like Kate in *The Partisan* or Bess Mathews in *The Yemassee* (1835), such women are typically the beautiful and chaste daughters and nieces of noble, elderly gentlemen who can no longer fully protect them. They represent the epitome of true (Southern) womanhood, inspirational paragons of virtue and self-sacrifice.

A central aspect of Simms's romances revolves around the transfer of protective authority from the father to a suitor and soon-to-be husband. This process usually involves a series of tests in which the gallant cavalier must provide physical protection from such things as poisonous snakes, ruthless savages, bloodthirsty bandits, and calculating con men. Always respecting the rules of fair play, what wins the woman's heart is not her suitor's battlefield valor or his ability to woo her, but his fulfillment of his duty to the community no matter the personal cost. When *The Partisan*'s Major Singleton speaks to Kate about his "purely selfish" love for her, she chastises his "idle thoughts."[16] It is only after Singleton defeats the British, securing the safety of the town of Dorchester and Kate's family, that he earns her love and respect.

If the male lead in such romances is defined by his sense of duty, those occupying the lower levels of this hierarchical society are judged by the degree of their loyalty. In Simms's novels and similar works by William A. Caruthers and Nathaniel Beverly Tucker, there is a "diverse body of merchants, artisans, farmers, and frontiersmen whose 'blood' and training prevent them from acting as leaders but who are more than willing to follow."[17] In *The Cavaliers of Virginia* (1834), Brian O'Reily's Irish blood and seemingly insatiable desire for alcohol make this "talking, blundering merry youth" an unfit leader, but his unwavering dedication to Nathaniel Bacon (a character loosely modeled on the historical figure) not only meets the criteria of the perfect squire, but also encourages him to display bravery in his own right.[18] Likewise, the figure of Schwartz in Tucker's *The Partisan Leader* (1836) is an expert woodsman and leader of other frontiersmen, but when he encounters Captain Douglas Trevor, whose aristocratic pedigree and skill with a horse confirm his "chivalrous character," Schwartz immediately assumes the role of loyal advisor and confidant, never presuming that he could or should be more.[19] The lesson offered by such characters seems clear: By adhering to the proper rules of Southern society, especially sublimating one's individual ambitions to the 'natural' social order, the whole community is improved.

At the bottom of this hierarchy are slaves. For antebellum romance authors, fashioning an ideal South meant presenting slavery as part of an organic social system. In *The Partisan Leader*, for example, Tucker depicted whites and blacks in the South as two branches of an interrelated family, "united by similar ligaments . . . fibres from which the ties that bind man to man are spun."[20] The ties that bind slave to master are not forged in brutality and exploitation for Tucker; rather, they are nurtured through common experiences shared on the plantation. Likewise, for Simms, underlying slavery is a bond between master and slave. Speaking of his black cook Tom, Captain Porgy declares in *Woodcraft* (1854):

> We have fought and fed too long together, Tom, and I trust we love each other quite too well, to submit to separation. . . . I shall fight for you to the last, Tom, and you, I know, would fight to the last for me, as I am very sure that neither of us can long outlast the other.[21]

To illustrate the strength of such relationships, the climactic scenes of many romance novels see black slaves come to the rescue of the master, defending him with their lives or attacking his enemies. In the closing pages of Simms's *The Yemassee*, the final deathblow to the great chief, Sanutee, comes not from the sword of a cavalier, but from the "club of the negro," one of many slaves that had fought side by side with the white settlers to defend their homes.[22] More poignantly, when surrounded by Federal troops intent upon arresting him for treason, the Southern partisan leader, Bernard Trevor, declares his plan "to arm the negroes in defense of their master," which he is confident will prove "an exhibition of the staunch loyalty and heart-felt devotion of the slave to the master."[23] Such depictions of master/slave relationships are not presented as something separate from Southern society, but rather as true expressions of the natural social order. What the cavalier is to his men, and what a gentleman is to the members of his household, so the master is to the slave, namely a patriarchal leader that invites devotion by the nature of his intrinsic qualities.

In today's neo-Confederate publications, Simms's interpretation of Southern society and its gentleman patriarchs have become articles of faith, with numerous discussions about great Southern leaders who seemingly epitomize these ideals. In a *Southern Partisan* review of J. Steven Wilkins's work, *Call of Duty: The Sterling Nobility of Robert E. Lee* (1997), Byron Snapp describes the archetypal gentleman patriarch:

> In the second part of this volume the author examines Lee's life under manifold character lenses. Through these, the reader views Lee's devotedness to his family, his humility, his fight with bitterness, his unselfishness, and most importantly, his trust in God through Jesus Christ. This trust formed the basis for his willingness to do his duty whether such duty meant being a servant to his invalid wife or being a leader and formulating battle strategies.[24]

Like the heroes in Simms's works, Lee in the neo-Confederate mind is a man who rises above the rest; his natural leadership skills are derived from a character that finds its truest expression in his selfless response to the call of duty. By extension, neo-Confederates, as the descendents of men like Lee, have uniquely inherited these natural and superior talents.

The Southern Humorists

If the romance works of William Gilmore Simms and others served to advance the idea of a natural aristocracy in the South ruling over a loyal populace, the writing of Augustus Baldwin Longstreet, George W. Harris, Johnson J. Hooper, and other "Southwestern humorists" helped shape the Southern ideal of the independent, yeoman farmer. Identified as "crackers" by many neo-Confederates and celebrated by Grady McWhiney in *Cracker Culture* (1988), which became a central text for neo-Confederate appeals for an "Anglo-Celtic" South (see Chapter 4), "crackers" are understood by many neo-Confederates as the true cultural inheritors and rightful rulers of the region.[25] Often uncultured and lacking a family pedigree, "crackers" seemingly stand in marked contrast to the gentlemen heroes of Simms's romances; however, they represent the unpolished version of their more refined counterparts. In terms of respect for traditional Southern values and social norms, the two are more alike than at first they appear.

The author most often associated with such figures is Augustus Baldwin Longstreet, his most famous work, *Georgia Scenes* (1835), being widely imitated. Longstreet sought to capture in this collection of nineteen stories the real life experiences, manners, and expressions of the men and women of the interior South. To do so, he created a frame in which two gentlemen narrators describe the routines and habits of the people around them. Like in later works of Southwestern humor, the outcome is a collection of often graphic depictions of the local that, on one hand, are designed to shock and entertain the reader and, on the other, to validate and celebrate the lives of people who supposedly express the truest Southern values.

A clear example in *Georgia Scenes* is "The Fight," which recounts in gruesome detail a battle between two of the "very *best men* . . . which, in the Georgia vocabulary, means they could flog any other men in the county."[26] Watching from the periphery, the narrator, in keeping with his cultured upbringing, declares that such "scenes of barbarism . . . are a disgrace."[27] However, while the narrator is clearly appalled by the brutal contest, he fails to mention what happened to start "The Fight," namely that one of the men insulted the honor of the other's wife. Had this been a Simms romance, such an affront would have likewise resulted in a duel—probably with pistols, not fists.[28] While Longstreet's "Fight" is far from anything a cavalier would engage in, the motivation, protecting the honor of a woman, is consistent within such notions of Southern society. Despite their rough demeanors and coarse manners, these two men are truly honorable. To stress the importance of this point, the loser announces, "Bobby, you've *licked* me in a fair fight; but you wouldn't have done it if I hadn't been in the wrong."[29] As prominent neo-Confederate James E. Kibler notes in his introduction to *Georgia Scenes*, "I know no writer who better portrays the values of [Southern] rural people with greater understanding, especially their frankness, independence, straightforwardness, modesty, and loyalty."[30] It is for these reasons that Longstreet remains a favorite of neo-Confederates—he reveals nobility and honor in their beloved "cracker culture." In neo-Confederate circles, the most celebrated representative of this Southern "cracker" or Celtic culture is Nathan Bedford Forrest (see Chapter 3), subject of a 1996 James E. Kibler poem, "General Forrest Muses from the Second Floor of the Alabama Archives."[31]

Postbellum Literature

Where antebellum literature had pointed to an independent future for the South based on its supposedly unique culture, in defeat such aspirations seemed unattainable. Take, for example, the transformation of the poetry of Henry Timrod, commonly referred to as "the poet laureate of the Confederacy."[32] Where in an 1861 poem he declared about the South, "At last, we are / A nation among nations; and the world / Shall soon behold in many a distant port / Another flag unfurled!" by 1867 his poetry was much more somber: "Sleep sweetly in your humble graves, / Sleep, martyrs of a fallen cause; / Though yet no marble column craves / The pilgrim here to pause."[33] While the slowly receding reality of Southern independence left some disillusioned, this sentiment was soon replaced by warm nostalgia for a bygone age and valorization of those who fought for the Confederacy. In their attempt to preserve the integrity of their collective identity, Southern authors transformed antebellum romance into postbellum melodrama, presenting themselves as the heroic defenders of a noble "Lost Cause."[34] In the literature that ensued, the chivalric planter and beautiful Southern belle are joined by the honorable Confederate veteran and obliging old Uncle Remus in defense of their homeland against the marauding forces of Yankee aggressors and carpetbaggers. At its heart, such literature functions by means of a simple dichotomy: the South was right, in every sense of the word, and the North, although more powerful, was inarguably wrong. Wrapped in the comfort of self-justification, victimization, and righteous indignation, adherents of this myth, including current neo-Confederates, see the South as an enduring symbol of all that is to be celebrated. The brutalities of slavery are conveniently ignored.

The term "Lost Cause" gained currency following publication of Edward Alfred Pollard's *The Lost Cause: A New Southern History of the War of the Confederates* (1866). Pollard, a wartime journalist of Richmond, Virginia, was one of the first to argue that while the military struggle was over, the battle for the South would continue:

> Now a war of ideas is what the South wants and insists upon perpetuating. . . . In such a war there are noble victories to be won, memorable services to be performed, and grand results to be achieved. The Southern people stand by their principles. . . .
>
> It would be immeasurably the worst consequence of defeat in this war that the South should lose its moral and intellectual distinctiveness as a people and cease to assert its well known superiority in civilization, in po-

litical scholarship, and in all the standards of individual character over the people of the North.[35]

While Pollard's conception of a distinct and superior Southern civilization continues in the work of Simms and others, its importance lies in the vehemence of Pollard's pronouncements and the degree to which many still cling to this proposition. As Rollin Osterweis argues, in the postbellum environment, the essential ideas of antebellum Southern romanticism were "modified and adapted to the exigencies of defeat and mortification."[36] Pride in a perceived Southern identity turned into a strident defense of the Confederacy's "Lost Cause." As part of this transformation, the righteousness of the South is set more directly in opposition to the wickedness of North. In the resulting literature, Union soldiers, carpetbaggers, and Reconstruction-era Republicans are ruthless, conniving, and treacherous—everything the South is not. Furthermore, the essence of Southern identity was soon identified as racial. In Pollard's sequel, *The Lost Cause Regained* (1868), he asserts: "This new cause—or rather the true question of the war revised—is the supremacy of the white race, and along with it and strengthening it, the reassertion of our political traditions and the protection of our ancient fabrics of government."[37] While Reconstruction brought some hope to African Americans, for Southern whites, particularly the poor who saw themselves in competition with newly emancipated slaves, this was a time to demand that the Lost Cause was not lost and that it was rooted in their own racial superiority.

In the years following the Civil War, Lost Cause propaganda disseminated through magazines like *Scribner's* and *Century Illustrated Monthly Magazine*, which published stories, essays, sketches, and poems that glamorized the Old South. Among the contributors were a collection of talented Southern writers and poets, including Henry Watterson, George W. Cable, Paul Hamilton Hayne, Sidney Lanier, and Joel Chandler Harris, who, beginning in 1882, published a series of songs and stories in *Century Illustrated* involving his most appealing literary character, Uncle Remus.[38] Speaking in a black regional dialect, this elderly slave tells a series of moralistic folktales about Brer Rabbit, Brer Fox, and other fanciful creatures to white children who come to visit him in his cabin. Critics have found fault with the way Harris characterizes Uncle Remus's "pleasant memories of the discipline of slavery."[39] Harris regularly depicted slave/master relationships in the Old South as cordial. In *Nights with Uncle Remus* (1883), Uncle Remus recalls his nightly meal given to him by his "thoughtful" former owner. He announces, "Ef she ain't one blessed white 'oman . . . den dey ain't none un um 'roun' in deze parts."[40] Although neo-Confederates like Clyde Wilson decry the fact that Harris and his Uncle Remus stories are no longer in favor, it is clear that the image of the happy, dutiful black slave living his simple life on a beautiful antebellum plantation has had a powerful effect on perceptions of slavery and has helped to further the myth of the Lost Cause.

Perhaps the greatest contributor to such sentimental idealizations of the Old South was Thomas Nelson Page in a series of stories for *Century Illustrated* and elsewhere, many of which were collected in *The Burial of the Guns* (1884).[41] Take, for example, "Marse Chan," in which the narrator describes a plantation with "numerous out-buildings and large barns and stables" that had "once been a seat of wealth." Sounding a note that resonates throughout the story, however, the fields have become, since the passing of the master and the collapse of slavery, a "wild waste of sassafras" and the plantation conveys "an air of desolation."[42] The narrator's lament is interrupted by an encounter with another remnant of this once-glorious place: Sam, a former slave who is looking for a lost dog. The dog had belonged to the son of the plantation, Marse Chan (Master Channings), and Sam has been caring for the animal and living on the plantation ever since Channing's death in the Civil War. Sam makes it clear that in his mind "Marse Chan's dawg" remains the property of the owner, just as, by implication, he does. In his rich, black dialect, Sam recounts for the narrator the story of his master whom he watched grow from birth into a true Southern gentleman, skilled with a horse and chivalrous: "Dem wuz good ole times, marster—de bes' Sam ever see!" Sam fondly recalls.[43] When the war came, Sam happily accompanied "de captain" as his cook and personal servant; he was even present at his last heroic charge into enemy cannon fire when Marse Chan picked up the fallen Confederate flag and yelled "Foller me!"[44]

In other stories, Page recalls with similar sentimentality the heroism of those who fought for the Confederacy. In "The Gray Jacket of 'No. 4,'" he recounts the ceremony surrounding the 1890 unveiling of Richmond's Robert E. Lee monument. Seemingly the entire South is gathered together to "glorify Lee" and "the volunteer soldiers of the South [who] had held the world at bay, and added to the glorious history of their race."[45] In the title story of his collection, "The Burial of the Guns," he tells of a Confederate battery entrenched in a mountain pass days after Lee's surrender at Appomattox on 9 April 1865. Having been ordered to hold the pass until instructed otherwise and to not let the cannons fall into Union hands, the Confederate colonel refuses to surrender even though he is surrounded and outnumbered. The struggle to defend their position against attack serves as a metaphor for the South's resistance to "Northern aggression." When Lee's surrender is confirmed, the colonel decides that he will not hand over his men or cannons and, after a final salute honoring the living and the dead, the cannons are buried in a ravine to hide them from the enemy. Before slipping away undefeated and ready to fight another day, the Confederate troops read a telling statement: "Now we're agoin home. We ain't surrendered; just disbanded, and we pledges ourselves to teach our children to love the South and General Lee; and to come when we're called anywhere's an' anytime, so help us God."[46]

Of all the literary works associated with the Southern post-war resistance, none are more strident than the three novels written by Thomas Dixon Jr. Entitled *The Leopard's Spots: A Romance of the White Man's Burden 1865–1900* (1902), *The Clansman* (1905), and *The Traitor* (1907), this trilogy presents one of most disturbing images of Southern identity ever written. In keeping with the spirit of Lost Cause literature, Dixon praises the old world of the plantation and celebrates the heroism of the Confederate soldiers; however, his real subject is Reconstruction, and with vitriol that is both shocking and appalling, he identifies the newest threats to Southern culture, "Negro domination . . . Negro deification . . . Negro equality and amalgamation."[47] What had once been a war between the North and the South has become a war between races. Instead of good Confederate soldiers fighting to protect their homes and families, Dixon tells of hooded members of the Ku Klux Klan riding to the rescue of white Southerners who are threatened with death and destruction by freed blacks and Northern politicians out for revenge. Melodramatic, nostalgic, and sentimental, these novels seek nothing less than to fashion a new Lost Cause of Southern white identity from the exploitation and propagation of racist beliefs.

Dixon is careful to address some of the issues that had once divided Northerners from Southerners. Not only does he mourn the death of Lincoln and pay tribute to the bravery of Union soldiers, but he also absolves the South of its claims to secession and the institution of slavery. Declaring that the "South did not fight to hold slaves," a position held sacred by most neo-Confederates, one Southern character concludes, "But for the frenzy of your Abolition fanatics who first sought to destroy the Union by Secession, and then forced Secession on the South . . . we would have freed the slaves before this without a war, for the very necessities of the progress of the material world, to say nothing of its moral progress."[48] Even so, for Dixon, if Northerners were wrong about anything, it was their lack of racial loyalty after the war. A central character in the story, the Preacher, asks a Northerner, "Why is it that you good people of the North are spending your millions here now to help only the Negroes, who feel least of all the sufferings of this war? The poor white people of the South are your own flesh and blood."[49] Those who have betrayed the nation are not the Southerners who fought to protect their land, but those in the Republican Party who, by creating The Freedman's Bureau and fostering the cause of black enfranchisement, threaten to impose a "Negro oligarchy" in the South.[50]

Dixon presents freed African Americans terrorizing white Southerners, drinking, looting, fighting, and seeking to satisfy their animalistic lust by raping white women. In one scene in *The Leopard's Spots*, a man's newlywed wife is seized by the "burly figure of a big Negro" and dragged out of the house. Her father calls out, "Shoot, men! My God, shoot! There are things worse than death." They do shoot and accidentally kill the girl, but her father concludes, "It might have been worse. Let us thank God she was saved from them brutes."[51] The fear that the father felt is based upon a strict notion of racial superiority and the need to keep one's white blood pure of the taint of "triflin' niggers."[52] As one character concludes:

> Amalgamation simply meant Africanization. The big nostrils, flat nose, massive jaw, protruding lip and kinky hair will register their animal marks over the proudest intellect and the rarest beauty of any other race. The rule that had no exception was that one drop of Negro blood makes a Negro.[53]

A "Negro," in the mind of Dixon, is a "human donkey," incapable of being educated or overcoming animalistic ways. As the Preacher incredulously states, "You don't believe that any amount of education can fit a Negro to rule an Anglo-Saxon, or to marry his daughter!" The conclusion that Dixon comes to is that the "Negro must ultimately leave the continent" to avoid a "race war." In the meantime, it is up to white Southerners, guided by the "instinct of self-preservation," to protect their homes and their families once again.[54]

• The salvation of the South comes not from the members of the old Southern aristocracy, but from its "Cracker Culture," the descendants of Scotch-Irish settlers. Speaking of the Piedmont area of South Carolina, Dixon notes, "It was settled by the Scotch folk who came from North of Ireland . . . the largest and most important addition to our population, larger in numbers than either the Puritans of New England or the so-called Cavaliers of Virginia and Eastern Carolina; and far more important than either, in the growth of American nationality."[55] Described as "sturdy, honest, covenant-keeping, God-fearing, fighting people," these Southern "Crackers" form the heart of the latest manifestation of the Southern knight errant, the Ku Klux Klansman.[56] In a passage charged with romantic intensity, Dixon presents the KKK as modern knights guided by only the highest intentions to right the wrongs done to their people:

This Invisible Empire of White Robed Anglo-Saxon Knights was simply the old answer of organized manhood to organized crime. Its purpose was to bring order out of chaos, protect the weak and defenseless, the widows and the orphans of brave men who had died for their country, to drive from power the thieves who were robbing the people, redeem the commonwealth from infamy, and re-establish civilization.[57]

In true melodramatic fashion, that is exactly what the Klan does in Dixon's books. In *The Leopard's Spots,* the local leader of the Klan, Charles Gaston, defeats his enemies and becomes the governor of North Carolina; in *The Clansman,* the story ends with "lights on the mountains" signaling victory in the shape of "the Fiery Cross"; and in *The Traitor,* the hero-Klansman John Graham ends up winning the hand of his sweetheart and receiving a pardon for his actions.[58]

  Dixon's trilogy had a dramatic cultural impact. The novels were greeted with enthusiastic approval by Southern readers of their day, and in 1915 Dixon assisted in transforming *The Clansman* into the script for D. W. Griffith's *The Birth of a Nation,* a landmark film in the history of the motion picture industry, both for its cinematography and its glorification of white supremacy. As Rollin Osterweis notes, "The contribution of this film to the later growth of the Myth of the Lost Cause, with its emphasis on black inferiority and white supremacy, must have been enormous."[59] Along with valorizing racism, Dixon's novels and the film helped to generate the cult-like following of General Nathan Bedford Forrest, who remains a darling of today's neo-Confederates. As recently as 1993, Sam Dickson, a leader of the racist and neo-Confederate Council of Conservative Citizens, argued in the introduction to a reprint of the trilogy that "Dixon's novels are as timely as ever" as they call into question efforts by liberals "to integrate the races already within the country."[60] In his own foreword to a reprinting of *The Clansman,* James P. Cantrell stresses Dixon's unappreciated "cultural liberalism" (including, strangely enough, his opposition to hunting) in an attempt to defend Dixon's racist works.[61] The League of the South's Clyde Wilson also overlooks Dixon's blatant racism, making only one criticism of the trilogy and Griffith's film:

The main thing wrong with "Birth" is too favorable a view of Lincoln. During the late 19th and early 20th centuries, Southerners like D. W. Griffith, the director, and Thomas Dixon, who wrote the novel that was used as a base, went out of their way to be good Americans and give some respect to the prevailing Northern sentiments.[62]

The Southern Agrarian Era

While adherents of the Lost Cause myth continued to write books well into the twentieth century, and themes of glory, loss, and defiance remain popular with neo-Confederates (such as Margaret Mitchell's *Gone with the Wind*, which appears on *Southern Partisan*'s list of the top fifteen Southern books ever written), if any theme defines neo-Confederate literature in the first half of the twentieth century it is an impassioned rejection of modernity.[63] Faced with the growing pressures of industrialization and liberalization, writers and thinkers who identified with traditional Southern values found themselves in a reactionary struggle against an array of outside cultural forces. In particular, a group of poets, writers, and critics known broadly as the Southern Agrarians (see Chapter 1) sought to counter what they perceived as the deadly threat of individualism, materialism, egalitarianism, and nihilism of modern American society by championing the cause of traditional Southern values, which they saw as grounded in agrarianism and regionalism. Of Southern Agrarians, which included at various times John Crowe Ransom, Andrew Lytle, Frank Owsley, Robert Penn Warren, and others, the two held most dearly by today's neo-Confederates are Allen Tate and Donald Davidson.

Outside of his work with the Southern Agrarians in *I'll Take My Stand* and in fostering literary symposiums on the subject of the South, Allen Tate's biggest contribution to the Southern cause came in the form of his novel *The Fathers* (1938). The story recounts the interaction of two families, the Poseys and the Buchans, during the lead-up to the Civil War. As Arthur Mizener notes in the introduction to the 1984 edition, the central tension in *The Fathers* is between "the order of civilization" created through ritual, ceremony, and tradition and the "disorder of the private life," which, lacking the proper guidance, is "at the mercy of its own impulses."[64] Tellingly, it is the Southern patriarch of the Buchan family, Major Buchan, who embodies the highest qualities of civilization, and the well-meaning George Posey, without a father or a sense of tradition, who acts with little regard for the outcome of his actions. The novel traces how the Buchans' Southern world is superseded by that of the Poseys, signaling Tate's disillusion with the form and direction of modern culture. However, the ending suggests this tragic lapse into individualism, materialism, and self-indulgence does not necessarily have to be the future of the South.

Major Lewis Buchan has a family history that stretches back generations and is firmly rooted in the Virginia soil of the story. He is the grandson of a "Scots adventurer" who married the daughter of a local landowner in 1741 and thus became part of "that unique order of society known latterly as the

Virginia aristocracy."[65] Everything the major does is informed by his strong sense of proper social order. When the family enters public places, as they do on a trip to Alexandria, it is in single file: first the major, then his wife, then the children, and then "old Lucy Lewis, my mother's maid."[66] Yet, as a true Southern gentleman, the major's loyalty and support for those under his care is nearly boundless.

In comparison to Major Buchan, George Posey represents what Tate feels will happen when the personal is allowed to dictate one's actions. The Poseys, like the Buchans, have a historic tie to the region, but in their case, they "left the land" during George's boyhood and moved permanently into a house in Georgetown.[67] The agrarian nature of Tate's conception of the true South clearly comes into play in this dichotomy between city dwellers and country people. In the climactic scenes of *The Fathers,* George's black half-brother, Yellow Jim, attacks his sister in her room; Semmes Buchan, in conformity with Southern custom, avenges this egregious violation of his fiancée's honor by shooting Yellow Jim.[68] In response, George shoots Semmes in a fit of passion, putting his feelings for Yellow Jim ahead of his duty to uphold racial and gender boundaries. George's actions signal a larger breakdown in the novel's social order, which symbolically culminate in the death of Major Buchan. Union soldiers visit the Buchan plantation and, instead of Major Buchan, George Posey tells them to "get off this place." When the troops return, however, it is Major Buchan who is duty bound to resist them and ends up paying with his life.

Among the Southern Agrarians, Donald Davidson is most heralded by neo-Confederate scholars. Subject of a biography entitled *Where No Flag Flies* by League of the South Institute director and Clemson University professor Mark Winchell, Davidson's career was marked by a steady move toward a radical pro-Southern position, a process that arguably began with *The Tall Men* (1927) and matured a decade later with *Lee in the Mountains and Other Poems* (1938). The title poem of *Lee in the Mountains* takes as its subject not Robert E. Lee's battlefield heroics, but the time after the war when he served as president of Washington College in Lexington, Virginia. It begins with Lee walking to his office, passing a group of children. In a tone replete with weariness, he remarks:

> The young have time to wait.
> But soldiers' faces under their tossing flags
> Lift no more by any road or field,
> And I am spent with old wars and new sorrow.
> Walking the rocky path, where steps decay

And the paint cracks and grass eats on the stone.
It is not General Lee, young men . . .
It is Robert Lee in a dark civilian suit who walks,
An outlaw fumbling for the latch, a voice
Commanding in a dream where no flag flies.[69]

The image is one of loss and decay, highlighting the fallen South where "General Lee" is reduced to being a simple "civilian" or, worse, an "outlaw" in a land where "no flag flies." The poem then moves to the distant past when Lee recalls the sad fate of his father, a Revolutionary War hero who endured bankruptcy and imprisonment before he died and was buried in a "lone grave."[70] Out of a sense of duty to his father and respect for the "sacred cause[s]" each of them fought for in their respective wars, Lee works to complete his father's memoirs. In doing so, he contemplates his own trials and the indignities that the South continues to face as a result of his surrender at Appomattox. With stoic resolve, Lee rejects self-pity for himself or the South and instead places his trust in God to redeem the future:

And in His might He waits,
Brooding within the certitude of time,
To bring this lost forsaken valor
And the fierce faith undying
And the love quenchless
To flower among the hills to which we cleave,
To fruit upon the mountains whither we flee,
Never forsaking, never denying
His children and His children's children forever
Unto all generations of the faithful heart.[71]

In Davidson's mind, the South was never defeated in the Civil War; it endured the humiliation of Reconstruction; and it stands ready to battle against forces of industrialism out to yet again transform the culture of the region from something beautiful to something crass and meaningless.

Whether it was battling against industrialism, federal authority, or desegregation, the politically defiant Davidson took an increasingly reactionary stance to defending the South in his poetry. This led him to adopt a very patronizing attitude toward African Americans. His poem "Old Black Joe Comes Home," for example, recalls Thomas Nelson Page's "Marse Chan" in its focus on the tragic consequences of emancipation for ex-slaves. As Paul Conkin, author of *The Southern Agrarians*, notes:

For Davidson, the Negro issue seemed to bring out his worst traits—a defensive rigidity or dogmatism. His fears went well beyond the prospect of northern intervention. He revealed a type of resentment against blacks, or at least a resentment against the solicitude shown them by writers, musicologists, and reformers. He took pains, in his writings on folklore, to deny any originality or creativity to blacks, even for their spirituals, and steadfastly refused to give any credit to Negro writers.[72]

This racial bias finds it way into poems like "Sequel of Appomattox," which pictures a "phantom cavalry" of Confederate soldiers returning for a midnight ride:

> And the hoofbeats of many horseman
> Stop and call from the grave:
> Remember, I was your master;
> Remember, you were my slave.[73]

In "Sanctuary," a poem calling for future generations to seek refuge in the world of their fathers, Davidson declares, "This is the secret refuge of our race" from which its members can "smite" their enemies or repose with one another in natural harmony.[74] Davidson's obsession with race ultimately led him to outspokenly defend segregation and insist upon the natural inferiority of black people in the civil rights era.[75]

Contemporary Neo-Confederate Authors

While no one of Davidson's literary stature has emerged in recent years to give voice to current neo-Confederacy, there have been a number of novelists who, in keeping with past traditions, seek to convey their ongoing battle to preserve and defend what they see as a distinctly Southern way of life. Neo-Confederate authors such as James E. Kibler, Lloyd Lenard, Ellen Williams, and Franklin Sanders have written fiction that still depicts the South as a unique cultural entity, employing literary devices that characterize earlier Southern works, namely the celebration of the local and veneration of the Old South. What stands out in these contemporary narratives is a pervading sense of Southern victimization. Heritage, tradition, culture, in fact all that is of real value in the world, is shown as being destroyed by the relentless forces of capitalism, consumerism, and liberalism.

James E. Kibler is one of the best-known contemporary neo-Confederate writers. A professor of English at the University of Georgia who serves on the editorial board of *Southern Partisan,* Kibler has authored numerous books and essays on Southern architecture, art, folklore, and literature. In Kibler's view, since the Civil War the South has been engaged in a relentless struggle to preserve its cultural integrity. Out-financed, outgunned, and unwilling to resort to the low-handed tactics of their Northern adversaries, Southerners have witnessed the near destruction of all they hold dear. In *Walking Toward Home* (2004), a satiric novel of local color on the clash between traditional Southern culture and modern American culture, Kibler writes, "We tried for our new July Fourth with all that we had, but got killed and invaded and burned out for our pains. Now we are still paying the price. From the looks of it, we . . . still ain't free. Free to get put out of business. Free to starve maybe, but not free."[76] Victims of Northern tyranny, true Southerners take pride in their distinctive ways, refusing to adapt to modern sensibilities, determined to mount a noble resistance and, as one character in *Walking Toward Home* notes, to "endure."[77]

For Kibler, the current fate of the South is part of a tragedy that extends back to the Civil War. In *Our Father's Fields* (1998), he envisions the Hardy Plantation, a South Carolina property he purchased in 1989 and refurbished, and its antebellum world as nothing short of an earthly paradise. Unlike frigid Northern cities, the Hardy Plantation exuded a warmth, beauty, and vitality that "magically gentled the manners of its people," bringing all into natural harmony with each other and the land.[78] Kibler tells of the "paterfamilias" William Eppes Hardy, the native-born son of a noble family line who presided over what "might be described as a small kingdom, with himself as its feudal overlord, with his vassals, loyal retainers, and bondsmen."[79] Overall, Kibler's descriptions of the plantation world express a chivalric sensibility worthy of a William Gilmore Simms narrative:

> For Hardy and his era, however, the end result by which success would be measured from the family's endeavor on the land, would not be merely material fortune but the degree of physical and spiritual wholeness and well-being of the plantation's people and of how they measured up to the codes of gentlemanliness, self-control, kindness, loyalty, fidelity, honesty, duty, decency, generosity, patience, and graciousness.[80]

These "good attributes" in Southern antebellum society "cut across lines of race, class, and gender,"[81] uniting all the members of the community. Slave and master worked together, prayed together ("Most ex-slaves, however, reported enjoying going to church with 'our white folks,' as they called them"),[82] and partook of the fruits of their labor if not together, at least in shared bounty: "The recollection of Hardy slave descendants is that when it came to food, they were 'treated like kings.'"[83] As Kibler notes, "These were indeed enchanted times."[84] All of this, of course, ends tragically with the conclusion of the Civil War and the coming of Reconstruction. When Confederate veterans returned home, they witnessed a South victimized by "financiers and industrialists" and "unprincipled opportunists" who steal from and exploit both blacks and whites alike.[85] Faced with such "tyranny," good Southerners like William Dixon Hardy were forced to defend themselves by joining the "Knights of the White Camellia" to protect their fellow citizens from further abuse. While Kibler acknowledges that the Klan administered a "brutal form of justice," he denies any racial motivation and presents Reconstruction as a master plan to destroy the South:

> The policy's aim was obviously to wrest money and property from the once prosperous planters, to punish them, to take away their political power and leadership, and thus totally to restructure society.[86]

According to Kibler, Reconstruction left the South poor and defenseless, unable to "support its own population" and faced with famine: "Where there had been no hunger, now it was widespread, particularly among blacks."[87] As descendents of the Hardys, driven by "the pressures of the modern world," scatter to the cities, the plantation became "haunted by a grief and loss."[88] Where once the South had been defined by families like the Hardys and their plantations, the region has been forced to abandon this heritage and adopt the materialistic, impersonal, and sterile culture of the North. Kibler ultimately calls on true Southerners to "resist the . . . impersonal World City of America, or Global Village—the nightmare at its most intense," and protect Southern culture against ongoing acts of Northern cultural aggression.[89]

Whereas Kibler looks to the past to recall the victimization of the South, neo-Confederate writers such as Ellen Williams and Lloyd E. Lenard focus on the near future. In his aptly titled novel *The Last Confederate Flag*, Lenard tells the story of Stonewall Bedford of Forest, Georgia (a play on two neo-Confederate heroes), and his struggle to defend from assault his beloved Confederate flag and the heritage he feels it represents. In what quickly descends into a racial persecution fantasy, Bedford finds himself at odds with the federal government, civil rights activists, and liberal media groups intent on distorting true Southern history and desecrating the sacred symbol of Confederacy. His greatest enemy, however, is the Black Muslim leader Abdul Karim, who uses the flag issue to incite black hatred of Southern whites. As Bedford notes, however, Karim is not an anomaly because "hating white people is in their bones":

> The hatred blacks feel has coursed through their blood for centuries, but they were not in a position to fight back. But now that they have the power of public opinion and the federal government on their side and with the Justice Department and the civil rights attorneys to run interference for them, they're no longer afraid of the white man. Thus, they feel free to let all of their pent up fury fill the air with constant rain of hatred's arrows. And we members of the white race are the targets.[90]

While Bedford is quick to assert that "I certainly don't hate blacks, because I have no reason for hating them," he must fight against anyone who threatens his Southern heritage. After battling attempts to remove the Confederate battle flag from city hall, Bedford has to defend his home and family against black militant assailants; he kills several of them and is put on trial for his life. The resulting courtroom process turns into a Kafkaesque nightmare in which Bedford is condemned in the name of political correctness while Karim hurls the country ever closer to a "war of genocide."[91] The Confederate dream has clearly turned into a nightmare for Lloyd Lenard, in which white Southerners face relentless persecution, especially from a vengeful black population. Ironically, Bedford's comments on African Americans' hatred of whites "for centuries" inverts the common neo-Confederate myth of slaves having loved their masters.

In her novel, *Bedford, a World Vision*, Ellen Williams presents a similar tale of Southern persecution, but this time it is at the hands of multicultural, globalizing forces intent on destroying the region's Southern Christian heritage. In the preface, Williams, who has belonged to both the Council of Conservative Citizens and the League of the South, writes:

> *Bedford, a World Vision* gives the reader a future look at life in a small Alabama town when statehood had disappeared and national sovereignty is waning. Multiculturalism has reached even Bedford, Alabama, and with it, the demise of Christianity's predominance; accompanied by the embrace of many religions all in the name of tolerance.[92]

The novel recounts how the small town of Bedford is purged of its heritage and traditional Christian values in the name of imposing "World Vision," a totalizing, secularized religion designed to eradicate all cultural differences and ensure "the future of the global neighborhood."[93] Horace and Virginia

Pruitt, proud Southerners and devout members of the Bethel Baptist Church, are put on trial by the multiculturalists for violating their son's rights under the United World's Children's Rights Treaty. By forcing their son Adam to regularly attend church, they "have arrogantly set themselves up to impose their values, ideals, and principles on their minor child and to brainwash his young mind into accepting their religious philosophy, values, and beliefs."[94] According to the law, they are guilty of child abuse. In the resulting trial, the prosecution details the "hate teachings" of the Bethel Baptist Church, specifically its rejection of "the gay and lesbian lifestyle."[95] In school, Adam must submit to multicultural indoctrination in the name of "the ever present, all prevailing and unquestioned concept of egalitarianism." Students are taught about the "War of Southern Racist Rebellion," and encouraged to feel guilty about the actions of their "degenerate Rebel ancestors." African American students are allowed to vent their rage at white students because of "past injustices," while the "Euro" students must remain silent as they have been taught in sensitivity training.[96] Lesbians and pedophiles are in charge of the schools, devout Christians are rounded up and put in "regulated religious residences," and, in the end, the Bethel Baptist Church is converted into Bedford's Historic Pink Triangle Bed and Breakfast.[97]

For another neo-Confederate novelist, Franklin Sanders, Southern persecution leads to a new civil war in the year 2020. In *Heiland*, Sanders details the growing divide between Southern traditionalists and those who pledge their allegiance to the "messianic state."[98] The traditionalists, or Freemen, are obedient to their Christian God, devoted to their families and communities, and forever tied to the Southern soil and the values it represents. Claude Heiland, the title character, declares when surveying his property in Tennessee:

> The land was *His,* but in *him* too, from his father's fathers for three hundred years. If he left it he knew he would cease to be Heiland, cease to be a father and a man, cease to be even a part of the world, would shrivel and become like the dry, rotted husk of a walnut. . . . By God's good grace, no one would ever take this freedom or this land from him.[99]

In contrast, the adherents of the messianic state, or the Insiders, reject Christianity, embrace a culture of death through the practice of abortion and euthanasia, and are guided only by their greed and desire for power. Steadily over the years, the Insiders have extended their control over American urban areas, using the tax code, the legislative process, and the courts to create a docile, enslaved populace. They have promoted homosexuality to control population size, "encouraged women to work outside the home and abandon their children" to undermine the family, and "introduced the death cult in rock music" to foster suicide among young people.[100] Those who resist, including homeschoolers, tax protestors, and especially the Freemen are violently suppressed by the state. Ultimately moved to action by an unprovoked attack on a Freeman gathering, Heiland leads his fellow Southerners to war against the Insiders, killing all the inhabitants of Nashville with a futuristic freeze ray.

Although Sanders declares that "nothing in this novel should be construed as an endorsement of political violence as a solution to today's problems in America,"[101] the feelings of persecution and victimization expressed in works like *Heiland, The Last Confederate Flag*, and *Bedford, a World Vision*, and the vehemence with which neo-Confederates rail against their perceived enemies, set a dangerous tone. One hopes such works will remain fantasy and not become inspiration.

Conclusion: Neo-Confederacy in Literature—Past and Present

What defines neo-Confederate literature, and what distinguishes it from Southern literature in general, is a commitment to the idea that the South has an essential culture that remains fixed regardless of time and circumstances. As the die-hard and self-defined Southerner Richard M. Weaver notes, "[It is] not snobbery, but historical observation, to say that the South has a distinct and rooted culture."[102] While there is nothing wrong with celebrating local culture, and it is certainly true that the region has produced a variety of great literature that reflects the depth and complexity of the Southern experience, the idea that the South has a definitive monoculture which has remained unchanged since the first European settlers arrived is absurd. The South depicted in the historical romances of Simms, the Lost Cause literature of Page, and the fictional narratives of Tate, Davidson, and others is no more reflective of the South than is neo-Confederacy. It is a dated and distorted vision of the South, one that is infused with hierarchical, patriarchal, and white supremacist beliefs. The problem with such a narrow construction of the South is that it replaces history's struggles, failures, and achievements with stereotypes and myths that may give succor to neo-Confederates but ignore the vibrancy and diversity of reality.

Notes

1. Wilson, Clyde. "The Essential Clyde Wilson," *Southern Partisan,* 19 (2nd Quarter 1999): 46.

2. Fleming, Thomas. "Old Rights and the New Right," *The New Right Papers,* ed. Robert W. Whitaker. (New York: St. Martin's Press, 1982): 185.

3. Quinn, Richard. "Partisan View," *Southern Partisan,* 19 (2nd Quarter 1999): 7.

4. Genovese, Eugene D. *The Southern Tradition: The Achievements and Limitations of an American Conservatism.* (Cambridge, MA: Harvard University Press, 1994): xi.

5. Kreyling, Michael. *Inventing Southern Literature.* (Jackson: University Press of Mississippi, 1998): vii.

6. Ibid., xi.

7. Osterweis, Rollin G. *The Myth of the Lost Cause: 1865–1900.* (Hamden, CT: Archon Books, 1973): 9.

8. Malvasi, Mark G. "The Agrarians in Retrospect: Southern Tradition and the Modern Age," *Southern Partisan,* 17 (4th Quarter 1997): 16–20. In addition to his book *The Unregenerate South,* Malvasi's work assessing the Southern Agrarians includes "'No Second Troy': *The Fathers* and the Failure of Southern History," *Slavery, Secession, and Southern History,* ed. Robert Louis Paquette and Louis A. Ferleger. (Charlottesville: University Press of Virginia, 2000): 178–196.

9. Gray, Richard. *Writing the South: Ideas of an American Region.* (Baton Rouge: Louisiana State University Press, 1986): 45.

10. Ibid.

11. Wilson, Clyde. "The South and Southern History." On-line: http://www.dixienet.org/dn-gazette/south-and-southern-history.htm [accessed 8 December 2004].

12. Simms, William Gilmore. *The Partisan: A Romance of the Revolution.* (Spartanburg, SC: The Reprint Co., 1976 [1854]): viii–x.

13. Gray, *Writing the South,* (1986): 47.

14. Simms, *The Partisan,* (1976 [1854]): 21.

15. Ibid., 75.

16. Ibid., 166.

17. Gray, *Writing the South,* (1986): 49.

18. Caruthers, William A. *Cavaliers of Virginia,* vol. 2. (Ridgeway, NJ: Gregg Press, 1974 [1834]): 214.

19. Tucker, Nathaniel Beverly. *The Partisan Leader.* (Upper Saddle River, NJ: Gregg Press, 1968 [1836]): 89.

20. Ibid., 204–205.

21. Simms, William Gilmore. *Woodcraft or Hawks about the Dovecote: A Story of the South at the Close of the Revolution.* (New York: Norton & Co., 1971 [1854]): 183.

22. Simms, William Gilmore. *The Yemassee: A Romance of Carolina.* (Boston: Houghton Mifflin Co., 1961 [1853]): 369.

23. Tucker, *The Partisan Leader,* (1968 [1836]): 202–203.

24. Snapp, Byron. Review of *Call of Duty: The Nobility of Robert E. Lee,* by J. Steven Wilkins. *Southern Partisan,* 17 (4th Quarter 1997): 35.

25. McWhiney, Grady. *Cracker Culture: Celtic Ways in the Old South*. (Tuscaloosa: University of Alabama Press, 1988). James P. Cantrell's *How Celtic Culture Invented Southern Literature* (Gretna, LA: Pelican Publishing, 2006): 20, seeks to combat the "prejudice against the mass of white Southerners" perpetrated by "America's cultural Marxists and their liberal fellow-travelers" by arguing the region's literary heritage is Celtic. Despite a positive review by Clara Erath of the United Daughters of the Confederacy, "Celtic Culture and the South," *UDC Magazine*, 64.4 (2006): 13, Michael Newton dismisses Cantrell's book in the on-line journal *e-Keltoi* as a "tirade" that is both "erroneous" and "ridiculous," in which Cantrell "swaggers into the chasm of Celticity and attempts to plant his Confederate Flag firmly in its nebulousness." See Newton, Michael. Review of *How Celtic Culture Invented Southern Literature* by James P. Cantrell. *E-Keltoi: Journal of Interdisciplinary Celtic Studies*, 2006. On-line: http://www.uwm.edu/Dept/celtic/ekeltoi/bookreviews/vol01/newton03.html [accessed 31 August 2006].

26. Longstreet, Augustus Baldwin. *Georgia Scenes*. Southern Classic Series. (Nashville: J. A. Sanders & Co., 1992 [1835]): 53.

27. Ibid., 64.

28. Celebrating such violence, the League of the South sells a videotape, "Fighting, Feuding and Dueling in the Old South."

29. Longstreet, *Georgia Scenes*, (1992 [1835]): 64.

30. Kibler, James Everett Jr. "Introduction," *Georgia Scenes*, by Augustus Baldwin Longstreet. Southern Classic Series. (Nashville: J. A. Sanders & Co., 1992): xiii.

31. Kibler's poem appeared in *Southern Patriot*, 4.5 (1997): 39. For further discussion of the position of Forrest in current neo-Confederacy see Potok, Mark. "A Different Kind of Hero," *Intelligence Report*, Southern Poverty Law Center 116 (2004): 51–52.

32. Osterweis, Rollin G. *The Myth of the Lost Cause: 1865–1900*. (Hamden, CT: Archon Books, 1973): 9.

33. Timrod, Henry. *The Poems of Henry Timrod*, ed. Paul H. Hayne. (New York: E. J. Hale & Son, 1872). On-line: http://docsouth.unc.edu/timrod/timrod.html#timr221 [accessed 8 December 2004]: 100, 209.

34. Osterweis, *The Myth*, (1973): xi.

35. Pollard, Edward A. *The Lost Cause: A New Southern History of the War of the Confederates*. (New York: E. B. Treat & Co., 1866): 750–751.

36. Osterweis, *The Myth*, (1973): 12.

37. Pollard, Edward A. *The Lost Cause Regained*. (New York: G. W. Carleton, 1868): 154.

38. Osterweis, *The Myth*, (1973): 45–48. Harris is recommended to home-schooling parents by the League of the South (see Chapter 7).

39. Harris, Joel Chandler. *The Complete Tales of Uncle Remus*. (Boston: Houghton Mifflin Co., 1983 [1955]): xxvii.

40. Ibid., 111.

41. Children's books by Page are examined in Fahs, Alice. "Remembering the Civil War in Children's Literature of the 1880s and 1890s," *The Memory of the Civil War in American Culture*, ed. Alice Fahs and Joan Waugh. (Chapel Hill: University of North Carolina Press, 2004): 79–93.

42. Page, Thomas Nelson. *In Ole Virginia or Marse Chan and Other Stories.* (New York: Charles Scribner's Sons, 1906): 2.

43. Ibid., 10.

44. Ibid., 34.

45. Page, Thomas Nelson. *The Burial of the Guns* (New York: Charles Scribner's Sons, 1894): 105.

46. Ibid., 80.

47. Dixon, Thomas Jr. *The Reconstruction Trilogy: The Leopard's Spots, The Clansman, and The Traitor.* (Newport Beach, CA: Noontide Press, 1994 [1902, 1905, 1907]): 69–70.

48. Ibid., 172.

49. Ibid., 24.

50. Ibid., 173.

51. Ibid., 64.

52. Ibid., 189.

53. Ibid., 197.

54. Ibid., 237.

55. Ibid., 337.

56. Ibid., 331.

57. Ibid., 77.

58. Ibid., 417.

59. Osterweis, *The Myth,* (1973): 18.

60. Dickson, Sam "Preface," *The Reconstruction Trilogy: The Leopard's Spots, The Clansman, and The Traitor,* by Thomas Dixon Jr. (Newport Beach, CA: Noontide Press, 1994 [1902, 1905, 1907]): xix.

61. Cantrell, James P. "Foreword," *The Clansman,* by Thomas Dixon Jr. (Gretna, LA: Pelican Publishing, 2005 [1905]): xiii–xiv.

62. Wilson, "The South and Southern History."

63. "The Top 15 *Southern* Books of All Time," *Southern Partisan,* 19, (2nd Quarter, 1999): 30–31.

64. Mizener, Arthur. "Introduction," *The Fathers,* by Allen Tate. (Athens, OH: Swallow Press, 1984 [1938]): xi.

65. Tate, Allen. *The Fathers.* (Athens, OH: Swallow Press, 1984 [1938]): 4.

66. Ibid., 17.

67. Ibid., 5.

68. Ibid., 279.

69. Davidson, Donald. *Lee in the Mountains and Other Poems, including The Tall Men.* (Boston: Houghton Mifflin Co., 1938): 3.

70. Ibid., 4.

71. Ibid., 7.

72. Conkin, Paul K. *The Southern Agrarians.* (Nashville: Vanderbilt University Press, 2001): 151.

73. Davidson, Donald. "Sequel of Appomattox," *Lee in the Mountains and Other Poems, including The Tall Men,* (1938): 43.

74. Davidson, Donald, "Sanctuary," in ibid., 57.

75. Conkin, *The Southern Agrarians,* (2001): 149.

76. Kibler, James Everett Jr. *Walking Toward Home.* (Gretna, LA: Pelican Publishing Co., 2004): 181.

77. Ibid., 75.

78. Kibler, James Everett. *Our Fathers' Fields: A Southern Story.* (Columbia: University of South Carolina Press, 1998): 59. League of the South founding director Clyde Wilson praised Kibler's book in *Southern Patriot,* 5.3 (1998): 3, as "an instant classic that ought to be on the shelf of every Southerner." Kibler, who also publishes under the name Jim Kibler, has provided the League of the South with a series of vocabulary lessons—see his "Verbal Independence: A Tutorial Series on Southern Orthography and Language," (1997–2000). On-line: *http://www.leagueofthesouth.com/ spatriot/verbal_independenc.htm* [accessed 24 October 1999 and 2 May 2000].

79. Kibler, *Our Fathers' Fields,* (1998): 29–30.

80. Ibid., 134.

81. Ibid., 135.

82. Ibid., 142–43.

83. Ibid., 130.

84. Ibid., 59.

85. Ibid., 325, 330.

86. Ibid., 330–331.

87. Ibid., 362.

88. Ibid., 375.

89. Ibid., 396.

90. Lenard, Lloyd E. *The Last Confederate Flag.* (Baltimore: America House Publishers, 2000): 33.

91. Ibid., 431.

92. Williams, Ellen. *Bedford, a World Vision.* (Belleville, ON: Guardian Books, 2000): 5.

93. Ibid., 10.

94. Ibid., 13.

95. Ibid., 23.

96. Ibid., 65–66, 71.

97. Ibid., 44.

98. Sanders, Franklin. *Heiland.* (Bermuda: Machrihanish Ltd., 1986): 100.

99. Ibid., 61–62 (original emphasis).

100. Ibid., 177–178.

101. Ibid., n.p.

102. Weaver, Richard M. *The Southern Essays of Richard M. Weaver,* ed. George M. Curtis III and James J. Thompson Jr. (Indianapolis: Liberty Fund, 1987): 60.

CHAPTER 9

You Ain't Just Whistlin' Dixie: Neo-Confederacy in Music

JON BOHLAND AND BRIAN TONGIER

In the essay "Jimmie Davis and his Music," Grady McWhiney, one of the central theorists of neo-Confederacy and founders of the League of the South (LS), and his co-author Gary B. Mills detail the life and times of the Southern folk artist and author of the well-known American ballad "You are my Sunshine."[1] Davis, who served two terms as governor of Louisiana, during which he fought strenuously to resist desegregation, is, for McWhiney and Mills, "America's most versatile and enduring singer and song writer [and] . . . lucky enough to have been born one of the Southern plain folk," namely a white Southerner. Following typical neo-Confederate arguments regarding the supposed connection between white Southern and Celtic cultural identities, McWhiney and Mills state that Davis "has written and sung the kinds of song that they [Southern plain folk] appreciate — songs close to and derived from their Celtic tradition."[2]

McWhiney and Mills's assessment of Jimmie Davis and his musical connection to the culture of the American South highlights the critical role music plays in the construction and imagination of this region as somewhere fundamentally different from elsewhere in the United States. Alongside Confederate flags, music is thus a key marker through which proponents of neo-Confederacy represent their Southern identity and, as outlined above, its status as a supposedly Celtic ethnicity.

Cultural geographers have demonstrated the multiple ways in which music serves to construct and reinforce the meanings of particular places.[3] As John Connell and Chris Gibson argue, music is "linked to particular geographic sites, bound up in our everyday perception of place, and part of movements of people, products, and cultures across space."[4] Often replete with landscape imagery and discussions of everyday life in a particular location, certain styles of music often come to be associated with specific areas. The lyrical content of American bluegrass music, for example, often alludes to the hard life of poor white farmers and coal miners within the Appalachian Mountains, and American country music demonstrates an extended thematic fascination with the Civil War.[5]

Assessing Musical Neo-Confederacy

In this chapter, we demonstrate how today's neo-Confederates use music both to perpetuate the supposedly Anglo-Celtic cultural folkways of the South and to articulate and disseminate the principal tenets of current neo-Confederacy.[6] We examine neo-Confederacy in music and musical performances in three ways. First, we review some of the most popular performers in what has become an active circuit of bands playing songs that could be identified as representative of neo-Confederacy.[7] This cottage music industry, typically promoted on neo-Confederate web sites and Internet bulletin boards, involves primarily amateur musicians playing Civil War period pieces and new neo-Confederate-themed music at events throughout the American South such as at Civil War reenactments, heritage rallies, and Confederate memorial celebrations. In many cases, the musicians themselves are Civil War reenactors who dress in full Confederate military uniforms both for scheduled concerts and impromptu "campfire jams" during reenactment weekends.

Second, we assess *Stonewall Country*, the longest running professional theatrical performance in Virginia. A musical tribute to Confederate hero General Thomas J. "Stonewall" Jackson, *Stonewall Country* ended its over twenty-year run at Lime Kiln Theatre in Lexington, Virginia, in 2004. Although the authors of the script and lyrics are not neo-Confederate sympathizers, the text of the musical displays many of the same Civil War heritage myths and falsities promoted by neo-Confederacy. As such, it suggests just how embedded these are within the popular narratives of many former Confederate states. After the Civil War, Robert E. Lee and Stonewall Jackson were reevaluated through the lens of the Lost Cause and were seen to represent ideals of Southern masculinity. Lee served as the archetype of the graceful Southern aristocrat, devoted to God, his family, and his "country" of Virginia; Jackson, on the other hand, epitomized the hard-working common man.[8]

Third, as music is a component of what Michael Hill calls the "regeneration of Anglo-Celtic cultural solidarity in the South," it is central to the politics of neo-Confederacy.[9] Neo-Confederate activists argue that it is only in the

South that cultural and thus musical innovation can occur, because Southern (Celtic) culture is considered a real culture, in contrast to U.S. mainstream culture, seen as an inauthentic, transient, and mongrelized multiculturalism. In addition, the assertion of the Celtic roots of Southern music whitens the diverse musicological heritage of the South, downplaying the African American and other traditions to the point where neo-Confederates suggest that nonwhite musical influences have been absorbed by the dominant Anglo-Celtic culture. We suggest that if the multicultural nature of music originating in the Southern states is clearly noted, this whitening of the U.S. South's musical heritage must be seen as part of the wider neo-Confederate project of ethnicizing and racializing a white Southern identity.

Words and Music: Performing Neo-Confederacy

Of the music that can be broadly defined as exhibiting elements of neo-Confederacy, much is performed by amateur bands with little or no national recognition. Self-produced CDs by these neo-Confederate musicians typically include cover images of the Confederate battle flag alongside portraits of heroic Confederate soldiers. Performances tend to be held at local heritage festivals and Civil War reenactments throughout the South in front of predominantly white audiences. Many musicians style themselves as "military bands" or folk artists and dress in nineteenth-century costumes. Throughout the summer in Staunton, Virginia, for example, the Stonewall Brigade Band, which has remained in existence in some form or another since the end of the Civil War, plays Confederate military music to a small crowd every Monday evening.[10] This outdoor event is sponsored by the local chapter of the United Daughters of the Confederacy (UDC) as part of their community outreach mission. In addition to sponsoring events like the performances in Staunton, the UDC regularly promotes Confederate music (often termed "Southern music"), as a 1986 UDC report documents:

> Various activities have encouraged the use of Southern music. Tapes, song-
> books, and sheet music have been donated to schools, libraries, nursing
> homes, and VA hospitals. Musical booklets have been made for [UDC] chap-
> ter use. A new member in one division composed and presented to her chap-
> ter "The Battle of Malvern Hill," the story of a young Confederate soldier.
> At parades, memorial services, and reenactments, tapes of Southern music
> were played and offered for sale. Chapters in two divisions sponsored con-

tests for young people with prizes for voice and instrumental performance of Southern music.

· Music used for any UDC occasion should be selected with care and only Southern music chosen; i.e., "God Save the South." . . . "The Battle Hymn of the Republic" should not be used at a UDC function even though it is a stirring marching tune.

Southern music, beautiful as well as nostalgic, is being used more than ever not only in UDC programs but throughout the land. Let us keep in mind that it is a part of our heritage, a cohesive force binding us together as sons and daughters of the South. As we acquaint our new members with its beauty and love, let us cherish it and thus help keep alive the cause for which it was written.[11]

The concerts of these amateur musical acts, whether under the auspices of the UDC or otherwise, are usually of small scale, with musicians performing to crowds of under one hundred. Despite their relative public anonymity, however, these performances serve as important sites for the localized dissemination of neo-Confederate doctrine, attracting new people to neo-Confederacy and providing a sense of commonality and shared experience.

Many in the audience at these amateur musical performances become aware of these concerts from word-of-mouth testimonials from fellow Civil War reenactors, and if the amateur band is deemed to be suitably pro-South, performances are promoted on neo-Confederate web sites. One of the leading sources of such information is the Y'all Come Back Music Center. Housed on the Apologia Book Store web site—which also promotes a "Christian World View" and displays advertisements advocating the eradication of abortion rights and the dismantling of the United Nations—the Y'all Come Back Music Center recently included an extended review of the music of the Twelfth Louisiana String Band, members of which were pictured in full Confederate costume beside women in Old South hooped skirts. The band's music, according to the review, "predates 1865, and includes many favorite songs of the period, mostly with a Celtic origin and hoe-down flavor":

Since their humble beginnings, the band has recorded two cassette tapes of music and one CD. *Songs of the Celtic South, Southern Songs of Love and War* and *Songs of the Southern Highlands* have been well received. A review in *Southern Heritage Magazine* states, "Here is a lively bunch of Southern gents who revel in their Celtic history." Their music is true to their roots and often includes both the original words brought over the sea, and the newer Southern version.[12]

Titles of Twelfth Louisiana String Band albums such as *Songs of the Celtic South* and tracks such as "Scots Wha Hae / Confederate Song," promote the Celtic South thesis, and their web site logo merges Scotland's blue and white national flag with the Confederate battle flag.

The Celtic South thesis, as articulated by McWhiney and Mills in their explanation of the music of Jimmie Davis, underpins an intertwining of folk, Civil War–era, Scottish, Irish, and contemporary neo-Confederate music into a potent mix of neo-Confederate politics and performance. The League of the South CD *Confederate Spirit—The Great Songs of a Proud South*, largely composed by LS member J. Pat Baughman, offers listeners "Confederate Piper" alongside Confederate Civil War songs like "The Bonnie Blue Flag" and "Dixie." Advertising this CD, the LS identifies the importance of both continuing past musical traditions and the ongoing process of making their own Southern culture to advance their political agenda. The CD is described as "a legitimate weapon to counter the princes of darkness arrayed to destroy the movement for a free Southland," and the LS recommends that it be played to peers and at LS meetings. The new recordings, such as "Hurrah for Davis and Lee," use "traditional musical styles," and one such track, "Southern Anthem," is described as providing listeners with "a rousing message for today that expresses our sentiments exactly."[13] As the *Confederate Spirit* CD evidences, songs, lyrics, and performances of neo-Confederate music, as well as CD artwork, commonly synthesize current neo-Confederate political concerns with Confederate Civil War imagery and Celtic themes. This synthesis was evident at the Southern Heritage Celebration held in Columbia, South Carolina, in January 2000. At this event, kilt-wearing bagpipers and drummers in tartan plaid were followed by marchers, often in replica Confederate gray uniforms, carrying Confederate battle and Scottish blue and white flags, ethnically coding the event and identifying its Celtic character.[14] The presence of Scottish musician Carl Peterson at neo-Confederate events, such as the Seventh Annual Southern Heritage Conference in Laurel, Mississippi, in August 2002 and the Southern Heritage Celtic Festival at Tannehill State Park, near Birmingham, Alabama, in April 2003, along with Peterson's albums *Songs of the South* and *Scotland Remembers the Alamo*, are also emblematic of the importation of Celtic elements into Southern music to the exclusion of other cultural themes.[15]

Other bands also perform songs in a fashion that links Southern and Celtic music. At a neo-Confederate rally to launch the Declaration of Southern Cultural Independence on 4 March 2000 in Montgomery, Alabama, a band named Un-Reconstructed performed.[16] According to a review of their music, the band primarily play[s] period music from the War Between the States but also a lot of Celtic folk songs. They try to combine the two into a sound that will be pleasing to the ear and maybe help someone to learn a little bit about that hard time in our history. They hope that through their music they can do their part to honor their ancestors and help keep the memories alive!![17]

One Un-Reconstructed album title merges a Scottish national emblem with the Confederacy: *Thistle 'N Dixie*.[18] In addition to promoting an Anglo-Celtic identity in synthesizing Civil War and folk music, some neo-Confederates state their ideological beliefs through their actions. The Border Ruffian Band, for example, donates income from their CD sales to the "heritage defense fund" of the Sons of Confederate Veterans (SCV), the UDC, and the Order of the Confederate Rose (OCR).[19]

The Rebelaires, who have an adult-contemporary sound, and the Free South Band, performers of contemporary country-rock, both espouse neo-Confederacy through fiercely political lyrics.[20] The former, a Georgia-based band whose members are also active in the Waycross chapter of the SCV, regularly play at Confederate festivals throughout the South. They were featured performers at the 1996 Southern Heritage Ball in Plant City, Florida, an evening sponsored by the local chapter of the Society for the Preservation of Southern History, which saw couples dressed in Old South costumes.[21] The majority of Rebelaires' music features Civil War and Confederate heritage themes. Self-produced cassettes and CDs feature songs such as "Stonewall Standin' His Ground," "Confederate Man," and "For the Cause."[22] Women are imagined as beautiful and courteous defenders of the homeland, dutiful wives whose love sustains Southern military masculinity in songs like "Georgia Belle," "Hey, Pretty Miss (from Mississippi)," and "Sweet Southern Lady." In their song "Southern Soldiers," the Rebelaires imagine themselves as contemporary soldiers, masculine Christian warriors ready to take up arms for the South.[23]

Like the Rebelaires, the Free South Band is a favorite of the contemporary neo-Confederate community, and their songs feature lyrics that support a neo-Confederate worldview. The web site selling Free South Band CDs, for example, includes a number of testimonials from neo-Confederate activists praising the pro-Southern themes in their music. Larry Baldwin, the ex-chair of the Southern Party, wrote, "I love [the song] 'Toast to Dixie.' [I am] sending your CD info to my friend who has about 1000 names in his address book."[24] Similarly, John Thomas Cripps, chairman of FreeSouth.org, notes the importance of neo-Confederate bands taking a do-it-yourself approach for the release of their music.[25] By self-producing music and selling it either on-line or at heritage festivals, groups like the Free South Band subvert mainstream distribution mechanisms which are believed by neo-Confederates to purposely exclude these bands because they "tell the truth" about Southern history and heritage. In regards to the Free South Band, Cripps states:

> [They] really address a void in contemporary "Southern music." Nashville has become so politically-correct that songs can no longer be produced that address "Southern" or "Confederate" issues. This CD, will be a lesson to the Nashville CEO's: "This is what our people want! When you don't give it to us—we'll produce it ourselves!" This is an exciting time for all lovers of "Southern music."[26]

Cripps's testimonial highlights how neo-Confederate activists use music to disseminate their message. Free South Band songs, for example, express themes of white Southern rebellion and defense of Southern and Confederate heritage. The lyrics of "1865," a song on their CD *Free South Project,* is an effort to remind listeners that the Civil War "still rages" in America. It suggests that white Southerners should still feel aggrieved over the defeat of the Confederacy almost a hundred and fifty years ago:

> She was born on that Mason Dixon line,
> Caught in-between two worlds, where north and south collide,
> Grandma was a southern belle, grandpa a Yankee spy,
> Battles still rage from a war supposed to end in 1865 . . .
> 1865: How did we survive?
> Think it all was over, been a long, long time.
> I can tell you brother that's a lie,
> More here to see than meets the eye.[27]

Lyrics by the Free South Band and The Rebelaires, amongst others, clearly distinguish between North and South both during and after the Civil War, emphasizing the virtue of the Confederacy and the Southern Cause, as well as the depravity and godlessness of Yankees. Robert Lloyd plays a slow ballad style of music with passionately sectional lyrics that invoke many neo-Confederate themes. His song, "Lest We Forget", echoes the familiar neo-Confederate assertion of the theological basis for the Civil War:

> A time not forgotten, a cause still not lost,
> As long as we're living, no matter our cost,
> We'll speak for the soldiers, for truth they have fought,

Forgive and forget we will not,
With devils in blue; the Lord's men in gray,
They clutch to their bibles, and kneel down to pray,
To vanquish the heathen, and rid from the land,
A call to arms, for every man.[28]

Like The Free South Band, Lloyd's song suggests that the Civil War continues in the mind of true (white) Southerners and that the heroic memory of the Confederacy must be preserved. Today's Southern men, he urges, must take up "arms" in the battle of their ancestors and "speak for the soldiers for the truth they have fought." This type of hyper-masculine discourse silences women, implicitly rendering them to support positions in this struggle while the men fight in the continuing battle for independence. As is typical in neo-Confederate discourse, Lloyd links the South to evangelical Christianity, imagining the "men in gray" as soldiers for Christ who "clutch to their bibles" and, like Stonewall Jackson, "kneel down to pray" before battle. In this religious binary, the North is imagined as a godless land and the South becomes home to a chosen people "baptized in blood" during the Civil War.[29]

In addition to calling for the continued distinctiveness of Northern versus Southern states, the lyrics of amateur neo-Confederate musicians attempt to reclaim Civil War memory from the historical "revisionists" whom they believe to have excluded Southern heroes from the history books. Atrocities during the Civil War, often retold from a highly partisan perspective, serve the divisive agenda of some neo-Confederate artists. Chris Edwards, for example, describes Confederate guerilla actions in "Centralia Train Massacre."[30] His lyrics counter common narratives of events in Missouri in 1864 and propose that "Bloody Bill" Anderson and his followers, who in cold blood killed several uniformed Union soldiers on furlough, were merely avenging the victims of Union aggression in Kansas. Terry Warren and Clint Lacy, featured on the *Dixie Broadcasting Southern Anthology,* take a similar view of the Civil War in the West.[31] In a relatively rare example of a female neo-Confederate artist, contemporary folk-singer Linda Carlton sings lyrics steeped in Lost Cause myths of the Civil War. Highlighted by the Dixie Broadcasting Company on their web site as a featured artist, she describes her music as part of an effort to

spread truth about Confederate history. If your listeners research the topics and people represented in the songs, they will find them historically documented but not necessarily politically correct. I hope my music speaks to listeners from the viewpoint of the people who lived through those terrible times. Generic battle songs don't do the War Between the States justice.

An example of the way in which Carlton's songs "spread truth about Confederate history" is her ballad the "Sword of Robert E. Lee." The lyrics eulogize Lee as a Christian soldier whom all Southern men should admire and aspire to be like. He is imagined as the ultimate and infallible Southern gentleman, a pious Christian defending the heroic Confederacy against Northern aggression.

Many neo-Confederate bands agree with Carlton that "generic battle songs don't do the War Between the States justice."[32] The lyrics of the Louisiana Tigers String Band, for example, are fiercely political and revisionist, and their albums such as *Songs of the Celtic South* include a number of traditional Scotch-Irish ballads, providing musical support for the neo-Confederate claims concerning the supposedly Celtic roots of Southern cultural identity. The Louisiana Tigers String Band was the featured act at a Southern Historical Conference in 2004, which presented speakers arguing that slavery was not a factor in the Civil War.[33] The String Band's web site has numerous links to neo-Confederate sites, and they have become favored performers on the "Dixie Ball" circuit, playing *Gone with the Wind* simulations throughout the Southern states.[34]

In addition to articulating Lost Cause views about the Civil War past, the neo-Confederate pantheon of contemporary complaints also plays a major role in neo-Confederate lyrics. Bobby Mountain's "Dixie Died in Georgia," for example, references neo-Confederate grievances about former Georgia governor Roy Barnes's downplaying of the Confederate battle flag emblem on Georgia's state flag while in office from 1999 to 2003.[35] The Free South Band's songs stress many such themes:

New York bankers see ya later,
Wall Street lies Yankee dimes,
It's just a thang MTV,
UN crap clean up your act,
It's just a thang, a southern thang,
Tell ya friends in DC mind their own store,
I don't see no white in their rainbow . . .

LA movie makers know where you can go,
Don't forget your fruitcake on the stove,

Your unborn child is all planned out,
It's just a thang, a Southern thang,
("SOUTHERN THANG," 2003)[36]

I said the South ain't never gonna go away,
The people band together stand up and say,
You ain't gonna change the way we feel,
Our souls run deep in these Southern hills.
("AIN'T GONNA GO AWAY," 2003)[37]

Hey don't mess with the boy from Dixie,
Unless you would like to feel,
A Southern raging fire,
Burning up the hills,
Hey don't mess with the man down in Alabam',
Or the folks in Tennessee,
'Cause the people gonna band together,
And the whole world is gonna see,
A free south by the grace of God is what they'll be.
("DON'T MESS WITH DIXIE," 2003)[38]

In these three songs, the Free South Band espouses a number of neo-Confederate themes. "Southern Thang" demonstrates a clear distrust of the United Nations and other forms of contemporary governance, as well as banks, corporations, free trade, and globalization. They express antagonism toward all things that supposedly threaten the South: the Hollywood film industry, abortion rights activists, and homosexuals all are derided. "Don't Mess with Dixie" spells out just what will happen if these powerful "Yankee" forces continue to "mess with the boy[s] from Dixie." They suggest a new form of resistance will take place among Southern whites, a "Southern raging fire" which "the whole world is gonna see." Lastly, the Southern cause is again linked to Christianity, as a "free" and independent South—the major political goal of current neo-Confederacy—will be achieved through "the grace of God." Linking their performances to those of mainstream acts hailing from the South such as Elvis Presley and Lynyrd Skynyrd, and stating that they are not racist in much the same way as neo-Confederate authors often include disclaimers disavowing racism, the Free South Band's web site further evidences their neo-Confederacy:

Song is the purest form of free speech and expression. Fear is the result of ignorance and the unknown. Some say if you write or sing songs about the

South and Southern Heritage you are a racist. That sounds like a lazy excuse and you need to do some homework. Tell that to Travis Tritt, Charlie
Daniel's [*sic*], David Allen Coe, and of course Hank, Jr., Lynard Skynard
[*sic*], Alabama. Allman Brothers, Randy Travis, Elvis Presley and on and on.
Our message to all is "Heritage"![39]

In addition to concerts, these musicians and their recordings reach sympathetic audiences through on-line music stores specializing in neo-Confederate
music, such as the Y'all Come Back music center and retailers in the "buy
Southern" network.[40] The LS also hosts performances, such as the Musical
Showcase at the Tenth Annual National League of the South Conference and
the First Annual Southern Rock/Blues/Country Jam, both held in 2003.[41]
The LS jam featured a folk music ensemble called Basic Gray, who declared
themselves dedicated "to reliev[ing] frustration over the social decay and the
threat of the 'New World Order', and to protest the long time domination of
folk music by the Left."[42] The League of the South's *Southern Patriot* identified members of Basic Gray as "our own Larry Smith and Nat Rudulph,"
the duo having met at a League of the South event in Alabama in 1998.[43]
The jam's musical categories included "Celtic" and "'Real' Country," and at
another LS event on Labor Day weekend 2004, performers were rhetorically
asked to select appropriate songs: "If you have doubts whether any song is
appropriate, then ask these questions of it: Does it honor God? Does it honor
the South? Does it honor the League of the South? Does it respect my hosts
and their guests?"[44]

Neo-Confederacy, the Musical:
A Trip to Stonewall Country

The musical *Stonewall Country*, which ran each summer from 1985 to 2004
at Lime Kiln Theater in Lexington, Virginia, illustrates how the content of a
musical performance can serve neo-Confederate mythology without the direct endorsement of any neo-Confederate organizations. The lyrics and supporting dialogue of *Stonewall Country* feature pro-Confederate ideology and
are based on long-standing Lost Cause myths that glorify Southern nationalism. The long popularity of the work amazed Don Baker, who wrote the play
and directed the original production, as well as Robin and Linda Williams,
who wrote the music and lyrics.[45] After not seeing the musical for over ten
years, all three attended the penultimate performance in 2004, which played
to a sold-out crowd of over 350 people (entirely white apart from two African

Americans who worked for the theater company).[46] The *Roanoke Times* described the closing of the musical:

> Tonight at Lime Kiln Theatre in Lexington, the ground will shake, the sky will fall, and the theater will slowly sink into the sea. Or maybe it just seems that way. This much is certain . . . one of the picturesque outdoor theater's first and surely its best-known production, synonymous in many minds with Lime Kiln itself, shuts down tonight after a 20-year run.[47]

Stonewall Country details the life and times of Thomas J. "Stonewall" Jackson, Confederate general and former professor at the Virginia Military Institute in Lexington. It depicts Jackson as a pious man of "Scotch-Irish stock" (a synonymous precursor to the recent ethnicization of white Southerners as Celtic) and a soldier who saw no contradiction between his staunch Christianity and his passion for warfare. As is typical in musicals, the narrative relies upon songs to recall complicated historical events in a somewhat simplistic fashion. The split between North and South and the ultimate secession of the Southern states, for example, is explained through a rousing musical number entitled "Battlin' Anthems." In the song, the Northern chorus chastises the Southerners for being poor examples of Christianity who are sinful, commit adultery, and debase African American women. Conversely, the Southern chorus dismisses the Northerners as hypocritical atheists who sell slaves to the South and disrespect women. Though this back-and-forth repartee attempts to provide some balance between Northern and Southern viewpoints prior to the war, it nonetheless utilizes neo-Confederate theological war arguments to make its points. Given the fact that a Confederate is the musical's hero, audience members can easily read the Southern argument as the favored one, aligning themselves accordingly.

In *Stonewall Country,* Jackson is portrayed as unwillingly pulled into the Civil War. Consistent with Lost Cause doctrine, he enlists in the Confederate army in order to fulfill his sacred Southern and manly duties of honor and sacrifice to God and to his homeland of Virginia. He is not fighting to preserve slavery, an institution he describes in one monologue as

> both a responsible and a troublesome one. It is not a desirable thing but is allowed by Providence for ends which it is not my business to determine. I prefer to see the Negroes free, but the Bible teaches that slavery is sanctioned by the Creator himself who maketh man to differ and instituted laws for the bond and the free.

, Jackson's monologue presents him as a conflicted Southern slave master, a man whose Christian beliefs teach him that slavery is a moral and justified practice. Such a narrative echoes current neo-Confederate arguments that slavery is supported by Christian doctrine (see Chapter 2). The song "Duty" explains Jackson's sense of obligation to God, its lyrics again providing support for neo-Confederate claims concerning both the piety of Confederate heroes and the South as a heartland of Protestant Christianity. In *Stonewall Country*'s battle scenes, Jackson is depicted as an eccentric and fearless warrior who once picked blueberries during a battle as bullets whizzed by his head. The legendary moment when Jackson earns the nickname "Stonewall," refusing to retreat his inexperienced soldiers from a Union advance at Manassas in 1861, comes across on stage as but the first of many examples of Jackson's heroism and valor in the field. The musical suggests that Jackson made his reputation during the 1862 Shenandoah Valley Campaign, a series of battles that comes alive during the song "Proud Valley Boys." Describing Confederate triumphs and determination to fight to the death to oust Union troops from Virginia, the song also highlights the supposed deep connection that Southerners have with their land. Indeed, throughout the musical, Virginia (the titular "Stonewall Country") is presented as an idyllic rural *heimat* that must be protected from Yankee invaders.

The last act features Jackson's final battles in 1862 and 1863, and includes scenes with his second wife, Anna, before his death in the Battle of Chancellorsville. Confederate general A. P. Hill is introduced to the audience as one of Jackson's best friends, though in his solo number, "A. P.'s Blues," Hill questions how Jackson can call himself a Christian yet seemingly enjoy the killing of so many Union soldiers. Indeed, *Stonewall Country* does not place Jackson above criticism. The song "Seven Day Freakout," for example, details Jackson's tactical errors during the 1862 Seven Days Campaign. Despite this, Stonewall Jackson emerges at the end of *Stonewall Country* as a pious, mythical figure who heroically served God and his homeland. His funeral scene includes a speech from his sister-in-law Maggie:

> My heart overflows with sorrow, never have I known a Holier man. He lived only to please God; his daily life was a daily offering up of himself. How fearful the loss to the Confederacy! The people made an idol of him, and God has rebuked them!

The beauty and mystical power of Virginia's Shenandoah Valley, a place presumed, much like the entire American South, to have been permanently marked as a Confederate space, is highlighted in the final scene as the entire cast joins in a reprise of the opening number "Stonewall Country." With Jackson's legend seemingly eternal, a last solo voice emerges from the chorus to extol his beloved homeland, which the soul of the Confederate soldier will gaze upon from heaven in perpetuity.

The musical provides an example of the kind of textual and visual performance that typifies neo-Confederate representations of the Civil War. It does so through the framework of the Lost Cause, constructing a mythical version of the Confederacy through a series of legendary tales and heroes. The extended popularity of the work suggests the lasting power of such narratives, with tens of thousands attending performances of *Stonewall Country* during its long run. As such, it served to influence, indoctrinate, and reinforce certain key themes concerning the meaning and legacy of the Civil War, myths that have gained legitimacy through repeated articulation and performance.

Overall, *Stonewall Country*'s depiction of the Confederacy is similar to other neo-Confederate texts and lyrics that idealize the antebellum South. Such texts claim the Civil War was a justified sectional affair fought between two different nations and cultures.[48] They also attempt to put a positive modern spin on Southern slaveholding, arguing, like neo-Confederates Clyde Wilson and Steve Wilkins in *Southern Slavery: As It Was*, that revisionists and abolitionists have depicted Southern slavery to be much more oppressive and violent than it was in reality.[49] As depicted in *Stonewall Country*, Stonewall Jackson is a pious man deeply troubled by the slave system. Echoing current neo-Confederate theological understandings of the Civil War, he ultimately concludes that since slavery is permitted in the Bible, it is an institution sanctioned "by God himself." Jackson's religious beliefs can thus be read as a justification for his involvement in the protection of the slave system during the war, an argument that can be extended to many equally "pious" Southern soldiers. Jackson's kindness to slaves is also lauded in the musical, including his bravery in defying the slave codes by operating a Sunday school for black children. It is also suggested that Jackson bought three slaves simply out of a desire to let them buy their own freedom. As such, the narrator refers to these slaves as "good investments," given that they rarely missed their payments to Jackson, who thereby profited from the transactions. As such, Jackson represents the normative values of the archetypical "good massa," the paternalistic and loving slave owner who hopes to instill in his slaves Christian values and self-reliance.

The lyrics of *Stonewall Country* also glorify the virtues of Southern culture and masculinity. In neo-Confederate discourse, the Southern man is said to embody loyalty, honor, duty, patriotism, and valor, and is imagined, according to Alan Nolan, to be "heroic, indefatigable, gallant, and law-abiding."[50] In *Stonewall Country,* Jackson's piety and duty to the Confederate cause, for example, are not characteristics suggested to be unique to his personality. Rather they are presented as intrinsically normative Southern masculine qualities that every Southern man can identify with and hope to embody themselves. Further, Jackson is depicted as a natural leader who demanded and received unquestioning loyalty from his men.

Though Jackson is depicted in *Stonewall Country* as an eccentric with several bizarre personality quirks, the play should not be read as an attempt to minimize the mythical legacy of Jackson. Following his tragic and melodramatic death scene, Jackson emerges at the end of *Stonewall Country* as a saint-like Christian who fought and died for his country and cause. As such, he is a model for contemporary neo-Confederates to follow in their holy mission to free the South from Northern hegemonic control.

Whiteness, Regional Identity, and Neo-Confederate Views on Southern Music

Writing about the most successful contestants in the hit television program *American Idol,* Neely Tucker notes that "seven of the eight top-two finishers in the first four years were from states that once formed the Confederacy, and five of the seven remaining finalists this season [2006] are, too."[51] Tucker suggests this is partly because viewing audiences (and thus potential voters for the contestants) are disproportionately drawn from former Confederate states, but also proposes a heartland thesis—the notion of "the South as influence, both as a geographic entity and as an idea," in American music, be it blues, gospel, jazz, or country. Noting a similar trend on *American Idol,* Chris Kromm argues that the South is commonly idealized within American popular culture as a region that still protects and nurtures "authentic" forms of music and folk culture. As such, it is imagined as a location where the "roots" of American music remain vibrant within a globalizing world of consumerism and mass marketing.[52]

It is arguments such as these that help to explain how neo-Confederate musicians can frame themselves as sustainers of an authentic culture free from the stains and sins of industrial, Northern modernity. Echoing Tucker, many neo-Confederates propose that all forms of American music are fundamentally Southern creations. This is because, to proponents of neo-Confederacy such as Clyde Wilson, only genuine cultures can be creative, and thus the United States "is incapable of producing a culture—art, music, literature, manners—although it will parasitically consume and distort what our Southern people produce."[53]

These "Southern people," Wilson maintains elsewhere, are the only producers of "real culture" in the United States. Mainstream America and its corporate distributors of music, it seems, mar this authentic Southern musical culture:

> Imagine the flowering of Southern arts that we would have, not by government subsidy, not a culture "poured in from the top," to use Donald Davidson's expression, but *real culture* rising up from a free people. Imagine what our musicians in Nashville and New Orleans could do if they didn't have to kow-tow to New York and Hollywood corporations.[54]

This Southern cultural expression, seemingly more authentic than elsewhere in the United States, is that of the "plain folk" whose everyday lives, as McWhiney and Mills intimate in their assessment of Jimmie Davis, comprise the basis of Southern music. It is a sentiment with which LS president Michael Hill concurs, arguing that music is

> firmly rooted in the folk culture of the South, these men and women who make this beautiful and soulful music have kept in touch with those permanent things—family, friends, faith, place, and the poetry that is everyday life down here in Dixie.[55]

This idyllic image of deep connections between people and place in the South, and their timeless qualities as "permanent things," in implicit contrast with the transient aspects of everyday life elsewhere in the United States, helps to construct the "real culture" epitomized by and through musical performances. Non-Southern states, it seems, cannot produce the same standard of cultural (and thus musical) performance and creativity, nor can they stimulate similarly heartfelt songs about their region. This suggests that Southern states have a sense of place that is unmatched by other U.S. regions:

> We even write songs about our places. . . . Ever heard Lynyrd Skynyrd sing about "Sweet Home Alabama," or Ray Charles' soulful rendition of "Georgia On My Mind?" . . . But why are there no heartfelt songs about Massachusetts or Minnesota?[56]

The mention of African American musician Ray Charles here is typical of the periodic lip service paid to nonwhites by advocates of neo-Confederacy. Neo-Confederate commentators, for example, do not celebrate black gospel music as a key part of the music of the American South and tend to see African American performers as contributors who are absorbed within the dominant Anglo-Celtic Southern culture:

> Over the centuries, our culture has been enriched in subtle ways by the influences of other non-dominant, cultural groups, particularly by black Southerners and the French-speaking Cajuns of Louisiana, but at its essence, the South has always remained a predominantly Anglo-Celtic civilization.[57]

The Celtic South thesis arguably now permeates every aspect of neo-Confederacy as deeply as the color line of the American South permeated life prior to the civil rights movement. Almost every detail of cultural life in the South is held by proponents of neo-Confederacy to stem from Celtic culture, a culture that is able to absorb and incorporate other ethnicities and cultural practices into itself without changing its fundamental character. Within this, music is no exception. Neo-Confederate performers play up the connections between Celtic and Southern music to the exclusion of other ethnic traditions, and combine new neo-Confederate lyrics with older Scottish and Irish songs. Incorporating bagpipes and other symbols of Celticness, current neo-Confederate music exhibits a whitened musical heritage and performance. This whitening of musical roots all but purges the significance of other influences upon "Southern" music.

Neo-Confederate music is inseparably tied to a political and social ideology that attacks multiculturalism (i.e., at least partially nonwhite). Proponents of neo-Confederacy explicitly overemphasize the Celtic roots of Southern culture and, therefore, the white roots of Southern music, while ignoring, downplaying, or even deliberately removing other sources of musical influence. Performers, for example, add distinctively Celtic instrumentation and themes in a way that can be seen as removing African American and Hispanic influences. This exclusionary project ties into broader patterns of ethnic/racial construction based on Celtic conceptions of whiteness in the American South. Consequently, neo-Confederate claims that some decidedly non-Anglo-Celtic musicians are part of the pantheon of Southern music, such as the New Dixie Manifesto's noting of Louis Armstrong and Ray Charles,[58] does not change the fact that the core source of music in America is, in the neo-Confederate worldview, Southern and white, with members of other cultures operating within the practices and patterns laid down by this Anglo-Celtic cultural core.

Any U.S. music that is regarded to belong to a particular race or ethnic group is, of course, most likely to be the result of collaboration among musicians of multiple races and ethnic backgrounds.[59] Racial boundaries in music are typically created by musicologists and a recording industry that commonly classifies music by race.[60] Sociologist John Shelton Reed, a regular contributor to *Southern Partisan,* sees music in mutually exclusive categories of black and white. Reviewing maps of the birthplaces of prominent country musicians, Reed noted that most were from Appalachia, the Ozarks, and Texas with a "near-vacuum" in the Deep South. He explains:

> When one of my students did a similar map of the origins of blues singers and we overlaid it on the country-music map, it filled in the Deep South nicely. The two maps together clearly showed the South—black and white, separate but equal—to be the great seedbed of American music.[61]

The distinction that Reed draws here between "white" country and "black" blues musicians suggests that he envisions music in the Southern states to be both categorically and geographically segregated. Yet he contends that "country music has been *Southern* music," racializing both the music, and its identification as "Southern," as white.[62] Reed emphasizes this racialization of musical styles when he proposes that white musicians in the mid-1950s Deep South preformed "half hillbilly, half black rhythm and blues, a wild half-breed music" that ultimately became rock and roll.[63] Thus music takes on a racial nature through a process of being categorized racially.[64] Such binary conceptions of race and music have long been part of the structure of race relations in the United States, but, in contradistinction to these understandings, Southern music has long incorporated multiple cultural influences, including Celtic, English, African, and Cajun sources.

The goal of neo-Confederates, however, is not merely to acknowledge that there are Anglo-Celtic elements within a multicultural musical form but rather to promote the Anglo-Celtic basis of music to the exclusion of virtually all other sources of musical inspiration. The key distinction between the neo-Confederate use of Celtic music and other uses of Celtic music lies in how the influence of Celtic music is understood and, thereafter, performed.[65] In particular, is the use of music as an expression of identity used to include or exclude others? Most groups that perform Celtic and/or Southern music, if race enters their consciousness at all, perform Celtic music out of preservation motives, preserving an arguably white form of music but not excluding other forms of music or ethnic or racial performers or influences. Yet given the broader context of neo-Confederate racial, ethnic, and cultural theory, it becomes clear that many neo-Confederate groups use music and emphasize its Anglo-Celtic origins to challenge the multiculturalism inherent in today's music and to homogenize so-called Southern culture as a white culture.

Conclusion: Musical Neo-Confederacy

Throughout the late nineteenth and early twentieth centuries, the UDC fought to have pro-Southern textbooks adopted in local schools, raised monuments to heroic Southern generals, and archived Confederate documents in an attempt to preserve and promote their pro-Confederate version of Civil War memory.[66] "Memory," Kevin Phillips notes, "became a battlefield," and it was in the realm of popular culture where this new Civil War was fought.[67] Modern neo-Confederates follow this tradition of waging a "culture war" in the South as part of an effort to glorify the Confederacy and the Old South. Music, as one of the most important forms of cultural expression, is central to these efforts, and our analysis demonstrates that the music supported and promoted by contemporary neo-Confederate organizations is one cultural "battleground" in the long-standing culture war over Southern history and memory.

Given the range of musical performances that could potentially be labeled neo-Confederate, from songs performed in a style labeled as "Southern" to songs with "Southern" themes articulated in lyrics, what definition of neo-Confederacy best captures the nature of this music? The underlying factor that links all neo-Confederate music together is its promotion of the neo-Confederate worldview (political, social, and racial/ethnic) through both the creation of new songs and in the reinterpretation of older songs through a pro-Confederate lens. This common thread ties together such musically disparate acts as Civil War reenactor bands, Southern rock bands, overtly neo-Confederate singer/songwriters, folk musicians, and other performers. According to Brian Britt, neo-Confederate music "ranges from traditional favorites like 'Dixie' . . . to country music and Southern rock" and includes performances such as those by the Charlie Daniels Band ("South's Gonna Do It Again"), Confederate Railroad (which performed at a Southern Heritage Jam in 1993), and by more overt neo-Confederates like the Rebelaires.[68]

The League of the South and other proponents of neo-Confederacy promote musical acts they believe articulate pro-Southern themes. Under the link "Southern Lyrics" on the LS web site, for example, a range of songs from white rock and roll acts, including Lynyrd Skynyrd, ZZ Top, Molly Hatchet, and the Allman Brothers, are listed as being appropriately pro-Southern.[69] At the First Annual League of the South Jam, songs performed included popular mainstream hits like "Sweet Home Alabama," "Free Bird," Blue Suede Shoes," and "Proud Mary."[70] Through such performances, neo-Confederate activists can claim particular songs as intrinsically Southern and use these as further evidence for their arguments concerning a preexisting and thriving (white, Anglo-Celtic) Southern culture. Many of the musicians whose songs are appropriated in this manner by proponents of neo-Confederacy do not publicly align themselves or their music with neo-Confederacy. For example, the LS recommend Creedence Clearwater Revival for their pro-Southern lyrics. Yet Creedence Clearwater Revival, a 1960s and 1970s rock band, seems an odd choice for the LS to claim as pro-Southern; the majority of the members hailed from the liberal bastion of Northern California, and their politics, as poignantly expressed in the anti-Vietnam war song "Fortunate Son," could be broadly described as left-leaning.[71] Despite this, the LS endorsement of Creedence Clearwater Revival marks their music as "Southern" simply because some of their lyrics describe events that took place in the South. As such, the LS strips these and other songs of the original writers' intended political and cultural meanings and reassigns them as Southern nationalist anthems.

In much the same manner, although some of the amateur reenactor bands that perform Civil War–era music do so in a manner that does not actively promote neo-Confederacy, many of them are applauded on neo-Confederate web sites as "heritage acts" and thus are claimed as supporters of neo-Confederacy. These bands often see themselves, like most reenactors, as "living historians" who perform the music of the past in order to keep it alive for today's audiences, yet proponents of neo-Confederacy claim this music as indicative of Confederate heritage and values. Bobby Horton and the Second South Carolina String Band, for example, perform period pieces with lyrics that are not overtly neo-Confederate.[72] Indeed, some members of the Second South Carolina String Band are from Northern states, and the band performs campfire songs that were favorites of both Union and Confederate soldiers. Yet on more than one occasion, Horton has been lauded in *Southern Partisan* for his recordings of *Homespun Songs of the CSA*, which are "familiar to the ears of any good Confederates, now or then," with "lyrics [that] will invigorate any Southern partisan's soul." *Southern Partisan* advises listeners to turn up the volume when playing Horton's music and "imagine how nice it would be if things had all worked out."[73] Further, Horton's music has been used as evidence of the Celtic identity of the Confederacy, with *Southern Partisan* regularly noting Horton's performance of Scottish tunes and the Irish origins of many songs, although Horton himself has made clear that "the black influence is so incredible in our music."[74]

Neo-Confederate music and songs typically provide both direct and tacit support for Lost Cause mythology that glorifies the Confederacy and memorializes its heroic leaders. It sometimes forwards current neo-Confederate positions, as in the case of the Free South Band, espousing the need for secession and reassertion of Southern (white, Anglo-Celtic) identity. In sum, many neo-Confederate artists use music and lyrics to air their paleoconservative grievances and spread their views to a wider audience through the Internet and live performances. Music, as a form of popular culture, provides neo-Confederate activists a platform for the articulation of their beliefs, and it should not be ignored as a critical element in the current practice, performance, and dissemination of neo-Confederacy.

Notes

AUTHORS' NOTE: This chapter was a highly collaborative effort. Thanks are due to Euan Hague and Cotten Seiler (in many ways the third and fourth authors of this piece) for their invaluable input on previous drafts and partnership in presenting this research. Although the following list certainly can't include everyone who helped develop this chapter, Brian Tongier would also like to thank Bob Antonio, Aziza Khazoom's research seminar at UCLA for extensive and invaluable input (extra thanks to Jennifer Winther in particular), and Bill Roy and the entire UCLA Sociology of Music Seminar.

1. McWhiney, Grady, and Mills, Gary B. "Jimmie Davis and His Music: An Interpretation," *Journal of American Culture*, 6.2 (1983): 54–57. Gary B. Mills (1944–2002) was a professor of history at the University of Alabama. He published essays in neo-Confederate venues defending the Confederate battle flag—see Mills, Gary B. "Dispelling Southern Myths—The Flag," *Southern Patriot*, 1.1 (1994): 4; "Group 2—Confederate Battleflag: A Symbol of Heritage and Independence," *Southern Partisan*, 20 (2nd Quarter 2000): 19–21.

2. McWhiney and Mills, "Jimmie Davis," (1983): 54–55.

3. See Leyshon, Andrew, Matless, David, and Revill, George, ed. *The Place of Music*. (New York: Guilford Press, 1998); Symon, Peter. "From Blas to Bothy Culture: The Musical Remaking of Celtic Culture in a Hebridean Festival," *Celtic Geographies: Old Cultures, New Times*, ed. David C. Harvey, Rhys Jones, Neil McInroy, and Christine Milligan. (London: Routledge, 2002): 192–207; "The Sounds of Manchester," *The North West Geographer*, 2.2 (2000).

4. Connell, John, and Gibson, Chris. *Sound Tracks: Popular Music, Identity, and Place*. (London: Routledge, 2003): 1.

5. Smith, Andrew K., and Akenson, James E. "The Civil War in Country Music Tradition," *Country Music Goes to War*, ed. Charles K. Wolfe and James E. Akenson. (Lexington: University Press of Kentucky, 2005): 1–25.

6. Neo-Confederate assertions of Anglo-Celtic culture refer to English-speaking people of Celtic descent (see Chapter 4).

7. Copyright permission was sought to reproduce lyrics. It was not granted in every case, and as a result some songs could not be quoted.

8. The Lost Cause myth emerged after the Civil War in the South as an attempt on the part of ex-Confederate politicians and pro-Confederate writers to come to terms with defeat and justify the Confederate cause during the war—see Foster, Gaines M. *Ghosts of the Confederacy: Defeat, the Lost Cause, and the Emergence of the New South, 1865–1913.* (New York: Oxford University Press, 1987); Gallagher, Gary, and Nolan, Alan, ed. *The Myth of the Lost Cause and Civil War History.* (Bloomington: Indiana University Press, 2000); Wilson, Charles Reagan. *Baptized in Blood: The Religion of the Lost Cause 1865–1920.* (Athens: University of Georgia Press, 1980).

9. Hill, Michael. "Extreme Traditionalism," *Southern Patriot,* 3.2 (1996): 9–10.

10. This information was gained from fieldwork conducted by Bohland in and around Staunton, Virginia, during October 2004.

11. Cowley, Miriam C. (Mrs. John R.). "Music of the Confederacy," *Minutes of the Ninety-Third Annual Convention of the United Daughters of the Confederacy.* (Richmond, 1986): 131–132.

12. "Twelfth Louisiana String Band," Y'all Come Back Music Center. On-line: http://www.pointsouth.com/Merchant2/merchant.mvc?Screen=CTGY&Store_Code=ABS&Category_Code=12TH-LA [accessed 8 December 2004 and 20 May 2006].

13. League of the South. "Southern Anthem," On-line: http://www.dixienet.org/linkads/merchandise.htm [accessed 8 December 2004] and http://leagueofthesouth.net/static/merchandise/merchandise.htm [accessed 9 August 2006]. See also *Confederate Spirit: The Great Songs of a Proud South.* On-line: http://www.pointsouth.com/yallcome/confederate/index.htm [accessed 8 December 2004]. Proceeds from the sales of the *Confederate Spirit* CD "help to support future work of the League of the South"—see "Miscellaneous Titles." On-line: http://www.pointsouth.com/Merchant2/merchant.mvc?Screen=CTGY&Store_Code=ABS&Category_Code=MISC-MUSIC [accessed 5 October 2006].

14. A video of the event is available: *Southern Heritage Celebration 2000, January 8, 2000 Rally.* Sons of Confederate Veterans, available from SCV, PO Box 11719, Columbia, SC 29211.

15. See "Carl Peterson—One Man, One Guitar, One Incredible Concert," Y'all Come Back Music Center. On-line: http://www.pointsouth.com/Merchant2/merchant.mvc?Screen=CTGY&Store_Code=ABS&Category_Code=CARL-PETERSON [accessed 14 December 2004 and 2 October 2006]. See also Society of Southern Celts. "Peterson, Reese to Bring Talent to Conference," *Society of Southern Celts,* (August 2002): 1.

16. "The Band Un-Reconstructed," *Southern Patriot,* 7.2 (2000): 2; "Declaration of Southern Cultural Independence," *Southern Patriot,* 7.2 (2000): 4. On-line: http://www.petitionOn-line.com/cripps/petition.html [accessed 1 November 2004].

17. "Un-Reconstructed," Y'all Come Back Music Center. On-line: http://www.pointsouth.com/Merchant2/merchant.mvc?Screen=CTGY&Store_Code=ABS&Category_Code=UNRECONSTRUCTED [accessed 8 December 2004].

18. "The Band Un-Reconstructed," *Southern Patriot,* 7.2 (2000): 2.

19. "The Border Ruffian Band presents . . . Live from Mole Church, Border Ruf-

fians." On-line: http://www.dixieinternet.com/border [accessed 8 December 2004]. The Border Ruffians are named after a group of settlers who entered Kansas in the 1850s and supported its entry to the Union as a slave state. See Fine, Gary Alan. "John Brown's Body: Elites, Heroic Embodiment, and the Legitimation of Political Violence," *Social Problems*, 46.2 (1999): 225–249.

20. Following cultural geographer Mike Crang we suggest that it is reasonable to analyze lyrics from the position of "a presupposed consumer of music who both understands and receives the dominant textual messages embedded within the content." See Crang, Mike. "On Display: The Poetics, Politics, and Interpretation of Exhibitions," *Cultural Geography in Practice*, ed. John May, Miles Ogborn, David Pinder, Alison Blunt, and Pyrs Gruffudd. (New York: Edward Arnold Press, 2003): 255–271.

21. Scherzer, Amy. "Rainbow Ball Hopes to Net Pot of Gold." *Tampa Tribune (Upscale Section)*, (20 April 1996): 4.

22. These CDs and the music of many other neo-Confederate acts are sold on-line at the Y'all Come Back Music Center. On-line: http://www.pointsouth .com/Merchant2/merchant.mvc?Screen=CTGY&Store_Code=ABS&Category_ Code=MUSIC [accessed 8 December 2004 and 12 May 2006].

23. The Rebelaires, "Southern Soldiers," on CD *P'litically Incorrect* (2001). Lyrics described from song sample at "The Rebelaires," Y'all Come Back Music Center. On-line: http://www.pointsouth.com/Merchant2/merchant.mvc?Screen=CTGY&Store_ Code=ABS&Category_Code=REBELAIRES [accessed 12 May 2006]. Copyright permission to reproduce lyrics of "Southern Soldier" was denied.

24. Reviews and testimonials for the Free South Band on-line: "Free South Band: Free South Project." On-line: http://www.cdbaby.com/cd/rhc [accessed 12 May 2006].

25. Cripps was listed in 2002 by the Southern Poverty Law Center as a prominent leader of the radical right and a hate group leader. See Beirich, Heidi, and Potok, Mark. "40 To Watch," *Intelligence Report*, Southern Poverty Law Center, 111 (2003): 20. He became leader of the Mississippi chapter of the League of the South in 2000 and was pastor of the so-called Confederate Presbyterian Church in the town of Lumberton. His Free South group runs a store in Florence, Mississippi, that sells Confederate paraphernalia, and in 2003 he ran for governor of the state as part of the far-right Constitution Party, finishing third with 6,317 votes (0.17 percent). In 2007, running as a Republican for State House Representative for District 93, Cripps received 1,693 votes (24.62 percent).

26. "Free South Band: Free South Project." On-line: http://www.cdbaby.com/cd/ rhc [accessed 12 May 2006].

27. Free South Band. "1865," *Free South Project*. (Waverley, TN: CSA Records, 2003). Lyrics by C. Robertson. On-line: http://www.freesouth.net/lyrics.htm [accessed 22 May 2006 and 9 August 2006] and also transcribed from Y'all Come Back Music Center. On-line: http://www.pointsouth.com/Merchant2/merchant .mvc?Screen=CTGY&Store_Code=ABS&Category_Code=FREESOUTH-BAND [accessed 12 May 2006]. Copyright permission to reproduce lyrics granted by Cornelius "Popcorn" Robertson, Free South Band, www.freesouth.net.

28. Lloyd, Robert. "Lest We Forget." *Rebel Private*. (Ft. Myers, FL: New World Enterprises, 2004). Copyright permission to reproduce lyrics granted by Robert Lloyd.

29. Wilson, Charles Reagan. *Baptized in Blood: The Religion of the Lost Cause 1865–1920.* (Athens: University of Georgia Press, 1980).

30. Edwards, Chris. "Centralia Train Massacre." *Blood on the Border.* (Columbia, MO: The Orchard, 2000).

31. Warren, Terry. "Border Ruffians," *Dixie Broadcasting Southron Anthology Volume I.* (McDonough, GA: Dixie Broadcasting, 2004).

32. DixieBroadcasting.com. "Musical Groups Featured on WDXB: Linda Carlton." On-line: http://www.wdxb.net/playlist.shtml [accessed 14 December 2004 and 3 October 2006].

33. "Southern Historical Conference August 29–30th." On-line: http://southern grace.web.aplus.net/bonnieblue/4_our_goal.htm [accessed 12 May 2006]. The Louisiana Tigers String Band was also scheduled to perform at a Confederate Ball in Winnsboro, Texas, planned for December 2006. See "Sincerely Southern—East Texas Christmas Ball Y'all." On-line: http://www.sincerelysouthern.com [accessed 3 October 2006].

34. "Southern Historical Conference August 29–30th: The Louisiana Tigers String Band." On-line: http://southerngrace.web.aplus.net/bonnieblue/15_louisiana_ tigers_string_band.htm [accessed 8 December 2004]. Political information, in particular revisionist histories of slavery, can be found through the group's participation in the "Southern Historical Conference August 30th: Southern Historical Conference and Bonnie Blue Ball." On-line: http://southerngrace.web.aplus.net/bonnieblue/6_ agenda_page.htm [accessed 8 December 2004]. Others appearing at this event were neo-Confederate activists H. K. Edgerton and Thomas E. Woods Jr.

35. Mountain, Bobby. *Dixie Bound.* (Talking Rock, GA: Bobby Mountain Music, 2001). Agenda of song on-line: http://www.wdxb.net/playlist.shtml and http://www .starsofmusic.com/bobby-mountain.html [accessed 14 December 2004].

36. Free South Band. "Southern Thang," *Free South.* (Waverly, TN: CSA Records, 2003). Lyrics by C. Robertson. On-line: http://freesouth.net/lyrics.htm [accessed 22 May 2006 and 9 August 2006]. Copyright permission to reproduce lyrics granted by Cornelius "Popcorn" Robertson, Free South Band, www.freesouth.net.

37. Free South Band. "Ain't Gonna Go Away." *Free South.* (Waverly, TN: CSA Records, 2003). Lyrics by Craig Hendrix. On-line: http://freesouth.net/lyrics.htm [accessed 22 May 2006 and 9 August 2006]. Copyright permission to reproduce lyrics granted by Cornelius Robertson. Craig Hendrix, Free South Band, www.freesouth .net.

38. Free South Band. "Don't Mess with Dixie." *Free South.* (Waverly, TN: CSA Records, 2003). Lyrics by Craig Hendrix. On-line: http://freesouth.net/lyrics.htm [accessed 22 May 2006 and 9 August 2006]. Copyright permission to reproduce lyrics granted by Cornelius Robertson. Craig Hendrix, Free South Band, www.freesouth .net.

39. Free South Band. On-line: http://www.freesouth.net [accessed 9 August 2006].

40. Y'all Come Back Music Center. On-line: http://www.pointsouth.com/ Merchant2/merchant.mvc?Screen=CTGY&Store_Code=ABS&Category_ Code=MUSIC [accessed 8 December 2004 and 12 May 2006].

41. "Musical Showcase: The First Annual League of the South Musical Showcase," *South Carolina Patriot*, 6.3 (2003): 33–36.

42. "Basic Gray." Y'all Come Back Music Center. On-line: http://www.pointsouth .com/Merchant2/merchant.mvc?Screen=CTGY&Store_Code=ABS&Category_ Code=BASIC-GRAY [accessed 8 December 2004].

43. "The Band Un-Reconstructed," *Southern Patriot*, 7.2 (2000): 2. The band's name is inconsistently spelled. In this column, it is "Basic Grey" but the "Basic Gray" spelling is more common.

44. League of the South. "The League of the South's Fourth Annual Big Event of the Year: The Most Bodacious Hoedown and Southern Music Jam." On-line: http:// www.dixienet.org/Hoedown.html [accessed 8 December 2004].

45. Permission was sought to reproduce the lyrics written by Robin and Linda Williams. It was not received.

46. This is based upon fieldwork observations by Jon Bohland, who attended the performance. Unfortunately, no photography was allowed during the performance of *Stonewall Country*.

47. Kittredge, Kevin. "Stonewall Country Closes Tonight," *Roanoke Times (Extra Section)*, (3 July 2003): 1.

48. Foster, *Ghosts of the Confederacy*, (1987).

49. Wilkins, Steve, and Wilson, Douglas. *Southern Slavery: As It Was*. (Moscow, ID: Canon Press, 1996).

50. Nolan, Alan T. "The Anatomy of the Myth," *The Myth of the Lost Cause and Civil War History*, ed. Gary W. Gallagher and Alan T. Nolan. (Bloomington: Indiana University Press, 2000): 17.

51. Tucker, Neely. "Who Put The Y'all In 'Idol'?" *Washington Post*, (18 April 2006): C01. On-line: http://www.washingtonpost.com/wp-dyn/content/article/2006/04/17/ AR2006041701758_pf.html [accessed 10 August 2006].

52. Kromm, Chris. "Facing South: Why Southerners Rule American Idol," *Southern Studies.Org Friday Music Watch*, (5 May 2006). On-line: http://southern-studies.org/facingsouth/2006/05/friday-music-watch-why-Southerners.asp [accessed 5 May 2006].

53. Wilson, Clyde. "The Montgomery Declaration," *Southern Patriot*, 7.2 (2000): 2.

54. Wilson, Clyde. "After Independence," *Southern Patriot*, 3.4 (1996): 30 (emphasis added).

55. Hill, Michael. "An Alabama Boy's Reflections on Southern Music," (2005) On-line: http://www.chroniclesmagazine.org/www/News/Hill/NewsMH072505 .html [accessed 10 August 2006]. Hill also describes here his admiration for the All-man Brothers in a nostalgic recollection of a chance conversation with Duane Allman in 1970.

56. Hill, Michael. "A Reply to Mark Strauss' *Let's Ditch Dixie: The Case for Northern Secession*," (2001). On-line: http://www.dixienet.org/ls-press-releases/ LS-special-reports/ls-special-index.html [accessed 8 December 2004].

57. Hill, Michael. "Southern Cultural Defence: The League of the South Approach," On-line: http://www.dixienet.org/ls-homepg/cul-def.htm [accessed 8 December 2004].

58. Hill, Michael, and Fleming, Thomas. "New Dixie Manifesto: States' rights will rise again," *Washington Post*, (29 October 1995): C03. The role of African American performers in post–World War II U.S. popular music is examined in Werner,

Craig. *A Change Is Gonna Come: Music, Race and the Soul of America.* (Edinburgh: Payback/Canongate, 2000 [1998]).

59. Ward, Brian. "Racial Politics, Culture and the Cole Incident of 1956," *Race and Class in the American South since 1890*, ed. Melvyn Stokes and Rick Halpern. (Providence: Berg, 1994): 181–208; Ware, Vron, and Back, Les. *Out of Whiteness: Color, Politics, and Culture.* (Chicago: University of Chicago Press, 2002).

60. See Filene, Benjamin. *Romancing the Folk: Public Memory and American Roots Music.* (Chapel Hill: University of North Carolina Press, 2000); Frith, Simon. "The Discourse of World Music," *Western Music and Its Others: Difference, Representation, and Appropriation in Music*, ed. Georgina Born and David Hesmondhalgh. (Berkeley: University of California Press, 2000): 305–322; Peterson, Richard A. *Creating Country Music: Fabricating Authenticity.* (Chicago: University of Chicago Press, 1997).

61. Reed, John Shelton. *Whistling Dixie: Dispatches from the South.* (Columbia: University of Missouri Press, 1990): 110, 111.

62. Ibid., 110 (original emphasis).

63. Ibid., 111.

64. See also Reed, John Shelton. "The South: What Is It? *Where* Is It?" *The South for New Southerners*, ed. Paul D. Escott and David R. Goldfield. (Chapel Hill: University of North Carolina Press, 1991): 18–41; Peterson, Richard A. *Creating Country Music: Fabricating Authenticity.* (Chicago: University of Chicago Press, 1997).

65. It is indicative to compare neo-Confederate Celtic music with Celtic music performed in Scotland, described in Symon, "From Blas to Bothy," (2002).

66. Cox, Karen L. *Dixie's Daughters: The United Daughters of the Confederacy and the Preservation of Confederate Culture.* (Gainesville: University Press of Florida, 2003).

67. Phillips, Kevin. *American Theocracy: The Peril and Politics of Radical Religion, Oil, and Borrowed Money in the 21st Century.* (New York: Viking Press, 2006): 138.

68. Britt, Brian. "Neo-Confederate Culture," *Z Magazine*, (December 1996). On-line: *http://www.zmag.org/Zmag/articles/dec96britt.htm* [accessed 27 January 1999 and 2 December 2004].

69. The list of contemporary artists endorsed by the League of the South is found in the "Southern Lyrics." On-line: http://www.leagueofthesouth.net/index .php?module=Lyrics [accessed 12 May 2006]. The list includes The Allman Brothers, Black Crowes, Creedence Clearwater Revival, Jimmy Buffett, Johnny Cash, Lynyrd Skynyrd, Stevie Ray Vaughan, The Band, Tom Petty, Willie Nelson, and ZZ Top.

70. League of the South. "First Annual League of the South Jam." On-line: http:// www.dixienet.org/ls-press-releases/Jam.htm [accessed 8 December 2004]. The event took place on 29 August 2003. On-line: http://www.dixienet.org/ls-press-releases/Jam .html

71. For discussion of the politics of Creedence Clearwater Revival songs, and their connection to the imagery of the U.S. South, see Werner, *A Change Is Gonna Come*, (2000 [1998]).

72. It should be noted that Bobby Horton has performed at neo-Confederate events in the past, such as the Second National Conference—documented in Hill, Michael. "President's Message [The Southern League: Past, Present and Future]," *Southern Patriot*, 2.3 (1995): 17–18. The extent to which Horton subscribes to neo-Confederate ideology, however, is unclear, although he told Oran P. Smith in a *South-*

ern Partisan interview, "In late 1984, I was asked by my Sons of Confederate Veterans camp to present a program of Confederate Music. And like so many people, I knew 'Dixie,' I knew how 'The Bonnie Blue Flag' went and I had sung 'Goober Peas' in grammar school in music class. But the tunes I knew were few. I got hooked on the War in 1961 when I visited Chickamauga Battlefield. Since then, I've accumulated a pretty good library. Confederate books. History books looking through gray shades" ("Partisan Conversation: Bobby Horton," *Southern Partisan*, 13 [1st Quarter 1993]: 31). Gray was the color of Confederate military uniforms in the Civil War.

    73. Walker, Redbone T. "New Offerings from the Troubadour Laureate of the South," *Southern Partisan*, 23.4 (2004): 29.

    74. Smith, "Partisan Conversation: Bobby Horton," (1993): 34.

CHAPTER 10

The Struggle for the Sons of Confederate Veterans: A Return to White Supremacy in the Early Twenty-First Century?

HEIDI BEIRICH

During the 108th annual reunion of the Sons of Confederate Veterans (scv), held in July 2004 in Dalton, Georgia, Walter C. ("Walt") Hilderman III was ejected from the event by scv lawyers Burl McCoy, then serving as the group's Judge Advocate General, and Sam Currin, a prominent former U.S. attorney and superior court judge from North Carolina who had chaired that state's Republican Party from 1996 to 1999.[1] Hilderman, a South Carolinian with a fondness for reenacting Civil War battles and tidying up Confederate cemeteries, had publicly asked the scv to remove white supremacists and secessionists from its ranks. After forcibly removing Hilderman from the convention, the scvers present voted nearly unanimously for a resolution to consider revoking Hilderman's scv membership. In November 2004, that resolution passed the scv's General Executive Council (GEC), the scv's leadership committee comprising officials appointed by the elected Commander, all living past Commanders, plus two elected officials from each of the three major scv divisions: the Army of Northern Virginia, the Army of Tennessee, and the Army of the Trans-Mississippi—divisions named after the components of the Confederate military.

Hilderman's ejection from the Dalton reunion symbolized the end of a fifteen-year attempt by moderates and Civil War history buffs to modernize the scv by renouncing segregation and race hatred. Having passed its first anti–Ku Klux Klan resolution in 1989, the scv by 2004 considered its experiment with racial tolerance over. This change of heart came as the result of a concerted effort by extremists, predominantly from the white supremacist neo-Confederate organizations the Council of Conservative Citizens (ccc) and the League of the South (ls), to infiltrate the scv and move it toward their own positions. This infiltration strategy was clever. It targeted a conservative group of men with deep nostalgia for the antebellum South and defensiveness for "The Cause" and its symbols. By sympathizing with this nostalgia and pointing the finger at African Americans and liberal whites for attacking their beloved Confederate battle flag, which civil rights organizations including the National Association for the Advancement of Colored People (NAACP) had asked be removed from public buildings, extremists manipulated these men's sentiments, turning the SCV into an organization more amenable to their racial goals. The conservatism of the SCV's membership helped the extremists in another way—it made the group disinclined to publicly admit to infiltration, to the point of suspending and threatening to expel some 300 members, including Hilderman, who called for an end to extremism in the ranks. The upshot of this strategy is that the SCV is returning to its roots, which were firmly planted in the soils of Southern white supremacy.

For nearly three years, Hilderman had been crusading for a nonracist SCV, founding the group Save the SCV in 2001 with another member, North Carolina restaurant manager Gilbert Jones. Jones had run unsuccessfully on an antiracist platform for Lt. Commander of the SCV's North Carolina division at the 2002 convention. His campaign message was to the point: "I think we ought to take the neo-Nazis, the white supremacists, and the skinheads and show them to the door."[2] Jones's and Hilderman's calls would have been seen as benign in the early 1990s when the SCV was distancing itself from its segregationist and racist past. In 1989, the group passed a resolution, clearly aimed at the Klan, condemning the use of the Confederate flag by groups or individuals espousing "political extremism or racial superiority."[3] This resolution was backed up by a stronger one passed by the SCV's General Executive Council in 1992 that denounced "the KKK and all others who promote hate among our people."

The SCV was expanding rapidly in the late 1980s and early 1990s, experiencing membership growth driven by popular interest in genealogy. Many men were drawn to the organization by an interest in their Confederate ancestors, but others, more radical, were drawn by Confederate history. These radicals included members of extremist organizations such as the CCC and LS, whose constituents wanted to create an "Anglo-Celtic" society in a seceded South.

In the early 1990s, the SCV's some 20,000 members each paid $33 a year to participate. With the increase in popularity, SCV membership surpassed 33,000 and the organization's financial assets grew accordingly, with the group taking in more than $1 million per year and building an endowment. Its ranks were filled with powerful politicians including Trent Lott, Jesse Helms (Sam Currin, who helped throw Hilderman out of the Dalton convention, was once a Helms aide), and Pat Buchanan. Lott was particularly enamored of the scv, having received its Order of the Southern Cross for his successful efforts to posthumously restore U.S. citizenship to Jefferson Davis, the Confederate president. Lott even narrated the group's 1991 recruiting video.

Jones, Hilderman, and hundreds of other scvers were byproducts of this modernization push, believing the scv should be dedicated to its historical mission and should reject all associations with extremist groups. But another prominent scver was pushing the group in the other direction, toward its segregationist past. Since the late 1990s, Kirk Lyons, a white supremacist lawyer from North Carolina who was married at the Aryan Nations compound, has led a crusade to radicalize the scv. His allies have been the white supremacists and secessionists that the scv had condemned earlier in the decade. The extent to which the antiracist crusade has failed was revealed in a March 2004 email Lyons penned to fellow radicals on an scv mailing list. "Mere Klan membership should not be sufficient to remove a member," Lyons replied to a question asking if it would be acceptable to take scv membership dues from Indiana klansman Railton Loy, given that the scv had denounced the kkk in 1989. When the email was made public in the Southern Poverty Law Center's (splc) *Intelligence Report,* there were no repercussions for Lyons during the subsequent scv convention, only for Walt Hilderman.[4] Ironically, at the 2004 Dalton convention the scv once again passed a resolution denouncing "racial and political extremists"—but now that term no longer specified the Klan, but the naacp and Jesse Jackson.

One Hundred Years of Segregation

In the late 1800s, Southern men began to organize groups of Confederate veterans into camps, many of which held annual reunions. In June 1889, these camps became official components of the United Confederate Veterans (ucv).[5] According to historian Karen L. Cox, the rise of these associations was a phenomenon of the ebb of Reconstruction and came in tandem with a nationwide reassertion in the 1880s of "states' rights and white supremacy."[6]

The ucv group eventually morphed into the scv, which was founded in 1896 in Richmond, Virginia, under the name United Sons of Confederate Veterans. Lt. Gen. Stephen Dill Lee, then Commander of the United Confederate Veterans, charged the group with "the vindication of the Cause for which we fought" and "the defense of the Confederate soldier's good name." The group changed its name to Sons of Confederate Veterans, dropping the "United," when members realized that the acronym—uscv—might be confused with that of the United States Colored Volunteers.[7] Membership in the scv remains based on descent from a Confederate soldier, and the parallel fraternal organization, the Military Order of Stars and Bars (mosb), comprises descendants of Confederate officers. A female equivalent of the scv, the United Daughters of the Confederacy (udc), represents female descendants of Confederate veterans.

In the late nineteenth century, the scv was inspired by the same Lost Cause nostalgia that animated most white Southern organizations of the day, including the Democratic Party. The scv disparaged blacks and questioned attempts to extend equality to the black community. These views were preached through what would become the group's house organ, *Confederate Veteran* (cv), founded by Sumner Archibald Cunningham in Nashville, Tennessee, in 1893. According to historian David Blight, the magazine featured "the common soldier's story, the western theatres of the war, and a rising tide of white supremacy."[8] Well into the early 1900s, the cv defended the Ku Klux Klan, argued that the founding fathers created the United States for "white people," and complained of how "when a Negro has learned to read he ceases to work."[9] The importance of the *Confederate Veteran* to rewriting the Civil War cannot be underestimated. The magazine was critical in presenting the views of the war that are now touted by neo-Confederates—such as the war having nothing to do with slavery and that slaves were generally happy with their plantation existence. *Confederate Veteran* reached over twenty thousand readers by the end of the 1890s and was, explains Blight,

> the clearing house for Lost Cause thought, and the vehicle by which ex-Confederates built a powerful memory community that lasted into the 1930s. Many veterans wrote to Cunningham expressing their love for the journal, which with "every succeeding year," wrote a Tennessean, "adds luster to the Lost Cause." . . . Cunningham made white supremacy central to the magazine's vision, welcoming to its pages frequent tributes to "faithful slaves" and denouncing the racial equality attempted during Reconstruction.[10]

The scv's strong defense of white supremacy actually paled in comparison to its sister organization, the udc, which was even more forceful in defending "The Cause." It was the udc that perpetuated the teaching of Lost Cause mythology and its attendant white supremacy in schools and to udc women. The group

> believed that if white children were properly instructed, they would become "living monuments" to the Confederacy. Unlike marble statues, these children served as future defenders of the "sacred principles" for which their

Confederate ancestors had died—namely, states' rights and the preservation of white supremacy.[11]

To this end, the UDC committed itself to eradicating unacceptable textbooks and ensuring that their version of history was taught. UDC members also placed Confederate flags and portraits of Confederate heroes in schools and worked directly with teachers to plan history lessons. This radicalism has remained in the UDC. In 1989, an article in UDC *Magazine* by Walter W. Lee argued that "the enslaved African lived an idyllic existence in an unspoiled Disneyland, complete with self-mowing lawns. The inhabitants seemed to have had an existence that only just failed to reach that of Adam and Eve before the Fall."[12] In January 2000, the group's president, Mrs. William Wells, shared the podium with white supremacists, including Lyons, during the 6,000-strong Columbia, South Carolina, pro-Confederate flag rally.[13]

The CV and the SCV reached their first apogee around the turn of the century, but it was short-lived. As the first generation of veterans passed away, the group began to stagnate. In 1932, production of CV was suspended as the SCV had few camps (local chapters) and only about 1,000 members. The group would languish until after the war, when a new leader reinvigorated its racist Lost Cause mythology.

The McCain Years, 1953–1993

The SCV's fundamental white supremacy did not disappear in the latter half of the twentieth century as the civil rights movement spread throughout the South. Dr. William D. McCain, who deservedly is considered within the SCV as its true founder, ran the organization with an iron fist until the late 1980s. A staunch segregationist opposed to civil rights, McCain was unwavering in his defense of the Confederacy and its politics. Even as the SCV passed resolutions condemning white supremacist groups in the 1980s and 1990s, the organization was simultaneously naming its library archives after McCain, and later created a Major General William D. McCain fund. Until 2005, the SCV was incorporated in McCain's home state of Mississippi in his honor and he remains a revered figure in the group.

From 1953 until 1993, McCain served as Adjutant-in-Chief for the SCV, a powerful administrative position that put him in charge of its day-to-day operations. McCain was an accomplished academic. While holding his SCV post, he also served as director of the Mississippi Archives and president of the University of Southern Mississippi. He remained president emeritus of the university until his death in 1993. McCain was a prominent supporter of the Mississippi State Sovereignty Commission, which spied on citizens and compiled information on anyone involved in the fight against segregation. He was a close personal friend of many of the commission's leaders, and often spoke on the evils of desegregation at commission-supported events. In a 1960 speech in Chicago sponsored by the commission, McCain explained Mississippi life to people in Illinois. "We insist that educationally and socially, we maintain a segregated society. . . . In all fairness, I admit that we are not encouraging Negro voting," he said. "The Negroes prefer that control of the government remain in the white man's hands." McCain claimed that blacks attempting to desegregate Southern universities were "imports" from the North, not Southerners fighting for equal access to public institutions.[14]

McCain backed up his words with actions, working hard to keep blacks out of the University of Southern Mississippi. In 1959, McCain enlisted local law enforcement and Sovereignty Commission officials to prevent Clyde Kennard from enrolling at the all-white school.[15] Thanks in part to McCain's efforts, Kennard would end up in the Sovereignty Commission's files listed as a "Race Agitator," and not long after his application to the university was rejected, Kennard was framed for the theft of five bags of chicken feed, convicted by an all-white jury, and sent to prison for seven years.

The fight for segregation did not interfere with McCain's work for the scv, which he transformed into a powerhouse. When McCain took over the scv in 1953 the group was about the same size as it had been in the 1930s, with thirty camps, a thousand members, and $1,053 in its bank account.[16] By 1993, when McCain died, the scv had hundreds of camps, 18,253 members, and a substantial endowment. McCain relaunched *Confederate Veteran* in the early 1980s and raised enough money to purchase a headquarters for the group— Elm Springs, a former plantation mansion in Columbia, Tennessee.

During McCain's long tenure, neither his segregationist views nor his work with the Sovereignty Commission was denounced by the scv. In fact, McCain's views were in line with those of many people who joined the scv while he ran the group. These included many prominent racists, including members of White Citizens' Councils, which fought vehemently against desegregation in the 1950s and 1960s. In fact, at the time of writing, the leader of the Alabama Division of the scv is Leonard Wilson, once a leader of the Tuscaloosa White Citizens' Council. Wilson also led violent protests against the desegregation of the University of Alabama when Autherine Lucy attempted to attend school there in 1953. Described as "presiding over a full-scale riot" by journalist Diane McWhorter in her celebrated memoir of segregationist Birmingham, *Carry Me Home*,[17] Wilson earned the nickname "Flagpole Wilson" for leading the anti-Lucy protests, chanting "Keep Bama white!" and "Hey, Hey, ho, ho Autherine's got to go" while climbing a campus flagpole.[18] Wilson's segregationist politics, like McCain's, were not out of step with the SCV's membership in the 1950s, 1960s, and 1970s.

The Move to Moderation

In the late 1980s, as McCain's power was dwindling along with his health, there was a push within the SCV to distance itself from its racist legacy by enforcing provisions in the group's constitution that require members to be apolitical during sponsored events. As a result, in 1989, the SCV passed a resolution against groups that "espouse political extremism or racial superiority." The resolution did not condemn racist hate groups or require that SCV members not join them; it simply rejected the use of the Confederate flag by extremists. This was an attempt by the SCV to differentiate itself from the Confederate flag wavers of the Ku Klux Klan. A 1992 resolution was more forthright, condemning all who "promote hate." At least once, in 1993, an SCV camp counter-demonstrated against the Klan.

The SCV also began to distance itself from the views of organizations that claimed part of its mandate. In particular, the SCV discouraged the involvement in CCC events of members acting in an official capacity. The CCC had been founded in 1985 out of the mailing lists of the White Citizens' Councils by a leadership that had been active in efforts to stop desegregation during the 1950s and 1960s. The CCC's abject racism was not well known nationally in the early 1990s, and its meetings featured important political figures such as Mississippi Republican senator Trent Lott. A 1998 exposé by the Southern Poverty Law Center revealed the group's white supremacist views and led the Republican Party to demand its members stay away from the CCC.[19] The fact that the SCV was already aware of the CCC's nature shows how strong its antiracism was in the early 1990s.

As part of this clean-up effort, the SCV leadership was purged of extremist elements. In 1994, P. Charles Lunsford, a popular SCV leader and originator of the neo-Confederate movement's 1990s slogan, "Heritage, Not Hate," was forced to step down from his post as Chief of Heritage Defense after speaking to the CCC. Norman Dasinger (SCV Commander, 1994–1996), the man who tried hardest to rid the SCV of racists, demanded that Lunsford not attend such events in his official SCV capacity. In a subsequent *Southern Heritage Magazine* article, Lunsford remarked that if members such as he were being reprimanded, then "the SCV will no longer be fighting the fight for Southern heritage," complaining that "those of us who made the scv famous by fight-ing these battles and swelling the ranks are being purged."[20] Despite such ac-tions, prominent members of the ccc retained their scv memberships, and a decade later, in an 18 August 2004 email posted to the scv's in-house mailing list, Lunsford insisted that race remained central to scv identity:

> Those who say that the scv has somehow changed in recent years are full of it. Our great mentor Gen. William D. McCain was a lifelong segregation-ist, never repenting until the day he died. Our cic [Commander-in-Chief] during the early 1900s was Nathan Bedford Forrest II, and he simultaneously held the position of Grand Dragon of the kkk. So what?![21]

The scv under Dasinger's leadership also chose to distance itself from the white supremacist and secessionist League of the South (ls), which was founded in 1994 on a platform of restoring the South to its rightful "Anglo-Celtic" owners. The ls grew quickly and many board members were also prominent members of the scv, but the scv resisted pressure to move in a secessionist direction. In 1995, Perry Outlaw, then Commander of the mosb and a close ally of Dasinger, wrote a scathing article in *Confederate Veteran* denouncing members who advocated secession.[22] Dasinger echoed Outlaw's comments in the scv's newsletter *The Gray Line*. In 1996 the scv leadership went so far as to ban all discussion of secession on its new email listserv, the scv Dispatch.[23] It should be noted, however, that what the scv was not willing to do was expel members for their membership in or association with white supremacist or other extremist groups, and scv Commander Ed Deason confirmed in a 2001 interview that no scv member had ever been charged with being a seg-regationist or expelled for participation in a racist organization.[24]

The Reemergence of White Supremacy in the SCV

These moves to ban discussion of secession did not sit well with scv mem-bers who were on the ls board. In 1996, Walter Donald "Donnie" Kennedy, coauthor with his twin brother James Ronald of the neo-Confederate screed and slavery apologia *The South Was Right!* resigned from the scv's General Executive Council (gec). Kennedy, who had served as Commander of the Louisiana division, complained in his resignation letter that the determina-tion by the scv that "discussion of secession today is 'political' and therefore prohibited by the Constitution of the scv," meant that he could no longer serve at the national level.[25] In Kennedy's estimation, secession should not be considered the same as political activity, because secession was a notion supported by the founding fathers and the Confederacy, which the scv was founded to honor.

Kennedy's opinions resonated with many scvers. George Kalas, the ls Web Master in the late 1990s, wrote on the ls web site that "there is a struggle now underway for the heart and soul of the scv."[26] Kalas said that he had had it with the "Eat, Meet and Retreat (em&r) Confederates" who "see the scv as a sort of Civil War Roundtable with a Southern accent" and "agree with the Yankees that the South waged war to defend slavery." Kalas was in the camp of the "Unreconstructed Confederates," a name often used now by scv extremists who "support a State's right to secede," and he had some advice for likeminded scvers: "I strongly urge you not to resign" from the scv and instead join with other "unreconstructed" camps in "actively resisting the em&r crowd's effort to impose a 'politically correct' regime upon the scv."[27]

While Kennedy and Kalas were denouncing the scv in print, white supremacist lawyer Kirk Lyons was coming up with ways to tap the group's more radical elements in a fight for a Southern revolution. Lyons had a record reaching back into the mid-1980s of serving as the lawyer for the racist right.[28] Through his Texas law firm, first called the Patriots Defense League and later renamed cause (which stood for Canada, Australia, the United States, South Africa and Europe—the places where white people live), Lyons had represented notorious white supremacists including Klan leader Louis Beam, known for introducing military training to the kkk and harassing Vietnamese fishermen in Texas (and being Lyons's best man at his Aryan Nations wedding),[29] and Richard Butler, head of the Aryan Nations, the country's largest white supremacist organization in the 1980s and 1990s. Lyons was also active in litigating in favor of some of the families of the Branch Davidians who died during the firestorm that engulfed David Koresh's compound near Waco, Texas, in 1993.

In 1996, Lyons, his brother-in-law Neill Payne (who was married to Lyon's wife's sister in the same ceremony as Lyons at the Aryan Nations compound), and another man incorporated the Southern Legal Resource Center (slrc), abruptly shifting Lyons's politics from defending racists to defending neo-Confederates. With the founding of the slrc, Lyons began selling himself as a defender of "Confederate Southern Americans," an "ethnic" term that Lyons created. Its web site described the slrc as "a nonprofit legal foundation waging a counteroffensive to preserve Southern Heritage" and committed to halting the "Ethnic Cleansing of Dixie."[30] Its most important issue would be protecting the display of the Confederate battle flag and other Confederate symbols from "heritage violations," which are defined on the scv web site as "any attack upon our Confederate Heritage, or the flags, monuments, and symbols which represent it."[31]

In the late 1990s, around the same time as he was setting up the slrc, Lyons was quietly ratcheting up his activism in the scv, reaching out to potential allies. In a 2000 speech to the neo-Nazi organization American Friends of the British National Party (afbnp), a group that raised funds for the white supremacist British National Party (bnp), Lyons told the racist crowd that he planned to turn the scv into a more radical organization. Sharing a podium with former Klan leader David Duke and Nick Griffin, head of the bnp, Lyons described "heritage coalitions" as a new way for scv members to cooperate with other neo-Confederate groups to fight "heritage violations," such as taking down Confederate battle flags.[32]

"Theoretically, it's a citizen's coalition, anybody can join," Lyons explained to a room full of listeners, as documented in a 22 April 2000 videotape. His point was a lawyerly one. Following the passage of the 1992 resolution, scv members were constitutionally prohibited from working with groups that "promote hate," but only in their capacity as scv members. In their personal lives or, as Lyons put it, as mere "John Q. Publics" working within autonomous "heritage coalitions," they can do as they like. These coalitions, which at that point were in place in Alabama, Georgia, North Carolina, Oklahoma, South Carolina, and Texas, offered a loophole that was already being used by hundreds of scv members to work with racist activists from organizations identified by the Southern Poverty Law Center as "hate groups," including the ls, the ccc, and others.

During his afbnp speech, Lyons described the ongoing battle within the scv, saying he had spent most of his twenty-two years of membership "cursing the organization . . . for [its] spinelessness and cowardice." He mocked the "granny" faction that "hide[s] in their shirts at the mention of the R-word [racism]." He talked about how a group of "unreconstructed Southerners" or "white trash," including himself, had helped to move the scv toward a white "nationalist perspective" that was reintroducing a "keen understanding of the historical elements of the Old South and the Old Confederacy." As proof of that success, Lyons pointed to a January 2000 pro-Confederate flag rally in Columbia, South Carolina, during which scv officials worked openly with udc, ccc, and ls members. Some 6,000 neo-Confederates attended this protest against plans to remove the Confederate battle flag from its position atop the Capitol. "The civil rights movement I am trying to form seeks a revolution," Lyons told his extremist colleagues that day. "We seek a return to a godly society with no Northernisms attached to it—a majority European-derived society." He ended his speech excitedly, "It's a new day in Dixie. I am very proud of the scv. They are finally standing up!"[33]

Given that the scv was led for nearly forty years by the openly segregationist McCain, it is not surprising that its somewhat limited moves toward the mainstream in the 1990s were short-lived. The resignation of Walter Donald Kennedy and the anger of the "unreconstructeds" ultimately affected the selection of a new Commander during the 1996 convention. Elections for scv posts are held every two years, and when Norman Dasinger stepped down he was replaced by the more radical Peter Orlebeke (scv Commander, 1996–1998). Orlebeke's views parroted neo-Confederate apologies for slavery and other positions presented in Kennedy and Kennedy's *The South Was Right!* After his selection, Orlebeke reiterated the theological war thesis, telling Steve Blow of the *Dallas Morning News* that slavery had biblical sanction and that the South did not have "problems with racial relationships until Reconstruction."[34] He went on to say that slave owners "took care of them [slaves]—all their clothes, all their food, all their medicine. It wasn't great conditions. Don't get me wrong. But there have been times that I wished someone had said to me, 'I'll give you a job for the rest of your life.'" By 2000, this view of slavery was preached from the scv's own pulpit after the group appointed as Chaplain-in-Chief John Weaver, a reverend from Fitzgerald, Georgia, whose essay "Biblical View of Slavery" claimed, "African slaves blessed the Lord for allowing them to be enslaved and sent to America."[35]

By 1998, the scv's apolitical stance had shattered under the weight of denunciations from within the ranks by the unreconstructeds and other extremists, particularly those in the rapidly growing ls, which had reached some 9,000 members by that time. The scv's more radical elements had been reenergized by the fall of Dasinger and the leadership of the far more extremist Orlebeke. In their convention that year, they rescinded Dasinger's policy mandating that scv members were "not affiliated with any organization in the world," which was put in place to ensure that the public would not confuse the scv with others who displayed the Confederate battle flag, like the kkk or "anybody who wants to secede from the United States."[36] In its stead, a new affiliation policy was passed that loosened the restrictions on working with other organizations while in an official scv capacity. The new policy allowed scv camps and divisions to participate in activities put on by other groups and permitted them to advertise the activities of other neo-Confederate organizations at local camp meetings. Although the new policy stated that "members and officers shall not promote or endorse the activities or goals of organizations with explicit or implicit racial motives during meetings or events of the Sons of Confederate Veterans," it was seen by neo-Confederate groups as a move in the "right" direction. Writing in *Southern Patriot,* LS founder Michael Hill joyously proclaimed that this new SCV affiliation policy would allow cooperation with other "pro-South" groups like the LS on "non-political matters" and would enhance the "prospects of protecting and advancing Southern culture." He proceeded to rejoice in the "good news long overdue" that the SCV "old guard" was "on its way out."[37]

This policy change ushered in an era in which the LS and the SCV would work together. The increasingly radical stance of the SCV that resulted from this development was reflected in the *Confederate Veteran* published just after this policy change was enacted. The magazine was filled with advertisements for extremist publications such as *The South Was Right!* and web sites for the LS and other more radical "heritage" organizations. The policy shift was also evident in the SCV's enthusiastic participation in various "heritage coalitions," as Lyons had proposed. Most prominent was the SCV's decision to let its leaders openly participate with well-known extremists from the CCC and the LS during the January 2000 Confederate flag rally in Columbia, South Carolina. Some 6,000 people attended the event. R.G. "Ronnie" Wilson, then Lt. Commander of the South Carolina division, shared the stage with Michael Hill and state senator Arthur Ravenal, who during his speech called the NAACP the "National Association for the Advancement of Retarded People" because of their boycott of South Carolina over its prominent display of the Confederate flag. The South Carolina SCV sponsored a videotape to commemorate the event, which featured interviews with leaders from both the CCC and the LS as well as Kirk Lyons, who hosted a barbecue following the Columbia rally.[38]

In August 2000, seven months after the Columbia rally and four months after Lyons spoke to the AFBNP, Lyons was elected to the SCV's GEC as a Councilman for the Army of Northern Virginia.[39] Lyons had been politicking for years behind the scenes in the Army of Northern Virginia, the largest division of the SCV, which included his home in Black Mountain, North Carolina. In 2000, Lyons maneuvered his friend and ally in the North Carolina Heritage Coalition, Roger McCredie, into the national position of SCV Chief of Heritage Defense, even though McCredie had never held a position higher than local Brigade Commander. McCredie was subsequently appointed as executive director of the SLRC in 2004.

The participation in events hosted by white supremacist organizations and racist hate groups has not let up since the 1998 affiliation policy change was made. In March 2000, the SCV participated in a Confederate flag rally in Montgomery, Alabama, organized by the LS.[40] Just over a year later, in April

2001, the scv held a joint rally in support of the Mississippi state flag with the ccc and a radical neo-Confederate group called FreeMississippi.org, run by the former head of the ls in Mississippi, John Cripps. scv leaders started appearing at conferences held by organizations identified by the splc as hate groups. For example, Ron Casteel, then the scv's National Chairman of Public Affairs, spoke at the 2001 annual ls convention. The scv became more active on another front: heritage violation cases. While serving as chief of that department, McCredie funneled heritage violation cases to the slrc, which received several donations from the scv to fund its work.

Commander Ed Deason, who was elected in 2000, reflected the new tolerance of hate group activities. When asked in 2001 whether or not membership in extremist groups as crude as the ccc could be consistent with scv membership, Deason said:

> [There is] not a lot of difference between the Council of Conservative Citizens and the Republican Party. The Council of Conservative Citizens is basically a political party, the League of the South is a political party, the Southern Party and so forth, so as long as they abide by the rules of the scv that we have in our established constitution and bylaws then they are free to join the organization.[41]

Little has changed in terms of policy for the scv since then, and its membership includes activists from the ccc, the ls, and the Heritage Preservation Association (hpa), a group P. Charles Lunsford established after the scv demoted him (and which had a Klan member as its Alabama state leader in 2003). But there was one prominent member ousted permanently from the scv: Ken Burns. The celebrated documentary filmmaker who first came to national prominence for *The Civil War*, broadcast on pbs in 1990, was expelled for suggesting that Robert E. Lee was responsible for more deaths than the Japanese in World War II.[42]

The Radicalization of the SCV and Its Aftermath

Reports of scv extremism in the splc *Intelligence Report*[43] led to a schism in the scv in the fall of 2001 and to the founding of a "Save the scv" movement. Walt Hilderman, who co-founded the movement with Gilbert Jones, wrote in November 2001, "We must develop a network of members and camps throughout the nation that will publicly condemn the infiltration of the scv by racists and secessionists, and who will work toward their removal" in the

2002 scv elections that were to be held in Memphis. "We intend to build a movement within the scv that will identify the extremists and vote them out of office or obtain their resignations. If they are secessionists, let them join the League of the South. If they think racism is a virtue, let them join the Ku Klux Klan."[44] Instead of a broad-based movement forming around Save the scv to take on the racists, however, following the Memphis convention, Hilderman, Jones, Charles Hawks, and some 300 other North Carolinians who were allied with Save the scv received letters notifying them that their scv memberships were to be suspended.

For those who had worked so hard to remove racists from the ranks of the scv, this turn of events was depressing. In a 2001 interview, Perry Outlaw lamented what was happening to his beloved organization, blaming it on infiltration by radicals:

> Well, I think it would be more accurate to say that the organization has been cross-pollinated by people who have membership in other groups. And they don't seem to be able to draw the line between what these other groups want and what the scv should be doing or not doing as the case may be. It's a trend I don't like.[45]

Outlaw's close friend, Norman Dasinger, expressed the same grief, "I love the organization, but when you cozy up to folks and they cozy up to you, you got to fish or cut bait with them."[46]

The scv did not cut bait. Instead a showdown election was held in Memphis's famous Peabody Hotel from 31 July to 2 August 2002. As horses in Confederate regalia wandered the hotel hallways, the scv moved further toward the radicals. Once again, Lyons was the principal protagonist. During the planning for the January 2000 rally in Columbia, South Carolina, Lyons apparently began a close relationship with R. G. "Ronnie" Wilson, who would take the scv Commander's position in 2002. Both men were key organizers of the Columbia demonstration and helped to produce a videotape of the day's events to sell under the aegis of the South Carolina scv, where Wilson was second in command. That same year, tax records reveal, Wilson joined the board of Lyons's slrc, the first of many ties that would soon knot together Wilson, Lyons, and the slrc.

After his August 2000 election to the scv General Executive Council, Lyons politicked within the scv incessantly, establishing a secretive network of scv extremists who often refer to themselves as "Lunatics." Lyons further cemented his bond with Wilson when he hired Wilson's daughter, Allison Schaum, as a legal assistant in November 2001. During the same period,

Lyons's SLRC appraised growing numbers of cases detailing attacks on the Confederate battle flag and other "heritage violations."

Toward the end of 2001, Lyons announced his candidacy for a top-tier SCV post: Commander of the Army of Northern Virginia, a position that is traditionally the stepping-stone to the highest position in the organization, SCV Commander. With widespread support for Lyons at the state level, gag orders that prohibited talking about internal matters to the press (meaning talking about Lyons's white supremacy) were rammed through in eight states: Alabama, Kentucky, Louisiana, Maryland, Missouri, South Carolina, Tennessee, and Virginia. In addition, men in the extremist wing of the SCV won important victories in state conventions leading up to the 2002 SCV elections in Memphis. In Alabama, David Allen, a member of the LS, was elected Commander and Charles Yow, who worked with Lyons's SLRC, became state division Judge Advocate. In Louisiana, Chuck Rand, a prominent LS member, became state Commander. In Virginia, Michael Masters, a CCC leader, won two state SCV posts. In South Carolina, Christopher M. Sullivan, editor of the glossy neo-Confederate *Southern Partisan* magazine, received a lesser leadership post. Similar results were seen elsewhere. Men like Allen and Rand were not the only LS members who were also in the SCV. Although their number is not known, McCredie said in a 2001 email, "I am a member of the League of the South, as are several thousand members of the Sons of Confederate Veterans, including other members of the General Executive Council."[47] McCredie's point was echoed a few months later by Lyons. "We are not some minority anomaly," Lyons told *The Independent* of North Carolina in January 2002. "The reform faction has been moving to essentially managerial control of the organization for several years now."[48]

Meanwhile, Ronnie Wilson was running for Commander in Chief in an election that received little press coverage. In the early 1990s Wilson had written numerous op-ed pieces for the CCC tabloid warning of Communist plots and praising Joseph McCarthy, and on his web site between 2002 and 2003 he sold an anti-Semitic work called *Barbarians Inside the Gates* that praised the *Protocols of the Learned Elders of Zion*.[49] In 1997, Wilson shared the stage at the CCC's annual convention with white nationalist Samuel T. Francis and, since the late-1990s, worked with CCC activist Jerry Creech in heading the South Carolina Heritage Coalition. Wilson's campaign web site marked him as an extremist, opposed to "the homosexual agenda, abortion and other Godless causes." If he were to win, Wilson vowed, the SCV would "teach the truth and culture of Confederate heritage," attack the "anti-Confederate climate," and redirect a "drifting, wobbly American society." He asked supporters to help him "put some muscle" into the SCV's political efforts: "May the spirit of resistance that lived in [our ancestors'] long-still hearts always live in ours!" As the campaign heated up, Wilson went further, promising to punish those who had had the temerity to criticize racists and other extremists in the scv.

And they were punished. Gilbert Jones, who denounced neo-Nazis in the scv on the *cbs Evening News* before the Memphis convention, was hounded off the stage during the annual oratory contest by scvers booing and throwing trash. The man who beat Lyons in the race for Commander of the Army of Northern Virginia, Charles Hawks, a friend of Jones's, was called a "traitor" on the scv Dispatch email list. In a matter of months after his election as scv Commander in August 2002, Wilson appointed members of white supremacist groups to a series of key national staff positions in the scv. They included David Allen, head of the Alabama ls, who was named Aide-de-Camp to the general staff; Charles Kelly Barrow, another ls member, who became the organization's Historian-in-Chief; Ronald Casteel, head of the Missouri ls, who was named Chief of Staff; Charles "Chuck" McMichael, a member of the radical neo-Confederate FreeMississippi.org group, who was appointed Genealogist-in-Chief; and segregationist Leonard "Flagpole" Wilson, a national director of the ccc, who became staff Parliamentarian. Wilson also decided to retain Chaplain Weaver, even though his pro-slavery tract had now been made public. Arguably, even more noteworthy was Wilson's choice of North Carolinian Boyd Cathey as a second general staff Aide-de-Camp. Since 1989, Cathey had been a member of the Editorial Advisory Committee of the *Journal of Historical Review*—an anti-Semitic periodical published by the world's leading Holocaust denial outfit.[50] Wilson also packed the scv's Media/Public Relations Committee with extremists, amongst them Virginian Bragdon Bowling. Bowling is connected to Kirk Lyons through an apparently clandestine circle within the scv—the "John Wilkes Booth Camp" whose membership overlaps with Lyons's "Lunatics." Although there is no official scv recognition of this camp, the group named after Abraham Lincoln's assassin came to light after photographs of its meetings appeared on a web site recounting the scv Virginia state convention in Roanoke in 2001.

Wilson also appointed Allen Sullivant, who had built his and Lyons's campaign web sites, to the key position of Chief of Heritage Defense. Sullivant was best known within the scv as the founder of a web site called the Order of White Trash, a gossipy collection of writings about the scv that strongly sided with Wilson and Lyons in the 2002 elections and has long carried a downloadable graphics section full of racist caricatures. Sullivant has also operated an unofficial scv email list called "The Echo" since 1996— the year Dasinger banned discussion of secession from the official scv Dispatch email listserv. There would be no such bans on "The Echo," Sullivant vowed, describing his list as "an uncensored free-speech forum, serving Sons of Confederate Veterans members and the Electronic Confederate Community at large." This uncensored "community" exchanged crudely racist jokes and comments until an *Intelligence Report* exposé made the postings public in 2002.[51]

Another outcome of the 2002 Memphis elections was the passage of a ban on scv members speaking to the press. It was proposed by Leonard "Flag-pole" Wilson, who, according to several accounts from those who attended, waved his cane in the air as he hotly advocated its passage, shouting, "The enemy is outside the door!" The ban mandated that it was scv "official policy that no member under any circumstance is authorized or permitted to attack a fellow member in any public forum" and "in particular, the generally hostile news media." If any member ignored the order, he would be "subject to disciplinary action," and "officers of the Confederacy are hereby instructed to initiate such procedures." By November 2002, actions had been brought against Gilbert Jones and at least two other "treasonous" scv members.

Wilson's appointments left the extremist faction just shy of a majority on the General Executive Council (GEC). This became apparent during the GEC's March 2003 meeting when appeals against the suspension of scvers were to be heard. Much to the surprise of Wilson, who assumed he controlled a majority of GEC votes, several former scv Commanders, all of whom are *ex officio* members of the GEC, arrived unexpectedly and voted against him. Among them was Norman Dasinger. As a result, final decisions on the expulsions of Gilbert Jones and others were delayed, except in the case of Hilderman.

The extremist faction then changed tactics, proposing constitutional amendments, primarily drafted by Lyons and to be voted on at the 2003 convention, which would reduce the power of the past Commanders who had defied Wilson's attempts to expel Save the scv supporters from the scv. One measure would strip past scv Commanders of their right to vote on the GEC, another would put the scv's Heritage Defense Chief, an appointee of the Commander, on the GEC, and a third amendment would remove from the GEC the Commander of the Military Order of the Stars and Bars. These amendments to the scv constitution were opposed by just over a third of those who came to Asheville, North Carolina, for the 2003 convention. This meant they failed because amendments needed a two-thirds majority for adoption. The most important measure to Wilson—removing past Commanders' voting rights—was rejected by just fifty-one votes, but the fact that more than sixty percent of those in attendance at Asheville had voted for the changes reveals the depth of pro-extremist sentiment.[52]

Despite this, the extremist faction was disappointed by the failure of its amendments during the Asheville convention. James M. McManus of the John Wilkes Booth camp of pro-Wilson hard-liners within the scv lamented:

> The overall result of Saturday's business meeting was a general waste of time, as the grannies and their lawyers filibustered and delayed any real constructive business from being done. So while our enemies are advancing . . . we leave many important actions on the table.[53]

Although Wilson's reforms failed in Asheville, he took his message to schools and churches as part of an "educational outreach program," which included the launch of the *Southern Mercury* in July 2003, a magazine subtitled "Unpardoned, Unrepentant, Unreconstructed" and described by Wilson as "the latest weapon in the war for our Southern heritage."[54] The magazine, which is filled with articles by white supremacists and other extremists, is published under the rubric of the then newly created Foundation for the Preservation of American Culture, a nonprofit arm of the scv.

The *Southern Mercury* is thick with nostalgia for the antebellum South, and features revisionist takes on slavery. In one article, Frank Conner, a well-known segregationist and author of *The South Under Siege (1830–2000)*, argued that the scv should fight to protect the "unique belief-system of the Old South" that has been undermined by desegregation:

> Beginning in the late 1950s, under the guise of providing the Southern blacks with civil rights, the Northern liberals sent the federal government to invade the South and systematically destroy the Old South and crush and suppress its belief system.[55]

The magazine's board was stacked with Wilson allies, including James Ronald Kennedy of the ls and Boyd Cathey of the Institute for Historical Review, and was part of Wilson's effort to radicalize the scv and to take on its perceived enemies.[56]

In February 2004, scv Commander Wilson, and his Lt. Commander Denne Sweeney, proposed staging an emergency scv convention. The idea was to surprise the membership with the convention in the hopes that few would be able to attend. Because voting in the scv is based on those who show up at conventions, radicals would thus dominate the special convention and pass the amendments that failed in Asheville. The plan never came to fruition, however, as it was voted down by local scv units, thus deferring the contest between the radicals and more moderate scv members to the 2004 annual convention in Dalton, Georgia.

By the time of the Dalton convention, the scv's politics had become even more complex. The Commander's race had broken into three factions: Save the scv's Walt Hilderman running on an antiracist platform, Denne Sweeney representing the extremists, and J. Troy Massey representing "moderates" (in their own words) affiliated with former Commander Peter Orlebeke. The blocs fronted by Hilderman and Massey rejected the Wilson faction, led by Sweeney, but the "moderates" would not openly denounce racism and did not work openly to stop the expulsions Wilson initiated against the Save the scvers.[57]

It was thought that the over one thousand scv delegates at Dalton would decide the balance of power between these groups, but instead the rancorous divisions continued. No faction emerged as the total victor, although the Orlebeke faction managed to win in tight votes all six open leadership positions in the scv's three geographic divisions, plus the national Lt. Commander post, meaning "moderates" secured seven positions on the GEC. The amendments to the scv constitution designed by Kirk Lyons were again defeated, but the battle over the future of the scv was postponed to the group's summer 2005 Nashville convention.[58] One thing, however, was decided at the Dalton meeting in 2004. The resolution demanding Hilderman's expulsion confirmed the scv would not dedicate itself to rooting out the racists in its midst.

SCV Radicals Expand Their Efforts

The extremists did not leave Dalton empty-handed. Most important, they won the Commander's post, electing former Texas division Commander and Wilson's ally Denne Sweeney by just 129 votes. Sweeney's reign looked to resemble that of his predecessor. On his campaign web site, Sweeney proposed creating a web site to challenge "Enemies of the South," including both the Anti-Defamation League and the Southern Poverty Law Center, and vowed to continue the purge of Save the scv members begun by Wilson.[59] Every person who was suspended received a McCarthyesque letter in June 2004 that demanded that they formally renounce their criticisms and "see the error of their ways."[60] At Dalton radicals also passed several key resolutions. One condemned "political and racial extremism" that "includes an all out war against all things Confederate and those of Confederate ancestry including the fomenting of race hatred against Southerners and Confederate Southern-Americans." Its target was "The NAACP, Jesse Jackson, Al Sharpton and Muslim terrorists." Another resolution "demanded" that the attorneys general of the United States and Alabama investigate the Southern Poverty Law Center, and further measures awarded Lyons's SLRC $20,000 for future legal battles and proclaimed all SCV members to be part of the "ethnicity" Lyons created, "Confederate Southern Americans."[61]

After his July 2004 election in Dalton, Sweeney moved swiftly, appointing several hard-liners to key leadership positions. H. Rondel Rumberg, a member of both the CCC and the LS, became the SCV's new Chaplain-in-Chief. Paul Gramling Jr. was appointed Chief of Heritage Defense. A past Louisiana Commander, Gramling has praised Lloyd E. Lenard's novel *The Last Confederate Flag* (see Chapter 8), which describes black violence against whites defending the Confederate battle flag. James "Jim" Dark, a close Sweeney ally, became the new Adjutant-in-Chief. Another hard-liner, Bragdon Bowling, was named National Press Officer.[62] In his first week, Bowling issued a series of press releases, including one charging that the NAACP had "lost its course as a true civil rights organization" and demanding that its tax-exempt status be revoked.[63]

Sweeney looked to face stiff opposition, particularly from past national Commanders, in his two-year term. After the 2004 Dalton convention, fellow radical James McManus in an SCV Dispatch email said that Wilson, the outgoing Commander, told him, "It's going to be a long next two years. You are going to see a lot of 9-to-11 votes going against Denne."[64] Another radical, identifying himself in a Dispatch email as "Roger Ramjet," agreed that future votes would be contentious, but said he expected the SCV to continue moving to the right. "There is a hodgepodge group on the GEC, roughly 50% 'reform' and 50% 'granny' [the radicals' favored name for SCV moderates], or 'old school,'" he wrote.[65] John Adams, GEC member and Florida division Commander until 2004, when he was ejected from his jobs as SCV Web Master and Adjutant-in-Chief in 2003 following revelations that he had vindictively signed up the present author for an array of pornographic Internet services.[66] He summed up the radical view of the Dalton elections in an August 2004 SCV Dispatch email: "Palatka [where Florida division elections were held earlier in the year] and Dalton solved nothing," he wrote. "If anything, they gave false hope to a dying breed of do-nothing grannies, who actually think they have a snowball's chance in Hell of turning back the clock to the 'good old days.'"[67]

By November 2004, Adams seemed to be correct given what the SCV decided to do with former self-declared warrior for the Aryan race, Floridian

Michael Tubbs. It was revealed in a fall 2004 *Intelligence Report* story that Tubbs, the scv's Florida Chaplain and the ls Vice Chairman of its Northeast Florida chapter, had stolen weapons from Fort Bragg, North Carolina, in 1987, claiming they were "for the kkk." Three years later, federal law enforcement found five of Tubbs's weapons caches, filled with machine guns, several pounds of tnt, land mines, grenades, and forty-five pounds of c-4 plastic explosives. Also found were lists of intended targets, including newspapers, television stations, and businesses owned by Jews and blacks. Tubbs had penned a Knights of the New Order pledge dedicating his life "from this moment forward to fostering the welfare of the white Aryan race."[68]

The scv's decision regarding Tubbs was distressing for those hoping for a nonracist organization. The Florida division scv Commander, Douglas Dawson, sent out a letter on 18 October 2004 that criticized the *Intelligence Report* article for being "based on sensationalized newspaper articles of the time" and said that Tubbs's "debt to society was paid in-full when he was released." Dawson also said that Tubbs "has served the organization without reproach."[69] Dawson left the decision on expulsion up to Tubbs's local camp, which took no action. At the time of writing, Tubbs remained active in the ls.

The battle between the moderates and Sweeney's allies accelerated in late 2004 and came to a head in January 2005, when Sweeney suspended three moderate members of the scv's gec. After the three sued for reinstatement in a Tennessee court, the judge in the case barred Sweeney from the gec and reinstated the three moderates. A later ruling reinstated Sweeney, but forbade him to suspend any gec members until the case was resolved. As the case progressed, it became apparent that the scv was falling apart as radicals continued to increase their power and moderates began to leave the scv. The power of the racist radicals was reflected in 2005 when scv official Jim McManus posted "Apology to the Black Race" on the scv Dispatch. Versions of this "apology" have also appeared on Klan and other white supremacist web sites. In it, members of "the Adamic, pink complexioned race (better known to you as the White race) that came to these shores from Europe, England, Scotland, Ireland, and Iceland" mockingly apologize to "the entire Black race living in America" for, amongst other things, ending slavery, "thinking we could civilize you," and "teaching you to add and subtract," the latter supposedly enabling members of "the Black race" to "count your children . . . on your fingers and sometimes toes."[70] After the *Intelligence Report* made McManus's posting public, he faced no sanction for his actions and retained his scv leadership position.[71]

It was at this point that Sweeney made a smart tactical decision. Once Sweeney and his allies were put back in power by the Tennessee court, they began soliciting signatures requesting a special convention to amend the SCV constitution. Sweeney claimed authority for this maneuver under Mississippi, not Tennessee, law—a law that allows private groups like the SCV to call constitutional conventions when five percent of the group's membership signs a petition. Although the SCV files its annual reports in and is chartered in Tennessee, it is also chartered in Mississippi—a legacy of the McCain era. The radicals gathered enough signatures to call the special constitutional convention for 23 April 2005 in Concord, North Carolina.

Just forty percent of the SCV membership was represented through their camp commanders at the special convention, and it soon became clear that most were supporters of Sweeney, who had strongly urged his allies to attend. The 1,701 delegates, representing 379 camps, passed two key changes. The first, passed by ninety-six percent of the vote, removed all past SCV commanders, save the three most recent, from the GEC. The second, passed by ninety-three percent of the vote, removed from a nonvoting GEC position the commander of the MOSB.

Now that moderate voting power on the GEC had been undermined by eliminating GEC members' ex officio positions, Sweeney led a move that same day to eject Anthony Hodges as SCV lieutenant commander. Sweeney replaced Hodges with an ally, Christopher M. Sullivan, editor of the *Southern Partisan*. Also stripped of their elected posts were key moderates including Thomas Tarry Beasley, commander of the Army of Tennessee, Beasley deputy John French, and Beau Cantrell, commander of the Army of the Trans-Mississippi. Beasley and Cantrell lost their posts on the GEC as a result, leaving only staunch Sweeneyites on the governing board. The now-purged GEC also voted to negotiate a formal break with the MOSB, remove Louisiana leaders Ed Cailleteau and Beau Cantrell, whose GEC membership had just been stripped, as co-chairs of the upcoming July 2005 convention, and donate a further $10,000 of SCV funds to Lyons's law firm, the SLRC.[72]

The events at Concord left moderates throughout the SCV furious, and key leaders denounced what they saw as Sweeney's devious tactics. "In the Missouri division," that state's commander, John Christensen, wrote in an email addressed to Sweeney,

> we believe we can disagree on an issue without being vile. . . . We believe
> that with free speech and assembly, discussion affords protection against the
> spread of noxious doctrine. . . . The personal vendettas, purges, recrimina-

tions and rancor sown by your administration are not good for any organization and may become the seeds of destruction for our beloved Sons of Confederate Veterans.[73]

The scv, which recently had as many as 36,000 in its ranks, began to bleed members. Some started new groups: Robert E. Lee societies were established as history clubs by expelled scv members, and in April 2005, moderate Robert Murphree in Mississippi chartered a new group called the United Sons of Confederate Veterans. Stripped of his leadership post at the Concord special convention, John French had a warning for those who remained in the scv, saying that they "will awaken one morning to [find] nothing left of the scv. All assets will be gone and the once proud organization left to rot."[74]

French's words were prophetic. The two years of Sweeney's reign would lead to an exodus of twenty-five percent of the scv's membership, which was down to 27,000 by early 2006 according to the group's executive director, Ben Sewell. The group's reduction in size actually made many radical scv members happy. "The slackers and the grannies have been purged from our ranks," Lyons exulted in December 2005. Now, Lyons added, the scv needs to become "a modern, 21st century Christian war machine capable of uniting the Confederate community and leading it to ultimate victory."[75] It became commonplace for scv members to simultaneously maintain membership in extremist groups, so much so that in January 2006, Gene Andrews, commander of an scv camp in Brentwood, Tennessee, casually boasted in a newsletter that he belonged both to the ccc and the ls. He went on to describe as "first class men among men" a group including Jared Taylor, who edits *American Renaissance,* a racist periodical devoted to the idea that whites are smarter and less "pathological" than blacks.[76]

None of this bothers Denne Sweeney. He said in February 2006 he would be concerned only if scv members also belonged to a group that "espouses violence and overthrow and killing of black people" and added that he saw the ccc and ls as mere "borderline" groups.[77] That is not a view shared by the Republican National Committee or the Conservative Political Action Committee, both of which have described the ccc as a racist group that their members should avoid.[78]

As members continued to pour out of the scv in 2005–2006, new antiracist Confederate heritage groups began to pop up throughout the South. These included the Sons of the Confederacy in Triune, Tennessee; the Descendants of Confederate Veterans in Seabrook, Texas; and other groups in Florida, Louisiana, Mississippi, Oklahoma, and Virginia. The scv, meanwhile, continued to move rightward.

In February 2006, Sweeney, aided substantially by Lyons, produced a proposed new constitution for the scv to replace the one adopted in 1896. Deleting the original prologue, the new constitution removed all mention of a reunited United States and also all references to the Pledge of Allegiance, which many scv radicals despised as an oath to the godless, anti-Southern North. It removed impediments to scv members taking on political causes, ended the original constitution's strongly apolitical flavor, and vastly expanded the power of the scv Commander.

During the August 2006 scv convention, a version of this constitution, with some amendments, was accepted by the membership. The document gave unprecedented power to the national Commander, now the newly elected Sweeney acolyte, Christopher M. Sullivan. Other Sweeney allies were elected to top posts in the scv's three armies. The election also solidified the hold on the scv of Lyons and his slrc. Two of the law firm's board members, Roy Burl McCoy and Bragdon Bowling, won posts on the scv's executive board.

Between the election of Sullivan and the passing of a new constitution, the radicals had finally consolidated their hold on the scv. The ls saw it the same way, enthusing on its web site that "the Sons of Confederate Veterans have endorsed a radical direction." Discouraged moderates continue to trickle out of the scv, as they have for several years. "Our convention committee presided over the funeral of what we all once thought of as the scv," lamented the commander of the New Orleans scv camp that hosted the 2006 annual convention. "The scv that we knew was dumped as a rotting carcass in a dung heap."[79]

Conclusion: White Supremacy in the Sons of Confederate Veterans

Since its inception in the late 1800s, the scv has existed to glorify the Confederacy, a regime built on the bastions of white supremacy and slavery. For decades, the scv was an active participant in efforts to keep the South white, with its leaders, in particular Dr. William D. McCain, avidly participating in efforts to keep the South segregated. This was the case until the 1980s, when the waning power of McCain led to new leadership and an attempt to distance the organization, if not from the Confederacy's racist roots, at least from modern variants of white supremacy, particularly the Klan.

The period from the late 1980s until the mid 1990s was one of major reforms for the scv. The organization condemned racist and other extremist groups and passed a resolution asking that its membership steer clear of white supremacist organizations such as the Klan, the ccc, and the ls. One scv Chief of Heritage Defense, P. Charles Lunsford, even lost his high post for cavorting with the ccc in 1994. But this antiracist era did not last long. Radical racial activists like Kirk Lyons realized that their hopes for pushing white supremacist ideas into the mainstream were becoming more and more difficult. Nearly all Americans in the 1970s and the 1980s were disavowing racism in the wake of the civil rights movement, but an organization filled with conservative, Southern, white men devoted to memorializing the Confederate soldier appeared to be a riper target than Middle America—and indeed it was.

The scv continues to shed members who cannot countenance the idea of being involved with members of organizations such as the ccc and ls that the splc describes as hate groups, but these hardcore extremists are tightening their grip nevertheless. The scv may not have as many members or as much money in the years to come, but it will certainly belong to the extremists.

Notes

1. Ironically, Sam Currin was at one time an ally of the scv's nemesis, the Southern Poverty Law Center (splc). He helped the splc sue the White Patriot Party in the 1980s and appears on the splc's introductory videotape filmed in 1988.
2. Beirich, Heidi, and Potok, Mark. "A House Divided," *Intelligence Report,* Southern Poverty Law Center, 105 (2002): 44.
3. The full text of the resolution, passed unanimously and adopted at the scv General Convention, Oklahoma City, Oklahoma, 19 August 1989, was printed in the scv magazine, *Confederate Veteran.* See "Resolution," *Confederate Veteran,* (March–April 1990): 3.
4. Beirich, Heidi. "Heritage Group Leaders Welcome Back the kkk," *Intelligence Report,* Southern Poverty Law Center, 114 (2004): 5.
5. This history is recounted in Foster, Gaines M. *Ghosts of the Confederacy: Defeat, the Lost Cause, and the Emergence of the New South, 1865–1913.* (New York: Oxford University Press, 1987).
6. Cox, Karen L. *Dixie's Daughters: The United Daughters of the Confederacy and the Preservation of Confederate Culture.* (Gainesville: University Press of Florida, 2003): 14.
7. Sebesta, Edward H. "Sons of Confederate Veterans (scv) How They Got Their Name." On-line: http://www.templeofdemocracy.com/SCV.htm [accessed 2 December 2004]. Sebesta refers to Foster, *Ghosts of the Confederacy,* (1987): 108.
8. Blight, David W. *Race and Reunion: The Civil War in American Memory.* (Cambridge, MA: Harvard University Press, 2001): 181.
9. Beirich, Heidi, and Potok, Mark. "A House Divided," *Intelligence Report,* Southern Poverty Law Center, 105 (2002): 45.
10. Blight, *Race and Reunion,* (2001): 277.

11. Cox, *Dixie's Daughters*, (2003): 120.

12. Lee, Walter E. III. "The African Slave Trade," *UDC Magazine*, 52.4 (1989): 18–19.

13. A video of the event is available: *Southern Heritage Celebration 2000, January 8, 2000 Rally* Video Sons of Confederate Veterans, available from scv, PO Box 11719, Columbia, SC 29211.

14. The event's costs were picked up by the Mississippi State Sovereignty Commission. See McCain, W. D. [William D.] "Address by Dr. W. D. McCain, President of Mississippi Southern College, Hattiesburg, Mississippi, before the Pro-American Forum at Chicago, Illinois, 9 September 1960." Text of the speech is found in Sovereignty Commission document 99-105-0-1-1-1-1. On-line: http://www.mdah.state .ms.us/arlib/sovcomm.html [accessed 10 September 2006].

15. Katagiri, Yasuhiro. *The Mississippi State Sovereignty Commission*. (Jackson: University Press of Mississippi, 2001): 58–61.

16. Hawkins, Robert L. "Obituary: William D. McCain," *Confederate Veteran*, 41.5 (1993): 45.

17. McWhorter, Diane. *Carry Me Home, Birmingham, Alabama: The Climactic Battle of the Civil Rights Revolution*. (New York: Simon & Schuster, 2002): 97–99.

18. Wilson was a master organizer in the White Citizens' Council, essentially creating the entire pro-segregationist infrastructure in middle Alabama—see McMillen, Neil R. *The Citizens' Council: Organized Resistance to the Second Reconstruction (1954–1964)*. (Urbana: University of Illinois Press, 1971): 48–49.

19. Potok, Mark. "Sharks in the Mainstream," *Intelligence Report*, Southern Poverty Law Center, 93 (1999): 16–21. Even with the Republican ban, more than twenty state-level Republican officeholders, including the governor of Mississippi, Haley Barbour, and Mississippi congressman Roger Wicker, spoke to ccc events in the South between 2000 and 2004—see Beirich, Heidi, and Moser, Bob. "Communing with the Council," *Intelligence Report*, Southern Poverty Law Center, 115 (2004): 10–18.

20. Lunsford, Charles. "Heritage Defense in the scv: A Comment," *Southern Heritage Magazine*, 2.4 (1994): 17.

21. Lunsford, Charles. "Hilderman's Attack in the Media Yesterday," scv Dispatch email list, (17 August 2004).

22. Beirich and Potok, "A House Divided," (2002): 47.

23. Ibid.

24. Deason, Ed. Interview by Heidi Beirich, 2001.

25. Beirich and Potok, "A House Divided," (2002): 48.

26. Ibid. Kalas left the neo-Confederate movement after the 11 September 2001 attacks on the World Trade Center and Pentagon, saying it had become too radical even for him.

27. Beirich and Potok, "A House Divided," (2002): 48.

28. The only detailed profile of Lyons that exists is Mark Potok's "Into the Lyons Den," *Intelligence Report*, Southern Poverty Law Center, 99 (2000): 18–23.

29. For more on Beam, see Potok, Mark. "The Firebrand," *Intelligence Report*, Southern Poverty Law Center, 106 (2002): 11–21.

30. Lyons's law firm has never won an "ethnicity" case and he has been thrown out of several courtrooms for lacking the legal basis for a suit. In 2003, Lyons was

personally fined $10,000 by a Virginia federal court for refusing to drop a case in which he was arguing that his clients had suffered discrimination because they were "Confederate, Southern Americans." For more on the Southern Legal Resource Center's lawsuits, see Beirich, Heidi, and Potok, Mark. "Cashing in on the Confederacy," *Intelligence Report,* Southern Poverty Law Center, 109 (2003): 61–67, and Beirich, Heidi. "Neo-Confederate Attorney Gets Slapped Down-Again," *Intelligence Report,* Southern Poverty Law Center, 113 (2004): 4.

31. Sons of Confederate Veterans. "How to Report a Heritage Violation." On-line: http://www.scv.org/heritageReporting.php [accessed 2 December 2004 and 10 September 2006].

32. American Friends of the British National Party. (Arlington, VA: 22 April 2000). Transcribed from videotape.

33. Ibid.

34. Blow, Steve. "Confederate Sons Defends Use of Flag," *Dallas Morning News,* (6 October 1996): 33A.

35. Weaver's booklets caused an uproar in late 2000 and early 2001 when they were found in Maurice Bessinger's barbecue restaurant, Piggy Park, in Columbia, SC. Most major supermarket chains refused to carry Bessinger's barbecue sauces as a result. The theological war thesis is outlined in Chapter 2, and Bessinger's neo-Confederate position and the controversy over his barbecue sauce are reviewed in Chapter 6. See also Southern Poverty Law Center. "Racist Lawyer Joins scv Leadership," *Intelligence Report,* 101 (2001): 3.

36. Dasinger, Norman. Interview by Heidi Beirich, 2001.

37. Hill, Michael. "Late Development," *Southern Patriot,* 5.4 (1998): 2.

38. *Southern Heritage Celebration 2000, January 8, 2000 Rally.* Sons of Confederate Veterans, available from scv, PO Box 11719, Columbia, SC 29211.

39. Southern Poverty Law Center. "Racist Lawyer," (2001): 3.

40. For coverage of this rally, which was billed by the League of the South as a "Southern Independence Day Celebration," see Reevers, Jay. "Confederate Flag Rally Held in Ala.," *Associated Press,* (4 March 2000); cnn News Service. "Marchers Rally at Alabama's Capital to Demand Respect for Cultural Rights." On-line: http://www.cnn.com/TRANSCRIPTS/0003/04/wv.06.html [accessed 2 December 2004]; cnn News Service. "Marchers Want Confederate Flag to Fly Again in Alabama," (4 March 2000). On-line: http://www.cnn.com/2000/US/03/04/confederate.rally [accessed 5 October 2006].

41. Deason, Ed. Interview by Heidi Beirich, 2001.

42. Southern Poverty Law Center. "Rebels with a Cause," *Intelligence Report,* 99 (2000): 11.

43. The first exposés of extremists in the scv's ranks were run in the *Intelligence Report.* The stories were by Heidi Beirich and Mark Potok—see "A House Divided" (105, 2002), and "A War Within" (108, 2002). According to former members of the group, including Jones and Hilderman, many scvers were aware that Lyons and his allies represented something radical in the scv, but it was not until they read of the extent of the infiltration of the group in the *Intelligence Report* that they became fully aware of the situation.

44. Quoted in Beirich, Heidi, and Potok, Mark. "A War Within," *Intelligence Report,* Southern Poverty Law Center, 108 (2002): 45.

45. Outlaw, Perry. Interview by Heidi Beirich, 2001.

46. Dasinger, Norman. Interview by Heidi Beirich, 2001.

47. Beirich and Potok, "A War Within," (2002): 39.

48. Elliston, Jon. "Uncivil War," *The Independent,* Durham, NC (16 January 2002). On-line: http://www.indyweek.com/durham/2002-01-16/cover.html [accessed 2 December 2004].

49. Beirich, Heidi. "Hijacking Heritage," *Intelligence Report,* Southern Poverty Law Center, 111 (2003): 48. *Protocols of the Learned Elders of Zion.* Trans. Victor E. Marsden (1934) is an infamous anti-Semitic Czarist-era Russian forgery that purports to reveal a Jewish plot to take over the world.

50. Cathey has written articles for *Southern Partisan,* the Council of Conservative Citizens' *Citizens Informer,* and the scv's *Southern Mercury.* He is a leading figure in neo-Confederacy—see Beirich, Heidi, and Potok, Mark. "40 To Watch," *Intelligence Report,* Southern Poverty Law Center, 111 (2003): 18.

51. Beirich and Potok, "A War Within," (2002): 41.

52. More details regarding the Asheville results can be found in Beirich, Heidi, and Potok, Mark. "Unfinished Business," *Intelligence Report,* Southern Poverty Law Center, 111 (2003): 57–58.

53. Quoted in ibid., 58.

54. Ibid.

55. Conner, Frank. "Death of a Nation? The Almost Forgotten Body and Soul of the Sons of Confederate Veterans," *Southern Mercury,* 1.1 (2003): 13. See also Conner, Frank. *The South Under Siege (1830–2000): A History of the Relations Between North and South.* (Newnan, GA: Collards Publishing Company, 2002), where Conner makes the same arguments but at much greater length.

56. See Cathey, Boyd. "Merchants of Hate, Morris Dees, The Southern Poverty Law Center, and the Attack on Southern Culture," *Southern Mercury,* 1.1 (2003): 14–18, 22–26. On-line: http://www.dixienet.org/Cathey1.html [accessed 2 December 2004]; Cathey, Boyd. "Merchants of Hate: How the Southern Poverty Law Center Is Attacking Southern Heritage," *Citizens Informer,* 35.3 (2004): 1, 4, 7–10.

57. Jeff Massey, head of the mosb from 2002 to 2004 and J. Troy Massey's brother, contacted the splc several times to discuss the extremist faction and its activities. In 1998, Jeff Massey, an Oklahoma attorney, denounced Kirk Lyons and the Oklahoma Heritage Coalition's demand to fly a Confederate battle flag over the Oklahoma statehouse. Massey directed reporters to alleged links between Lyons and Oklahoma City bomber Timothy McVeigh, who allegedly phoned Lyons's office the day before the April 1995 bombing—see Sewell, Dan. "Confederates' Activist Has Klan Tie," *Associated Press,* (12 September 1998).

58. Beirich, Heidi. "scv Standoff," *Intelligence Report,* Southern Poverty Law Center, 114 (2004): 29.

59. Ibid., 30.

60. Save the Sons of Confederate Veterans. "Purge Letter," (21 June 2004). On-line: http://www.savethescv.org/Purge_Letter.htm [accessed 2 December 2004 and 10 September 2006].

61. These measures are addressed in Beirich, "scv Standoff," (2004): 30–31.

62. These appointments can be found at the Sons of Confederate Veterans national web site: http://www.scv.org.

63. Bowling, Bragdon. "Press Release: NAACP Engaging in Politics—501(c) 3—A Level Playing Field," *Sons of Confederate Veterans Press Release*, SCV Dispatch email list (2 August 2004).

64. Quoted in Beirich, "SCV Standoff," (2004): 31.

65. Beirich, "SCV Standoff," (2004): 31.

66. Potok, Mark. "Dirty Tricks," *Intelligence Report*, 112 (2003): 6–9.

67. Beirich, "SCV Standoff," (2004): 29–31.

68. Potok, Mark. "C-4 and the Confederacy," *Intelligence Report*, Southern Poverty Law Center, 115 (2004): 31.

69. Dawson, Douglas. Letter addressed to "Florida Division Membership." 18 October 2004.

70. The entire "apology" is over two thousand words long.

71. Potok, Mark. "The Year in Hate," *Intelligence Report*, Southern Poverty Law Center, 117 (2005): 50.

72. Beirich, Heidi, and Potok, Mark. "Uncivil War," *Intelligence Report*, Southern Poverty Law Center, 118 (2005): 48–49.

73. Quoted in Beirich, Heidi, and Potok, Mark. "Into the Wild," *Intelligence Report*, Southern Poverty Law Center, 121 (2006): 16.

74. Ibid.

75. Ibid., 17–18.

76. Ibid., 18.

77. Sweeney was interviewed by Heidi Beirich in February 2006. Parts of those interviews are published in ibid., 16–21.

78. Ibid., 18.

79. "SCV Once Again Elects Radical National Leaders," *Intelligence Report*, 123 (2006) 3.

Afterword: Nationalizing Neo-Confederacy?

EUAN HAGUE AND EDWARD H. SEBESTA

As we were developing this manuscript in November 2004, George W. Bush was reelected president of the United States.[1] Following the election results, the neo-Confederate League of the South (LS) published two maps on its web site. Under the heading "two nations?" each map showed the United States divided into blue Northern states and red Southern states, one labeled "1861" the other "2004."[2] Gleefully quoting the evaluation by British journalist Simon Jenkins that the election was the "Confederates' revenge," the neo-Confederates' implication was clear.[3] The United States was once again "two nations." In 1861 this division had resulted in secession and the attempt by Southern states to gain independence and establish their own nation-state — why not secede once more in 2004?[4]

A week before the election, James Webb, writing in the *Wall Street Journal,* also warmed neo-Confederate hearts by identifying the "Scots-Irish" as the decisive ethnic group in the upcoming vote.[5] The LS web site exuberantly proclaimed its familiar neo-Confederate message with an illustration of a sword-wielding, kilt-wearing Celtic warrior accompanying the text:

> With the decline of the 20th century megastate, culture and ethnicity are re-asserting themselves as organizing principles. So, for us, Anglo-Celtics of the South, this probably marks the first "mainstream" recognition of this phenomenon in the Americas.[6]

In his essay, Webb simplistically conflated culture and ethnicity to argue that Scots-Irish ethnic culture has produced "for 16 centuries" a "mix of fundamentalist religion and social populism," the members of this ethnic group being "tested through constant rebellions against centralized authority." Sounding like neo-Confederate ideologues Michael Hill and Thomas Fleming, Webb argued that during the civil rights era of the 1950s and 1960s the Republican Party became the electoral beneficiaries of the Scots-Irish ethnic group, which "was the dominant culture in the South."[7]

⌐ Despite Webb's antiquated conceptualization of culture, the article made one important point—there is a significant bloc of voters in the United States, many of them in so-called swing states, almost all of them white, who can fundamentally shape the result of an election. Whether they actively acknowledge it or not, many of these voters align themselves with neo-Confederate beliefs. Their political attitudes, claimed by Webb to be inherent in their Scots-Irish culture, include opposition to federalism and support for the patriarchal nuclear family, conservative Christianity, and the right to bear arms. Because Webb and others identify these political positions as cultural attributes, they are often not subjected to thorough analysis or critique. Rather because they are cultural, they are presumed to be intuitive or beyond the realm of conscious political thought. Yet, as Don Mitchell reminds us, "culture is politics by another name," and as a result the connections between an appeal to culture and the real political and material impacts of such an assertion must be explored.[8] It is imperative, therefore, that when we discuss culture we know what we are actually talking about. Culture is *not* an explanation for a belief—it is what must be explained.

This is the approach that we have taken in *Neo-Confederacy*. When advocates of neo-Confederacy invoke their Anglo-Celtic or Southern culture as a rationale for their beliefs, rather than accept this as an explanation, we have interrogated this articulation and its meaning. We have explored the development of neo-Confederacy and proposed that it is underpinned by ideas of irreconcilable racial and ethnic difference, white dominance, patriarchy, social Darwinism, and so-called orthodox Christianity. The Civil War, which destroyed the slave-owning society of the Confederacy, is understood by neo-Confederate activists to be the beginning of the decline of American society and even Western civilization, a decline accelerated by the civil rights gains initiated in the 1950s and 1960s. The involvement of the federal government in ensuring equality, equal rights, and the right to vote for all is perceived as an intolerable disruption of human inequalities that are both God-ordained and natural.

This current iteration of neo-Confederacy began in the late 1970s with the appearance of *Southern Partisan* magazine and the attractive Celtic South thesis of ethnic and cultural identity, which was used to underpin a belief in the distinctiveness of the Southern white population. It became public in the mid-1990s with the foundation of the League of the South on 25 August 1994 and the launch, in the *Washington Post*, of the New Dixie Manifesto on 29

October 1995. To explain and assess these developments, we have sought to demonstrate how current invocations of neo-Confederacy build on past ideas, be these from the Old South, the Lost Cause, or the segregationist White Citizens' Councils of the 1950s and 1960s. Our contributors have shown the understandings of race, gender, and religion in neo-Confederacy and demonstrated how these beliefs are practiced through music, literature, education, heritage organizations, and even in the sales of barbecue sauce.

Our collection has further evidenced that in the United States there is a curious acceptance of and reverence for the short-lived Confederacy and its legacies of racism and white supremacy. This is not confined to the Southern states. Brian Britt notes that "there is also a hard core of politically-motivated, right-wing neo-Confederates from the North as well as the South." One of these, Al Benson Jr. from Illinois, Britt quotes as saying, "There are a lot more of us Northern Confederates out there than most people realize."[9] Michael Hill stated in 1995 that his nascent LS had "a core membership from 38 states and the District of Columbia."[10] In uniting around symbols of the Confederate States and calling for the defense of so-called Southern heritage, neo-Confederate activists throughout the United States position themselves as supporters of tradition. Yet their intentions are hardly benign. In 1995 author Tony Horwitz compared a ten-person Ku Klux Klan march which was attended by many more police and reporters to a neo-Confederate rally ten miles away, which attracted thousands of supporters but no media presence:

> The Klan didn't come, but the scene was far more menacing, with several skinheads in the crowd and speakers who spewed venom at the state and its presumed agents among liberal and minority groups. Michael Hill, a professor who teaches history part time at the University of Alabama told several hundred cheering onlookers:
>
> > In remembering Randy Weaver in Idaho and the Branch Davidians in Waco, we must understand one thing above all else. Our enemies are willing to kill us. It is open season on anyone who has the audacity to question the dictates of an all-powerful federal government or the illicit rights bestowed on a deadly underclass that now fulfills a role similar to that of Hitler's brown-shirted street thugs in the 1930s.
>
> Such thinking seems eerily resonant in the wake of the Oklahoma bombing; if the state and its brownshirts are after you, better to strike first. And if the source of the nation's law is tyrannical, then lawlessness is justified. Yet this speech and others even more inflammatory didn't make the nightly news.

One reason: Mr. Hill wore a tie instead of a hood and took the podium as head of the blandly-named Southern League.[11]

In the second half of the twentieth century, "the South's sectional conscious-ness was resurging," noted veteran Republican Party observer Kevin Phillips.[12] Our analyses suggest that this resurgence is neither harmless nor marginal and that neo-Confederacy is playing an active role in American public life and political debate. Proponents of neo-Confederacy and neo-Confederate publi-cations demonstrate connections to prominent politicians, major universities and their faculties, and syndicated columnists like *Southern Partisan* contribu-tor Joseph Sobran and Charley Reese. Reese is lauded on neo-Confederate web sites and has stated in an manner echoing Michael Hill that "the cultural heritage of America that sets this country apart from all the others is Anglo-Celtic. . . . I prefer my own Anglo-Celtic culture to any other."[13] Another prominent essayist, Stanley Crouch, suggests that connections between neo-Confederate activists and members of the Republican Party have "real politi-cal import" but remain little discussed. Crouch continues:

What appears before us now is clear: Neo-Confederates with a disguised racial policy have risen to the top of the GOP. But this rise is something that has to remain under wraps, because in the era of Michael Jordan, one cannot just come out and be hardcore racist. That would be impolitic. . . . The racist of old would come right out and call an insulting name at those who raised his paranoia. But these guys are cagier. Or more cowardly.[14]

These prominent Republican politicians could be said to include those who have allowed themselves to be associated with neo-Confederate publica-tions like *Southern Partisan*, including regular contributor Pat Buchanan and interview subjects Trent Lott (former Mississippi senator and Senate majority leader), Jesse Helms (former North Carolina senator), Dick Armey (former Texas congressman and House majority leader), Phil Gramm (former Texas senator), Lindsay Graham (South Carolina senator), John Ashcroft (former Missouri senator and U.S. attorney general) and Thad Cochran (Mississippi senator). David Funderburk, a former U.S. House Representative for North Carolina from 1995 to 1997, was listed on *Southern Partisan*'s masthead as an advisor and contributor from 1986 to 1999; as noted in our introduction, Richard Quinn, owner and former editor of *Southern Partisan*, has close ties to Senator John McCain; and the *Partisan*'s former assistant editor, Richard Hines, once served in the South Carolina state senate and the Reagan ad-ministration. Other Republican officeholders, such as former Virginia senator

George Allen, have had contact with the Council of Conservative Citizens (ccc), and Senator John Cornyn of Texas, the chairman of the Senate Judiciary Subcommittee on Immigration, Border Security, and Citizenship, held a September 2006 meeting on Capitol Hill with members of the Rockford Institute and publishers of *Chronicles,* including Thomas Fleming, to discuss "America's immigration crisis."[15] Recognizing such trends in 2005, W. Fitzhugh Brundage noted a broad alliance promoting a "reactionary agenda" that includes the ls, ccc, and sections of the Republican Party.[16] In addition, there are many elected representatives at the state level who have sympathy with neo-Confederacy and have participated in groups like the League of the South. Neo-Confederacy is also entering mainstream media venues with Thomas E. Woods Jr.'s *Politically Incorrect Guide to American History* being promoted on Fox News, and Donald W. Livingston outlining a neo-Confederate secessionist agenda in *Harper's Magazine.*[17] Further, on cnn's *Lou Dobbs Tonight* the host utilized information on immigration provided by the ccc,[18] an organization that Thomas B. Edsall described in the *Washington Post* in 1999 as having "strong ties" to both Republican and Democratic Party members across the U.S. South.[19] And when the lyrics on Bob Dylan's *Modern Times* (2006) were noted by the *New York Times* to echo the work of the pro-Confederate poet Henry Timrod, whose "Ethnogenesis" was quoted on the first page of the first issue of *Southern Partisan,* neo-Confederate James Everett Kibler Jr. provided comment.[20]

Much of the authority of neo-Confederacy comes from the social standing of those making the arguments—pastors, academics, teachers, columnists, and others in the middle class.[21] Further strength is gained by the acknowledgment of neo-Confederate positions in the national media and by prominent politicians and, as a result, neo-Confederate activists can identify like-minded figures in positions of power in the United States. Senator Trent Lott, for example, through his words and actions over a thirty-five-year career in Washington, such as installing Jefferson Davis's desk in his Capitol Hill office, made his sentiments known to supporters, but he did not overtly state his Confederate sympathies. Yet, as James Webb pointedly comments in his articulation of a conservative Scots-Irish ethnic group and culture, "those inside the culture know how to read such code words,"[22] a contention echoed by Kevin Phillips, who argues that theocratic ideas increasingly invoked by Republicans "are especially tricky to discuss publicly, so they are instead quietly promoted in clandestine briefings or loosely signaled by phrases and citations that reassure the attentive faithful."[23] Neo-Confederate activists make precisely such appeals. Although at face value they may seem to articulate a distinctive ethnic culture and call for reverence for their ancestors, these mask neo-Confederacy's extremism and its advocacy of social and ethno-racial hierarchy, patriarchy, and theocracy—positions much closer to the white nationalism espoused by people such as Jared Taylor, publisher of the extreme *American Renaissance* magazine.[24]

Although it is fundamentally political, neo-Confederacy is often presented as a fringe debate about competing interpretations of history or a cultural issue, or dismissively reduced to petty arguments about the meanings of flags and school names.[25] This downplays the controversies and glosses over the wider political context, not just of the beliefs of neo-Confederate activists, but over the meaning of the Confederacy in the United States. As theorists of nationalism and political analysts have often argued, historical narratives give meaning to our nations and contests over these narratives are struggles over the meaning of society. In 2002, after reviewing the emergence of neo-Confederacy, Christopher M. Centner concluded:

> The Neo-Confederates' power is in their conviction and their dedication to ancestral, religious, and ethnic pride. History is a full contact sport and Neo-Confederates take their evangelism seriously. Neo-Confederates are well organized, educated, and have a vision. They have heard the call to battle, and wage it relentlessly with revisionist zeal. Those more loyal to historical accuracy need to defend historical truth or lose the future to an ugly past. While Neo-Confederates must be allowed to express their opinions it is up to those who oppose them to show, with equal vigor, where, how and why they are wrong.[26]

We hope that this collection is a suitably vigorous contribution to these debates.

Notes

1. George W. Bush is also identified as having connections to neo-Confederate groups. See "Bush's 'Close Ties' to Neo-Confederate Groups Questioned," Common Dreams Progressive Newswire, (18 February 2000). On-line: http://www .commondreams.org/news2000/0218-04.htm [accessed 6 December 2004].

2. League of the South. "Two Nations?" (2004). On-line: http://www.dixienet .org [accessed 15 November 2004]. The map of 1861 added Missouri and Kentucky as "red" Confederate states in 1861—though neither seceded. It also added Oklahoma, which was "Indian Territory" at the time of the Civil War. The 2004 map also correctly included Ohio and Indiana as "red" states won by President Bush.

3. Jenkins, Simon. "The Inevitable Triumph of Guns, God and a Large Slice of Apple Pie," *The Times*, (4 November 2004): 20. On-line: http://www.timesOn-line .co.uk/article/0,,1059-1343277,00.html [accessed 15 November 2004].

4. Emboldened by a White House that aligned with many neo-Confederate positions, LS leader Michael Hill inverted his usual call for Southern secession by suggesting that either the Democratic Party supporting Northern "blue" states secede, or at least the major cosmopolitan cities do: "I've always liked the city-state idea," Hill mused. "It worked quite well in the Middle Ages." See Hitt, Jack. "Neo secessionism", *New York Times*, section 6, (12 December 2004): 84.

5. Webb, James. "Secret GOP Weapon: The Scots-Irish Vote," *Wall Street Journal*, (19 October 2004): A18. Webb reiterated his views and expanded upon them in his subsequent book, *Born Fighting: How the Scots-Irish Shaped America*. (New York: Broadway Books, 2005). In 2006, as the Democratic candidate for the Senate in Virginia, he defeated the Republican incumbent, Senator George Allen.

6. League of the South. "Secret GOP Weapon: The Scots-Irish Vote," (2004). On-line: http://www.dixienet.org [accessed 22 November 2004].

7. Webb, "Secret GOP Weapon," (2004): A18.

8. Mitchell, Don. *Cultural Geography: A Critical Introduction*. (Oxford: Blackwell, 2000): 3.

9. Britt, Brian. "Neo-Confederate Culture," *Z Magazine*, (December 1996). On-line: *http://www.zmag.org/Zmag/articles/dec96britt.htm* [accessed 27 January 1999 and 2 December 2004].

10. Hill, Michael. "President's Message [The Southern League: Past, Present and Future]," *Southern Patriot*, 2.3 (1995): 17.

11. Horwitz, Tony. "Rebel Voices: The Faces of Extremism Wear Many Guises— Most of Them Ordinary," *Wall Street Journal*, 95.83 (28 April 1995): A1. Michael Hill responded to Horwitz's article—see Hill, Michael. "Letters to the Editor: A Scavenger Hunt for Villains," *Wall Street Journal*, (5 June 1995): A15. Others taking issue with Horwitz were neo-Confederate author James Ronald Kennedy, David Hays from Louisiana, and Russell Brew, who described himself as a "Displaced Confederate" writing from Patchogue, New York.

12. Phillips, Kevin. *American Theocracy: The Peril and Politics of Radical Religion, Oil, and Borrowed Money in the 21st Century*. (New York: Viking, 2006): 134.

13. Reese, Charley. "America's Anglo-Celtic History." On-line: http://www.anu .org/news_americasangloceltichistory.html [accessed 22 October 2002]. Reese has appeared at neo-Confederate events such as the 1998 LS national conference, where he spoke on "The Rebirth of the Southern Community." See League of the South. "1998 National Conference Audio Tapes," *Southern Patriot*, 5.5 (1998): 6.

14. Crouch, Stanley. "Neo-Confederates of the GOP Rise Again," *San Francisco Examiner*, (5 January 1999): A15.

15. Blumenthal, Max. "Beyond Macaca: The Photograph That Haunts George Allen," *The Nation*, (29 August 2006). On-line edition: http://www.thenation.com/ doc/20060911/george_allen [accessed 18 September 2006]; Blumenthal, Max. "Sen. John Cornyn Meets the Racist Right," *The Huffington Post*. On-line: http://www .huffingtonpost.com/max-blumenthal/sen-john-cornyn-meets-th_b_29835.html [accessed 20 September 2006]; PRNewswire. "Senator Cornyn (R-Tex.) to Address Conference on Immigration on September 19." On-line: http://biz.yahoo.com/ prnews/060918/nym163a.html?.v=1 [accessed 19 September 2006].

16. Brundage, W. Fitzhugh. *The Southern Past: A Clash of Race and Memory*. (Cambridge, MA: The Belknap Press of Harvard University Press, 2005): 340.

17. Livingston, Donald W. "Dismantling Leviathan," *Harper's Magazine,* 304.1824 (2002): 13-17.

18. Southern Poverty Law Center. "Using Hate Materials, Dobbs Slams Illegal Immigration," *Intelligence Report,* 122 (2006): 10. CNN stated that a "freelance field producer in Los Angeles" had found the map on the Internet and had been disciplined for using it. The program was broadcast on 23 May 2006. Dobbs has a track record of often vitriolic broadcasts opposing immigration.

19. Edsall, Thomas B. "Controversial Group Has Strong Ties to Both Parties in South," *Washington Post,* (13 January 1999): A02.

20. Rich, Motoko. "Who's This Guy Dylan Who's Borrowing Lines From Henry Timrod?" *New York Times,* (14 September 2006): E1.

21. Evelyn Schlatter makes a similar point when she notes that although "downwardly mobile lower-middle-class men" are often identified as the constituency of white supremacist groups, white supremacy at the end of the twentieth and start of the twenty-first centuries has a wide range of followers, attracting "educated, middle-class professionals" and participants from "upwardly mobile households." See her *Aryan Cowboys: White Supremacists and the Search for a New Frontier, 1970-2000.* (Austin: University of Texas Press, 2006): 159.

22. Webb, "Secret GOP Weapon," (2004): A18.

23. Phillips, *American Theocracy,* (2006): 96.

24. Readers can compare the quotations from neo-Confederate publications presented here with the statements made by Taylor and other white nationalists interviewed in Swain, Carol M., and Nieli, Russ, ed. *Contemporary Voices of White Nationalism in America.* (Cambridge: Cambridge University Press, 2003).

25. A common media phrase when reporting on struggles over historical narratives around the role of the Confederate flag in public life is to dismiss the incident as a "flag flap"—see, for example, CNN's Cabell, Brian. "Confederate Flag Flap Triggers Boycott of South Carolina." On-line: http://www.cnn.com/US/9908/13/south .carolina.flag [accessed 6 December 2004].

26. Centner, Christopher M. "Neo-Confederates at the Gate: The Rehabilitation of the Confederate Cause and the Distortion of History," *Skeptic,* 9.3 (2002): 66.

Contributors

HEIDI BEIRICH is the Director of Research and Special Projects for the Southern Poverty Law Center's Intelligence Project, which tracks America's hate groups. Dr. Beirich also pens feature articles for the *Intelligence Report*, the Southern Poverty Law Center's award-winning quarterly on the American radical right.

JON BOHLAND is an Assistant Professor of International Studies and Political Science at Hollins University. His research fields are in critical geopolitics and nationalism, with a particular interest in how everyday cultural forces impact and shape national identities.

EUAN HAGUE is an Associate Professor of Geography at DePaul University. His research on neo-Confederacy and Celtic identity in the United States has appeared in *Cultural Geographies, Annals of the Association of American Geographers, Canadian Review of Studies in Nationalism, Scottish Affairs* and *Hagar International Social Science Review*.

KEVIN HICKS is an Associate Professor of English at Alabama State University, where he serves as the Director of Writing Across the Curriculum.

JONATHAN I. LEIB is an Associate Professor of Geography at Old Dominion University. His research fields are political geography, cultural geography, and geographies of "race" and ethnicity, with an emphasis on electoral systems and political representation, political and cultural change in the American South, and the politics of representation on the American South landscape involving Confederate and civil rights iconography. His research has appeared in *Political Geography, Cultural Geographies, Journal of Cultural Geography, Journal of Race & Policy, Geographical Review, Journal of Geography, Geojournal,* and *Southeastern Geographer.*

JAMES W. LOEWEN is a professor of sociology who has taught at Tougaloo College, the University of Vermont, and Catholic University of America. His books include *Lies My Teachers Taught Me: Everything Your American History Textbook Got Wrong* (1995), which won the American Book Award, and *Lies across America: What Our Historic Sites Get Wrong* (1999). He was recently honored with a Gustavus Myers Human Rights Book Award for *Sundown Towns: A Hidden Dimension of American Racism* (2005).

EDWARD H. SEBESTA is an independent researcher examining neo-Confederacy. He has contributed to articles for the Southern Poverty Law Center's *Intelligence Report* and has been a consultant for numerous journalists on this topic. His academic analyses of neo-Confederacy have appeared in *Scottish Affairs, Canadian Review of American Studies,* and *Cultural Geographies.* He is currently working on *"The Great Truth": Confederates and Neo-Confederates in their Own Words* for publication in 2009.

BRIAN TONGIER received his master's degree in Sociology from UCLA in 2002.

GERALD R. WEBSTER is Professor of Geography at the University of Wyoming, where he serves as the chair of the Department of Geography. His research interests are largely in political geography and focus on political redistricting, electoral geography, secessionist groups, political iconography, and nationalism. He has published over five dozen articles and book chapters in such outlets as *Political Geography, Professional Geographer, Geographical Review, Journal of Geography,* and *Southeastern Geographer.*

Index

Page numbers in italics refer to images

Abbeville Institute, 13, 19n58, 73n67, 202, 220n2
abolition, 78, 85, 217. *See also* slavery
abortion, 26, 63, 83, 140, 262, 294
ACA. *See* Alabama Celtic Association
Adams, John, 299
"An Address to Christians throughout the World," 65
AFBNP. *See* American Friends of the British National Party
affirmative action: as anti-white, 143; effects of, 144; and King holiday, 140; and miscegenation, 141–142; and neo-Confederacy, 4, 12, 131, 159; works on, 163n46. *See also* quotas
African Americans: and affirmative action, 143–144; and Confederate flag, 169, 177, 280; and conservative thought, 160n4; empowerment of, 134–135; and federal government, 135; in film, 174; hostility toward, 55, 160n1; as inferior, 77, 179, 243; and Ku Klux Klan, 122n29; in literature, 28, 132, 228, 235–236, 237–238, 241, 242–243, 246; lynching of, 81, 82; and music, 255, 268–269, 270, 272, 277–278n58; and neo-Confederacy, 102; and Reconstruction, 235; rights of, 134, 142, 157; role of, 213; sexuality

of, 81, 94n19, 151–152; stereotypes of, 93–94n18, 137, 150–151; and violence, 135, 151, 165n84, 238
agrarianism, 7, 25, 31. *See also* Southern Agrarians
AIDS, 91, 135
Aiken, David, 229
Alabama: and Confederate flag, 170, 171, 175, 180; state legislature of, 199n132
Alabama (band), 263
Alabama Celtic Association (ACA), 122n23
The Alamo (1960), 215
alcohol, 105, 124–125n48
Allen, David, 294, 295
Allen, George, 313, 315n5
Allman Brothers, 263, 271, 277n55, 278n69
Altman, John, 209
America: The First 350 Years, 214
American Friends of the British National Party (AFBNP), 289
American Idol, 267
American Renaissance, 10, 105, 164n84, 302
American Review, 29
American Revolution, 30
Anderson, Alister C., 66

busing, 141, 142
Butler, David, 215
Butler, Richard, 288
Byrd, R. Wayne, Sr., 9

Cable, George W., 235
Cailleteau, Ed, 301
Calhoun, John C., 3, 24, 217
Cantrell, Beau, 301
Cantrell, James P., 239, 250n25
Carlson, Wayne, 99–100, 132
Carlton, Linda, 260–261
Carmichael, Stokely, 138
Carter, Jimmy, 24, 48
Caruthers, William A., 231
Carver, George Washington, 162n39
Cash, Johnny, 278n69
Casteel, Ron, 292, 295
*Catechism on the History of the Confeder-
ate States of America*, 205–206
Cathey, Boyd, 295, 297, 307n50
Catron, James, 106
Caucasians. *See* white people
CAUSE, 288
Cavaliers, 98, 101, 111, 238
The Cavaliers of Virginia, 231
Cawthon, William, Jr.: on immigration,
155; and integration, 117, 142; and
League of the South, 163n66; on
racism, 132; on segregation, 136; on
Southern nationalism, 145; works of,
160n6
CCC. *See* Council of Conservative
Citizens
Celtic ethnicity: and alcohol, 105, 124–
125n48; and Anglo-Saxon ethnicity,
101; appearance of, 110–111; and
Celticization, 104; culture of, 112–
113; definition of, 112; and education, 211, 216, 217–218; and farming,
106; as fictional, 109–110, 128n93;
food of, 110; history of, 102, 104,
109–112; language of, 106; and Lega
Nord, 128–129n105; and literature,
250n25; as masculine, 106, 114; music
of, 105–106, 110, 253, 269, 270–271,
278n65; and neo-Confederacy, 99,

102; stereotypes of, 110; as symbolic,
102; and violence, 108–109, 110. *See
also* Anglo-Celtic ethnicity; Celtic
South thesis
Celtic Scotland, 110
Celtic South thesis: criticism of, 127n88;
history of, 103–105; McWhiney and,
12, 45n47, 104, 105, 106, 107, 112,
124n44, 128n95, 149, 257; and music,
257; and natural order, 116–118; and
neo-Confederacy, 99–101, 103–107,
112–115, 119–120, 269, 310; and vio-
lence, 108–109; works on, 112n21,
123–124n39, 127n86. *See also* Anglo-
Celtic ethnicity; Celtic ethnicity
Century Illustrated Monthly Magazine,
235, 236
Chalcedon Foundation, 51, 57, 62
Chalcedon Presbyterian Church, 58
Chalcedon Report, 57, 58, 61, 62
Charles, Ray, 268, 269
Charlie Daniels Band, 271. *See also*
Daniels, Charlie
Children of the Confederacy, 205, 219
chivalry. *See* code of honor
Chodes, John, 122n29
Chodorov, Frank, 44n46
Christensen, John, 301–302
Christianity: and biblical literalism, 7;
Confederate soldiers and, 54; and
education, 208–209; and gender
roles, 84; and literature, 228, 247–
248; and Lost Cause movement, 175–
176; and music, 260, 262; and neo-
Confederacy, 5, 6, 7, 11, 31, 86; and
"New Dixie Manifesto," 1, 50; and
science, 55; and slavery, 52, 54, 55, 60,
63–64, 66, 67, 188, 190, 199n132, 266;
and the South, 59, 62, 64, 70n38, 98;
Southern Agrarians and, 28. *See also*
theoconservatives; theological war
thesis; *and specific denominations*
Christian nationalism, 50, 52, 57, 58, 61,
64
Christian Reconstructionism, 57, 58,
62, 65
Chronicles: A Magazine of American

Sons of Confederate Veterans, 287–288; on Southern identity, 100–101; works of, 35–36, 170

Kentucky, 1, 314n2

Kershaw, Jack, 46n61, 88, 212

Kershaw Foundation. *See* Mary Noel Kershaw Foundation

Kibler, James, 243–245; and Abbeville Institute, 220n2; and *Georgia Scenes*, 233; and music, 313; praise for, 252n78; and *The Simms Review*, 229; works of, 78, 250n31

Killian, Lewis, 42n18, 42n23, 98, 160n1

King, Henry, 215

King, Martin Luther, Jr., 23, 138–141, 159, 165n90

King holiday, 31, 139–140, 159, 162n38

Kirchner, Paul, 149–150, 164n80

Kirk, Russell, 24, 207

Knights of the New Order, 300

Knights of the White Camellia, 245

Koresh, David, 288

Ku Klux Klan: and civil rights, 135; condemnations of, 102; and Confederate flag, 174; in film, 174; and Forrest, 87; in literature, 35, 237; and neo-Confederacy, 122–123n29, 311–312; praise for, 137, 224n52, 238–239, 283; and Reagan, 42n18; revival of, 27; rise of, 81; and Sons of Confederate Veterans, 280, 281, 282, 286, 287; violence and, 82; and women, 94n26

Lacy, Clint, 260

Ladies' Memorial Associations, 176, 177

Lady Baltimore, 214

Lamb, Kevin, 151

Landess, Thomas H., 30, 155

Lanier, Sidney, 235

The Last Confederate Flag, 245–246, 248, 299

Latané, John Holladay, 214

Layden, James, 162n38

League of the South (LS), 181–185; and Bessinger, 190; and Christianity, 50, 52; and Confederate flag, 12, 170, 178, 184, 185; criticism of, 17n42,

73n67; and education, 202, 203, 206, 217–219; and ethnicity, 104; and gay rights, 185; and gender roles, 86, 91; and home schooling, 203, 212–217; Home Schooling and Secondary Education Program, 212; and immigration, 165n98, 185; and King holiday, 162n38; and literature, 213–215, 216, 226–227; membership of, 183; and multiculturalism, 152; and music, 257, 263, 278n69; name change from Southern League, 13n2; National Conference of, 62; and neo-Confederacy, 3, 10, 170, 178, 310; origin of, 14n5; and politics, 292, 309; and racism, 8, 132, 289; and Red Shirts, 123n29; and secession, 11, 281, 287; and separation of church and state, 185; and Sons of Confederate Veterans, 280; and Southern Celtic conference, 107; and Southern Poverty Law Center, 8, 219; and "Summer Institute for Young Men," 91, 203; and theological war thesis, 51; videos made by, 250n28; and violence, 109; web site of, 183, 184–185; and white supremacy, 287

League of the South Institute for the Study of Southern Culture and History (LSI), 73n67, 202, 203, 206, 211–212, 216, 217, 223n45, 223n48, 223n50, 226–227

Leamon, Warren, 143

Lee, Robert E.: citizenship of, 49n89; criticism of, 292; as ideal Southerner, 232; legacy of, 58, 184; in literature, 241–242; and Lost Cause movement, 176; as masculine ideal, 86–87, 140, 254, 261; societies for, 302; statue of, 196n68, 236; surrender of, 236–237

Lee, Stephen Dill, 282

Lee, Walter W., 284

Lee Institute. *See* Stephen D. Lee Institute

Lee in the Mountains and Other Poems, 241–242

Lega Nord, 33, 45n58, 114, 128–129n105

Nation of Islam, 148
NATO. *See* North Atlantic Treaty
Organization
Nazis, 42n31, 103; neo-Nazis, 102
Nelson, Willie, 278n69
neo-Confederacy: and affirmative
action, 4, 12, 131, 159; and Anglo-
Celtic identity, 12, 45n58, 102, 119,
273n6, 312; and Celtic ethnicity, 99,
102; and Celtic South thesis, 99–101,
103–107, 112–115, 119–120, 269, 310;
and Christianity, 5, 6, 7, 11, 31, 86;
and civil rights movement, 12, 85,
159; and Confederate flag, 8, 12, 24,
30, 83, 169–170, 177–178, 191–192,
253; and Confederate iconography, 2,
8, 12, 169; and culture, 5, 12, 149, 151,
159–160; definition of term, 9–10;
and desegregation, 9, 12, 117, 159; and
education, 202–204, 207–211; and
gender, 11, 76, 77–78, 84, 91; homophobia and, 5; identity of, 11–12, 98;
ideology of, 3; immigration and, 12,
43n34, 153–157, 159; and Ku Klux
Klan, 122–123n29, 311–312; and Lost
Cause movement, 311; major figures
of, 10; and masculinity, 76, 78–79,
82; and natural order, 116–118; and
race relations, 11, 147–153, 159–160;
racism and, 2, 131–133; and Republican party, 4, 5, 6, 8–9, 13, 286, 292,
302, 305n19, 310; and secession, 1,
97; and theological war thesis, 11, 50,
61–67, 290; and white supremacy, 5,
122–123n29, 136; and women, 88–89
neo-Confederate literature, 13, 34, 226–
228, 248; characters in, 227–228, 230–
231, 240–241; and Christianity, 228;
humor, 228, 232–233; melodrama,
234–240; modern literature, 243–248;
reprinting of, 35, 138, 224n55, 239; romances, 228–232, 248. *See also specific
authors, publishers, and works*
neo-Confederate periodicals, 12, 37. *See
also specific publications and publishers*
neoconservatives, 25, 26
New Century Foundation, 164–165n84
New Deal, 85

"New Dixie Manifesto," 1–2, 11, 50, 111,
269, 310–311
New Right. *See* neoconservatives
Newsweek, 104
New World Order, 179, 184, 192, 263
Nights with Uncle Remus, 235. *See also*
Uncle Remus
1965 Immigration Act. *See* Hart-Celler
Act
1965 Voting Rights Act. *See* Voting
Rights Act
nonwhites, 148, 160. *See also specific
ethnicities*
*North Against South: The American Iliad,
1848–1877,* 214
North Atlantic Treaty Organization
(NATO), 26
Northern ethnicity, 98, 99, 104. *See also*
Yankees
Northern League. *See* Lega Nord

Obama, Barack, 136
OCR. *See* Order of the Confederate
Rose
Ohio, 314n2
Oklahoma, 1, 289, 311, 314n2
"Old Black Joe Comes Home," 242
Old Man (1997), 215
Order of the Confederate Rose (OCR),
258
Order of White Trash, 295
Orlebeke, Peter, 290, 298
Our Fathers' Fields: A Southern Story, 78,
244
Outlaw, Perry, 287, 293
outsourcing, 143
Owsley, Frank, 29, 110, 240

Page, Thomas Nelson, 236, 242, 248,
250n41
paleoconservatives: and community,
26; and hierarchy, 27; and neo-
Confederacy, 11, 23, 25–27; and Reagan, 26; and Republicans, 29; and
Southern Agrarians, 27, 31
Palmer, Benjamin Morgan, 51, 53–54,
60, 61, 66
The Partisan, 230

65–66; influence of, 58, 60, 66, 67; and slavery, 59; and theological war thesis, 51, 53–54, 57, 66
Thurmond, Strom, 4, 10, 37, 48n89
Timrod, Henry, 234, 313
Tomorrow (1972), 215
The Tragic Era, 137
The Traitor, 237, 239
Transcendentalism, 62
Travis, Randy, 263
The Trip to Bountiful (1985), 215
Tritt, Travis, 263
True Grit (1969), 215
Tubbs, Michael, 300
Tucker, Nathaniel Beverly, 231
Twelfth Louisiana String Band, 256–257. *See also* Louisiana Tigers String Band
"Twelve Southerners," 28

UDC. *See* United Daughters of the Confederacy
UN. *See* United Nations
Uncle Remus, 215, 216, 234, 235–236. See also *Nights with Uncle Remus; Tales of Uncle Remus*
Union Army, 54, 55, 235, 237
United Confederate Veterans, 9, 282
United Daughters of the Confederacy (UDC): Children of the Confederacy, 205, 219; and Civil War, 271; and Confederate iconography, 176; and education, 205–206, 207, 219; and ethnicity, 98; as "heritage defenders," 7; and Lost Cause, 283–284; magazine of, 37; membership of, 48n85, 283; and monuments to Confederacy, 177; and music, 255–256, 258; as neo-Confederate, 8, 10, 13; and neo-Confederate historical committees, 9; praise for, 101; and white supremacy, 283–284
United Nations (UN), 7, 26, 262
United Sons of Confederate Veterans, 282, 302
United States: and Celtic culture, 115; culture of, 62, 102, 111, 255, 267–268; as empire, 33; and ethnicity, 97; flag

of, 171–172; as multicultural, 145, 146, 163n63; racism in, 131
Universal Rights of Man, 90
Un-Reconstructed, 257–258
The Unregenerate South, 117, 249n8
Up from Slavery, 214
U.S. Circuit Court, 191
U.S. Constitution. *See* Constitution of the United States
USSR. *See* Soviet Union
U.S. Supreme Court, 169, 191. *See also* specific cases

Vanderbilt Agrarians. *See* Southern Agrarians
Vanover, J. R. *See* Reed, John Shelton
Vaughn, Stevie Ray, 278n69
Vinson, John, 117, 152, 165n90
violence: and African Americans, 135, 151, 165n84, 238; and Celtic ethnicity, 108–109, 110; and code of honor, 80; proponents of, 83; in the South, 82, 98; and white supremacy, 93n18
voting, 158, 166n112, 208
Voting Rights Act (1965), 23, 36, 141, 158, 166n112

Walking Toward Home, 244
Wallace, George C., Jr., 175, 181
Wall Street crash of 1929, 56
Wall Street Journal, 309
Wal-Mart, 12, 190
Warren, Robert Penn,: as agrarian, 27, 46n61, 56; and neo-Confederacy, 240; on violence, 82, 84; writings of, 28, 29
Warren, Terry, 260
The War the Women Lived: Female Voices from the Confederate South, 214
Washburn, Michael, 146
Washington, Booker T., 162n39, 213, 214
Washington Post, 1, 4, 310, 313
Was Jefferson Davis Right?, 36
WASPS (white Anglo-Saxon Protestants), 124n44
Watson-Brown Foundation, 19n58
Watterson, Henry, 235

Lightning Source UK Ltd.
Milton Keynes UK
UKHW01f0824270518
323273UK00001B/114/P